Translating Shakespeare

A Guidebook for Young Actors

TRANSLATING SHAKESPEARE
A Guidebook for Young Actors

David Montee

Smith and Kraus Publishers

2014

ISBN: 1-57525-889-7
ISBN: 978-1-57525-889-8
Library of Congress Control Number: 2104936833

Typesetting and layout by Elizabeth E. Monteleone
Cover by Borderlands Press

A Smith and Kraus book
177 Lyme Road, Hanover, NH 03755
editorial 603.643.6431 To Order 877.668.8680
www.smithandkraus.com

Printed in the United States of America

For my students, who have translated Shakespeare for me so magically over the past 26 years through their inspired work and dedication;

For my mom, who read to me;

And for my wife, Robin: partner in life and art.

ACKNOWLEDGMENTS

All photographs depicting my own staged productions of Shakespeare plays in this book are used courtesy of the Interlochen Center for the Arts. Thank you to Terri McCarthy of Interlochen's Photo Archives for helping me to track them down.

My thanks to former teachers (particularly Jack Wright, Bill Kuhlke, Robert McGill, Ron Willis, and Charlie Suggs, who each shaped my own approach to acting in unique and inspiring ways), colleagues and students over the years, virtually all of whom influenced this book in some manner; attempting to list them all here would invariably lead to unfortunate omissions. I can only hope that I've let most of you know in some way over the years how important and influential you have been to my life and profession.

A special thank you to Adam Immerwahr for an important introduction.

Thanks also to Kathy Ziege, secretary extraordinaire . . . and friend.

TABLE OF CONTENTS

David Montee as Shylock in *The Merchant of Venice*

When I was in junior high school—I know, today it's called "middle school"; but I'm nostalgic and showing my age—I first encountered Shakespeare. This occurred before I even knew on a conscious level that I wanted to be an actor; although I'm convinced that on a deeper level, there was rarely any doubt of it. Fortunately, this initial encounter happened for me in the best possible way: by seeing Franco Zefferelli's breathtakingly lovely and moving film of *Romeo and Juliet*. Even while viewing it in a run-down, damp-smelling movie theatre in a small Oklahoma town, I knew that I was experiencing something very, very special.

Not long after, with that film's images and passions still emblazoned in my memory, I came across a battered paperback on my older sister's bookshelf. Sharon was in her sophomore year of college at the time, and the small anthology of Shakespeare's great tragedies (containing *Hamlet, Julius Caesar, Romeo and Juliet,* and *Macbeth,* as I recall) was one of her required texts for a literature class. Paging through it, I was dazzled by the beauty of the language as I read it aloud. Most of the time, I had no clear idea of precisely what it meant—but it *sounded* so beautiful, and those words tasted wonderfully exciting on my tongue. I had to know more about the works of this man that most of my teachers claimed was the greatest poet/playwright ever in the history of the English language. Maybe the greatest writer ever in *any* language.

Jumping forward about five years, I found myself finally in an acting workshop/master class with touring professionals, focused on the fundamentals of "how to" act Shakespeare on stage. Now a freshman in college, still struggling socially with my somewhat embarrassing decision to major in theatre (I kept assuring my worried family and friends that it was only an offbeat preparation for law school), I was eager to finally hear from working actors—from *experts*—how to begin the journey toward becoming as good as those actors in the Zefferelli film whose names I had memorized, although I had encountered them only rarely in other films at local theatres. (Remember, this was Oklahoma, and long before Netflix, the Internet Movie Database, or even VHS tapes, much less DVD's and Blu-Rays.) Leonard Whiting . . . John McHenry . . . Milo O'Shea . . . Robert Stephens . . . and of course, burned irrevocably in my adolescent hormonal memory, Olivia Hussey on that moonlit balcony, one of the loveliest young ladies I could remember ever seeing. Here, I thought, I would begin to gather the skills that would help me to inspire others with Shakespeare, just as those actors had inspired me.

What I mostly recall from that workshop experience was my frustration at hearing phrase after phrase tossed about without explanation: meter, scansion, antithesis, Quarto and Folio, etc., etc. Whenever one of us would raise our hand to ask for some clarification about these terms, the usual response from the guest teachers was, "Don't worry about that now. That's a little too advanced. For the moment, let's just continue with this improvisation exercise." I began to get the sinking feeling that learning to act Shakespeare was something akin to joining a secret society: you had to be vetted, groomed, and eventually voted into the club before anyone would really tell you anything practical about it.

This book has been written for those young actors—like me, some four decades ago—who are attracted to the idea of tackling Shakespeare on the stage, but fear that his plays contain too many secret and specialized facets that are beyond their grasp for them to ever achieve satisfaction or success in understanding them, much less *acting* in them. What I eventually learned is this: all of those terms and techniques that were so glibly touched upon in that long-ago workshop are not only comprehensible—even for beginning actors—they're actually fun to learn about and explore. All one has to do is provide the appropriate contextual framework for transferring Shakespeare from page to stage—using the same basic fundamentals that actors use for all scripts (with a few more specialized principles thrown in)—and most of those inquisitive and ambitious young actors can soon find the Bard of Avon's work emotionally inspiring, intellectually stimulating, and ultimately quite thrilling.

I've never felt the need to "talk down" to young actors in my classes and rehearsals. I try to treat them like fellow artists—albeit with fewer years of life under their belts, and thus less experience—and expect them to follow up with their own investigations. Most who will enjoy successful long-term careers in the art are naturally curious; they have to be. Teaching, for me, has always been a journey of personal creative exploration and discovery alongside energetic young artists in a studio situation who share my own curiosity and drive. Teaching acting is simply a methodology of explaining, as clearly as one can, what fascinates you personally about the discipline in a manner that inspires the student's desire to find out more for himself. The student takes it from there.

And that's how I've approached this book.

(Incidentally, on a quick side note: throughout this book I usually fall back on the generic male pronoun when talking of the student actor: *him, he, himself.* No sexism is intended, only succinctness; constantly using the double pronoun in such writing [i.e., *him or herself*] seems clumsy and tedious when done on a continuing basis. So I now ask absolution for that practice from what [I hope] will be my many young female readers!)

This is not a step-by-step "how to" book. There seem to be so many of those on the shelves devoted to Drama in various bookstores: How to Improvise, How to Act, How to Audition, and on and on. As most experienced artists recognize, there really is no effective "how to" system in such theatrical endeavors. There may be proven principles, accepted theories, beneficial and enlightening experiences to share and pass on . . . but no sure-fire formula for success and proficiency. Perhaps in time, and with their own personal encounters with Shakespeare in production, many young actors who read these chapters now will eventually find things to disagree with, ideas to dispute. I hope so. That will be a sure sign that they've grasped what I've tried to suggest here, and are now forging their own new paths ahead to benefit future generations of eager Shakespearean thespians.

This is also not a book that tries to go into great depth and detail for the working professional (although hopefully, even they might find parts of it interesting and provocative). There are already good examples of such books, and I talk about a few of them in my Afterword. Neither does it seek to be a scholarly treatise on the plays or their writer. There are plenty of those as well, and have been for about four centuries now. Critical and scholarly studies of William Shakespeare have evolved into a cottage industry, made even more so by the recent arguments concerning "whether Shakespeare was really Shakespeare." I also note a couple of what I believe are good "starting point" books for such critical studies in the Afterword as well.

With *Translating Shakespeare*, I hope to pique the interest of the younger actor in pursuing further this most rewarding of playwrights in a way that doesn't threaten, yet also doesn't patronize. Ideally, it will also serve as a practical reference work for well-intentioned young teachers with limited experience in imparting to their charges the magic of Shakespeare's stories and language. For those teachers who might be using the book as such, I suggest that they always remember this: it's never wrong to respond to a student's question with "I don't know . . . but I'll try to find out." I've found that the more a student hears those words from their teacher—if the teacher, along with them, is genuinely interested in investigating and uncovering more information, hand in hand with the student—the more possibility exists that all involved will actually learn lasting lessons, both about the subject as well as about basic human interaction on a variety of levels. As the saying goes, the only stupid question is one that never gets asked.

Finally, a word about the title, *Translating Shakespeare*. In a later chapter of the book, I anecdotally reveal where the title came from. But let's take a moment to look at that word "translating."

We usually think that this refers to taking a passage of text in one language and transcribing it—or verbally speaking it—in a different language. However, the Roman poet Ovid—one of Shakespeare's own favorites, by the way—uses the idea of "translation" a bit differently. In the beginning passages of his masterwork of poetic mythology, *Metamorphoses*, he notes that all aspects of life itself, as well as the mortal world that contains it in forms both animate and inanimate, exist in a perpetual state of change. There is never stasis: youth translates into old age, vitality into decay, sadness into happiness (and vice versa), life into death, and death into rebirth. In this sense, "translate" means "to convey from one form to another"; or even, in more overtly spiritual terms, "to transport; to enrapture."

So, the main purpose of this book is not simply to translate the challenging language of William Shakespeare into an accessible context—verbal and behavioral—that a young actor can more easily understand; additionally, it is intended to translate the young actor's understandable fear and intimidation of "the greatest of playwrights" into admiration and respect— and hopefully, an increased eagerness to grapple with him in class, in rehearsal, and in performance. Most of the time, the outcome of such a theatrical encounter "translates" into one of an actor's more enduring stage memories.

May you find yourself translated by Shakespeare many times over the course of your future stage experiences!

"Hold the Mirror Up to Nature":
Where We Begin

Although this book deals with a young actor's initial encounters with Shakespeare in acting classrooms and rehearsal studios, an initial understanding about acting in general is in order before we truly begin that work.

First of all: there is no getting away from the Stanislavsky system. Although William Shakespeare's plays were written three centuries before the Russian actor/teacher trod the boards, Stanislavsky's goal of truthfulness in performance is one that spans all eras of the theatre, even though our aesthetic standards of "truthfulness" may change from generation to generation. If you doubt the relevance of Stanislavsky's basic approach to our work on Shakespeare, you should read Hamlet's advice to the players (which we will touch on more fully in the first chapter) very carefully. Accepting this, it's important before we begin to explore an actor's approach to Shakespeare that we briefly remind ourselves of what Stanislavsky was all about.

It's always been my belief that to a large degree, actors are formed in the womb, not the classroom. Techniques can be shared between teacher and student, the latest theories and processes can enhance our way of seeing precisely what we do in rehearsal and performance, but "the actor animal" either exists in you from the earliest times of your childhood or it does not.

There are a couple of ways to tell if it exists in you.

When you were a child and were enacting your fantasy lives, either in the solitude of your own room or with the company of your friends, did the rules *really matter* to you? If you were imitating your favorite characters from television, films or comic books, creating new storylines or daring and exciting situations of your own imagining to place them in, did it frustrate you when those you were playing with seemed to fundamentally misunderstand what could and couldn't be *true*? When a comrade dropped the façade of the story's character and interjected something totally irrelevant from "real life"? When a soldier shot in battle refused to follow through with appropriate dying behavior? When a prince courting a princess seemed entirely ignorant of what to do next? When a neighborhood counterspy seemed completely oblivious to what James Bond would do in a similar situation?

When they decide what fantasy world they will inhabit today, children do not ask, "What is my character?" They ask, "Who am I today?" This is not simply a different choice of words; it is a pivotal variation in the way a developing actor *sees* the potentials of the world around him.

The importance of sustained consistency when enacting a fantasy situation—seen in childhood play—is an early sign in a child of "the actor animal." Another early indication of a potential actor in the forming is a keen sense of empathy, that most vital of acting tools. Were you unusually sensitive to the feelings of your playmates or your siblings, whether they were happy, sad, pensive or excited? Did you regularly wonder (and imagine) what it would be like to see the world from their perspective, to live their lives for a while, to walk in their shoes, look in their mirrors with their eyes? When they wept, did you feel similar stirrings in yourself? When they laughed, did you feel joy as well?

This is not to say that all children with these feelings and tendencies in life and play will develop into actors. Some measure of empathy lives in the majority of human beings who filter through our lives. (Even though our increasing interactions and relationships with computer screens and pocket technology may be altering this irrevocably, and not for the better!) And obviously, very few of us pursue acting as vocation or avocation. But it is my belief that these tendencies *must* exist in a child before there is any chance of an actor evolving forth.

So what does this have to do with Stanislavsky? Everything. The fundamental precept of the Stanislavsky system is self-use. An actor plays him or herself, because he/she knows no one else—or ever will—as intimately. We are forever trapped, held in our own bodies, minds, imaginings, perspectives. Contrary to the general public's clichéd perception, actors do not play other people; they play themselves in other situations, other lives, traveling on other paths from those that their own personal circumstances have led them in their "real" lives. Actors do not don masks; they take them off in order that their private, inner selves may be more clearly utilized and seen in their public characterizations. These intimate revelations require courage, boldness, and a self-knowledge that is hard-earned, perhaps only fully accessible after many years of living and experiencing grief, exultation, and everything in between. The revelation of those experiences in performance, although generally somewhat spiritually fulfilling, is not always easy or "fun"—at least not in the manner that we usually understand that word.

The truth, frustrating as it may be for young, impatient actors who want to *be there now*, is that the basic premise of acting is quite simple—*living truthfully in imaginary circumstances*—although it takes many, many years to learn and master. The benefit of that rule, however, is this: although dancers and athletes may have careers that are bounded by the limits of age on their physicality, if all goes reasonably well, an actor will only get better and better at his art with more age and life experience!

So: there is no separate, secret acting system to be used in approaching a Shakespearean text. The challenge lies in finding the most effective means of applying the techniques of Stanislavsky to the special needs of texts that rely heavily on heightened language, verse rhythms, and complex poetry and rhetoric.

Consequently, before we open our collected Shakespeare together and wade into the greatest dramatic works that any playwright has ever left to generations of eager actors, it is worthwhile to briefly review what an actor *does* when utilizing the Stanislavsky system upon beginning work with any dramatic text.

The first thing that an actor must do is find out as much as possible concerning the unique world that he is about to enter; that is, read the play again and again and again. Read it from all perspectives, yours and the other characters'. Read it as the author who may be considering revisions and rewrites. Read it as the audience member who is seeing it live for the first time, in three dimensions and with actors, settings, lights and costumes. Read it as a director or designer might read it, searching for all the clues and languages contained in this blueprint that will bring it to vibrant life. In sum, read it until you begin to see how it *works*. True, that is the director's job (and the designer's), but it is, first and foremost, yours as well. Theatre is a collaborative art, and everyone's informed input is vital in creating the special synergy that brings about the best stage experience. Do not wait for a director to tell you what to do, nor use the first read-through with your fellow cast members to meet the play for the first time. Bring your best game to the table, right from the first rehearsal. Do your homework. It is never a question of what to do with the line on the page; the question is what lies *behind* the line, the *con*text behind the text. The text is the icing, the context the cake. (However, as noted elsewhere, we'll soon see that with Shakespeare, his particular text is the most tasty and nutritious icing imaginable!)

Don't stop with just reading the play. Read other works by the same author, or other authors who were writing at the same time, or about the same things. Read all that you can (or that may be available) about the author's life, all that you can about the setting, era, and social milieu of the play. Ignore all of the lazy people (some of them, sadly, might be teachers and critics) who may tell you that the only thing you really need to know about is the play itself. If you're really going to live effectively and behave intuitively in an alternate reality for hours of rehearsals and performances, you can never know too much. Suppose someone were to play *you*, bringing your "character" to life on a stage? How much detail about you, your environment, and your background would they have to understand in order to portray effectively the complexity that exists in even the simplest moments of your daily life? Each speck of knowledge you accumulate helps you play the "rules" of the play's world and its individual people more completely—which is your artistic obligation and responsibility.

Where to begin? Start with the nearest library and the Internet. Gather as much information as you can to answer the following questions *in depth and detail*:

When and where does the play take place?

Who were the political and social leaders and philosophers of the time and country in which the play is set? What were they thinking, feeling, saying and writing? What made them popular with their contemporaries? (Or unpopular, whichever the case may be?)

What were the economic forces at work during the time and setting of the play? How poor were the poorest, how rich were the richest, and how economically secure were all of the people existing between those two poles? How do these factors compare with the world you're living in today? How was the political climate of the time dependent upon those economic circumstances?

What spiritual movements or religious institutions were thriving at the time of the play? How were they interconnected with or inspired by the political and economic conditions? How do those factors compare with your life today?

How were the momentous events of an "ordinary" life conducted in the era of the play—births, marriages, funerals? Discover all that you can about those rituals of love and death, for they will always be at the hub of every culture into which you seek an imaginative entry.

And perhaps the most enlightening (and certainly the most fun) of all: What artistic endeavors were enjoyed by the people living at the time and place of the play? What were the poets and writers saying, and how was their work received? What were the musicians composing, and what did people like to hear? What were the visual artists painting and sculpting? How were the arts influenced by the political, religious and economic events of the time?

But what should the actor do if the world of the play doesn't correspond to any known era or location in the "real" world?

An important question, and one that led Stanislavsky, provoked by the challenges of his own students such as Vsevolod Meyerhold, Evgeny Vakhtangov, and Mikhail Chekhov, to re-examine and refine the initial precepts of his early teaching system. The answer is simpler than one might expect, but not always easy to accomplish. For example, if you are working on a play like Samuel Beckett's *Endgame*, in a setting which shares little clear correlation to any actual reality presently in existence, the actor's duty becomes that of creating a virtual world out of his/her own imagination, one that is consistent with the events and characters of the play as the author presents them, and one with the unique qualities necessary to inspire and motivate the events of the action. The creativity necessary for such a task can usually be encouraged or provoked in a variety of ways by teacher and director—but can it be instilled if the seeds are not already present in the young, would-be actor? Probably not. The imagination is like a muscle that must be conscientiously massaged and exercised in a disciplined manner each and every day if it is to blossom, thrive and succeed. This is increasingly important in a world of technology that too often does a lot of the legwork once left to the human imagination. Ambitious young actors would be well served by turning off their laptops, their IPhones, their IPads, their televisions, or any other ready-to-use device that more often than not truncates and stunts the developing imagination. (This is something that experienced acting teachers understand, which lazy, bureaucratic administrators chasing after the latest corporate educational trends do not. So idealistic actors, be warned: Don't be seduced by creative shortcuts! Use the marvels of modern technology as a tool toward a creative solution, not as the solution itself.)

After setting up these basic parameters (the creative guidelines for your own fantasies at work) of the game you are about to embark upon, it's time to move from the general to the specific by examining carefully how the character that you are about to portray in this imaginary world is influenced, directly or indirectly, by all the factors that you have discovered in your initial readings and investigations. Begin by asking the following questions. Answer each of them *on paper*, exploring your thoughts, feelings and instincts along the way as fully as you can at this initial stage of the process.

What is the story of my character's life until that point in time when the play begins?

> What the text doesn't specifically give you, invent for yourself based upon hints by the playwright and what you have found in your own research into the play's era, the author's life, the context of the play's creation. REMEMBER: the more details you supply, the more your imagination will have as resources to work upon.

What religion (if any) was my character raised with?

> What is his spiritual foundation? Does he believe in a force higher than himself, and if so, how does he envision it?

What is my character's romantic history?

> How is love defined? How is sex viewed? How have his personal experiences up until this point in the fictional history shaped these views and perceptions?

What is my character's economic position, now and previous to the play's events?

> Is that the primary method for defining social position and class identification, or does this character make definitive distinctions between the two?

What educational experiences has your character received?

> How do those experiences unite him with or separate him from others in the play? Does he reflect or resist the general climate of the time?

What biological, physical, and emotional traits is the character given explicitly or implicitly by the playwright?

>Are any of them similar to my own personal characteristics? Do they seem extremely different? How does the character describe himself in the text of the play? What do other characters in the play say about him?

Once you answer these questions as thoughtfully and as completely as you can, letting your imagination lead you down unexpected paths toward surprising discoveries, you may begin to feel a blurring of the boundaries between your own personality and that of the character's. This is precisely what you want to achieve at this stage of your preparation: a unification of who you are and how you feel with who the "character" is and how he feels. Because ultimately, there can be no separation. It's worth saying one more time: Greek classical theatre and Commedia del'Arte styles notwithstanding, actors do not reveal character by putting on the mask of a separate persona—we reveal it by stripping those masks away from our own layers of personality that are hiding beneath. And when those masks are gone, there had better be personal truth and emotional honesty beneath if you want an audience to come along with you during your time of public pretending—the "two hours traffic of our stage", as the Prologue to *Romeo and Juliet* puts it. An actor's individual preparation—that careful blending of empirical textual research with free flights of daydreaming fantasy—is essential for making the magic of creative discovery happen in the rehearsal hall, where all of the collaborative elements (the creative input of fellow actors, the clarification of the narrative by the director, the vital contributions of the design team) begin to come together at last.

Ultimately, all good acting involves playing yourself, first and foremost. *You don't know anyone else as intimately and completely as you know yourself, nor will you ever.* Despite what some may tell you, there is nothing wrong with playing yourself (living in different times, places, and circumstances) in your various roles. This only becomes a problem when, as Charles

Marowitz neatly puts it in his inspirational book *The Act of Being*, you don't have access to enough of yourself to play. Once again, that's why actors generally get better as they grow older—life gives them larger reservoirs of experience, knowledge and emotion upon which to draw. Over the course of time, they have the opportunity to "be" more people in a widening variety of situations, with a plethora of different personalities with which they interact; and as a result, more "characters" begin to live and breathe inside of them. Good acting is controlled (and a very important word that is!) schizophrenia.

Which brings us back to Stanislavsky and the lever of the "magic if."

Once all of your initial research and preparation is compiled, and a clearer picture of the person whose world you are to occupy for a while begins to emerge, the next step is simultaneously the simplest and yet the most challenging: to *pretend*, with as much childhood abandon as you can muster. *What if* I (the actor) had been born into the context I've discovered within the circumstances I've outlined? How would I behave? How would I feel? What would I do? What would I dream? Most children are naturally gifted with the ability to journey into such imaginary realms almost at will. Most adults are not; it has been hammered out of them by well-meaning parents, teachers, bosses, and yes, even friends. I suppose there is something of a "Peter Pan syndrome" that encompasses the adults who are able to retain this quality into their older lives—and that gives them at least the potential to achieve a rich (yet carefully fostered and disciplined) "pretend" state, which is at the core of all fine acting: an ability to "believe" with a large part of your consciousness what you know to be a fiction—primarily because your careful research and preparation has made it so *real* for you, igniting your fantasy life into artistic expression.

I have yet to encounter any acting teacher who can truly teach the ability to *imagine to the threshold of belief* to a student in whom the seeds of it aren't already present before the lessons begin.

Make no mistake about it, however; even if you are blessed with such a creative imagination, it needs to be ridden through its paces every day in order for the process described above to become intuitive and of a second nature for you. Individual artists have different methods of doing that (and far be it from me to prescribe how it should be done), but here are some possible starting points: read lots, and a wide variety, of books of all genres, literary forms, and viewpoints; listen to music of all kinds; visit museums to see art and historical artifacts; spend time with nature; watch people and animals behave and interact; and reflect and write about what you observe and how you respond to all of these stimuli. As a result of these experiences, new perspectives about nearly everything will spring up and surprise you throughout the day, fueling your imagination and inspiration.

On the other hand, spending a large majority of your time with the various technological social media that have become increasingly more prevalent and available to all over the past decade can have the opposite effect on the imagination, as can indiscriminate and constant viewing of television and film. These things can easily dull our facility to fantasize, leading us into mind-numbing and predictable pathways of narrative that are simplistic, formulaic, linear, literal, obvious, and altogether unchallenging. They set too many restrictions that maneuver and control our subconscious mind's free flight; and this can prove deadening to the evolution of the inner creative state that any credible methodology of acting (and particularly Stanislavsky's) seeks, through the processes touched upon above, to promote, foster and release.

Above all . . . allow yourself to fully revel in the experiences that arise from these questions of self-exploration and discovery. When your acting work becomes a trial more than a joy for the greater percentage of the time you're engaged with it, it's a good indication that it might be time to take a rest from it, temporarily or indefinitely. Presumably, we all initially sought out the theatre for career or avocation because it was *fun*, however we may each choose to define that word.

Why else would they call it a "play?"

*What are the most common questions that young actors have
about acting Shakespeare?*

> Maybe: How do I make this strange language
> sound like *me?* And what about the verse?
> (Who speaks poetry in the midst of such intense
> feelings? I mean, *really!*) How do I recognize
> and bring to life the tricks of phrase and rhythm
> that I hear more experienced actors rhapsodize
> about? And once I've found them, how do I *use*
> them in performance to create the images that get
> those responses that I so desire from audiences,
> the moments that vibrate within them long after
> they leave the auditorium and return to their daily
> lives? How do I create lasting stage memories
> with what (as everyone "in the know" keeps
> telling me) are the most beautiful lines I will ever
> speak as an actor?

Wherever do I start?

> Why not at the beginning: with directions from
> the very man who wrote those plays that we seek
> to clarify on the stage in our performances?

So, here it is: our first acting lesson in acting Shakespeare,
from Shakespeare himself; direct, specific advice for actors from
the man.

✧

Imagine. (The fuse for everything that we do as artists, interpretive or creative.)

You are a playwright/director, bravely producing your own adaptation of a well-known story of murder and betrayal, with a carefully wrought "twist" (your own dramatic vision) at the heart of the imminent event. You pace nervously backstage in the moments that remain before the opening performance. The chaos around you is daunting, and doesn't bode well for your hopes of the play's success. And tonight, success promises more than critical acclaim; it could, in fact, deliver you from a hell of uncertainty about your own family members, the people closest to you in blood on this earth, whom you now suspect might be involved in murderous treachery too horrendous to contemplate without madness threatening.

You are Hamlet, the artist prince, and tonight you hope that your play will "catch the conscience of the king"—a man who is now your mother's husband, and who may have murdered your father.

And yet, completely unfazed by—to be fair, entirely ignorant of—the life-and-death stakes of the story they are about to enact, the actors chatter on as actors are apt to do in that nervous and exhilarating period before the curtain rises on this brief chronicle of their time; teasing one another, making last minute touch-ups to costumes and make-up, checking to make certain that runaway props have been captured and properly housed.

It's time for them to focus on the importance of what they are about to create, time to put their adrenaline-driven giddiness aside and remember exactly what they are here *to do*. So drawing their attention to him for a few concentrated moments, Hamlet—and by proxy, Shakespeare himself—reminds them of what they are to do with the following concise and tense directions:

> *Speak the speech, I pray you, as I pronounced it*
> *to you, trippingly on the tongue. But if you mouth*
> *it, as many of our players do, I had as lief the*

town-crier spoke my lines. Nor do not saw the air too much with your hand, thus, but use all gently; for in the very torrent, tempest, and, as I may say, whirlwind of your passion, you must acquire and beget a temperance that may give it smoothness. O, it offends me to the soul to hear a robustious, periwig-pated fellow tear a passion to tatters, to very rags, to split the ears of the groundlings, who for the most part are capable of nothing but inexplicable dumbshows and noise. I would have such a fellow whipped for overdoing Termagant, it out-Herods Herod; pray you avoid it.

Be not too tame neither; but let your own discretion be your tutor. Suit the action to the word, the word to the action—with this special observance: that you overstep not the modesty of nature; for anything so overdone is from the purpose of playing, whose end, both at the first and now, was and is, to hold (as it were) the mirror up to nature: to show virtue her feature, scorn her own image, and the very age and body of the time his form and pressure. Now this overdone, or come tardy off, though it makes the unskillful laugh cannot but make the judicious grieve, the censure of which one must in your allowance overweigh a whole theatre of others. O, there be players that I have seen play—and heard others praise, and that highly (not to speak it profanely)—that, neither having the accent of Christians nor the gait of Christian, pagan, nor man, have so strutted and bellowed that I have thought some of Nature's journeymen had made men, and not made them well, they imitated humanity so abominably. O, reform it altogether!

And let those that play your clowns speak no more than is set down for them; for there be of

*them that will themselves laugh to set on some
quantity of barren spectators to laugh too, though
in the meantime some necessary question of the
play be then to be considered. That's villainous,
and shows a most pitiful ambition in the fool that
uses it.*

Go, make you ready.

A brief speech, unwavering in its certainty (as tense directors facing an uncertain audience are apt to be when giving last-minute counsel to their nervous casts), and a treasure chest of practical, foundational instruction for an actor approaching Shakespeare's own texts—or any other play texts, for that matter.

So let's go through it, point by point.

*Speak the speech, I pray you,
as I pronounced it to you . . . .*

First and foremost, *do not paraphrase Shakespeare.* This is, of course, a golden rule to observe with *any* playwright you are serving, or creatively collaborating with, however you may prefer to regard it; but when working with the playwright whose dramatic works are considered the greatest in English literature, the rule becomes essential to follow. Shakespeare is spectacularly precise in his use of vocabulary; in fact, as etymologists are fond of pointing out, when faced with an idea or an image for which no word then existed, Shakespeare was not at all averse to creating one himself (or combining and compounding words already in use) to fit his needs. Almost every day we use or hear words in simple conversations that first appeared in the works of William Shakespeare.

We are often defined as distinct human personalities by the words that we choose in expressing our thoughts; so it generally follows that the deeper and wider our range of vocabulary, the more far-reaching will be our imagination and our ability to communicate what we envision to others. Words conjure images, and images give birth to metaphors and analogies, to different ways of seeing the world around us. As Shakespeare well knew, metaphors provide keys and insights into who we really are. We are how we see things, and the connections we then make, poetical or otherwise, between those things we perceive.

Our word usage defines us, as it defines the plethora of characters that Shakespeare gave us, from King Lear to Cleopatra's messenger. Do not choose to say their lines differently, approximately, or nearly. Shakespeare knew what he was doing, so trust him.

It's interesting to also note that our speaker/director says to his actors to speak the words precisely as he "pronounced" them, perhaps implying that he was not hesitant to utilize that bane of the actor's ego, the dreaded "line reading." While it is true that such a practice can be disrespectful to a working professional actor with years of experience, there is much a young actor can learn by simply listening to how seasoned actors handle Shakespearean verse in general and, yes, even how they phrase and inflect specific lines. *Always be open to learning from your more experienced collaborators, your fellow actors and your director, in whatever form that lesson might take.*

. . . trippingly on the tongue.

We might tend to immediately jump to the definition of "trip" as "a stumble or fall"; but we would also perhaps be fascinated to discover that a preferred alternate definition for the word listed in most dictionaries is " light or nimble tread." "Trippingly," therefore, is the adverb form of "tripping," defined as "moving or stepping lightly and briskly; easily; nimbly."

So, our speaker/director is certainly not suggesting that the actors "trip" themselves up when speaking their lines; instead, he is suggesting that speed and pace—without the loss of clarity and crisp pronunciation and diction—rules the day in a majority of instances. With Shakespeare's complex and rich poetry, where ideas and metaphors often stretch luxuriously out over numerous lines of verse, speed and clarity are usually of the essence in planting the correct clues for understanding in the listener. It's vitally important, as we'll see when we progress more deeply into these ideas in later chapters, that the actor working with Shakespearean verse identify precisely the word or phrase that expresses the concluding thought to which he is leading in his speech, often found at the end of a thorny and occasionally convoluted trail of metaphors. With too many pauses of phrasing or consideration, the actor can lose the listener in the tangles of that undergrowth; so, it's important that the actor move "trippingly" and surely through those tangles, emerging with the audience into the clearing of insight and discovery that lies at the end of that path—and more often than not, at the very end of the line.

In the course of the journey, never lose track of the destination, where the path of the verse and the ideas it contains is leading. The character may not know where it is heading as he speaks it (he may be in the process of discovering it himself), but the actor must *always* know. And knowing, he must take the listener's ears and imagination firmly and surely, leading them toward the conclusions he wishes them to share. *Speak swiftly, with precise and practiced diction and clarity of pronunciation, move with assurance toward the discovery and revelation that awaits your character at the end of each line of thought—and be sure to take the audience along for the ride.*

> *But if you mouth it, as many of our players do,*
> *I would as lief the town-crier spoke my lines.*

In the first pronouncement, our speaker/director tells his actors what they should do when speaking the words of the playwright (in this particular instance, Shakespeare). Here, he follows that up rather sharply, and with a touch of sarcasm, with what they should *not* do: *Don't over-enunciate the words to the point of theatrical affectation, nor confuse volume and force with specificity and clarity of expression.*

We all have some image of the town-crier in the eras of, and before Shakespeare; the civic official who patrolled streets of city and village, loudly proclaiming the time of day for all to hear, or delivering decrees and bits of news from various government officials and agencies, local, provincial or national.

Obviously, the primary requirement for such a position was a loud, declaiming voice, necessary in order to gain the restless crowd's attention without the benefit of modern microphones and amplification devices. Bugles and bells might draw the listeners, but then the crier had to speak loudly and slowly enough so that all could hear and understand.

Our speaker/director evidently doesn't want his actors to declaim overly loudly, nor does he want them to slow their speech unnaturally, thus "chewing" the words; that would not be speaking his lines "trippingly," as previously directed. From the earliest point of the direction, our actors are encouraged to follow a path toward naturalism in their vocal characterizations, to search for a conversational quality paired with verbal pace and clarity of thought. Although any theatrical experience is inherently artificial—and verse drama even more so—speak the lines with a sense of truth, not with affectation or falseness.

Nor do not saw the air too much with your hand, thus,
but use all gently . . .

One imagines with some amusement the specific demonstration our speaker/director (in this case, Hamlet) makes when delivering this bit of instruction. A teaching colleague of mine once deemed the awkward, habitual gestures that inexperienced, nervous actors fall back upon in rehearsals and (too often, unfortunately) performances as "sorting socks." However we describe it—sawing or sorting—the fact is that when actors have not immersed themselves in the type of imaginative research that I refer to in the earlier Introduction to this book, they are likely to quickly fall back into nervous patterns that fill in the gaps of their belief in the fictional world and situation with generalized activity. Moreover, the less specific their acting choices for any given moment, the more the unprepared actor may seek to compensate by melodramatic gesture, making them feel like they are "doing" something—even when they're not sure what that may be.

Avoid this trap, advises our speaker/director; don't seek to make up for specificity of choice with a lot of visual fireworks that aren't to the point. Instead, simplify and clarify. If you have done your work well and know *what* you're saying and *why* you're saying it, your instincts will begin to kick in. A little bit can go a long way. Bombast is not always called for, and it is rarely the more interesting choice on stage. Less is often more. *Don't wave your arms around to compensate for a lack of clarity.* It will only distract your audience from what you need them to attend to, particularly when paired with the declamatory style of speaking already noted and condemned.

> *. . . for in the very torrent, tempest, and, as I may say, whirlwind of your passion, you must acquire and beget a temperance that may give it smoothness. O, it offends me to the soul to hear a robustious, periwig-pated fellow tear a passion to tatters, to very rags, to split the ears of the groundlings, who for the most part are capable of nothing but inexplicable dumbshows and noise. I would have such a fellow whipped for overdoing Termagant, it out-Herods Herod; pray you avoid it.*

This peril of over-acting clearly appears to be a particular concern of our speaker/director for his performers, as he now continues at some length to stress his point. He recognizes that passion and nervous energy can combine at any juncture, leading actors astray into mistaking histrionics for an effective dramatic moment. This passion of an actor for such a cherished "moment" is aptly called a *whirlwind*—and he is counseled to *seek the calm in the eye of the storm and use it to achieve control of both story-telling and character revelation.*

He continues, utilizing specific examples from Medieval/ Elizabethan theatre to elaborate upon his point. Recognizing that such exaggerated melodramatic hysteria will often demand the spectators' attention (although not always for the effect that anyone might wish!), the speaker/director cites specific examples from his own contemporary theatre of what the actor should avoid. Without belaboring the point too much for modern readers, Termagant (a quarrelsome Moslem deity) and Herod (the paranoid and traditionally hedonistic governor of Galilee in the time of Jesus) were both familiar villains in the religious and morality plays of the era; actors who played these characters (often amateur craftsmen-turned-performers and members of trade guilds, forerunners of our modern-day unions in their work, and community theatre actors in their play) apparently enjoyed displaying their histrionic potential to its maximum. Thus, these characters were known as two of the primary "scenery-chewers" of their day, and were therefore familiar and popular to their common audiences (the "groundlings", those who stood at the edge of the platform stages, pressing forward for the best view); although, in the speaker/director's estimation, this success was often at the expense of the story and its proper aesthetic effect. (For Shakespeare's more light-hearted perspective on these kinds of things, we need look no further than the adventures of Bottom, Peter Quince, and their fellow "rustics" in *A Midsummer Night's Dream*.)

This elaboration also touches upon a theme to be examined more explicitly later in our study: the idea that a significant portion of the actor's audience in such venues may be ignorant, unsophisticated, and therefore incapable of appreciating the subtleties of the story being attempted; they are understanding of only spectacle and noise. (The Germans would call it *sturm und drang*—storm and stress.) *Avoid the temptation to "dumb down" what you're doing, to compromise your service to the play in order to gain the momentary personal approval of the ignorant.* Although theatre should entertain, it ought not to do so by completely surrendering the equally important goals of education and enlightenment.

> *Be not too tame neither;*
> *but let your own discretion be your tutor.*

Any director or teacher who has coached young actors— *any* actor for that matter—will surely smile at the sudden change of gears seen here. Our speaker/director appears to have suddenly recalled how eager to please actors are by their very nature, realizing that pulling back from all sense of flair and theatricality might result in "too much of a good thing" (as Rosalind puts it in *As You Like It*)—that is, an underplayed, dull performance. So attempting to encourage the proper balance, he advises: *Don't go so far in the direction of "realism" that you lose everything that might make your performance suitable to the high dramatic stakes of the play, and your characterization striking and memorable.* After all, we really don't go to the theatre to see people just like us, living through situations that we ourselves go through every day; even with the works of the so-called social realists like Chekhov and Ibsen, we go to see extraordinary people journeying through extraordinary lives. In the world of Shakespeare, a world of heightened passions, events, and languages, this is even more the case.

As an addendum to that advice, our speaker/director seems to remember that he must always engage in a creative collaboration with his actor, and that ultimately the final performance must be the actor's own and not something imposed from the outside by a director; guided, yes, but not dictated. As a Shakespearean actor, you must *embrace a sense of balance between flamboyance and subtlety in your performance; in so doing, trust your instincts.* You are seeking to honestly portray flesh-and-blood human beings who behave honestly in heightened situations, expressing themselves with some of the most beautiful poetry yet produced in the English language.

> *Suit the action to the word, the word to the action—with this special observance: that you overstep not the modesty of nature; for anything so overdone is from the purpose of playing, whose end, both at the first and now, was and is, to hold (as it were) the mirror up to nature: to show virtue her feature, scorn her own image, and the very age and body of the time his form and pressure.*

Ignited by his previous observations on balance, the speaker/director shares some broader perspectives on our role in general as theatrical artists, and the actor's duty in particular, the thespian being the primary focus of the dramatic experience for audiences.

Words are not enough in themselves to inspire a spectator's belief in character and story, especially in an age where "watching" has overtaken "listening" as the fundamental experience for both theatre and film audiences. Words are the cues and clues for actor behavior; but as renowned acting teacher Sanford Meisner once put it, "An ounce of behavior is worth a pound of words." Words are the icing on the cake in a performance; but actor behavior is the cake itself. Obviously, with a writer as brilliant as Shakespeare, this is very rich icing indeed, and the cake would not be nearly as gratifying in its absence—as many adapted texts and productions of Shakespeare that seek to make it "understandable" to modern ears by changing the language and vocabulary have demonstrated clearly over the years, in spite of the best intentions of their perpetrators.

What must the actor do? *Always make sure that what you're doing on stage complements and clarifies what you're saying.* Don't seek to demonstrate; but at the same time remember that *how* we say something is usually more important than *what* we say. Behavior reveals the truth when words do not.

It is almost a given that what passed for naturalistic and truthful stage behavior in Shakespeare's outdoor public theatres must have been far removed from what we seek as such in today's culture, especially since the cinema has replaced the stage as the most popular form of dramatic entertainment. Nonetheless, it is important to note that the actor's goal as set forth here by our speaker/director was substantially the same four centuries ago as it is today: *Even using the artifice of heightened language and verse drama, we seek to ring a bell of truth to resonate and remain with our audiences after the playgoing experience is over and they have returned to their everyday lives*; to hold a mirror to their souls whereby they may see themselves more clearly and (hopefully) learn something about themselves and those around them. The best theatre reminds us of the wonder of being alive, encompassing the wide range of human experience from exultation to despair.

Moreover, it's important for both the actor and producer of Shakespeare to remember that every age has its own concerns, its own social and political perspectives, its own truths. Only esoteric scholars (if even they) are interested in attending the theatre to experience a museum piece, a demonstration of "how it was done in Shakespeare's day." The mainstream of audiences desire, if not demand—as well they should—what they are seeing to have some relevancy to their contemporary lives, even if the text presented was written centuries ago. Times change, but some human experiences remain consistent through the ages; and actors must embrace that in their performances. *Actors should always seek to reflect the central truths of their era in their work,* even when enacting a tale from a different time.

> *Now this overdone, or come tardy off, though it makes the unskillful laugh cannot but make the judicious grieve, the censure of which one must in your allowance overweigh a whole theatre of others. O, there be players that I have seen play—and heard others praise, and that highly (not to speak it profanely)—that, neither having the accent of Christians nor the gait of Christian, pagan, nor man, have so strutted and bellowed that I have thought some of Nature's journeymen had made men, and not made them well, they imitated humanity so abominably. O, reform it altogether!*

For actors, the primary attraction of the stage is the immediate response that they receive from their audiences. A whispered line can bring a hush to the crowd; a well-executed movement or gesture elicits a gasp of surprise or recognition; and a perfectly timed gag can result in a roar of laughter. In the latter case, it is true that a *mis*-timed jest or gesture can also result in gales of mirth—and as the speaker/director notes, for some amateur performers the boundary between an appropriate audience response (one that advances and enhances the story being represented) and an inappropriate reaction (one that draws undue attention, desired by him or not, to an individual actor at the expense of story and mood) is a thin one.

It's undeniable that some actors are in the profession for the wrong reasons. Stanislavsky addressed this with admirable succinctness when he charged his pupils to "love the art in yourself, not yourself in the art." Three centuries prior to that statement of principle, Shakespeare appears to be saying the same thing through the words of Hamlet: *Don't play to the lowest common denominator in your audiences; and always support the shared purposes of the ensemble effort above your own personal gratification.* Laughs are often fun to receive for the onstage actor, and therefore the temptation is sometimes great to play specifically for that result at the expense of a moment's dramatic integrity. What can make this even more tempting for the young novice performer is his tendency to mistake this improper attention for personal critical approval. The speaker/director continues this counsel by citing his personal experience of such actors in his own prior theatrical experiences. He obviously feels quite strongly about it, as he even goes so far as to question their common humanity! Such bad habits (he declares) on the part of amateur performers need to be flushed away, once and for all. We must maintain the artistic integrity of our work, seeking for greater value than the immediate gratification of an "easy laugh"—even if this means focusing on one discriminating member of our audience over a "whole theatre of others."

> *And let those that play your clowns speak no more than is set down for them; for there be of them that will themselves laugh to set on some quantity of barren spectators to laugh too, though in the meantime some necessary question of the play be then to be considered. That's villainous, and shows a most pitiful ambition in the fool that uses it.*

This final directive from the speaker/director takes on something of a personal tone, perhaps giving us an insight into Shakespeare's own frustration with the primary comic actor (or clown) of his own company, Will Kempe. Documents and anecdotes from the playwright's time in late 16th Century London indicate that Kempe of the Lord Chamberlin's Men was featured prominently in some of Shakespeare's earliest plays, probably playing roles such as Launcelot in both *The Two Gentlemen of Verona* and *The Merchant of Venice*, as well as Peter in *Romeo and Juliet* and Dogberry in *Much Ado About Nothing*. All of these roles appear to have something in common: they all have speeches or moments delineated in the texts wherein the narrative of the play momentarily assumes a sideline status to the individual comic's private showcase (Launce's story of his dog's misbehavior in *Two Gentlemen*, Act IV, scene iv is a perfect example of this, as it doesn't advance the story at all). Although these plays as they have been left to us in their earliest editions (some of them perhaps printed from Shakespeare's own manuscripts—but more of that in the next chapter) contain circumscribed textual versions of these comic showcases (or *lazzis* as they are sometimes called in a term taken from the Commedia del'Arte), it appears by their nature that they could have been easily expanded by self-indulgent actors improvising for their eager fans in an Elizabethan public playhouse, where all levels of education and cultural experience mixed. One can imagine Shakespeare, the playwright/actor/company member standing offstage with grim expression as Will Kempe decided to "improve" his play by expanding on his individual showcased moment, spurred on by the chortling groundlings.

Don't change the play as written for your own personal gratification in the midst of a performance, instructs the speaker/director, quite firmly. *Serve the play, don't make it serve your own egotistical needs.* This means, of course, "speaking the speech" as it was written.

With this final advice, the speaker/director—Hamlet—has come full circle, re-emphasizing the point with which he began. It is near curtain time, the audience is settling in, and time is short. And the stakes are very high.

✧

So, to quickly summarize Shakespeare's advice to his players point by point, offered through the mouth of his most famous character:

1. **Don't paraphrase the text the playwright has given you.**
2. **Listen and learn from your director and fellow actors.**
3. **Speak swiftly and with clear and precise diction; don't declaim too loudly or over-enunciate with affectation.**
4. **Define and clarify the story you're telling, and your role within it.**
5. **Control your gestures and movement; stay relaxed, restrained, and in control in your acting, even while your character is experiencing the height of passion.**
6. **Don't "play down" to the lowest common denominator in your audience; instead, fashion your performances for the discriminating among them. Entertain, educate and enlighten.**
7. **While restraining from overacting, at the same time don't underplay climactic and dramatic moments in the play that demand appropriate physical energy and vocal support.**
8. **Seek to match your physical and vocal choices to what each scene, moment, and beat requires over the course of the play.**
9. **As an actor, always make truth your primary goal, however that may be defined by the world of the play and the time that it is presented.**
10. **Respect the ensemble, and serve the play; don't distort the text and the story in order to make the play serve you.**

Finally, after you have done your homework completely and your creative preparation conscientiously, using the points above as your navigational guide, *trust your own instincts and learn from every experience.*

And that, bounded in a nutshell, is the primary advice from Shakespeare himself, delivered through the words of Hamlet, to the actors of his plays, regardless of the era in which they are produced. So, with those precepts in mind, go make you ready. You should have all the tools you need to begin, right?

Well, yes and no. Would it were that easy!

CHAPTER II

"WHAT IS YOUR TEXT?":
CHOOSING THE BLUEPRINT

Some time ago, on the first day of one of my Acting Shakespeare classes, an eager young student asked me what "translation" we would be using for our work together.

Although this garnered the unfortunate young man a few smug snickers from some of his classmates, the question is not altogether absurd. Although Shakespeare's plays were written by an Englishman—in the English language—the language of the late 16th and early 17th centuries (not to mention their idiosyncratic, ever-changing spelling!) seems far-removed and foreign to our own spoken and written 21st century American English. Especially so now that we have evolved of late into simplistic, almost primitive phone texting messages like "How r u?", "LOL", and similar abbreviated communications. Nonetheless, human beings remain human beings (for the time being, anyway), and the emotional, philosophical, political and spiritual outlooks and concerns of Western civilization contain threads that weave consistently through the last four centuries. So, the initial challenge facing the young actor grappling with Shakespeare is uncovering those threads, attempting to define them, and in doing so, begin the process of illuminating the individual personality traits of the characters that they might suggest.

Additionally, there exist textual variations of many of the plays that are important to explore when preparing to perform them, and in some way these might indeed be viewed as different "translations" or interpretations of Shakespeare's creative intent. Sadly, no manuscripts in Shakespeare's hand (called "foul papers," due to the often messy state in which such documents apparently existed) have survived. The closest we have to that—and scholars continue to debate points of authenticity surrounding it—is a manuscript of the play *Sir Thomas More*, containing a passage of several pages that many believe were written by Shakespeare himself, in collaboration with several other Elizabethan playwrights. (*Sir Thomas More* has recently been accepted into the official canon by several modern editors, including a newly annotated edition from the Arden series. Although it doesn't approach the quality of Shakespeare's primary plays, it's an interesting work for its time and political circumstances, as demonstrated by its fascinating and comprehensive introduction.)

Without any such primary sources for the plays from the author's own hand, what is the nearest thing we have? Something called the First Folio, the initial edition of the "collected Shakespeare" in 1623, and a handful of individual play publications from Shakespeare's own lifetime, called "quartos." More about those in a moment.

In approaching any modern staging of Shakespeare, an actor or director should secure and consult at least three respectable modern editions of the play. There are several good reasons for that practice. For clarification of the most important reason, let's again turn to *Hamlet*.

The majority of modern readers and playgoers would probably be surprised to learn that there is, really, no definitive text of what is arguably the most famous work of Western literature. The reason for this is that there exist no fewer than three early versions of the play, two of which were published during Shakespeare's lifetime, and a third that made its debut as part of Shakespeare's earliest collected plays, the aforementioned First Folio. The earliest version, published in 1603, reveals some very surprising differences from the play that many of us have either read or seen: most of the famous verse passages are entirely different, even though the gist of them might be somewhat familiar; some character names are changed (Polonius is Corambis, in the most blatant example); and the play itself is much shorter than what we usually encounter on page or stage, lacking many of the famous incidents and scenes that we would know from the versions of the play most familiar to the general readership.

Here is one example of the remarkable differences between this 1603 *Hamlet* and the one we're likely to recognize: towards the middle of the play (Act III, scene i in modern editions . . . .or "translations"), Prince Hamlet delivers the most famous single soliloquy—a character's mental reflection while in physical isolation—in all of Shakespeare's writing: the text that begins with "To be or not to be." Here is the piece as we're likely to know it:

> *To be, or not to be; that is the question:*
> *Whether 'tis nobler in the mind to suffer*
> *The slings and arrows of outrageous fortune,*
> *Or to take arms against a sea of troubles,*
> *And, by opposing, end them. To die, to sleep—*
> *No more, and by a sleep to say we end*
> *The heartache and the thousand natural shocks*
> *That flesh is heir to—'tis a consummation*
> *Devoutly to be wished. To die, to sleep;*
> *To sleep, perchance to dream. Ay, there's the*
> *   rub,*
> *For in that sleep of death what dreams may*
> *   come*
> *When we have shuffled off this mortal coil*
> *Must give us pause. There's the respect*
> *That makes calamity of so long life.*
> *For who would bear the whips and scorns of*
> *   time,*
> *Th' oppressor's wrong, the proud man's*
> *   contumely,*
> *The pangs of despised love, the law's delay,*
> *The insolence of office, and the spurns*
> *That patient merit of th' unworthy takes,*
> *When he himself might his quietus make*
> *With a bare bodkin? Who would these fardels*
> *   bear,*

> *To grunt and sweat under a weary life,*
> *But that the dread of something after death,*
> *The undiscovered country from whose bourn*
> *No traveler returns, puzzles the will,*
> *And makes us rather bear those ills we have*
> *Than fly to others that we know not of?*
> *Thus conscience does make cowards (of us all),*
> *And thus the native hue of resolution*
> *Is sicklied o'er with the pale cast of thought,*
> *And enterprises of great pitch and moment*
> *With this regard their currents turn awry,*
> *And lose the name of action.*

Now, for modern readers and listeners, there are apt to be several thorny phrases or passages in this speech that will send the curious (and actors had better be the most curious of all!) to a dictionary, lexicon or editorial footnotes to determine intended meanings; but for the moment, let's overlook those textual puzzles, and take a look at an "alternate version" of the same speech, the one that appears in the very first version of Shakespeare's *Hamlet* as published in London in the third year of the 17th century, at the height of his acclaimed theatrical career:

> *To be, or not to be; aye, there's the point:*
> *To die, to sleep; is that all? Aye, all.*
> *No, to sleep, to dream, aye, marry, there it*
>   *goes;*
> *For in that dream of death, when we awake,*
> *And borne before an everlasting Judge,*
> *From whence no passenger ever return'd,*
> *The undiscovered country, at whose sight*
> *The happy smile, and the accursed damn'd,*
> *But for this, the joyful hope of this,*
> *Who'd bear the scorns and flatt'ry of the*
>   *world,*
> *Scorned by the rich, cursed of the poor;*
> *The widow being oppressed, the orphan*
>   *wrong'd,*

The taste of hunger, or a tyrant's reign,
And thousands more calamities besides;
To grunt and sweat under this weary life,
When that he may his full quietus make
With a bare bodkin? Who would this endure,
But for a hope of something after death?
Which puzzles the brain, and doth confound
*   the sense,*
Which makes us rather bear those evils we
*   have,*
Than fly to others that we know not of.
Aye, that. O, this conscience makes cowards of
*   us all.*

Clearly, although the thrusts of both speeches are the same, the differences in vocabulary and phrasing are significant. And for the actor approaching a characterization of Hamlet, these alternative speeches suggest remarkable variations in the prince's thought processes as well as in the complexity and dexterity of his verbal expression.

Which one is the preferable text? Well, in the case of *Hamlet*, the choice for most actors and scholars seems relatively clear and easy. Although both the versions of 1603 and 1604 claim William Shakespeare as their author, the speech as we best know it comes from the later version, printed only one year after the original version; and the title page of this 1604 text claims that the play contained in its subsequent pages is "newly imprinted and enlarged to almost as much again as it was, according to the true and perfect copy." Interpreting that final phrase, it would appear that this version is Shakespeare's last and best word on Hamlet and the expression of his internal turmoil.

Or perhaps not. For, in 1623 (seven years after Shakespeare's death in his home village of Stratford, after a relatively short retirement from the London stage), yet another version appears for our consideration, that text contained in the First Folio collection. This version, albeit similar to the "second edition" of 1604, omits 230 lines found in the earlier text. (Two of these deletions contain some of the most famous and oft-quoted of the play's passages, and we'll note them a little later on in the chapter.) Upon initial consideration of those deletions, it would seem obvious that the 1604 text contains the "real" *Hamlet*, the one with which we are most familiar, the best one to produce for the stage; but can we really be sure of Shakespeare's intention in that regard? Many scholars see evidence in the Folio version of a theatrical manuscript; and if Shakespeare indeed participated in this version (as would seem to be indicated by the claims of his fellow actors in the Folio's prefatory material), perhaps he felt that the play worked better on the stage without some of the passages in the second, longer version, in spite of our continuing admiration for them.

So, in summary: our first version of *Hamlet* (1603) is probably the least likely to be immediately useful to the modern actor/producer, or even the modern reader, as fascinating as it proves for the literary researcher and scholar; the verse is often clunky and the vocabulary vague, although the progression of the plot moves more swiftly and directly at times. In spite of the specific claims of authorship on the title page, scholarly debate continues regarding whether or not Shakespeare had much of a hand in its writing, or whether it is instead a badly-remembered "bootleg" edition of the famous play as (mis)remembered by a renegade actor working in collaboration with an over-eager printer. Or, perhaps it is a very early version of the play, written in Shakespeare's late 1580's theatrical apprenticeship period, and later refined into the masterpiece that we think of today when we refer to the play.

But which version is that masterpiece? Which is *the* play of *Hamlet* that we should read and trust as the definitive Shakespearean version, the remaining 1604 Second Quarto, or the Folio text of 1623? Well, both and neither. The versions of *Hamlet* you will most likely first encounter in your readings and studies of the play will contain individual editorial interpolations and patchwork versions of these last two original texts left to us by Shakespeare (or those connected with him), during his lifetime or shortly thereafter. Thus, for any serious actor, it becomes pretty important not to place his entire trust in one modern edition of *Hamlet*, particularly one that he pulls at random off the shelf of a bookstore or library.

As a further example of the importance of looking at more than one edition of a Shakespeare play, let's look again at a few small details of the "To be, or not to be" soliloquy, as it might be found in one of the many modern published versions of the play currently at your local bookstore. In many of those editions we might find the following variations: in line 17 of the soliloquy from the 1604 edition (the revised Second Quarto), "the pangs of despised love" becomes "the pangs of *disprized* love." In line 28, three words are added to make the line read "Thus conscience does make cowards *of us all*" (as found in the Folio version). And in line 31, the "enterprises of great pitch and moment" become ones of "great *pith* and moment."

Small variations to be sure; but the potential greatness in all acting is rarely seen in the broad brush strokes of a performance, but rather in its nuances and detail. Choosing between the words "despised" and "disprized" when describing love tells us something about the man who is Hamlet; and the Prince's observation that includes himself in the legion of cowards born from too much reflection—or conscience—seems a pretty significant direct self-criticism that shouldn't be glossed over. (Perhaps the omission of the phrase "of us all" in the Second Quarto is merely an oversight by the printers; but then again, perhaps not. As actors, we should not jump to immediate conclusions about the surviving text options without some thorough reflection.) And the different possibilities that spring from the actor's choice between "pitch" and "pith" at the close of the soliloquy also present subtle but interesting variations of Hamlet's intellect, emotional state, and thought processes.

Which is the *correct* choice? Eager young actors will always want to give the right answer; that is, until they accept as part of the healthy evolution of their artistic individualism that *there are rarely right answers when it comes to acting*. To slightly paraphrase a brilliant former professor of mine, "*Every* interpretation of a text is a mis-interpretation; however, some mis-interpretations are better than others!" In the case of these three choices in this most famous of Shakespearean soliloquies, it will be up to each actor that plays the Prince of Denmark to make his personal choice; and each such choice finally culminates in a unique portrayal of Hamlet. The awesome truth is that no actor has ever played the role exactly like you could play it; because no other actor who has ever lived, or will live, is exactly like you. No interpretation is right, no reading is wrong. However, the more informed the artist is about the material he is working with, the more certain his creative choice will be; and with bold choices are born effective stage characterizations.

What are the origins of these word variations in the different editions? And which words did Shakespeare actually choose? Unless some scholar discovers a manuscript of *Hamlet* at some future date that is provably in Shakespeare's own hand, we will never know. In fact, even if such a thing would happen, we could still never be sure what his final thought on the matter might have been. Perhaps he chose one word for his original composition, then later changed his mind; or perhaps the word was amended in the rehearsal collaboration between writer and actor (in this case, probably Shakespeare and Richard Burbage, the first actor to play this magnificent role). As already noted, the soliloquy as printed above is taken from the Second Quarto of *Hamlet*; the three text variations we have just discussed are found in the First Folio of the works of Shakespeare, published in 1623. So let's take a moment here to review a few facts about the various Quartos and the First Folio to which we've been referring.

Simply put, each one of the individual plays by William Shakespeare that were published in separate editions during his lifetime, and into the first half of the 17th Century following his death, is referred to as a "quarto." The name comes from the method by which the pages of the book were printed, gathered and bound: a larger sheet of paper was folded once from top to bottom, then folded again from side to side, leaving a page size that was approximately a "quarter" of the size of the original paper—thus the name. Each of these sheets would consequently comprise eight pages of the quarto, often designated by successive alphabetical letters at the bottom of each page (for example, the pages 1-8 would be marked A through A8, pages 9-16 would be marked B through B8, and so on). Once all these folded pages were printed and bound in proper order, the folds that still existed at the top of most of the pages would be cut by the first reader of the quarto upon its purchase.

The alert reader might note immediately what potential problems would arise during the layout and printing of a quarto. On one side of a printing block (the size of one of the large sheets of paper before folding), four pages would be set out by the printer, letter by letter, before the block was inked and page sheets were cranked through. On one side of the sheet, quarto pages 1 and 8 would be printed side-by-side on the bottom half of the paper, while above them on the upper half of the sheet—yet upside down to them!—would be pages 4 and 5. Once that side was printed in sufficient quantities, the printers went to work on the opposite side of the large paper, again mapped out into the quarters that would become the full pages of the quarto upon its eventual folding. Backing pages 1 and 8 would be pages 2 and 7, respectively; and, turning the larger paper upside down once again, pages 4 and 5 would be backed by pages 3 and 6. Once folded, pages 1 through 8 would then appear in the proper order. This procedure obviously produced some challenges for the Elizabethan printers, who were often setting their pages from handwritten manuscripts and theatre promptbooks, both presumably rather difficult to read in the indoor lighting of the time. Additionally—and students always enjoy hearing this part!—the machinery of these early printing presses needed to be regularly cooled against the building friction resulting from their operation. Since water in urban London was a precious commodity, and other potables no less so, many of the printers consumed large portions of beer and ale during their work in order to produce plentiful urine to store up and use as a "natural" cooling fluid for the heat generated by the incessant cranking of the machines. The consumption of copious amounts of ale, coupled with the intricacies of the quarto page layouts described above, obviously led to many potential errors in readings and printings from the original source material. In hopes of reducing these errors and miscalculations, a small clue was left at the bottom of each quarto page as a referral or reminder that consisted of the first word or words of the line of text that was to begin the top of the following page.

We have to accept that most printing from this historical period, even those documents overseen by the most careful of craftsmen, were fraught with error; and play scripts, however commercially popular some of them might prove, were seldom the most respected or revered of the era's literature. Nevertheless, the copies of the single quartos of Shakespeare's plays that have survived to the present time are vital documents for critical scholars, literary historians, director and actors, for they remain the earliest recorded versions of these famous plays that we will probably ever have.

Only about half of Shakespeare's plays have survived to our time in these quarto versions that were all published prior to the First Folio collection. Twenty plays in all, these include: *Titus Andronicus, The First Part of the Contention betwixt the two famous Houses of York and Lancaster* (we know it better as *The Second Part of King Henry VI*), *The True Tragedy of Richard Duke of York* (*The Third Part of King Henry VI*), *Romeo and Juliet, Richard II, Richard III, Love's Labor's Lost, The First Part of King Henry IV, The Second Part of King Henry IV, A Midsummer Night's Dream, The Merchant of Venice, Much Ado about Nothing, Henry V, The Merry Wives of Windsor, Hamlet, King Lear, Troilus and Cressida, Pericles* (a collaboration between Shakespeare and George Wilkins), *Othello,* and *The Two Noble Kinsmen* (a collaboration between Shakespeare and John Fletcher). Several other quartos exist of plays that may contain passages or fragments of Shakespeare's writing, but they are not generally included by scholars and editors in this list of "official" Shakespeare quartos; they are: *Edward III* (clearly a collaboration), and *The Taming of a Shrew, King Leir,* and *The Famous Victories of Henry V*, all three perhaps earlier plays by other authors that Shakespeare "appropriated" and revised. In spite of whatever authorship problems or printing errors that these quartos might contain (and the quartos of *The First Part of the Contention, Richard Duke of York,* the First Quarto of *Hamlet*, the First Quarto of *Romeo and Juliet, Henry V, The Merry Wives of Windsor,* and *Pericles* contain many, and are seen as "bad" quartos), they are our true first editions of these twenty Shakespeare plays. As we have seen with *Hamlet*, a Second Quarto sometimes quickly followed the First, making many changes and corrections; and the same happened with *Romeo and Juliet. Pericles*, although a very popular play of its time, never received a "corrected" edition, nor was it included in the First Folio collection of 1623; so this somewhat corrupted 1609 version of the play is all that remains.

So when Shakespeare died in 1616, these twenty plays (along with his published non-dramatic poems and sonnets) were his literary legacy at the time. If his fellow actors had not embarked upon a project to gather these plays into a single volume, along with the remaining ones that he had written and staged during his two decade theatrical career, fully eighteen of his titles would probably be lost and unknown to us, and four more would survive only in error-ridden versions. These include some of his most famous titles, such as *Macbeth, The Tempest, Twelfth Night,* and *As You Like It,* among many others. Obviously, the efforts of John Heminge and Henry Condell (the two actors who spearheaded the First Folio project) endowed posterity with an incomparable gift: nearly half of the Shakespeare canon!

An introductory essay in the First Folio of 1623, entitled "To the Great Variety of Readers:", describes its purpose and content as follows:

> *It had been a thing, we confess, worthy to have been wished that the author himself had lived to have set forth and overseen his own writings. But since it hath been ordained otherwise, and he by death departed from that right, we pray you do not envy his friends the office of their care and pain to have collected and published them, and so to have published them as where, before, you were abused with divers stolen and surreptitious copies, maimed and deformed by the frauds and stealths of injurious imposters that exposed them, even those are now offered to your view cured and perfect of their limbs, and all the rest absolute in their numbers, as he conceived them.*

In other words, Shakespeare's colleagues and friends were, with this volume, attempting to finally see in print all of the plays by their company's master playwright that had never been published prior to his death, while at the same time taking some care to offer the most "perfect" versions available of all his previously printed plays. There have been fascinating scholarly explanations offered about the origins of both "bad" and "good" quartos, and it is certainly worth any director or actor's time to seek out that information; but what is the prevailing academic opinion about the provenance of these thirty-six plays contained in the First Folio? Were their sources manuscripts in Shakespeare's own hand? Copies of such manuscripts by professional scribes? Prompt scripts owned and archived by Shakespeare's company, the King's Men? Collections of collated "sides" (which were the actors' individual lines, inscribed on rolls of paper and given them to learn—such as what is depicted in Act I, scene ii of *A Midsummer Night's Dream*, when the rustic apprentice players are all given their parts by their director, Peter Quince)? Previously printed "good" quartos, re-set by the printers for this new collection? Actually, the most likely answer is: all of the above, at various times. There are signs in the various plays that support all of those ideas, including the names of a few of the Company's known actors appearing next to their lines of dialogue in some of the texts, cues written in margins by (presumably) the playhouse prompter/bookkeeper, idiosyncratic spellings identified by some scholars with Shakespeare himself, and obvious quarto errors that are matched in the same Folio passages. The most important thing for young actors to remember about the First Folio, however, is this: it is the earliest appearance of all of Shakespeare's major works in a single collection, planned, assembled, and overseen by some of his closest friends and fellow-actors. As such, it trumps virtually all other collections of Shakespeare as the single most important source for a theatrical artist to consult when working on the staging of a play by the Bard of Stratford. A few quartos (the Second Quarto of *Hamlet*, most prominently) are also vital sources for consultation, but the First Folio of 1623 stands alone as the most authoritative edition of Shakespeare that we will ever have.

This brings us to the question of modern editions of Shakespeare, editions that endeavor to "translate" this rough 17th Century tome into texts with modern spellings and encompassing scholarly corrections of perceived mistakes and misprints contained within that volume. Some of these modern editions are painstakingly edited and thoughtfully reviewed; others are thrown together haphazardly, often with more care given to the attractive binding and covers than to the content therein. What are some of the better editions that serious young actors should seek as they make their creative preparations for the stage?

Leading the list for top honors would be three editions: the *Arden*, the *Oxford*, and the *New Cambridge*, all generally offered in single editions of each play (preferable) or in comprehensive collections of the Works. All three of the series have varying editors for each title, so the titles range widely in usefulness for the actor. Over the past decade, the Arden Shakespeare has been in the process of bringing out its Third Series of titles, issuing updated editorial versions of nearly two-thirds of the canon so far as of this writing; its careful attention to superb editing of less popular titles (*Timon of Athens*, *Troilus and Cressida*, *The Two Gentlemen of Verona*, and the *Henry VI* series) has been particularly useful to adventurous directors and their actors. Each of the newer Third Series Arden editions also goes far in rectifying a weakness of their prior editions by including historical surveys of the plays' production histories, complete with illustrations, photographs, and contemporary critical responses. For the most part, their literary and textual analyses (all encompassed in detailed introductions that span nearly half of each volume) and appendices also contain usefully inspirational ideas for performers, directors and designers. The Oxford Shakespeare adapts a similar approach to the Ardens; used in conjunction in pre-rehearsal research, they complement one another quite effectively, with one edition often filling in gaps left by their counterpart. The New Cambridge series also proves useful, but the completeness and availability of their newer editions falls short of the other two. The most important quality of these editions for actors—and one that they all share—

is the printing of illuminating explanatory and textual notes on each and every page, along with the Shakespearean text. (The popular *Folger* editions, used extensively in secondary schools across the country, share this important asset; however, the notes themselves are considerably more superficial, and often lack the insights of the other versions.) Footnotes on each page also delineate the variations and text options between Folio and quartos of the plays that have come down to us in both versions, an extremely valuable acting resource. There are also discussions of many editorial emendations of problematical text passages that have been attempted over the past four centuries by scholars hoping to look beyond possible printers' errors into Shakespeare's original intentions.

As for collections of the entire Shakespeare canon now available, several are worth exploring for actors and directors. *The RSC (Royal Shakespeare Company) Complete Works of Shakespeare* has just debuted recently; it uses the First Folio almost exclusively as its source material, and its notes and introductory material focus particularly upon what each text suggests as performance guides. It is perhaps the first Complete Works published that unabashedly courts actors, directors and audiences as its primary readers. *The Riverside Shakespeare*, currently in its second edition, is tried and true in classrooms and studios, offering solid and valuable text notes, introductions to each play as well as essays addressing facets of the Elizabethan/Jacobean era in general and Shakespeare's life in particular, and lovely illustrations, including color plates. David Bevington's *Complete Shakespeare* has also been a standard and respectable classroom edition for decades, offering comparable material to the Riverside. All of these editions offer clear explanatory notes on the same page as the pertinent text (although they sometimes contradict one another, highlighting the importance of an actor consulting at least three texts for each play!), and all three are reader- and actor-friendly.

An additional series of volumes worth searching the used bookstores and websites for: *The Variorum Shakespeare* edited by Horace Howard Furness. Approximately a third of the canon—most of the more famous plays—were published in separate, uniform, and inexpensive paperback editions by Dover Publications (known primarily for their no-frills printings of classic literature) in the mid-Twentieth Century, printed from Furness's edited texts of several decades earlier. Many of these editions offer original spelling texts of both quarto and Folio versions of the plays where both exist (for example, *Hamlet* and *Romeo and Juliet*), and they also offer comprehensive listings of all variant readings so that actors can easily compare them side by side. Moreover, they contain almost ridiculously detailed footnotes offering editorial comments from virtually every major edition of Shakespeare from the 17th Century through the time of their own publication; hence the name *Variorum*. Sadly, most of these Dover volumes are no longer in print (although the two-volume *Hamlet* has appeared once more of late in larger bookstores), but they can often be found online, and they are worth tracking down if you are working on one of the plays in the series.

Finally, several photographic facsimile editions of the First Folio as well as the quartos are available, some reasonably priced, some not. The Norton Facsimile, its pages assembled from the best extant copies available from the Folger Shakespeare Library in Washington D.C., is the best of these, both for readers and performers doing proper research. The Yale and Applause editions (the latter available in paperback) are less expensive, but both are photographed from a single source copy of the First Folio (instead of a composite of many copies like the Norton, assembling their best pages), and thus have some pages and passages that are difficult to read and full of errors. As accustomed as we are to modern printing practices, where thousands of books are printed from the same prepared source, it is sometimes difficult to get our minds around the idea that no two copies of the First Folios that have come down to us over the centuries are identical; but that is the case. This is what makes the work of editor/scholar Charlton Hinman in compiling the Norton Facsimile all the more admirable and valuable. Individual photo facsimiles of various quarto editions are also published intermittently for more serious scholars and collectors by such organizations as the Oxford University Press, the Shakespeare Association, and the Malone Society; and a nearly complete compendium of quarto photo facsimiles can be found in the pricey *Shakespeare Plays In Quarto*, published by the University of California Press. However, *as long as the actor has consulted a First Folio facsimile and at least three modern edited versions of the text to compare variations of interpretation and critical thought,* he has made a great start in the preparation of his role in the play; and many of these rare quartos are reprinted in their entirety in newer editions of the Arden, the Oxford, or the New Cambridge volumes.

Why is this so important? Are the variations between texts, once they are uncovered by the actor researching a role, so significant as to make a difference in his final performance? Well, yes—and we'll look at some specific examples shortly. An actor and a reader tend to look at a Shakespearean text in a fundamentally different way. A reader will almost invariably view the play in the printed edition he is consulting as the finished work of art, as that is how we tend to view all of the books that we read which are printed today. To suggest an important metaphor for a moment: when we read a book, it is like we are looking at a finished house; walking through the rooms, noting the color schemes, the view from its windows, the solidity of the structure as it has been built, etc. However, when an actor considers the text of a play, he is not looking at the house, he is looking at the blueprint of a house. *For an actor, a play text is a blueprint for behavior*; behavior that he will soon be responsible for bringing to truthful, believable life on stage, before witnesses.

Now, the chances are good that when we contract a house to be built as presented in a planned blueprint, we want to know a) that the proposed builder knows how to read such a blueprint, b) that he has enough knowledge and experience with reading blueprints to be able to anticipate and address issues of the construction as they arise, and c) that he has within his resources all the tools that might be necessary to see the house to its completion—or at least that he knows where to go for support if he encounters something that momentarily impedes him in his construction project. The actor is that builder. A serious (or casual) reader, teacher or critic may be able to read the blueprint insofar as recognizing the more literary elements that point toward the interpretation of the plot, the imagery, the symbolism, the broader character types (protagonist vs. antagonist), and so on; but the actor must interpret the *action* that is suggested by the text/blueprint, and the nuances of a character's psychology that propels him into the behavior that determines *how* he goes about that action. To do this job well, he needs to have all the tools he can gather right at the beginning—starting with as many possible ways to complete the blueprint before him that he has time to find. These would include a basic grasp of quarto and Folio differences and options, along with the historical/ critical resources to be gained by his exposure to at least three respectable modern editions of Shakespeare along the path of his preparation and process. Along with his continuing work in classes (and at home—very important!) on the fundamental voice and movement skills of his craft, the tools that such an actor/builder must bring to the process of acting Shakespeare include an informed perspective on which blueprint variant seems best to use for *his* house's construction, why, and how to fully realize everything that it suggests to him.

However, the actor should not confuse any of the above with a quest to find the "correct" reading or interpretation of a character within the play's narrative. (Remember: every interpretation is a mis-interpretation; but some mis-interpretations are better than others!) Many young actors struggle mightily in the early phases of their training with this concept, especially as our Western educational system in general has tended to stress the reward of finding "the right answer" as opposed to the larger gratification that comes with good critical thinking and reflection—even if that sometimes leads to more interesting questions than it does to "correct" solutions. The truth is, questions about art rarely result in right answers; rehearsal processes are not mathematical formulae. During rehearsals, you're not searching for the correct interpretation of Romeo, as Shakespeare saw it; you can never know that. *You're searching for the truth of Romeo that lives within yourself.*

Sometimes you might fear being bold in your choices; don't. Those daring acting choices that can reasonably exist within the carefully considered framework—or blueprint—that the Shakespearean text provides can be exhilarating and memorable, for both artist and audience. Your sense of truth—what Hamlet referred to as "your discretion" in his advice to the players we examined in Chapter I—must be your guide. (And that guide will become even more valuable and dependable as your life progresses alongside your development as an actor!) Don't worry unduly about harming the play in your explorations. Shakespeare's plays will surely survive for the next production, wherever your interpretation during your own creative encounter with them might lead.

In fact, let's conclude this part of the discussion with another couple of metaphors. Let's assume that the text of a Shakespeare play can be compared with a "sculpture" that consists of a couple of sticks and four rubber bands. Those are the materials that comprise the finished form to be created, and Shakespeare provides these items to arrange in whatever way that might please you, or your audiences. These components will remain basically the same in their essence and their qualities, no matter how they are arranged, stretched, distorted or connected by any number of "sculptors," all working with these same six pieces. Thus, as actors, as directors, as designers, we actively collaborate with Shakespeare by responsibly manipulating and composing the elements he offers us.

Or perhaps a better comparison is this: a Shakespeare play is much like a fine diamond. If we provide the proper light, an appropriate background for it (or someone who wears it well), turn it this way, then that, we can offer our audiences a different way of seeing something they have perhaps seen before, finding freshness in the familiar.

And there are plenty of facets to work with in the diamond that is a Shakespeare play.

Let's now look at a few examples of the differences found between Folio and quarto texts in some of the Bard's most famous plays, differences that provide fascinating creative choices for the actor and director when preparing to bring a play to breathing life on the stage. These examples should help to illuminate why your consultation of multiple modern editions of Shakespeare—coinciding with a little bit of research into the Folio and extant quartos—should be an essential preparatory step before rehearsals even begin.

Earlier, we touched upon some very significant cuts in the script of *Hamlet* as printed in the authoritative First Folio, key passages that, for whatever reason, were determined unnecessary for a performance's success. However, two such passages were utilized for great effect in the screenplays of two very famous 20th Century film adaptations of the play. Presumably after careful study and comparison of Second Quarto and First Folio texts, Laurence Olivier used an abridged version of this passage from the quarto as the voiced prologue of his acclaimed 1948 film, thus showcasing it as a vital thematic element of his character interpretation of the troubled Prince.

> *So oft it chances in particular men*
> *That, for some vicious mole of nature in them—*
> *As in their birth, wherein they are not guilty,*
> *Since nature cannot choose his origin,*
> *By the o'ergrowth of some complexion,*
> *Oft breaking down the pales and forts of reason,*
> *Or by some habit that too much o'erleavens*
> *The form of plausive manners—that these men,*
> *Carrying, I say, the stamp of one defect,*
> *Being nature's livery or fortune's star,*
> *His virtues else be they as pure as grace,*
> *As infinite as man may undergo,*
> *Shall in the general censure take corruption*
> *From that particular fault.*

In the context of the passage as it exists in the Second Quarto (Q2), Hamlet is speaking of how Claudius's court's revelry is the "defect" in the body that is the state of Denmark, corrupting it steadily from within. Olivier, by using portions of the passage as a disembodied Prologue, seems to focus the metaphor on young

Hamlet himself, concluding the quotation with the statement: "This is the tragedy of a man who could not make up his mind." Thus, a passage from Q2, excised from Shakespeare's company's final edited version of the play, is inserted into the film in this pivotal manner to significant effect.

With similarly strong effect, Kenneth Branagh determined to replace another previously mentioned excised passage from Q2 in his own filmed performance of *Hamlet* in 1996. After the Prince's brief encounter with Fortinbras's Captain in Act IV, scene iv of Q2, he lingers for a moment alone to speak the powerful soliloquy that begins, "How all occasions do inform against me/And spur my dull revenge!" and ends over thirty verse lines later with the declaration, "O, from this time forth/ My thoughts be bloody or be nothing worth!" For many Hamlets down through the past several centuries, this soliloquy has been seen as a key (perhaps *the* key) turning point for the man's emotional journey through the play. Indeed, Branagh seemed to feel it so, for his filming of it is done with a grandeur that borders on excessive, and he places a rare cinema intermission directly after its delivery. Yet Shakespeare's company—perhaps Shakespeare himself—determined to leave the passage out of their arguably authoritative "final" version of the play, the one in the First Folio. In formulating their text "blueprint" for a guiding vision, the modern actor and director must decide for themselves whether this passage—or others—is crucial (or not) for their own staging. Clearly a knowledge of all their textual options, and an intelligent and informed sifting of them, will be vital factors in those artistic decisions.

A final difference between the Q2 and Folio texts of the play that we'll glance at (although there are many, many more that could, and should, be considered when preparing a production) comes at the moment of the Prince's death in the play's conclusion. In Q2, Hamlet's last moment of life is released in a dying line of dignity and acceptance, the famous sighing breath of "the rest is silence." In the Folio, however, his parting from this world appears to occur with more roughness, pain and despair; for following the above line, another line appears that reads simply: "O, O, O, O!" Was this Shakespeare's change? Or an improvised (and presumably effective) performance moment from the company's leading actor, Richard Burbage, which was subsequently added to the text? Or some combination of the two? We shall never know; but for an actor shaping the role's final moment for himself and the audience, the theatrical effect suggested by this variation seems considerable.

Another of Shakespeare's most famous plays has a textual history that somewhat parallels *Hamlet*. *Romeo and Juliet* first appeared in print in quarto form in 1597. Two years later, it appeared in a Second Quarto with this claim on its title page: "Newly corrected, augmented, and amended." Although scholars have deemed the 1597 first edition as a "bad quarto", it really isn't at all comparable in its so-called "badness" to Q1 of *Hamlet*, which we touched upon earlier. In fact, many passages of Q1 of *R&J* are the same as the later Q2 and Folio versions, or only show minor variations. In some cases, Q1's lines have become the more familiar version; for example, in the famous balcony scene of Q1's Act II, scene 1, Juliet declares "That which we call a rose/By any other name would smell as sweet." In Q2, the line is altered to "By any other *word* would smell as sweet." Over the years, the Q1 line has been used so often in production that actors often believe that "word" must be a misprint when they encounter it in many modern editions.

There has been substantive discourse and disagreement among scholars through the years about the origins of Q1 and Q2. For a long time, one theory accepted by a rather surprising number of academics was that some of the actors who had participated in the original stagings of the play (representing the roles of Capulet, the Nurse, Benvolio, Romeo, Paris and Mercutio, since their lines in Q1 and Q2 seem most alike) assembled together with an unscrupulous scribe, presenting their memorial reconstruction to a printer without authorial permission. But the title page of Q2 suggests a more straightforward scenario: that Shakespeare himself probably revised the play after its initial success for his own artistic reasons.

Other than numerous variations of words, phrases and lines throughout (well exemplified by a quick comparison of the

Prologues of both versions), a major difference between Q1 and Q2 of *R&J* can be found in the treatment of Juliet's character. In Q1 she is much less verbose and "poetic" than she appears in Q2, more direct and blunt in the expression of her feelings and desires. Almost every well-known soliloquy of Juliet throughout the play is substantially expanded in the First Folio/Second Quarto, and a quick comparison of the following passages offers ample evidence of this:

Juliet impatiently awaits the return of the Nurse, whom she has sent to meet with Romeo on her behalf and arrange an elopement.

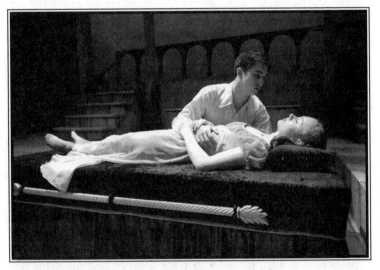

Romeo and Juliet from *Romeo and Juliet*

(First Folio/Second Quarto, Act II, scene iv)

JULIET: The clock struck nine when I did send the Nurse;
    In half an hour she promised to return.
    Perchance she cannot meet him—that's not so.
    O she is lame! Love's heralds should be thoughts,
    Which ten times faster glides than the sun's beams,

Driving back shadows over louring hills.
Therefore do nimble-pinioned doves draw Love,
And therefore hath the wind-swift Cupid wings.
Now is the sun upon the highmost hill
Of this day's journey, and from nine till twelve
Is three long hours, yet she is not come.
Had she affections and warm youthful blood,
She would be as swift in motion as a ball;
My words would bandy her to my sweet love,
And his to me.
But old folks, many feign as they were dead;
Unwieldy, slow, heavy, and pale as lead.
O God, she comes! O honey Nurse, what news?
Hast thou met with him?

(And here is the same passage from the First Quarto, Act II, scene iv)

JULIET: The clock struck nine when I did send my Nurse;
    In half an hour she promised to return.
    Perhaps she cannot find him—that's not so.
    O she is lazy! Love's heralds should be thoughts,
    And run more swift than hasty powder fired
    Doth hurry from the fearful cannon's mouth.
    O now she comes! Tell me, gentle Nurse,
    What says my love?

In this next passage, Juliet excitedly awaits the arrival of her new husband, Romeo, anticipating their first night together.

(First Folio/Second Quarto, Act III, scene ii)

JULIET: Gallop apace, you fiery-footed steeds,
    Towards Phoebus' lodging. Such a wagoner
    As Phaeton would whip you to the west,
    And bring in cloudy night immediately.
    Spread thy close curtain, love-performing night,
    That runaways' eyes may wink, and Romeo

Leap to these arms, untalked of and unseen.
Lovers can see to do their amorous rites
By their own beauties; or, if love be blind,
It best agrees with night. Come, civil night,
Thou sober-suited matron all in black,
And learn me how to lose a winning match,
Played for a pair of stainless maidenhoods.
Hood my unmanned blood, bating in my cheeks,
With thy black mantle, till strange love grow bold,
Think true love acted simple modesty.
Come night, come Romeo, come thou day in night;
For thou wilt lie upon the wings of night
Whiter than new snow upon a raven's back.
Come gentle night, come loving black-browed night,
Give me my Romeo; and when I shall die,
Take him and cut him out in little stars,
And he will make the face of heaven so fine,
That all the world will be in love with night,
And pay no worship to the garish sun.
O, I have bought the mansion of a love,
But not possessed it; and though I am sold,
Not yet enjoyed. So tedious is this day
As is the night before some festival
To an impatient child that hath new robes
And may not wear them. O, here comes my Nurse—
And she brings news, and every tongue that speaks
But Romeo's name speaks heavenly eloquence.
Now, Nurse, what news? What hast thou there,
The cords that Romeo bid thee fetch?

(Now, the passage from First Quarto, Act III, scene ii)

JULIET: Gallop apace, you fiery-footed steeds,
    To Phoebus' mansion. Such a wagoner
    As Phaeton would quickly bring you thither,
    And send in cloudy night immediately.
    But how now, Nurse? O Lord, why look'st thou sad?
    What hast thou there, the cords?

Finally, here Juliet prepares to take the drug, given to her by Friar Laurence, which will put her into a death-like coma, thus allowing her to avoid the arranged marriage to the County Paris.

(First Folio/Second Quarto, Act IV, scene iii)

JULIET: Farewell.—God knows when we shall meet again.
    I have a faint cold fear thrills through my veins
    That almost freezes up the heat of life.
    I'll call them back again to comfort me.
    Nurse!—What should she do here?
    My dismal scene I needs must act alone.
    Come vial. What if this mixture do not work at all?
    Shall I be married then tomorrow morning?
    No, no! This shall forbid it.
    (Lays aside knife)
    Lie thou there.
    What if it be a poison which the Friar
    Subtly have ministered to have me dead,
    Lest in this marriage he should be dishonoured,
    Because he married me before to Romeo?
    I fear it is—and yet methinks it should not—
    For he hath still been tried a holy man.
    How if, when I am laid into the tomb,
    I wake before the time that Romeo
    Come to redeem me? There's a fearful point.
    Shall I not then be stilled in the vault,
    To whose foul mouth no healthsome air breathes in,
    And there die strangled ere my Romeo comes?
    Or, if I live, is it not very like,
    The horrible conceit of death and night,
    Together with the terror of the place—
    As in a vault, an ancient receptacle,
    Where for this many hundred years the bones
    Of all my buried ancestors are packed;
    Where bloody Tybalt, yet but green in earth,
    Lies fest'ring in his shroud; where, as they say,
    At some hours in the night spirits resort—

Alack, alack, is it not like that I,
So early waking—and with loathsome smells,
And shrieks like mandrakes torn out of the earth,
That living mortals hearing them run mad—
O if I wake, shall I not be distraught,
Environed with all these hideous fears,
And madly play with my forefathers' joints,
And pluck the mangled Tybalt from his shroud,
And in this rage with some great kinsmen's bone,
As with a club, dash out my desp'rate brains?
O look! Methinks I see my cousin's ghost
Seeking out Romeo that did spit his body
Upon a rapier's point. Stay, Tybalt, stay!
Romeo, Romeo, Romeo! Here's drink—I drink to thee.

(And here, the variant from First Quarto, Act IV, scene iii)

JULIET: Farewell.—God knows when we shall meet again.
Ah, I do take a fearful thing in hand.
What if this potion should not work at all?
Must I of force be married to the County?
This shall forbid it.—Knife, lie thou there.—
What if the Friar should give me this drink
To poison me, for fear I should disclose
Our former marriage? Ah, I wrong him much,
He is a holy and religious man;
I will not entertain so bad a thought.
What if I should be stifled in the tomb?
Awake an hour before the appointed time?
Ah, then I fear I shall be lunatic,
And playing with my dead forefathers' bones,
Dash out my frantic brains. Methinks I see
My cousin Tybalt welt'ring in his blood,
Seeking for Romeo. Stay, Tybalt, stay!
Romeo, I come! This do I drink to thee.

What might the actor or director, researching these source texts of this most famous play, draw from these variations that might affect their decisions for staging the play? First, it is undeniable that Juliet's poetry from the First Folio/Second Quarto is more mature, more laden with beautifully expressed imagery and extended metaphors, and much richer and more expressive of her emotional state than that of the First Quarto. If we consider only the quality of the writing itself for Juliet, it's difficult not to gravitate instinctively toward Q2/Folio. But as we've noted before, the actor/director's job is to focus primarily upon behavior and stage life, and what a given text might suggest for that; so let's step back for a moment, let go of the indisputable beauty of the poetry alone, and look at one option for telling the story of the two star-crossed lovers, and what the First Quarto might suggest about Juliet that is somewhat lost in the later versions.

When Shakespeare introduces us to Romeo, we receive an immediate first impression of a young lad in love with Rosaline (a young lady who's apparently not interested in reciprocating his feelings toward her), in love with his own passion, in love with poetry, in love with teenage angst and drama—in short, in love with love itself. When Romeo learns from Benvolio about the brawl in the Verona street between the Montagues and Capulets that began the play, he immediately launches into a rather self-conscious poetic reflection of the ongoing family feud.

> *Here's much to do with hate, but more with love.*
> *Why then, O brawling love, O loving hate,*
> *O anything of nothing first create;*
> *O heavy lightness, serious vanity,*
> *Mis-shapen chaos of best-seeming things,*
> *Feather of lead, bright smoke, cold fire, sick*
>   *health,*
> *Still-waking sleep that is not what it is:*
> *This love feel I, which feel no love in this.*
>   (Act I, scene i)

Later on, as the hormone-driven Montague boys prepare to crash the Capulet party in search of girls and mischief, Romeo again expresses an articulate, self-aware poetic premonition of his fate, the "consequence, yet hanging in the stars" that he feels hovering over him. In the garden encounter with Juliet after meeting her at the party (Act II, scene i), he rhapsodizes wordily over Juliet in the shadows before she becomes aware of his presence for some 20+ lines of verse, speaking some of Shakespeare's most enduring passages, beginning with "But soft, what light through (or *forth* in Q1) yonder window breaks?/It is the east, and Juliet is the sun." It might strike the actor doing his text research that, in spite of all of the differences noted between Q1 and F1 in the length and quality of Juliet's poetry, Romeo's verse remains much more consistent in both texts.

Perhaps the reason might lie in Shakespeare's original dramatic vision of the differences in personality between these two young lovers, delineated quite clearly in all versions of the text (Q1, Q2, and F1) of this II,i "balcony" scene. Romeo, already presented as the young teenage poet infatuated with his own feelings and possessing an admirable talent for poetic metaphor, meets his match in the practical young Juliet, the personification of anti-metaphor. If fact, Juliet speaks directly against the frivolity of metaphor, coming down firmly on the side of practical reality in some of her earliest lines of the scene:

> *'Tis but thy name that is mine enemy.*
> *What's Montague? It is nor hand nor foot,*
> *Nor arm nor face, nor any other part*
> (Belonging to a man. O be some other name! Q2/
> F1; not in Q1)
> *What's in a name? That which we call a rose*
> *By any other name would smell as sweet;*
> *So Romeo would, were he not Romeo called,*
> *Retain the divine* (that dear Q2/F1) *perfection*
>   *(which) he owes*
> *Without that title.*

Still later in the scene, Juliet startles the poetic, dreamy Romeo with a bluntness that sharply delineates their personalities, he the dreamer, she the doer. "Farewell, compliment," she exclaims; she cares little for the expected coy games most new lovers play. "Dost thou love me?" She goes on to admit that she knows men are apt to lie in response to such a direct question in order to get what they want. (Such shrewd directness in a 13-year old girl; Romeo has clearly met his match!) And ultimately, when the Nurse threatens to appear on the scene and time is short, she directly tells her newly professed lover that if he intends an honorable marriage to seal his declarations of this night, he should send her word on the morrow about marriage arrangements.

As Shakespeare presents her in these pivotal moments, this is an astoundingly plain-speaking young lady! The contrast between these two young lovers charms and endears; and in many ways, it helps set up the events of the tragedy to come. Moreover, the spare, lean quality of Juliet's verse in the Q1 versions of the three speeches we've compared above actually serves to emphasize that behavioral contrast. Although Shakespeare heightens the literary quality of Juliet's verse in his revisions for Q2 and F1, in the process he arguably muddies the clarity of the fascinating, no-nonsense young lady that the text "blueprint" of Q1 reveals.

Whatever the actor or director approaching this play may conclude from their research—and it might very well legitimately dispute the points I've drawn here—such active engagement with the possibilities and options presented by the variations of Shakespeare's source texts can only lead them to clearer, more detailed acting choices; and consequently, a better performance.

Even very small details can matter a great deal in the actor's preparatory research. Let's take a quick look at Othello's final speech in Act V, scene ii, just before he commits public suicide in atonement for the murder of his beloved Desdemona. Remarking that he is "one that loved not wisely but too well," he goes on (in the First Quarto of the play, published in 1622) to note that his hand, "Like the base Indian, threw a pearl away/Richer than all his tribe." However, in the First Folio, Othello's assertion is changed by one word, thus reading "Like the base Judean, threw a pearl away/Richer than all his tribe." This alters the metaphor rather starkly. In the first version, the example is of an uncivilized Indian who, finding a gem held valuable in "higher" societies, discards it ignorantly, without recognizing its true worth. In the second version, Othello compares himself to Judas Iscariot, who maliciously discarded a jewel (Jesus of Nazareth) who was richer than all his fellow Hebrews. Besides raising the important consideration of Othello's religion—Christian or Moslem?—this variation also reveals something essential about his self-perspective. Does he pity himself for the abysmal ignorance that led him to mistrust the love of his life, with tragic results? Or in his final moments, does he condemn himself mercilessly as maliciously traitorous to Desdemona, making him in his own view the moral equal of Iago? There is no correct answer, and we will never know for certain if this textual contrast results from a simple printer error or a later authorial revision of the play (there are many such differences between Q1 and F1 of *Othello*); but thoughtful examination of the question will lead both actor and director toward important creative explorations and pivotal character decisions about the play's protagonist.

Richard III was an exceedingly popular play with Elizabethan audiences; perhaps it was this play more than any of his other early works that paved the path to Shakespeare's commercial success. One of the most challenging scenes that actors can explore in this exciting historical melodrama is that of the wooing of the widow Lady Anne Neville by the would-be king (and, incidentally, the murderer of King Henry VI and his son Prince Edward, Lady Anne's husband). This outrageously bold courtship occurs over the very corpse of Anne's father-in-law; it strains the audience's credulity that Richard could achieve that successful seduction in the span of 15 stage minutes, and it has proven daunting and frustrating particularly to modern actresses who understandably wonder: "How could I be so trusting as to believe this lying, deformed creature who now professes love for me after literally destroying my family, my hopes, my life?!" A good question, indeed; and a good answer might be found in a passage of the scene that only appears in the First Folio of the play, not in the First Quarto of 1597. Richard tries all tactics with young Anne—flattery, gallows humor, outright fabrication, political justification of his murderous deeds—and all prove useless in persuading her to forgive and marry him. As if suddenly inspired by his own imagination (and the

Lady herself), Richard tries a final gambit—he appeals to her empathy. He is the Beast, and she Beauty; his only guilt is in having never learned how to express his true feelings for her, and for others. The following lines appear in the First Folio, but are absent from Q1:

> *These eyes, which never shed remorseful tear—*
> *No, when my father York and Edward wept*
> *To hear the piteous moan that Rutland made*
> *When black-faced Clifford shook his sword at*
>   *him;*
> *Nor when thy warlike father like a child*
> *Told the sad story of my father's death*
> *And twenty times made pause to sob and weep,*
> *That all the standers-by had wet their cheeks*
> *Like trees bedashed with rain. In that sad time*
> *My manly eyes did scorn an humble tear,*
> *And what these sorrows could not thence exhale*
> *Thy beauty hath, and made them blind with*
>   *weeping.*
>
> (Act I, scene ii)

In other words: "I've been too macho for my own good, and now I'm caught forever in that trap; I've watched people close to me die all of my life, and held all my responses to those losses inside. I don't know how to express my true feelings . . . help me! Your beauty has softened me, and now I don't know how to deal with myself!" Although modern actresses might still struggle with Anne's gullibility, it is up to the actor playing Richard to persuade her, with his passion, his vulnerability, his naked "honesty"—all yet another charade by this masterful, amoral actor. If he succeeds in winning Anne, he will also enthrall the audience, putting them in the palm of his hand by the close of the second scene of the play. These lines will help him to do just that; and they're not even found in some versions of the play!

Many literary critics consider *King Lear* to be the earliest example of a play that deals directly, and often with harrowing effect, with existential questions of life's meaning in what can often seem an indifferent universe. The finale of the play, depicting the death of a devastatingly humbled old man over the corpse of his wronged and loving daughter, is perhaps—when effectively staged and performed—the most moving scene in Western dramatic literature. But in fact, there are two versions of *Lear*, the First Quarto of 1608 (called *The Chronicle History of King Lear*) and the First Folio text (called *The Tragedy of King Lear*). Although the events of both versions follow parallel paths of story and character, there are enough differences between them to merit consideration of both as separate entities; in fact, the collected edition of *The Oxford Complete Works of William Shakespeare* publishes both plays in the same volume (instead of trying to conflate them as some modern editions do) so that readers and theatre artists can examine the variations in detail if they are so inclined. Actors and directors should have that inclination.

Take the death moments of Lear himself, just mentioned: in Q1, it is as follows:

LEAR: And my poor fool is hanged. No, no life.
    Why should a dog, a horse, a rat have life,
    And thou no breath at all? O, thou wilt come no more.
    Never, never, never.—Pray you, undo
    This button. Thank you, sir. O, O, O, O!
EDGAR: He faints. My lord, my lord!
LEAR: Break, break, I prithee break.
EDGAR: Look up, my lord.
KENT: Vex not his ghost. O, let him pass. He hates him
    That would upon the rack of this tough world
    Stretch him out longer.
    (LEAR dies)

                                        (Scene 24; or, Act V, scene iii)

Here is the version in the First Folio:

LEAR: And my poor fool is hanged. No, no, no life?
    Why should a dog, a horse, a rat have life,

And thou no breath at all? Thou'lt come no more.
Never, never, never, never, never.
Pray you, undo this button. Thank you, sir.
Do you see this? Look on her! Look, her lips.
Look there, look there!
(LEAR dies)
EDGAR: He faints. My lord, my lord!
KENT: Break, heart, I prithee break.
EDGAR: Look up, my lord.
KENT: Vex not his ghost. O, let him pass. He hates him
That would upon the rack of this tough world
Stretch him out longer.

(Act V, scene ii)

Little needs to be said here; performances of the play bring out clearly the difference in dramatic effect between the two passages. The five repetitions of "Never" are heartrending; and what does Lear see in his final moments of life in the latter version? Is it what he mistakes as a slight breath in Cordelia? Is it a metaphysical vision at the instant of his final breath that no one else shares? Is it joyful? Despairing? Which passage that is staged, and the choices that the actor and director make with its performance, will greatly affect how an audience will respond to the ultimate moments of this monumental play.

(And might the Q1 "O, O, O, O!"—echoing the Folio version of Hamlet's final moment—be an attempt by the playhouse scribe to immortalize in textual form a famous performance trademark of the tragedian Richard Burbage when playing death scenes in the Globe Theatre? The similarities seem to me more than mere coincidence.)

Now we'll conclude with a comparison of the First Quarto and First Folio versions of a key passage in the final scene of *A Midsummer Night's Dream*, one of Shakespeare's most oft-staged plays; I think this example, perhaps more than any other we've examined, illuminates the value of this kind of textual research for actor and director when preparing to stage one of the plays.

One of the three parallel plots of *Midsummer* involves the misadventures of two pairs of adolescent lovers over one long, magical and amorous summer night in the woods surrounding Athens. The conflict, in brief: Hermia is in love with Lysander, but her father, Egeus, has arranged a marriage for her with Demetrius. Hermia's best friend, Helena, has had a prior romantic relationship with Demetrius, and is still in love with him. Hermia defies her father, and makes plans to elope with Lysander that very night. Helena, trying to gain favor with Demetrius, informs him of their plans. (Apparently, the young lady is *very* obsessed with her former lover to concoct such a seemingly self-defeating scheme!) Demetrius follows Lysander and Hermia into the woods with the intent of preventing their elopement; and of course, Helena follows him. In the forest that night, the lovers fall under the spell of the fairy kingdom, and love potions are mistakenly administered. Both men become infatuated with Helena, leaving Hermia completely baffled and heartbroken. Eventually it all works out with appropriate comical energy, and the lovers are matched with their proper counterparts. Asleep in the woods in one another's arms, they are discovered the next morning by Duke Theseus and Hermia's father, Egeus. Egeus is furious at his daughter's rebellion and contemptuous of her true love, Lysander, but Theseus decides to overrule the father's opposition to what is clearly meant to be. A triple marriage is arranged, with Theseus and Hippolyta, the Duke and his newly-conquered lady, comprising the third couple. In the First Quarto, at this point, unhappy papa Egeus vanishes from the play, never to reappear in the text.

At the beginning of the wedding scene in the Q1 text of Act V, Theseus calls forth Philostrate, his Master of Revels, to consider the post-ceremony entertainment. Then occurs the following passage.

THESEUS: Come now, what masques, what dances shall we
    have
  To wear away this long age of three hours
  Between our after-supper and our bedtime?
  Where is our usual manager of mirth?
  What revels are at hand? Is there no play
  To ease the anguish of a torturing hour?
  Call Philostrate!

PHILOSTRATE: Here, mighty Theseus.

THESEUS: Say, what abridgement have you for this evening?
    What masque, what music! How shall we beguile
    The lazy time if not with some delight?

PHILOSTRATE: There is a brief how many sports are ripe.
    Make choice of which your highness will see first.
    (Hands him a scroll.)

THESEUS: *(Reading the scroll.)*
    "The battle with the centaurs to be sung
    By an Athenian eunuch to the harp."
    We'll none of that. That have I told my love
    In glory of my kinsman, Hercules.
    "The riot of the tipsy Bacchanals
    Tearing the Thracian singer in their rage."
    That is an old device, and it was played
    When I from Thebes came last a conquerer.
    "The thrice-three Muses mourning for the death
    Of learning, late deceased in beggary."
    That is some satire, keen and critical,
    Not sorting with a nuptial ceremony.
    "A tedious brief scene of young Pyramus
    And his love Thisby. Very tragical mirth."
    'Merry and tragical'? 'Tedious and brief'?
    That is hot ice, and wondrous strange snow.
    How shall we find the concord of this discord?

PHILOSTRATE: A play there is, my lord, some ten words long,
    Which is as brief as I have known a play;
    But by ten words, my lord, it is too long,
    Which makes it tedious. For in all the play
    There is not one word apt, one player fitted.
    And tragical, my noble Lord, it is; for Pyramus
    Therein doth kill himself, which when I saw
    Rehearsed, I must confess, made mine eyes water;
    But more merry tears the passion of loud laughter
    Never shed.

THESEUS: What are they that do play it?

PHILOSTRATE: Hard-handed men that work in Athens here,
    Which never labored in their minds till now,

And now have toiled their unbreathed memories
With this same play against your nuptial.
THESEUS: Go, bring them in.

(Act V, scene i)

Now, the same passage in the First Folio text of the play:

THESEUS: Come now, what masques, what dances shall we have
To wear away this long age of three hours
Between our after-supper and our bedtime?
Where is our usual manager of mirth?
What revels are at hand? Is there no play
To ease the anguish of a torturing hour?
Call Egeus!
EGEUS: Here, mighty Theseus.
THESEUS: Say, what abridgement have you for this evening?
What masque, what music! How shall we beguile
The lazy time if not with some delight?
EGEUS: There is a brief how many sports are ripe.
Make choice of which your highness will see first.
(Hands Lysander a scroll.)
LYSANDER: (Reading the scroll.)
"The battle with the centaurs to be sung
By an Athenian eunuch to the harp."
THESEUS: We'll none of that. That have I told my love
In glory of my kinsman, Hercules.
LYSANDER: "The riot of the tipsy Bacchanals
Tearing the Thracian singer in their rage."
THESEUS: That is an old device, and it was played
When I from Thebes came last a conquerer.
LYSANDER: "The thrice-three Muses mourning for the death
Of learning, late deceased in beggary."
THESEUS: That is some satire, keen and critical,
Not sorting with a nuptial ceremony.
LYSANDER: "A tedious brief scene of young Pyramus
And his love Thisby. Very tragical mirth."
THESEUS: 'Merry and tragical'? 'Tedious and brief'?

> That is hot ice, and wondrous strange snow.
> How shall we find the concord of this discord?
> EGEUS: A play there is, my lord, some ten words long,
>   Which is as brief as I have known a play;
>   But by ten words, my lord, it is too long,
>   Which makes it tedious. For in all the play
>   There is not one word apt, one player fitted.
>   And tragical, my noble Lord, it is; for Pyramus
>   Therein doth kill himself, which when I saw
>   Rehearsed, I must confess, made mine eyes water;
>   But more merry tears the passion of loud laughter
>   Never shed.
> THESEUS: What are they that do play it?
> EGEUS: Hard-handed men that work in Athens here,
>   Which never labored in their minds till now,
>   And now have toiled their unbreathed memories
>   With this same play against your nuptial.
> THESEUS: Go, bring them in.
>
> (Act V, scene i)

For actors, directors and audiences, the preference between which text to use in production seems obvious. The latter Folio text has many advantages: More of the passage takes the form of dialogue, which is inherently preferable onstage; while a character extraneous to the play's central narrative (Philostrate) is eliminated, and a supporting character's (Egeus's) dramatic journey is resolved, one whose objection to the marriage of his daughter to Lysander incites the play's action. What is classically desirable in such romantic comedies happens on stage: an angry father finally accepts as his new son-in-law the man his daughter truly loves, symbolized by his handing of the scroll to Lysander to read and consider along with Theseus, thus honoring him as a new member of his family on this special day. Father and daughter are reconciled. In the First Quarto, this does not happen, and a small cloud hangs over the happy ending of the play in the person of the absent father.

When first staging *A Midsummer Night's Dream* some twenty years ago, I was rather shocked to discover that at that time, there were virtually no major modern editions of the play that printed the First Folio text of this scene; all of the readily available printings of the play utilized the Q1 version, with Philostrate present and Theseus's solo reading of the entertainments. Moreover, in many of these standard editions, used in classes and stagings throughout the country, there weren't even any notations or discussions of the Folio variant. Upon further research, I discovered that Q1 had been considered the preferable text by traditional literary Shakespeare scholars for most of the four centuries since the play's composition. Why? Because when studying most texts as literature, there is a natural academic prejudice toward the earliest edition as being the closest to the author's own hand, and thus truer to his purest intentions.

As the 20th Century drew to a close, and the idea of "performance criticism" became more acceptable in mainstream academic writing, more editions of the play began to follow the lead of the Oxford series and include the option of considering both passages, sometimes with accompanying critical commentary. As alluded to elsewhere, the source material for the 1623 First Folio texts are often difficult to pin down from the evidence available; scholars have debated them for decades. For some of the Folio plays, however, there appears to be some clearer basis upon which to determine their textual provenance; and *Midsummer* is one of those plays. Throughout the printed Folio text, there are character entrances marked in advance; some very specific stage directions not found in Q1 of the play; and, in one specific instance, a stage direction that actually gives the name of an actor/musician of Shakespeare's company. Thus, the source of the Folio version of *Midsummer* was apparently a promptscript—or the "Book" of the play—used in its latter stagings at either the Blackfriars or the Globe, the two theatres owned and operated by the King's Men. Did Shakespeare himself write or approve the revisions of Act V? Or were they, as some scholars insist, "corruptions" of the play made by the actors for their own non-literary purposes?

William Shakespeare was, first and foremost, a practical working artist in the commercial theatre of his time. He knew what played well in his theatre, what attracted audiences. I believe that, being an actor himself and having professional theatre artists as friends and colleagues, he embraced the principle with which we began this chapter's exploration: the playscript, as composed by any playwright, cannot be seen by the actor as the finalized work of art, the last word. Instead, it is the blueprint for the performance to come. Today's actors and directors who determine to bring the script to life on stage are the active collaborators—in Shakespeare's case, the *posthumous* collaborators, four centuries after the fact—with the playwright.

A serious Shakespearean actor must therefore become a bit of an historical detective and a scholar when preparing to tackle this greatest of all Western playwrights. He left us no personally annotated explanations of the origins of his quartos, and no map with which to determine the possible misprints and variants of the Folio copies that have survived. Committing to the research necessary in order to decide the best textual options available for a given Shakespeare play is an essential pre-requisite for any staging and performance; an informed actor is an actor best equipped to make the most interesting textual choices, which in turn should lead to a more thoughtful, dynamic, nuanced and memorable performance that will linger in the audience's mind for years, and perhaps send them back to another reading of a play they thought they already knew well enough . . . before they experienced your striking interpretation!

Again: Even as we hold it in appropriate respect—even reverence—every Shakespeare play text is your blueprint for your performance. Plan it well, make informed choices of your options, lay your foundations with the proper research—and begin to build!

CHAPTER III

"THE CUE FOR PASSION"
FILLING THE ROLE

Your blueprint is in place: you've done your basic research on the origins of and the options offered by the original Shakespearean texts, both in Folio and in Quarto (those plays that were published in that form). You've looked into what some of the best editorial minds, working from lifetimes of historical and literary research, have said about those textual possibilities, and as a result of this, you have begun to engage actively and creatively—yes, *collaboratively*—with the mind of Shakespeare himself, over a gulf of four centuries. Now it's time to *act* on all that thought and research.

But once more: where to begin? When compared to the plays and playwrights that you're probably most used to working with—the contemporaries, or near-contemporaries such as the Mamets, the Wassersteins, the LaButes, the Henleys, and so many others—Shakespeare seems so . . . well, *stiff. Artificial. False.*

Is it?

In spite of the of the grand poetry and metaphor encompassed by Shakespeare's compositional style; in spite of the particular Elizabethan historical context from which the plays arise; in spite of the four centuries that separate us from Shakespeare's pen scratching out his remarkable dramatic visions upon sheets of parchment, *it is not*. It is not only Shakespeare's literary style—so intimidating to most young students as well as the oft-befuddled educators who struggle to introduce the plays effectively to them—that has insured his plays' survival over 400 years; it is the psychology of the characters, the essential passion and universal humanity of the stories and how they are told.

And that's where the actor enters the scene. Psychology, passion and humanity are the tools of our trade, as they were Shakespeare's—a quintessential man of the theatre.

John Barton, in his wonderful video series of filmed workshops with members of the Royal Shakespeare Company entitled *Playing Shakespeare*, outlines quite succinctly the challenge facing modern actors tackling Shakespeare. The actor, he says, must find a way of marrying the naturalism and truthfulness of the modern stage with the heightened language of the plays.

The key to success in achieving this lies in two basic approaches that an actor must embrace: *importance* and *immediacy*. These aspects are crucial with all scripts and characterizations that an actor tackles, but they are especially vital in Shakespeare. His plot situations, and the active and emotional responses that his characters have towards them, are never "everyday." Shakespeare's people—certainly they that populate his tragedies and histories, but also the primary movers of his comedies—are in the midst of experiencing *the most important moments of their lives*. How they respond to those moments will determine all possibilities of future happiness, success in romance, potential triumphs, threats of defeat, and utter personal destruction. There is rarely room for passive reflection; they must examine, resolve and *act*, with urgency and passion. Not in the days to come, but *now*.

Let's look at a few examples to illustrate this point:

The poetry that Romeo speaks while voyeuristically viewing his newfound love—indeed, his newfound *obsession*—from her moonlit courtyard as she dreamily muses on the balcony of her bedroom, springs primarily from his adolescent lust; from a genuine awe of how her beauty has affected him to his very soul; from a heightened sense of physical danger of being discovered by the Capulets, who would do him bodily harm, even conceivably murder him; from the alcohol that he has consumed at the Capulet party that he and his "posse" crashed earlier in the evening; and from his frustration and anger at being ridiculed for his amorous feelings only moments before by his best buddies, Mercutio and Benvolio.

Given all these contextual elements, the words could hardly come out gently lyrical, self-consciously poetic. Instead, they are eager, sometimes breathless in their headlong and reckless emotional (and hormonal!) response to this beautiful young girl, draped in her nightgown, on the balcony above him—a spatial relationship that naturally would inspire metaphorical celestial images of suns, moons, stars, and clouds in the actor/ character who is Romeo. Predictably, Romeo's rhapsody is also filled with the earthier things that possess his thoughts as his eyes take her in, lit by her candles ("What light through yonder window breaks?") on the threshold of her bedroom: the sound of her sigh, the imagined touch of her soft cheek, her beautiful eyes—and of course, her virginity. (Speaking of the "vestal livery" of Diana, goddess of maidens, which Juliet still figuratively wears, he invokes her vigorously to "Cast it off!"—presumably for his own benefit!) Romeo's spoken tribute to Juliet's beauty and his own attraction to it, running for some 30 lines, jumps from metaphor to metaphor, image to image, feeling to feeling—precisely like a young man in the initial agonizing and ecstatic throes of falling in love and lust simultaneously. The emotions are extreme, and can only be expressed in poetry—the kind of poetry that we all wish we could create in those times when ordinary words fail us. For Shakespeare's characters, the passions are high, yet truthful— truthful with a capital "T"—and words rarely, if ever, fail them. Would our own lives' special moments could be so blessed with such beautiful articulate expressiveness!

A bit earlier in the play, at the Capulet's party, disguised party-crasher Romeo pulls Juliet aside to speak with her for the first time. In their brief exchange, they create a perfectly structured 14-line sonnet together. The actors portraying these characters are faced with answering a fundamental question in the playing of this important moment: do the young lovers consciously create the sonnet together, playfully challenging one another to supply the next line or couplet? Or is it entirely unconscious, a happy accident, something that the reader or audience might note appreciatively from a literary perspective but that Romeo and Juliet are unaware of? In working the scene in rehearsal and in class, I have seen it play well enough both ways—once again, there is no "right" answer. However, when the actors embrace this bit of dialogue as a *conscious* use of the poetic structure (sonnets sent between lovers were a common mode of lovemaking at the time of the play's composition—would that it were still so today!), a way of communicating their sudden discovery of one another in a way that is both romantic and witty, they make a bold and important step toward marrying a natural and truthful motivation—to win their partner's love, admiration, respect, attraction, etc.—with the intentional utilization of heightened language, rather than simply trying to make the verse—in itself an artifice—"sound" natural. One approach simply tacks the poetry on to the naturalistic behavior (proving quite a challenge for young, contemporary actors), while another seeks to make it an honest, self-aware, organic part of the lovers' meeting . . . which, it seems to me, should be much easier to actively play.

Let's take another quick look at that famous speech of Hamlet's that terrifies so many young actors: "To be or not to be." In spite of the intellectual depth of the famous soliloquy, the moment that it represents for the character in the play is anything but passively reflective. From a broad perspective, Hamlet's thoughts can be applied to a wide variety of existential moments of crisis in any human life. But if it is to be immediate and effective in performance, part of the driving action of the story, the actor must never approach it with such broad generalities in mind. Hamlet's crisis is personal, involving the highest possible stakes—and the actor must decide that it needs to be resolved now, at this very moment. Not after further thought, nor careful reflection, but now. The nature of his current situation demands it. To live, and continue to sort through all of this agonizing mess: his father's murder, his mother's marriage to his uncle, his problems with his girl friend, his feelings of inadequacy . . . in sum, his burdensome responsibilities; or to simply take the easiest avenue out of it all by ending his own life.

So he strides out onto the stage, to confront us, forcing us to share his moment of truth, demanding that we invest in it fully, along with him. Challenging us to feel exactly what he is feeling by consciously using the heightened language and stark poetic imagery almost as weapons, attempting to infect us with the same passion and turmoil he struggles with. Dependent upon where all of this shared examination leads him, the possibility of his own suicide is immediate; he could do it now. The "bare bodkin" could very well be in his hand, ready to fulfill the impulse. Emotions are at their highest, all possibilities hover over his shoulders. The story of Hamlet could really end right there, within the next few spoken lines. The actor must truly believe in this option at some level, even while he knows that the play as Shakespeare wrote it actually goes on for another three Acts. His belief in that urgency organically heightens both the stage moment and the language.

Lady Macbeth makes her first entrance into the play that bears her husband's name reading a letter that he has sent to her from the battlefield, where he has been putting down a rebellion against King Duncan's rule by the traitorous Thane of Cawdor. Scotland is embroiled in civil insurrections, apparently due to the age and increasing weaknesses of her monarch, who now, in his infirmity, relies on his Thanes (his titled and landed allies, among which Macbeth is numbered) to insure his continued rule of the country. The letter that so excites Macbeth's young wife relates the tale of her husband's encounter on the battlefield with three supernatural beings who deliver prophesies of his future climb to political power, which (they say) will culminate in his gaining the Scottish crown. This news electrifies her; it is exactly what Lady Macbeth has always believed her husband deserves! After all, he is the man most capable of subduing the current, unruly climate of war and revolt: a bold soldier, a well-trained killer, an assured and passionate husband and lover. The success and renown she believes has always been fated for them now actually seems within their reach, and metaphysical forces—whether benign or malignant—are clearly urging them to seize it with boldness and assurance.

But she fears her husband's reluctance to challenge the political *status quo*; and she is frustrated that, as a woman, she may not be able to persuade him adequately that *now is their time*. So, gripped by her enthusiasm for their partnership, as well as her devoted love for her husband, and wanting to help him gain what he so clearly deserves in her eyes, she makes a startling choice and puts it into practice on an impulse: she sells her soul to Satan, right there, right then. Like a child that plays naively with a Ouija Board, she jumps unthinkingly into an actual ritualistic summons of all of the Evil forces that she feels hovering over her, asking for their preternatural support in her ambition to secure the throne for her husband. Too often, this passage is played simply as theatrical rhetoric by the actress portraying the role. It is not; it is an invocation of Dark Forces, capped by the appearance of her husband (symbolically apt, as he will soon become the human embodiment of soulless malice) whom she rushes to embrace. Here is yet another example of passions which are too heightened to be confined within the bounds of ordinary language; only verse, rhythm and metaphor will serve to do them justice.

Over my years of teaching young actors on the stage, I've found this generalization to be mostly true about how they view themselves, at least early in their artistic development: they are either musical theatre devotees ("Broadway Babies" is the semi-derogatory term often used) or "serious" actors who pride themselves in their knowledge of literature and their range of classical experience and ability. Of course, such self-perceptions are unproductive and creatively limiting. If theatre is a true love for you, then all forms of it are worth your exploration. If the actors who love and respect musical theatre can be properly introduced to the challenges of Shakespearean verse—and find the inspiration that awaits them in that newfound experience— they will soon discover that the challenges of performing Shakespearean and musical theatre texts are surprisingly similar. With musicals, a song is not simply attached at certain points to passages of text; a character sings primarily because his emotional life is so intense at a given point that simple words and "normal" energy will no longer suffice to express those feelings. With Shakespeare, the actor must embrace a similar concept: his passions and needs are so intense that only the heightened language—the "music" of the verse rhythms and the beauty of that perfect metaphor—will suffice to communicate them. If he has not found this to be true in his work, then chances are he has not yet discovered the details and specific context necessary in order for him to fill the role as Shakespeare conceived it.

So, in creating your character's story, embrace the necessity of gaining what you desire *now*, making the vital choice *now*, fulfilling your essential need *now*. Embrace this idea *passionately*, and find the reason for *urgency*. (With Shakespeare, this isn't difficult to discover, and that's the reason why most actors love to work on his plays.) Your passion must feed the need for the heightened language you speak, and then you will speak it convincingly.

An actor tackling Shakespearean roles and text must also learn to adore the English language, with all its intricacies, eccentricities, possibilities and nuances. Tedious as the process may seem to young artists who long to leap into the flood and begin acting (particularly emoting!) on their feet as soon as possible, table work and written analysis is vital preparation, especially with thorny Shakespearean vocabulary. Shakespeare often seems giddily intoxicated with the English language, pushing its frontiers at every opportunity. Estimates vary as to how many words that Shakespeare either "invented" by coining them himself for the first time in written literary history, changing nouns to verbs, verbs to adjectives, or combining two or more words into one. Many words or phrases that we use every day can be originally traced back to a first recorded appearance in a Shakespeare play, including *assassination, amazement, champion, eyeball, gossip, label, negotiate, premeditated, remorseless, submerged, torture,* and *puking*. At least 1700 such examples have been accepted by experts over the course of their historical study of the English language.

With the text of the play before them, the actor needs to conscientiously identify and mark every word in his part—or in the parts of the characters that cue his responses—about which he is curious or with which he is unfamiliar. Part of the fun of acting Shakespeare resides in his deft use of words that can mean several things within the single context in which they appear; i.e., implied or explicit double meanings. The sonnets, with their higher emphasis on wordplay, are perhaps the best examples for exercising the actor's mind on Shakespeare's cleverness. For example, let's glance at the first two lines of Sonnet 92:

> *But do thy worst to steal thyself away;*
> *For time of life thou art assured mine . . .*

Consider his use of "steal"; it could mean that the lover/ friend in question is physically sneaking away from the speaker, "stealing" out of his life; or, it could mean that the lover/friend is robbing the speaker of the riches that his presence gives him by choosing to absent himself from company; or—by the sound of the word alone, when spoken—it could suggest that the lover/friend is "steeling" himself away, giving nothing in warm, emotional support to his needy partner.

Or here, in the first two lines of Sonnet 27:

> *Weary with toil, I haste me to my bed,*
> *The dear repose for limbs with travail tired;*

In this example, "travail" at its most direct certainly means "labor"; it also implies labor hampered by strife or perils. But moreover, the sound of the word links it to "travel", and did even more in Elizabethan parlance; and obviously the word "travel" works equally well for the poet/speaker in this particular context.

A last example of double meaning, also drawn from the sonnets, is particularly witty and clever. In Sonnet 138, the speaker/poet explores the differences between the flattering deceptions practiced by lovers and outright falsehoods. In the piece's final two lines, he concludes:

Therefore I lie with her and she with me,
And in our faults by lies we flattered be.

Here, to "lie" (in both lines) equally means: 1) to deceive by flattery, and 2) to lie down with a lover in a romantic context. Furthermore, the "faults" talked of encompass both the tendencies of lovers to fib to one another, as well as the "sin" of lusting after one another. In fact, the entire sonnet is packed with double meanings: "vainly" is used in a way that means both "futile" and "conceited" simultaneously; and "habit" can be seen as meaning a "repetitive action" as well as "a characteristic appearance or dress." Both are equally relevant within the context of the sonnet, as shown below in its entirety:

When my love swears that she is made of truth,
I do believe her, though I know she lies,
That she might think me some untutored youth
Unlearned in the world's false subtleties.
Thus vainly thinking that she thinks me young,
Although she knows my days are past the best,
Simply I credit her false-speaking tongue;
On both sides thus is simple truth suppressed.
But wherefore says she not she is unjust?
And wherefore say not I that I am old?
O love's best habit is in seeming trust,
And age in love loves not to have years told.
Therefore I lie with her, and she with me,
And in our faults by lies we flattered be.

While we're with this sonnet, let's pause for a moment to exercise another practice that all actors, beginning and experienced, should do when working with Shakespeare; let's paraphrase what the speaker/poet is communicating, using our own words and phrasing:

When my lover tells me that she would never,
ever lie to me (or even in my presence), I
believe her—even when I know she's lying as

she says it!—because I want her to believe that I'm a naïve truster in her charming ways, even though I've had lots of past experience with former lovers— quiet flirtations and deceptions. Consequently, I play along with her, pretending to believe that she thinks I'm young (even though we both know I'm not anymore!); and this makes her feel younger than she really is as well. So, why don't we just admit the actuality—that she's flattering me, and I'm really not very young anymore? Well, because that's the way lovers behave with one another: they tell one another flattering, happy lies, because they like to believe the fantasy that they're still as young and as vital as ever. Consequently, we continue to flatter one another—as well as sleep together—and by tacitly agreeing to share that fiction, we remain together, happy in our illusions.

Shakespeare says it so much more lyrically, mischievously, wittily, and lovingly, doesn't he? That's the beauty of heightened language: familiar and truthful human impulses ignite it (as with all well-written plays and characters), but Truth with a capital "T" results from the beautifully crafted artifice. So, when approaching Shakespeare's verse (as when approaching songs in musical theatre), take Hamlet's advice: "Be not too tame." As long as honesty remains your foundation, the passion will be organic and sustainable—and essential.

And as the character, choose your words carefully; to achieve this, an actor must personally connect with the word, both in meaning and in *sound*.

You might have noted that I referred to the poet of the sonnets also as the speaker; for the actor must always be concerned with the *sounds* of words as well as their meaning, particularly with Shakespeare. (He clearly was, as it is beyond dispute that his lines inevitably are clarified when read aloud in a manner that is not always the case when they are simply viewed on the page; after all, he originally wrote them to be *heard*, not read.) In truth, a word's meaning is often defined—in some cases, even originated—in their sound. Actors must *taste* the word's sound, even while he is thinking of its meaning.

Let's compare these examples: *grab, hold, clutch, seize.* In concept, all of these words are varying forms of a similar action. And yet, how differently they sound when spoken aloud! Take a moment to pronounce each one: first, in a normal tone and tempo. Then, articulate each sound of the word more slowly, luxuriating in the vowels and diphthongs, mapping out the harshness or looseness of their boundaries that the consonants provide. Taste the words; be aware of how your mouth, lips and tongue produce and caress each sound shape, how the interactions of your breath and your vocal folds are providing the engine for expression. Imagine that you must communicate the essence of the word simply by the sound you make saying it: your choice of pitch, volume, resonation; the wideness of the vowel sounds; the sharpness of the consonants.

Grab has a blunt sound, a kind of clumsy, blundering, animal quality, helped toward this effect by the combination of glottal and glide ("grrr") and the voiced plosive consonant that concludes it. Consonants play less of a prominent role in the voicing of *hold*; the open "o" vowel dominates, surrounded by the aspirant beginning and the tongue glide of the "l", ended rather gently by the barely heard stop of the softened "d." The hard glottal "k" sound that opens *clutch*, in combination with the tongue fricative of the word's ending, suggests in its sound a frantic scrabbling, as of fingernails searching for purchase on a solid surface, or the noise made by a closing trap. Finally, *seize* is entirely dominated at both the beginning and end of its pronunciation by hissing sibilants, the first unvoiced, the last voiced, providing a slightly firmer ending consonant sound; such a strong wrap-around "hiss" stimulates a visceral response in the listener, most often associated with an aggressive animalistic, even reptilian sound.

Although the examples above fall slightly short of onomatopoeia (defined as "the formation of a word that sounds like what it refers to"), they still provide legitimate examples of how the sounds of words in a skilled actor's mouth can help suggest, directly or subtly, the *feeling* that pervades a key moment in the play or the character himself. There are examples of this to be explored in every scene of every Shakespeare play. Again, there are no "right" conclusions to be reached in such siftings; the creative value for the actor lies primarily in the process of examination and experimentation. The soliloquies are full of sounds, like music, to suggest underlying moods that provide foundation for thoughts. Shakespeare enhances the uniqueness of his characters by the sounds that issue from them: the serpent-like sibilants of the conniving Richard III, the blunt barking consonants that can be associated with the savage Caliban, the physical imitation of the noise of the surrounding storm made by the maddened Lear. ("Blow, winds! Crack your cheeks! Rage! Blow!"—who can fail to hear the gusts of gales in those final two words, and the explosion of the thunderclap in "crack"?)

Shakespeare loved the sounds of the English language. Although fascinated by the intellectual debates and explorations of the ideas that the words represent, he was equally enamored with the emotional states evoked by the sounds of individual voices as they spoke those words aloud on the stage. He never lost sight of the fact that human languages originated in the expression of fundamental emotions before they ever concerned themselves with concepts and ideas. The Shakespearean actor must learn to love the *sounds* of words as well—and, like his characters, love them with a *passion*.

Another example of a "cue for passion" that the actor shouldn't ignore in Shakespeare often lies embedded in the structure of that most intimidating of forms, the soliloquy.

By definition, a soliloquy is a dramatic device in which a character examines and attempts to actively tackle a problem by verbally addressing it alone on the stage; this can take the form of either musing to himself aloud about the issue, or engaging the audience directly in the discourse. If the latter choice is made by director or actor, then the actor must decide whether or not he is personally addressing the audience as a separate entity made up of diverse personalities, or whether he is viewing the audience as merely a symbolic extension of himself, an alternate facet of his own personality.

Whatever that choice may be—and there are good arguments to support both options, and one may work better than another due to the nature and "tone" of the play that contains the soliloquy—the actor begins serious work on the soliloquy by identifying and defining what drives it toward its ultimate destination or resolution. After careful reading, he must identify clearly and specifically the engine that powers the thoughts and the resolution of the problem toward which the discourse leads; in other words, he begins to map the personal journey that the character travels in the text by clearly delineating where the journey begins and ends. Similarly to each individual line in Shakespeare (or any other good playwright, for that matter), this particular cue for passion is often baldly stated at or near the soliloquy's conclusion. Think of it as the open clearing that awaits the character at the end of a path through thick, tangled woods. The actor depicting the sequence of thoughts and discoveries that are the road signs of that journey must always maintain his focus upon that open glade, and not become lost or snagged by the clinging branches of complex images and parenthetical phrases along the way. He must keep his perspective and, to borrow another saying, he must not lose sight of the forest for the trees.

Let's look at a few examples, beginning with one of the more famous soliloquies in Shakespeare's history plays, from Act V, scene v of *Richard II*, justifiably celebrated for both the philosophical substance that lies at its heart, as well as the poetic beauty of its form. King Richard II, deposed by Henry Bolingbroke in open revolt against his rule, sits alone in his cell at Pomfret Castle, grappling with a new reality: he is a monarch no longer, only a common prisoner.

> *I have been studying how I may compare*
> *This prison where I live unto the world;*
> *And for because the world is populous,*
> *And here is not a creature but myself,*

I cannot do it; yet I'll hammer it out.
My brain I'll prove the female to my soul,
My soul the father, and these two beget
A generation of still-breeding thoughts;
And these same thoughts people this little world,
In humors like the people of this world;
For no thought is contented. The better sort,
As thoughts of things divine, are intermix'd
With scruples, and do set the word itself
Against the word;
As thus: "Come, little ones," and then again,
"It is as hard to come as for a camel
To thread the postern of a small needle's eye."
Thoughts tending to ambition, they do plot
Unlikely wonders: how these vain weak nails
May tear a passage through the flinty ribs
Of this hard world, my ragged prison walls;
And for they cannot, die in their own pride.
Thoughts tending to content flatter themselves
That they are not the first of fortune's slaves,
Nor shall not be the last—like seely beggars
Who, sitting in the stocks, refuge their shame,
That many have and others must [sit] there;
And in this thought they find a kind of ease,
Bearing their own misfortunes on the back
Of such as have before endur'd the like.
Thus play I in one person many people,
And none contented. Sometimes am I a king;
Then treasons make me wish myself a beggar,
And so I am. Then crushing penury
Persuades me I was better when a king;
Then am I king'd again, and by and by
Think that I am unking'd by Bolingbroke,
And straight am nothing. But what e'er I be,
Nor I, nor any man that but man is,
With nothing shall be pleas'd, till he be eas'd
With being nothing.

Beautiful verses, wonderful imagery, to be sure; but let's distill it down to the basic conclusion, the "clearing" toward which King Richard struggles, through the metaphorical undergrowth. It is simply this: no matter what our situation in life, our power, our social status, our wealth, we all share one basic truth: we will never be contented with our lot in life, and are fated to be perpetually dissatisfied. That, according to Richard, is the truth of the human condition, and his wrestling actively toward its clear realization and articulation is the passion that drives the soliloquy. He himself is understandably discontented, in view of his present situation; but upon examining those circumstances more closely, he discovers that he has *always* been discontented, throughout every phase of his life, regardless of his changing fortunes. More importantly, he realizes that this is also true of everyone else; and so we shall remain as long as we continue to draw breath in this difficult world.

Simple enough: "Man is fated to be unhappy with his lot in life, and I am not alone in that feeling." It is not as if Richard lacks an awareness of where he is journeying at the outset of the soliloquy; but along the way, he actively tests an initial hypothesis with the study of several examples, finally concluding that it is, indeed, a true perspective on the human condition. This is the fundamental structure of Richard's soliloquy, ignited by the passion arising from his struggle to find some comfort amidst his current despair and loneliness. But there are many twists and turns along the path that threaten to trap or detour the unwary and inexperienced actor, mostly taking the form of the various analogies Richard examines. The soliloquy is not about Richard finding a world in microcosm within his dungeon cell where he must learn to live; it is not a contemplation of the metaphysical relationship of mind and soul; it's not about how one thought leads to another thought, like uncontrolled breeders; or how contradictory the lessons of Christianity can be. All of these matters are touched upon in the course of the piece, but they are all the trees, not the forest. The glade at the end of Richard's journey of feeling and intellect is simply this: *We are all unhappy with our lot in life.* So the actor must remain focused upon that, using every metaphor and analogy available in the soliloquy for the purpose of illuminating that proposition, not getting lost or tangled along the way.

Another example: Helena's soliloquy at the close of the first scene of *A Midsummer Night's Dream*. After hearing her comrade Hermia's plan to elope into the woods surrounding Athens with her lover Lysander in spite of her father's desire that she marry Demetrius instead, Helena, herself in frustrated love with Demetrius, remains alone on stage to work out her dilemma through soliloquy.

> *How happy some o'er other some can be!*
> *Through Athens I am thought as fair as she,*
> *But what of that? Demetrius thinks not so.*
> *He will not know what all but he do know;*
> *And as he errs, doting on Hermia's eyes,*
> *So I, admiring of his qualities.*
> *Things base and vile, holding no quantity,*
> *Love can transpose to form and dignity.*
> *Love looks not with the eyes but with the mind;*
> *And therefore is wing'd Cupid painted blind.*
> *Nor have Love's mind of any judgment taste;*
> *Wings, and no eyes, figure unheedy haste;*
> *And therefore is Love said to be a child,*
> *Because in choice he is so oft beguil'd.*
> *As waggish boys in games themselves forswear,*
> *So the boy Love is perjur'd every where;*
> *For ere Demetrius look'd on Hermia's eyne,*
> *He hail'd down oaths that he was only mine;*
> *And when this hail some heat from Hermia felt,*
> *So he dissolv'd, and show'rs of oaths did melt.*
> *I will go tell him of fair Hermia's flight;*
> *Then to the wood will he tomorrow night*
> *Pursue her; and for this intelligence*
> *If I have thanks, it is a dear expense.*
> *But herein mean I to enrich my pain,*
> *To have his sight thither and back again.*

Where is the clearing in the woods to which this particular path leads? To *action*, pure and simple. "I will go tell him of fair Hermia's flight;/Then to the wood will he tomorrow night/ Pursue her." The actor has a choice: does she know what she intends to do at the beginning of the soliloquy? If so, then she uses all of her initial railing on the injustices of love simply to justify the course she already intends to take. Or, does she use all of the smoldering passion within herself in the initial lines of the soliloquy, exploring all the ways in which life and love are *just not fair . . . not right!,* to ignite a sudden emotional impulse that obviously would benefit from a little more reflection on her part? The former choice is a static one, not giving the actor much of a figurative trampoline upon which to jump; it will likely result in the report of a journey planned in advance, rather than a discovery of the *possibility* of the journey. The latter choice allows the actor to use the repetitive examples of Love's injustice and her resultant rising emotion—expressed in full for perhaps the first time, a passionate adolescent outpouring of hormonally fired emotions—as a springboard propelling her to *do something NOW!*—whatever that may be. So, the primary thing that the actor must focus upon is the journey toward action, however ill-defined that action might be when the soliloquy begins. This must not be lost in passive reflections that would sap the text's immediacy.

For a final example, let's look at the text that opens *Twelfth Night*. Although not precisely a soliloquy, it might well be; Duke Orsino rhapsodizes at some length about love, comparing it to the sound of music, food, the scent of flowers, rivers running into the sea, illusory, fantastical, protean shapes, even death—and all in a mere 15 lines! His attendants are present, but he seems to give them minimal notice as he speaks the following:

> *If music be the food of love, play on!*
> *Give me excess of it; that surfeiting,*
> *The appetite may sicken, and so die.*
> *That strain again, it had a dying fall;*
> *O, it came o'er my ear like the sweet sound*
> *That breathes upon a bank of violets,*

> *Stealing and giving odor. Enough, no more;*
> *'Tis not so sweet now as it was before.*
> *O spirit of love, how quick and fresh art thou,*
> *That notwithstanding thy capacity*
> *Receiveth as the sea; nought enters there,*
> *Of what validity and pitch soe'er,*
> *But falls into abatement and low price*
> *Even in a minute. So full of shapes is fancy*
> *That it alone is high fantastical.*

As famous as this particular Shakespearean passage might be, it remains a challenge for novices and veterans alike. Yes, Orsino is speaking about love; but with what tone, and precisely what is he saying about it? Unless the actor examines closely the answers to those questions specifically suggested by this text, he will run the risk of playing this very important passage (it is the opening of the play, after all!) in generalities rather than specificities.

First, all of the metaphorical referents that Orsino connects to love (with the possible exception of food) are intangibles, things that are hard to capture or contain: the fleeting tones of music, the scent of flowers blown on a breeze, a river's water flowing into the sea, hallucinatory shapes. Love, he says, which yields such concrete effects on our bodies and minds, seems virtually impossible to physically control, an inexorable force of nature. As noted, food is the most tangible metaphorical referent, and in the piece's opening lines Orsino seizes upon the possibility that if food is indeed comparable with love, he can control its power over him by over-ingesting it until it sickens him and kills his appetite for any further such nourishment. However, in Orsino's present restless, frustrated and impassioned state, he seems unable to stay with one metaphor for longer than it takes to discover it. Music and food are intermixed, as are the strains of melody with the perfume of flowers. The struggle for the proper expression of the agonizing obsession he feels for the Countess Olivia ultimately dissolves into the helpless recognition that there may be no remedy for this particular malady: his love/lust is like the sea in that it absorbs without apparent visible effect any volume of additional water flowing into it.

What is Orsino passionately and actively *doing* with these lines of verse? He is struggling mightily to understand the ache of longing he feels by trying to *name* it, as naming something gives one some power over it, some grasp, some comprehension of its processes and effects—and yes, some control. Orsino's cue for passion here lies in his emotional distress, and the soliloquy embodies his active journey toward controlling it; although in its final lines, he seems to be acknowledging that he will lose the battle, and fail to complete that journey. Love is too strong, and yet at the same time, too ethereal . . . not an opponent easily faced down and subdued. Orsino's struggle here with such an elusive foe, played by an actor who taps into the ardency of that fight, launches *Twelfth Night* onto the stage with force and vibrancy. Again, the actor must keep focus upon the core of the text's action as he brings the lines to life, and not be distracted from that central journey. Doing so, he makes the metaphors and heightened language serve his active purpose, *behaviorally*.

In summary: Young actors working with Shakespeare must not allow themselves to be intimidated by the heightened language of his plays; nor must they feel that making such language work on the stage is somehow a separate and additional challenge to the usual kind of honest, organic, behavioral acting analysis with which they engage contemporary plays. The actor of Shakespeare should work from the premise that *there is a truthful reason for why the characters speak in the manner that they do—and that reason lies in the play's story and context.* It is always there for the diligent, disciplined and curious young actor to discover. And remember: your goal isn't to find the proper *answer*, but rather to pose interesting *questions*, thereby engaging in a personally inspirational and detailed way with each component of your text. This will be the start of making the character uniquely your own.

Here are some final points to review and remember:

1. **Always choose to make a Shakespearean text that you speak immediate; never passive or reflective.**

Even if the text might suggest that you are simply "reporting" something, how you feel or respond to what you are reporting is every bit as important—perhaps even more so—as the information itself.

2. Define why your text is urgent! Determine precisely what makes it the most important thing you could possibly say at this moment, considering your character's circumstances. Always remember that Shakespeare's characters live in the present moment, usually more urgently than any other playwright's. They rarely, if ever, find themselves at a loss for words when expressing accurately and articulately what they need, and why they need it now.

3. Identify every word in the text for your character that you don't know the meaning of, or that you're unable to articulate the meaning of without using the word itself. Find all the possible meanings of the word, listing all the synonyms that you believe could apply. This will help you determine why you believe the character chooses this unique word at this particular moment in the action; and as a result, this will help you actively make the same choice that the character makes, giving you one more personal link to the character you are portraying.

4. Play with words. Explore their sounds in your mouth. Become aware of how you form them, and how you support their resonation when you speak them. Speak them broadly, shortly, loudly, in a whisper. As an exercise when learning your lines, try to communicate the meaning of key words in your text by their sound alone.

5. Jotting down whatever thoughts occur to you when working on your text, try to specifically map the journey where each passage seems to be leading. Avoid getting lost in the thickets (i.e., extended metaphors, parenthetical elements) along the way; yet at the same time, explore in your own imaginative thinking why the character is drawn

to—or even lingers over—each extended metaphor or parenthetical phrase.

6. Build each sentence one word at a time, exploring both sound and meaning. Check different editions of the text to compare different choices of editorial punctuation. What punctuation choices work best for your interpretation of the character?

Follow each of these steps as you begin your research, analysis and memorization of each Shakespearean text, personalizing your script further at every phase of your preparatory work. This close involvement with the language of your role at the earliest stages of your work will pay off handsomely in the long run. Be patient; don't try leaping to the end of your journey before you have taken these first steps. If you restrain that eagerness a bit, you will find that the next steps of your preparation—exploring the structure of the verse, its rhythms, and what they might reveal about the people of the play, their personalities, and their critical dramatic moments—will prove more rewarding and enlightening.

CHAPTER IV

"THAT WOULD BE SCANN'D":
VERSE SCANSION, AND THE RHYTHMS OF THE CHARACTER

The time has arrived to examine the most debated, maligned, and spoofed element of Shakespearean performance: How to scan the verse, and once scanned, how to effectively apply that information to your performances.

Before starting however, let's agree on this: scanning Shakespearean verse is a process, not a product; a means to an end, and not the end itself. And what is that end? A richly textured and inspiring performance, musically delivered, founded upon detailed character choices resulting from an informed and imaginative examination of the poetic rhythms of the text and what they might suggest to the actor.

Scansion is not a mathematical formula. It will not lead you to an inarguably *correct* answer. Instead, it will suggest paths toward interesting acting choices, and help you more effectively communicate the text you see on the page to the audience's ears. So, use your common sense; always test your scansion options aloud, and ultimately depend upon that most crucial point of Hamlet's advice to the players: *Let your discretion be your tutor.*

RHYMED AND BLANK VERSE

Let's begin by defining some terms.

Shakespeare's plays are written using various literary formats. Large sections of them are in prose, rather than verse. (*Much Ado*

About Nothing, for instance, is almost entirely in prose, rather unusual for one of his comedies.) The sections of his plays that are written in verse sometimes utilize rhyme, a device more heavily used in his earlier plays, such as *The Comedy of Errors, The Two Gentlemen of Verona, Love's Labour's Lost, A Midsummer Night's Dream,* and *Romeo and Juliet.* The rhyme scheme in these plays generally takes the form of repeated rhymed couplets, two adjacent lines linked by the similar sounds of the lines' final words. Here are some examples:

> *This will I send, and something else more plain*
> *That shall express my true love's fasting pain.*
> *O, would the King, Berowne, and Longaville*
> *Were lovers too! Ill, to example ill,*
> *Would from my forehead wipe a perjur'd note:*
> *For none offend where all alike do dote.*
>   (Dumain in *Love's Labour's Lost,* Act IV, iii)

> *The grey-ey'd morn smiles on the frowning night,*
> *Check'ring the eastern clouds with streaks of light,*
> *And fleckled darkness like a drunkard reels*
> *From forth day's path and Titan's fiery wheels.*
> *Now ere the sun advance his burning eye,*
> *The day to cheer and night's dank dew to dry,*
> *I must up-fill this osier cage of ours*
> *With baleful weeds and precious-juiced flowers.*
>   (Friar Laurence in *Romeo and Juliet,* Act II, iii)

Sometimes the rhymed couplets are shared between two characters, as in the following example:

JULIA: Why he, of all the rest, hath never mov'd me.
LUCETTA: Yet he, of all the rest, I think best loves ye.
JULIA: His little speaking shows his love but small.
LUCETTA: Fire that's closest kept burns most of all.
JULIA: They do not love that do not show their love.
LUCETTA: O, they love least that let men know their love.
                        (*The Two Gentlemen of Verona,* Act I, ii)

In all of these cases, the actors must decide whether they are *consciously* using the rhyming device, or whether it's all happening by accident. Deciding that they are fully aware of what they are doing—and what purposes are motivating that clever (or impassioned) choice—is yet another way of linking the artifice of the heightened language with the goals of naturalistic acting. Perhaps Lucetta enjoys teasing Julia by undercutting her haughty objections with a rapidly chosen rhyme; it builds Julia's comic frustration while providing Lucetta the opportunity to think on her feet, proving that she's not the uneducated servant that people sometimes assume she is! Perhaps Friar Laurence is so enchanted by the beautiful Verona morning that, in commenting on it, he finds delight in composing an impromptu ode to it for his private satisfaction. And maybe Dumain, having just spent some hours secretly structuring a sonnet for his beloved, still has poetry on his mind; for him then, the rhyme treads the line between conscious and subconscious. In all cases, instead of imposing the rhyme on the truth of the character's moment, *the actor makes the rhyme an essential component of that truth.*

Shakespeare uses a different rhyme scheme on some occasions in his plays, more often in his sonnets: the A/B/A/B format with the rhyme occurring at the end of every other line instead of in the couplet form. Here's an example:

> *Lend me the flourish of all gentle tongues—*
> *Fie, painted rhetoric! O, she needs it not.*
> *To things of sale, a seller's praise belongs;*
> *She passes praise, then praise too short doth blot.*
> *A wither'd hermit, fivescore winters worn,*
> *Might shake off fifty, looking in her eye:*
> *Beauty doth varnish age, as if new born,*
> *And gives the crutch the cradle's infancy.*
>
> (Berowne in *Love's Labour's Lost*, Act IV, iii)

In fact, many times over the course of the plays *Romeo and Juliet* and *Love's Labour's Lost*, the characters speak in a poetic form that's very similar to the author's sonnets, if they are not actually sonnets themselves. It's still a good practice for the actor to try to "own" that form by means of a motivational character choice that incorporates it into the circumstances of the moment, although the obviousness of the rhyme in this structure isn't as blatant to the audience's ears as it tends to be when presented in couplet form.

However often Shakespeare uses rhyme in his earlier plays—or caps off key soliloquies or public speeches with them, even in his more mature works—the predominant form he uses in his plays is called *blank verse*. Basically, blank verse is unrhymed verse. It contains all of the metaphors, imagery, rhythms, and wordplay that Shakespeare's writing is noted for . . . .but as a rule, no rhyming couplets or alternating rhyming lines. Although some may feel that the verse loses a bit of its cleverness with the absence of rhyme, most actors will find it more naturalistic and flowing in spoken delivery, mainly because it leads to fewer *end stops* (pauses occurring by phrasing or punctuation at the end of a verse line), and less artificiality, or self-conscious theatricality. After all, for better or worse, people don't generally speak in rhyme in their everyday conversational dialogue!

IAMBIC PENTAMETER AND ANOMALIES

Shakespeare's standard of rhythm for his blank verse—a norm that he shares with most of his playwright contemporaries—is something called *iambic pentameter*. Iambic pentameter is the heartbeat of Shakespearean verse; it's a bit like the drum and bass line of a jazz combo, what keeps the underlying beat of the music steady so that the instruments on top can improvise and "play" under, above and around that rhythm.

Let's break it down a bit. Spoken English generally works by using stressed syllables against unstressed syllables; it's one of the basic elements that our ears and brain use in listening and making sense of what is being said to us. If you read that last sentence aloud, you will begin to choose your stresses and contrasts instinctively, just by the act of speaking. For instance, one choice might sound like this (with stressed syllables capitalized): "It's ONE of the BA-sic EL-e-MENTS that our EARS and BRAINS USE in LIST-e-NING and UN-der-STAND-ing WHAT is BE-ing SAID to US." This is not the only way one might use syllabic stresses in saying this sentence aloud, but it gets the job done. Although unstressed and stressed syllables don't always occur one after the other—sometimes stresses occur in immediate sequence, and the same is sometimes true of non-stressed syllables—more often than not, a majority of the sounds in spoken English happen when stressed and unstressed syllables are used in immediate juxtaposition, such as in the final part of that sentence: "in LIST-e-NING and UN-der-STAND-ing WHAT is BE-ing SAID to US." Deciding this process when working with your script, using a mixture of instinct and reason (again remembering to "let your discretion be your tutor"), is one of the foundational performance tasks of the Shakespearean actor, and it should be explored as thoroughly as possible, both before rehearsals begin and continuing throughout the rehearsal process.

In an average line of Shakespearean verse, there are usually ten syllables. These syllables are divided into five sections, which we call *feet*. So, there are usually *five feet* in a standard Shakespearean verse line, whether it is blank verse or rhymed verse. How the stresses occur in each two-syllable foot determines the name of that foot. Although we will explore other variations presently, the kind of foot that we'll look at first is called an *iamb*. In an iamb foot, an unstressed syllable is followed by a stressed syllable, such as "I *can*" or "She *won't*." In fact, this is the most basic pattern of English speech: in the simplest of sentences that consist of only a noun and a verb (such as those two just noted), the verb will almost always receive more emphasis than the noun. Why is this? Because to stress the noun would subtly change the substance of what is being communicated in the speech. "*She* won't" shifts our focus from what she *won't do* to the point that although *she* won't do it (whatever "it" may be), someone else might!

So, an iamb is probably the most common two-syllable rhythm in English speech, and an iambic pentameter verse line has five of them. There have been many theoretical explanations offered as to why Shakespeare and his contemporaries preferred and developed the form of pentameter above other line lengths, such as hexameter (six feet per line), septameter (seven feet), etc. The most interesting idea I've heard proposed is the following: the phrasing in pentameter is simply the most natural to our everyday life. That is, if one were to record all of our speech over the course of a day, the average length of our natural phrasing for spoken communication with others would be ten syllables. Although this idea is probably never ultimately provable, it sounds intuitively right. For the actor, Shakespeare's phrasing, as controlled by the iambic pentameter structure, seems much more natural for English speech than any of the other metrical alternatives. In fact, we often find ourselves quite unconsciously speaking in iambic pentameter form.

Take this sentence: "I'll climb those stairs to get a candy bar."—a complete sentence in perfect iambic pentameter (if not great poetry!). Let's quickly map out the basic rhythm here—what actors call *scanning* the line, which is notating its inherent "beat" in the same way a musician will begin to score a piece of music on the page that he is about to bring to life by playing. Spoken, the sentence would sound something like this: "I'll CLIMB those STAIRS to GET a CAN-dy BAR." Now, take a moment and play with it. Try emphasizing some of the other syllables that I've left unstressed. Stressing "to", "a", or the "dy" syllable in "candy" is virtually impossible if one wants to maintain any semblance of natural speech. (Try it yourself and see.) The other two, however, might be possibilities to explore. Does stressing "I'll" or "those" improve the communication of the thought, or alter the meaning in any tangibly effective fashion? For my ears (and brain), it does not; but this does not necessarily mean it would be *wrong* to do so. Perhaps stressing "those" would differentiate one staircase from another; assuming there *is* a second staircase to consider. And stressing "I'll" might imply that the speaker's companions are unwilling to make the climb . . . so *he* will do it. The actor must weigh the possibilities.

But here is what is important to remember: Shakespeare was consciously choosing to work in iambic pentameter, and in doing so he was often using the very form itself to point the actor to what words and syllables should be noted and stressed. In this case, the form very much works to dictate the content, the very meaning of the line. That's what makes the understanding of iambic pentameter and how its rhythm works so fundamental to the work of a Shakespearean actor. In effect, it allows Shakespeare to offer his own thoughts and direction for character interpretation and performance—across four centuries and more—directly to the modern actor; intelligent and informed scansion can be the key to those messages.

In his earliest plays, Shakespeare's iambic pentameter rhythm is very regular; often, for actors preparing their truthful performances, it can seem rather heavily so. Comedy troupes spoofing classical actors in general and Shakespeare's works in particular have often had great fun satirizing the stilted, stentorian delivery to which a slavish over-emphasis to iambic patterns can lead. But the regularity of the iambic pentameter can serve the actor by helping them in line memorization; and, by drawing their attention to changes in rhythm when they occur. In turn, the actor's deft handling of these changes of rhythm can alert an audience to the points in the speech that are different, that "jump out" and demand attention. These are usually the pivotal factors of the text that are the most important to hear and ponder.

These changes in the regular flow of the iambic pentameter are called *anomalies*, or a deviation from the norm. When they occur, and the actor successfully highlights them (albeit often quite subtly) with his spoken performance, they stand out in a way that either helps to clarify a moment on stage or illuminates an important point that the character wants to make. To again use the allegory of music: the rhythm of the piece goes along fairly regularly until, at a point in the score specifically written by the composer, a change occurs. The change is musically intriguing and emotionally exciting for the listener; when words and ideas are involved, working in conjunction with the alteration in the "beat"—as is the case with the anomalies in Shakespearean iambic pentameter—the change is also intellectually stimulating or even enlightening, in ways both large and small. They may indicate an "ah ha!" moment of realization for both the character and the listeners.

Many of these moments are obviously embedded in the text as Shakespeare wrote it (and we'll look at some examples soon). Others may be only suggested and optional, and used by an actor much like a drummer or bass player will "punch" a note in syncopation or opposition to the dominant pattern. Let's take a quick look at such an optional syncopation in some of the verse lines that Shakespeare offers an actor at numerous times in the course of his plays.

SYNCOPATION

During her soliloquy at the close of Act I, scene i of *A Midsummer Night's Dream*, an exasperated Helena remarks of Demetrius: "He will not know what all but he do know." With the regular rhythm of iambic pentameter, the line would scan "He WILL not KNOW what ALL but HE do KNOW." But the actress might also choose the following scansion option: "He WILL not KNOW what ALL but HE *DO* KNOW." In other words, she might keep both of the stresses on the 8th and 10th syllables that the iambics suggest, while at the same time opting to give an extra little kick to that 9th syllable (the "do"), like a drummer gives an extra little kick at the close of a musical phrase, a "backbeat" that works against the main pulse of the music. Try it aloud both ways. Which do you think individualizes Helena's emotional state more, makes the line more striking, more strongly demands the hearer's attention? Neither option is the *right* answer; the acting choice is up to you. However, by simply examining the text in this close fashion—word by word, virtually—you are engaging with the character in a manner that will automatically maneuver you into making choices about what kind of person they are in living, breathing life, and set you on the path to making Shakespeare's play come alive and off the page.

This syncopated device that lurks as a possibility on the off beat—most often occurring on the 9th syllable of the 10-syllable line—is something that pops up fairly regularly in Shakespeare's verse. Here are a few other examples; the line with the possible "syncopation" on the final two syllables is in bold, and the syncopated syllable itself underlined. Try speaking them all aloud and experiment with what you think works best for you.

> *Pray you peruse that letter.*
> **You must not now deny it is <u>your</u> hand!**
> > (Malvolio in *Twelfth Night*, V,i)

> *Be it lawful that I invocate thy ghost*
> **To hear the lamentations of <u>poor</u> Anne**
> > (Lady Anne in *Richard III*, I,ii)

> *How these vain weak nails*
> *May tear a passage through the flinty ribs*
> *Of this hard world, my ragged prison walls,*
> **And for they cannot, die in their <u>own</u> pride**
> > (Richard in *Richard II*, V,v)

> *If th' assassination*
> *Could trammel up the consequence, and catch*
> **With his surcease, success; that but <u>this</u> blow**
> *Might be the be-all and the end-all here,*
> *But here, upon this bank and shoal of time,*
> *We'd jump the life to come.*
> > (Macbeth in *Macbeth*, I,vii)

It's important to note that even if the actor chooses to throw in that extra punch on the line's 9th syllable, this does not mean that the 8th and 10th syllables have to lose their own emphases and become unstressed syllables in compensation; the lines in question would simply have 6 stresses instead of the normal 5. Presently, we'll look at some examples of lines that have 5 stresses, but depart from the regular iambic pentameter rhythm—which is the standard *dee-DUM-dee-DUM-dee-DUM-dee-DUM-dee-DUM*.

MARKING SCANSION IN THE TEXT

Let's pause briefly here to outline a fairly standard method used by actors to mark their scansion on the pages of their script. Feet of verse are separated by a "/." A stressed syllable in a line of verse is most usually designated by a slightly slanted vertical mark above that syllable, like this: ´. An unstressed syllable is identified by a small horizontal mark above it, such as this: ¯. Here is an example of the opening two lines from *The Comedy of Errors* as spoken by Egeon, scanned using this system:

Prōcéed,/ Sōlí/nūs, tó/ prōcúre/ mȳ fáll,/

Ānd bý/ thē dóom/ ōf deáth/ ēnd wóes/ ānd áll.

Two very regular iambic pentameter lines: five regular iambic feet in both. Here's another example of notated scansion, this time from the opening of *Love's Labour's Lost*, as the King of Navarre proclaims:

Lēt fáme,/ thāt áll/ hūnt áf/tēr ín/ thēir líves,/

Līve ré/gīst'réd/ ūpón/ oūr brá/zēn tómbs.

Don't dwell too long upon the curious contraction—marked by an apostrophe—of the middle syllables of *registered* in the second line. These things crop up all the time throughout the printed Shakespeare plays. They're important for the actor when they suggest a change in pronunciation of the word (usually as a result of a contraction of two syllables) that might affect the overall rhythm of the line, and we'll look at a few examples of that a bit later on. In this case however, *registered* is still spoken with three syllables, with stresses on the first and the third.

FEMININE ENDINGS AND CAESURAE

Now, if you've already moved to any passages of verse in the Shakespeare plays and begun to try your own hand at initial "scans" of various lines, you'll probably notice almost immediately that there are *many* lines that seem arhythmical, or elusive to pin down. Some lines don't seem very iambic. Some don't have 10 syllables. Some have 11 syllables, or even 12 or more (or seem to, at any rate).

As mentioned before, one of the most famous lines in all Shakespeare is this one from *Hamlet*:

To be, or not to be: that is the question.

Count the syllables. (Not the words, the syllables; sometimes it's easy to confuse the two when you're starting to work with scansion.) There are not 10, but 11. Most of the line scans pretty regularly, although we might pause for a moment over the foot of verse that contains "that is." It seems that the actor might choose to stress *that* over *is*, thus in effect reversing the rhythm there; but it's not really necessary for communicating the thought effectively. But what about that 11th syllable?

It's called a feminine ending, presumably named as such because it signifies a weak, unstressed syllable at the end of the pentameter line. (Yes, it's a rather sexist designation in today's culture, but let's try to ignore that!) Feminine endings generally occur in lines of Shakespearean verse that have more than 10 syllables; and when, in those cases, there also don't seem to be any syllables that can be contracted or combined together earlier in the line to make the line come out in 10 syllables.

What effect does the use of feminine endings have in Shakespeare? For one thing, it breaks up the regularity of the iambic rhythms. The constant repetition of this rhythm in speech throughout entire scenes or plays (as comic spoofs of Shakespeare often emphasize) can be mind-numbing for both actors and audiences in performance. Thus, anomalies— wherever and however they may occur—lend the artifice of the verse form more naturalistic and interesting variations for the ear. As we'll soon see, it's one of many such techniques that Shakespeare mastered over his playwriting career that helped to set his plays a level above his fellow contemporaries. The anomalies not only help to focus our attention on appropriate dramatic moments both large and small throughout the plays, they help the characters sound more *real* to us, less self-consciously theatrical. A quick comparison between the plays of Shakespeare—even early examples—and Christopher Marlowe, an obvious inspiration for his initial dramatic writing, will show the theatrical value of Shakespeare's deft use of changes, shifts and anomalies; even smaller ones, such as feminine endings.

Feminine endings also give the actors subtle directions for phrasing the spoken word in performance. A pause for phrasing or meaning—sometimes specifically directed by a comma, colon, semicolon, dash, etc.—is called a *caesura*. The choices that an actor makes for when these brief pauses occur in his text will not only determine the appropriate times for him to take breaths that will successfully support his speech, they also will allow the audience to better understand the text that the character is expressing. Whereas a regular, unpunctuated line of iambic pentameter will tend to propel the actor naturally into the subsequent line with uninterrupted, or even increased tempo (much like the centrifugal force generated by a downward curve in a roller coaster), a feminine ending will almost demand a *caesura* of some kind. This is not to give the impression that caesurae only occur after a feminine ending, or at the end of a regular iambic line; they can occur anywhere in speech where the actor feels that they are needed in order to communicate the sense of what is being spoken to the hearer. Use your common sense: don't run your thoughts and phrases together, but don't chop them up too much either. The best phrasing works both with the rhythm of the line, as well as with its thought.

Here are a few examples of some scanned Shakespearean lines containing 11 syllables with an unstressed final syllable; all show feminine endings:

Ī knów/ thāt vír/tūe tó/ bē ín/ yōu, Brútūs,/
Ās wéll/ ās Í/ dō knów/ yōur oút/wārd fávōr.
(Julius Caesar, Act I, ii)

Īs thís/ ā dág/gēr thát/ Ī sée/ bē/fóre mē,/
Thē hán/dlē tóward/ mȳ hánd?/ Cōme, lét/ mē clútch thēe!
(Macbeth, Act II, i)

Ānd whát's/ hē thén/ thāt sáys/ Ī pláy/ thē víllāin,/
Whēn thís/ ādvíce/ īs frée/ Ī gíve,/ ānd hónēst?
(Othello, Act II, iii)

A PUNCTUATION PAUSE

As any actor, director or editor of Shakespeare quickly discovers, the punctuation we find in his plays is a "moveable feast"—that is, it varies from quarto to Folio, from one modern edition to the next. In the earliest Elizabethan and Jacobean printings, we often find a multitude of commas, colons, and semi-colons; and by contrast, an often peculiar (by our modern standards, anyway) lack of periods.

There might be a variety of reasons for the inconsistency of punctuation in these earliest printings: Shakespeare himself might have had his own distinct leanings about punctuating, and the printers followed what they found in his foul papers; they might be indicative of the various playhouse scribes' preferences, those scriveners who copied the manuscripts out for promptbooks; they might be actors' notations on their own written parts (their "sides"), marking where they would choose to phrase for sense, or pause for breath; or they may even represent the unique idiosyncrasies of the printing houses themselves. As with spelling, the Elizabethans yet followed no established rules of punctuating their written texts.

Whatever the facts of the matter may be, the actor is faced with some significant decisions when dealing with all of the options presented. How a line, a scene, or a soliloquy is punctuated will greatly affect how it is spoken, and therefore how the character is brought to life. This is yet another reason why several modern editions of a given play should always be consulted and compared by any serious Shakespearean actor before starting to work on his role. *Remember: in this, as in other matters of scansion and scoring, there is no "right" answer; but some choices will certainly be more thoughtful and better informed than others.* So try to be as well-informed in your punctuation options as possible when preparing your performance texts. Try them all by speaking them all aloud, with focus on what each edition's punctuation suggests to you. Then, make your choices; always remaining open to new options of phrasing and new discoveries as you journey through the rehearsal process.

NOT ALL STRESSES ARE CREATED EQUAL

Even when a line is scanned, the stressed syllables are identified, and the line determined to be either regular or irregular in its iambic format, with or without a feminine ending, the actor should yet keep in mind that all stresses are not created equal; so, it's important to additionally examine which words (or syllables) might deserve the strongest stresses of the 5 in the line. It's a good practice to try underlining the 2 stresses in each line of verse that seem to matter the most for communicating clear meaning or intent in the vocal delivery of each line; this will initiate the creative process of choosing which words or phrases are most essential for the character in effectively pursuing his dramatic action and expressing the emotional content of that particular moment of the play. Let's look at a segment of one of Proteus's soliloquies from *The Two Gentlemen of Verona*, Act II, vi:

> *To leave my Julia—shall I be forsworn?*
> *To love fair Silvia—shall I be forsworn?*
> *To wrong my friend, I shall be much forsworn!*

Opposites pre-dominate in these three lines (and more about that in the next chapter). "Leave", "love", and "wrong" all share an obvious relationship. Proteus struggles with what action he might take that would be true to his own feelings, and yet morally acceptable. Thus, in the first two lines, *leave* and *love* merit an extra emphasis. The two ladies in question, whose attributes Proteus compares in his imagination, also deserve a bit of vocal attention, although perhaps not as much as the action verbs that Proteus contemplates following.

For the vast majority of Shakespearean verse lines, the final stressed syllable (which basically encompasses the word that the stress occurs within) almost always works better when given an additional charge by the speaker; in the case of these lines, it helps that it, too, is an action verb. Actors working with Shakespeare should keep this general principle in mind: *Most of the strongest stresses in Shakespeare's iambic lines fall in the final syllable*. This gives the actor—and his audience—an additional and effective "kick" into the next line or thought.

The third line presents some interesting variations. The actor could again follow the pattern of the first two—with primary emphasis on for*sworn*, and secondary emphasis on *leave* and *love*—but let's examine another alternative. If the actor primarily stresses *much*, and secondarily *friend*, the change in pattern from the first two lines catches the audience's ear and communicates the following quite clearly: Proteus is more concerned with the sin of wronging his *friend* (Valentine) than he is with the feelings of the two ladies in question—which is, in fact, the rather controversial theme of the play. This is, of course, also underscored by the phrase "*much* forsworn."

Spoken aloud by Proteus, it would scan like this:

Tō *léave*/ mȳ Jú/līa—sháll/ Ī bé/ fōrs**wórn**?

Tō *lóve*/ fāir Síl/vīa—sháll/ Ī bé/ fōrs**wórn**?

Tō wróng/ mȳ *friénd*/—Ī sháll/ bē ***múch***/ fōrswórn!

(The alert actor reading this will note that the "ia" of both Julia's and Silvia's names are here treated like a single syllable;

we'll deal more with this kind of thing soon. The clever actor might also take advantage of the syncopated "backbeat" effect we were talking about a little earlier, although this time it might be utilized to good effect on the 3rd syllable of the second line instead of the 9th, giving the word "fair" an extra little punch; it is, after all, Silvia's beauty that draws Proteus's fickle attention away from his fiancée, Julia. His very name "Proteus" means "ever-changing"!)

Once again, this is not the *right* formula for speaking the lines; it's simply one option among several. Each actor will make his own individual choice for this, and every other line of Shakespearean text that he analyzes, scans, scores, and finally speaks. Every musician playing a composition will make it sound individual and unique, based upon his own skill, feeling and life experience. It's the same with actors and their roles.

You're not looking for *the* answer; you're looking for *your* answer.

ALTERNATE RHYTHMS

As we've already noted, when eagerly turning to some passages in Shakespeare to test some of these precepts outlined above, the young actor will quickly notice that very many of the lines he investigates don't fit neatly into the rhythms of strict iambic pentameter. Once again: *Shakespeare's verse works by setting up a foundational rhythm—that of iambic pentameter— and then varying it at key points in the lines in order to draw appropriate attention to these anomalies for the purposes of revealing significant story points, or character traits and relationships.* His skill at this practice was what set Shakespeare apart from his contemporary rivals, and what has helped to keep his plays sounding fresh and true in the mouths of able actors for over four centuries. If the actor attends to this with some diligence in his preparation, and uses it appropriately in his performance, the practical result is that an audience will most likely have an easier time fully understanding what is happening in that moment on the stage. With this in mind, let's examine some possible rhythmic variations to be discovered in the feet of

Shakespeare's verse, and how they change the actor's delivery and the overall flow of the lines in which they appear.

As we've established, an iamb is a foot of verse containing two syllables, an unstressed one followed by a stressed one. On the other hand, a *trochee* reverses that pattern; it is a foot of verse with a stressed syllable preceding an unstressed syllable, which is exactly the opposite of an iamb. Although trochees may appear anywhere in the course of a verse, they very often crop up right at the very beginning of the line. Here are some scanned examples, with the feet that contain the trochees italicized :

Nów, fāir/ Hīppó/lȳtá,/ oūr núp/tiāl hóur/

Drāws ón/ āpáce.

　　　　　　　　　　　(*A Midsummer Night's Dream*, Act I, i)

Nóthīng/ īn Fránce,/ ūntíl/ hē hás/ nō wífe./

　　　　　　　　　　　(*All's Well That Ends Well*, Act III, ii)

Tō whóm/ shōuld Í/ cōmpláin?/ *Díd Ī*/ *téll thīs*,/

Whó wōuld/ bēliéve/ mē? Ó/ *pérī*/lōus móuths,/

Thāt béar/ īn thém/ *óne ānd*/ thē sélf-/sāme tóngue.

　　　　　　　　　　　(*Measure For Measure*, Act II, iv)

And finally, this famous opening of *Henry V:*

Ó, fōr/ ā múse/ ōf fíre,/ thāt wóuld/ āscénd/

Thē bríght/ēst héa/vēn óf/ īnvén/tīón!

Here we also see yet a different kind of anomaly: the word *invention*, which we normally treat as 3 syllables is here treated as 4. Again, we'll talk more about why that might be later in this chapter.

A foot of verse that contains 2 stressed syllables together is called a *spondee*. Here are some scanned examples of spondees, with the relevant foot of verse again italicized and double stresses underlined:

Twó hóuse/hōlds, bóth/ ālíke/ īn díg/nītý
(*Romeo and Juliet,* Prologue)

Ó thát/ thīs tóo/ *tóo súll*/iēd flésh/ wōuld mélt
(*Hamlet*, Act I, ii)

Ónce móre/ ūntó/ thē bréach,/ *déar friénds*,/ *ónce móre*!
(*Henry V*, Act III, i)

This third example of multiple spondees in a single line from *Henry V* illustrates a general truth about Shakespeare rhythms that actors should also be aware of: polysyllabic words (words of more than one syllable) in a sequence are naturally spoken faster than monosyllabic words that follow one another. Thus, very often spondees occur in lines of verse that contain several sequential words of one syllable. This slows the speech down a bit and adds emphasis to each word being uttered. Actors should look for this very effective dramatic device when doing their initial scansions; Shakespeare uses it purposely many times throughout his plays.

This line also highlights another point that young actors wrestling with Shakespearean scansion for the first time should always keep in mind: *A common anomaly you will often discover is that there will be more than the usual five stresses in some lines of verse; especially when the action or emotional context of the moment in which the line is spoken is intense and heightened.* We'll pause here to look at this more closely before continuing, as this is one of Shakespeare's more common techniques for heightening the passionate context of a dramatic moment.

When a character's feelings are running high, quite often his verse rhythms become more excited and irregular, and any additional or irregularly stressed syllables in key lines tend to *stand out* to great dramatic effect. Here are a couple of examples (beginning with the *Henry V* text that began this slight digression), with suggestions for effective scansion of each:

Ónce móre ūntó thē bréach, déar friénds, ónce móre!

Ōr clóse thē wáll úp wīth oūr Énglīsh déad.

Īn péace thēre's nóthīng só bēcómes ā mán

Ās módēst stíllnēss ánd hūmílītý;

Būt whén thē blást ōf wár blóws īn oūr eárs,

Thēn ímītáte thē áctiōn óf thē tígēr;

Stíffēn thē sínēws, cónjūre úp thē blóod,

Dīsguíse fáir nátūre wīth hárd-fávōr'd ráge;

Thēn lénd thē eýe ā térrīblé áspēct;

Lét īt prý thróugh thē pórtāge óf thē héad

Līke thē bráss cánnōn; lét thē b">brów o'ērwhélm īt

Ās féarfūllý ās dóth ā gállēd róck

O'ērháng ānd júttȳ hís cōnfoúndēd báse,

Swíll'd wīth thē wíld ānd wástefūl ócēán.

(*Henry V*, Act III, i)

  There are some interesting things to note here. As previously shown, the first line begins with an unusual number of stressed syllables: 8 out of the 10 could legitimately be emphasized, as Henry desperately exhorts his weary and frightened troops to again charge the breach they have made into the besieged city wall under attack. Although subsequent lines don't show the same plethora of stresses as Henry's initial call to action, the energy continues to run high, evidenced by the irregular rhythms that persist: iambs remain the skeletal structure of the beat, but trochees and spondees also abound throughout Henry's call to action. The anomalies make the points of Henry's inspirational plea stand out *strongly*. Twice Shakespeare himself contracts—or *elides*—words for rhythmic effect (*o'erwhelm* and *o'erhang*, a device that both preserves the driving rhythm and propels the speech forward—more about such contractions in a moment). Several times he makes very effective use of *alliteration* and *assonance* (the close repetition of consonant and vowel sounds for musical effect)—"sti*ll*ness and humi*l*ity"; "*wh*en the *bl*ast of *w*ar *bl*ows in our ears"; "*st*iffe*n* the *s*inew*s*"; "*p*ry through the *p*ortage"; "*br*ass cannon/*br*ow o'erwhelm"; and "*w*i*l*d and *w*asteful." Also interesting is what he does with the scansion of "ocean" in the last line from the quotation above, stretching it to a full three syllables. We'll look at possible reasons for that later in this chapter.

It's also worth taking a moment here to recall our earlier point: when single syllable words (called *monosyllabic* words) follow one another in quick succession in a line, it will almost automatically force the speaker to go slightly more slowly while simultaneously emphasizing each word with a little stronger accent. We can hear it happening in King Henry's first line: "*Once more* unto the *breach, dear friends, once more!*" We can also note it in the first three lines of one of Shakespeare's most famous sonnets, 116: "*Let me not* to the marriage of *true minds*/ Admit impediments; *love is not love*/ That alters when it alteration finds." *Monosyllabic words following one another in quick succession demand special emphasis and dramatic force from the speaker, while polysyllabic words tend to roll off the tongue more quickly, with the usual alternating stressed syllables.*

Here's another piece of text, spoken by Edmund in *King Lear*:

Thóu, Nátūre, ārt mý góddēss; tō thý láw

Mȳ sérvícés āre boúnd. Whērefóre shōuld Í

Stánd īn thē plágue ōf cústōm, ánd pērmít

Thē cúrīósítý ōf nátiōns tō dēpríve mē,

Fōr thát Ī ám sōme twélve ōr fóurtēen móonshīnes

Lág ōf ā bróthēr? Whý bástārd? Whérefōre báse?

Whēn mý dīménsiōns áre ās wéll cōmpáct,

Mȳ mínd ās génerōus *(elided to two syllables)*, ánd mȳ shápe ās trúe,

Ās hónēst mádām's íssūe? Whȳ bránd thēy ús

Wīth báse? Wīth básenēss? Bástārdȳ? Báse, báse?

Whó, īn thē lústy stéalth ōf nátūre, táke

Mōre cómpōsítiōn ānd fiérce quálītý

Thān dóth wīthín ā dúll, stále, tírēd béd

Gó tō th' crēátīng ā whóle tríbe ōf fóps,

Gōt 'twéen āsléep ānd wáke? Wéll thén,

Lēgítimāte *(elided to three syllables)* Édgār, Í mūst háve yōur lánd.

Oūr fáthēr's lóve īs tó thē bástārd Édmūnd

Ās tó th' lēgítimāte *(again elided)*. Fíne wórd, "lēgítīmáte"!

Wēll, mý lēgítimāte *(elided)* íf thīs léttēr spéed

Ānd mý īnvéntiōn thríve, Édmūnd thē báse

Shāll tóp th' lēgítīmáte. Í grów, Í próspēr.

Nów, góds, stánd úp fōr bástards!

(*King Lear*, Act I, ii)

Just before this revealing soliloquy occurs, we have witnessed Edmund made the butt of several jokes about his illegitimate conception by his own father, the Duke of Gloucester, that are shared with a friend in his son's presence; so is there any wonder that the speech trembles with barely constrained rage?

For a final example, let's look at one of the most percussive and irregularly rhythmed speech in all of Shakespeare: one by King Leontes in *The Winter's Tale*:

Leontes and Paulina from *The Winter's Tale*

Ínch-thíck, knée-déep, o'ēr héad ānd eárs ā fórk'd ōne!

Gó pláy, bōy, pláy. Thȳ móthēr pláys, ānd Í

Pláy tóo, būt só dīsgrác'd ā párt, whōse íssūe

Wīll híss mē tó mȳ gráve: cōntémpt ānd clámōr

Wīll bé mȳ knéll.Gó pláy, bōy, pláy. Thēre hāve béen

(Ōr Í ām múch dēcéiv'd) cúckōlds ēre nów,

Ānd mány *(elided)* ā mán thēre ís (éven *(elided)* át thīs présēnt,

Nów, whíle Ī spéak thīs) hólds hīs wífe bȳ th' árm *(elided)*

Thāt líttlē thínks shē hás bēen slúic'd īn 's *(elided)* ábsēnce,

Ānd hīs pónd físh'd bȳ hīs néxt néighbōr—bý

Sīr Smíle, hīs néighbōr. Náy, thēre's cómfōrt ín't,

Whīles óthēr mén hāve gátes, ānd thóse gātes ópēn'd,

Ās míne, āgáinst thēir wíll. Shōuld áll dēspáir

Thāt háve rēvóltēd wíves, thē ténth ōf mánkīnd

Wōuld háng thēmsélves. Phýsīc fōr't thēre's nóne.

Īt ís ā báwdȳ plánēt, thát wīll stríke

Whēre 'tís prēdómīnánt; ánd 'tīs pów'rfūl—thínk īt—

Frōm eást, wést, nórth, ānd sóuth. Bé īt cōnclúdēd,

Nó bārrīcádō fór ā béllȳ!

(*The Winter's Tale*, Act I, ii)

The rhythms of this text clearly depict a tortured soul, and the circumstances of the story confirm that conclusion. Leontes is the King of Sicilia, married to a beautiful and generous Queen, Hermione; together they have a son, the young Prince Mamillius, still a boy. As the play opens, they have been hosting Leontes's childhood friend, Polixenes, now the King of Bohemia; having stayed in Sicilia for some months, Polixenes is preparing to return home. No one in the seemingly happy Sicilian court, however, is aware that Leontes suffers from a mental illness that fosters paranoid delusions about a non-existent adulterous relationship between his friend and his Queen, and these delusions give sudden birth to a murderous jealousy. The preceding speech is spoken in the presence of

Mamillius, who, too young to understand what troubles his sick father, plays happily at his sire's feet.

Leontes's diatribe shows some of Shakespeare's most impassioned and irregular verses; most of the initial lines of the quoted text all contain 6-7 strong stresses, with numerous spondees. No gentle, rolling rhythms here, leading easily from one thought to the next; instead, the tirade stutters and explodes like gunfire. The sexual imagery Leontes aims at his blameless wife is derogatory and degrading. The nearly total absence of lines in the speech that have full stops, or even easy caesurae at their conclusion, is also indicative of Leontes's tumultuous emotional state; the spoken thoughts of one line seem to literally crash against its own iambic pentameter structure, breaking like violent waves into the initial words of the following line. Thoughts that tend to phrase with the iambic pentameter of a line, leading to full stops or caesurae after the final syllable, are called *end-stopped* lines. Sentences and/or phrases that clearly "run on" from one line into the following are called *enjambed*. Leontes clearly speaks almost entirely in enjambed lines; his thoughts and emotions will not be reasonably bridled or contained. All in all, this is one of the most harrowing and charged texts in all of the Shakespearean canon.

This general guideline is worth remembering when young actors scan Shakespeare: *When characters are more in control of their own emotional state, more rational, more philosophically reflective, or more self-consciously lyrical (i.e., in love), Shakespeare's iambic pentameter will usually be more regular, with fewer striking variations in rhythm. More anomalies of rhythm indicate higher emotional states, increased passion, or new ideas (exciting or upsetting) in the process of discovery.*

But don't look for the anomalies first! Find the regular heartbeat of the line, establish it (if it's there), and only then look for the variations.

Keeping that in mind, let's quickly look at the few remaining alternatives to Shakespeare's regular iambic foot.

A final variation occasionally found in some feet of Shakespeare's pentameter verse is the *pyrrhic*. A pyrrhic by itself doesn't demand the audience's attention, at least on its own; instead, it usually (although not always) appears in juxtaposition with a spondee, offering a rhythmic balance to the line, as a pyrrhic is a foot of verse with no stressed syllables. Here again are a few examples of pyrrhics, *with the "weak" feet in question italicized*, beginning with the line of Edmund's from *King Lear* that we just examined:

Thóu, Ná/*tūre, ārt*/ mý gód/*dēss; tō*/ thý láw/

Mȳ sér/vīcés/ āre boúnd.
(King Lear, Act I, ii)

Ānd thē/ júst pléa/súre lóst/ whīch ís/ sō deémed
(Sonnet 121)

Tō thē/ swéet glán/*cēs óf*/ thȳ hó/nōr'd lóve
(The Two Gentlemen of Verona, Act I, i)

Fíe ōn't!/ Āh fíe!/ *'Tīs ān*/ ūnwéed/ēd gárdēn
(Hamlet, Act I, ii)

(We'll note something more about the "on't" in this last example in a moment.)

So in summary: the four potential variations of a 2-syllable foot of Shakespearean verse are as follows: an *iamb* (unstressed, stressed), which is the foundational rhythm that is literally the heartbeat of the line; a *trochee* (stressed, unstressed); a *spondee* (stressed, stressed); and a *pyrrhic* (unstressed, unstressed). The iamb, and these three anomalous variations, will be what the actor finds more than 99% of the time when scanning Shakespeare.

There are two other anomalies that appear only rarely in Shakespeare's verse; but it's worth noting them briefly. A *dactyl* is a foot of verse that is three syllables in length instead of two; in this, a stressed syllable is followed by two unstressed syllables (DUM-dee-dee). An *anapest* is a foot of verse that is three syllables in length, with two unstressed syllables followed by a stressed (dee-dee-DUM). Again, neither of these variations are likely to appear often in Shakespearean verse; the triplicate rhythm is more at home in classical French verse drama (particularly in the anapest form) than it is in English. (Ironically, when the word "anapest" is pronounced aloud [an' a pest], it sounds like a foot of dactyl verse!). One of the more famous examples of the rare use of the anapest form in English poetry is a narrative piece that we're all pretty familiar with:

'Twas the night/before Christ/mas, and all/through the house,/

Not a crea/ture was stir/ring, not e/ven a mouse.

This 12-syllable verse line form, utilizing anapests as its primary foundation, is called *Alexandrine*. French neo-classical dramas are composed in this rather restrictive scheme. Shakespeare and his fellow playwrights did not generally utilize the Alexandrine verse form, as spoken English doesn't sound natural with this repetitive rhythm pattern. However, this is not to say that there are no Shakespearean lines of verse containing 12 syllables; on the contrary, in his later plays, as he experimented with looser patterns and rhythms of speech on stage (yet always coming back to the iambic pentameter as his base), there are increased instances of 12- and even occasionally as many as 14-syllable lines. But in virtually all such examples, the beat of the line is still iambic; it's just iambic *hexameter* instead of pentameter (that is, six feet of verse instead of five).

Perhaps the most recognizable Shakespearean line that is sometimes cited as an example of Alexandrine verse that utilizes a combination of anapests and iambs for its poetic effect is the following, from Act III, i of *Macbeth*:

Tō bē thús/ īs nó/thīng; bút/ tō bē sáfe/lȳ thús.

There are two good arguments against this proposal. The first is that the line itself is actually two partial lines. That is "To be thus is nothing" is actually a shared line of iambic pentameter, properly connected with Macbeth's short direction to his servant: "Bring them before us." In this format, the line would scan:

Bríng thēm/ bēfóre/ ūs. Tó/bē thús/ īs nó/thīng;/

Būt tó/ bē sáfe/lȳ thús./ Oūr feárs/ īn Bánquō/

Stīck déep,/ . . . .

. . . and so on, into the rest of the soliloquy. Here, the only anomalies would be the minor ones of feminine endings at the close of each line, which as we've noted is fairly common in Shakespeare; so much so that they probably shouldn't be regarded as genuine anomalies. But according to the First Folio—the earliest printing of the play—"Bring them before us" is a separate line unto itself, followed by the proposed Alexandrine. Although the Folio should retain our respect as the earliest authoritative source of *Macbeth*'s text, the printers were clearly not infallible as we've noted earlier, and it's entirely likely that the methods of separating the verse lines for printing were, on many occasions, theirs and not Shakespeare's.

So . . . in beginning to work with scansion, the most important thing that young actors should keep in mind is that whenever the regular iambic rhythm changes and becomes irregular, it usually coincides with an intensity of feeling or passion in the character. *A point is being made by him*, and it will reward the actor's attention to it, giving him clues to the character's dramatic progression and emotional state, both in the scene and in the play. And if the actor incorporates this realization into his line delivery, the audience should take note of it too—either consciously or unconsciously.

ELISIONS AND "STRETCH-ED" WORDS

However, there's another good argument for this line example from *Macbeth* not being strictly Alexandrine, even if it's printed as an integral verse line: perhaps, when spoken, certain words in this line were meant to be pronounced together as one syllable rather than given their usual value as two. This is called *elision*, and is another essential tool for the actor to grasp when scanning Shakespeare's verse.

Even though the line we're examining from *Macbeth* is not the clearest, easiest elision for the speaker to effect—mainly because it has a troublesome voiced plosive (the "b" sound) smack in the middle of our proposed contraction—if we were to pursue that option, it would scan something like this:

T'bē thús/ īs nó/thīng; bút/ t'bē sáfe/lȳ thús.

In speaking the line this way, we're attempting to give the two syllables—*to be*—the vocal rhythmic value of only one—t'be. This achieved, the line falls easily into the regular iambic pentameter beat.

How often are elisions to be found and practiced in spoken Shakespearean verse? *Very often.* In fact, sometimes Shakespeare marks them specifically in his writing so that the actor doesn't even have to search them out: words such as even, ever, and never are regularly found in his texts as *e'en, e'er,* and *ne'er.* Here, a middle consonant for each word is left out in its articulation, and by this choice two beats become one. There may also be found in the plays many instances of two words combined into one by the elimination of a vowel; some are difficult to do easily, and take practice by the actor (*of the* elided to *o'th'*, for example). *Is it* becomes *is't, to it* becomes *to't, were it* becomes *were't,* and *on it*—as we saw in the previous example we cited from Hamlet when we were examining pyrrhic feet—becomes *on't.*

Very often, however, the elisions are not spelled out on the page, and it is up to the attentive actor to discover when they should happen, as well as where in a given line they are to be found. When they occur is mostly dependent upon how you determine that the line should be scanned. Thus, your careful and informed experimentation with the sound of each line's rhythm when spoken aloud—its drumbeat, as it were—should give you important clues as to where potential elisions might be lurking for you to find and utilize. As we shall see, when these rhythms and related elisions occur, they might also provide valuable hints about the characters themselves, as well as how to successfully play the scene.

Here is what to look for: count the syllables in a given line of iambic pentameter: when you find it to be more than 10 syllables—yet, at the same time, when you say it aloud it seems to call for a stressed syllable on the final beat in order for it to make sense to the ear—the chances are strong that somewhere in the line 2 syllables need to be elided in order to find the line's proper spoken rhythm. (Remember: an 11-syllable line with an *un*stressed final syllable has a feminine ending; that's a different matter. *Look for the 11- or 12-syllable line that has a final stress in it to sniff out possible elisions in the line.*)

As mentioned, there are many times when Shakespeare identifies the desired elision himself for the actor in the text left to us. Here are a few examples of that, all of them notable for other interesting anomalies as well:

Caésār/ sáid tō/ mé, "Dár'st/ thōu, Cás/siūs, nów
(Julius Caesar, Act I, ii)

Hīs cá/nōn 'gáinst/ sélf-slaúgh/tēr! Ó /Gód! Gód!
(Hamlet, Act I, ii)

Thē lóyal/l'st hús/bānd thát/ dīd e'ér /plīght tróth
(Cymbeline, Act I, i)

In the first example from *Julius Caesar*, the author-noted elision is obviously in the 3rd foot of verse, making the 2-syllable "darest" into the single syllable "dar'st"; additionally, this line has other striking anomalies for the actor to note: the first two feet are trochees and the third a spondee, before the line returns to a regular iambic rhythm in the final two feet. And, as is mostly the case throughout the play (so not precisely an anomaly), "Cassius" is pronounced as two syllables.

In the second example from Hamlet, Shakespeare elides (in fact, abbreviates) "against" into one beat by dropping the first syllable of the word altogether. The 4th foot works either as an iamb or a pyrrhic; it is the individual actor's choice. The final foot, however, is undoubtedly a spondee. (The emotion behind this change of rhythm at the end of the line is clearly very high.)

The final example from one of Shakespeare's last plays seems especially challenging. (Remember: the later Shakespeare texts contain the most anomalies in rhythm of any in the canon.) Without the printed elisions (presumably by Shakespeare himself), the line would run 12 syllables: "The loyallest husband that did ever plight troth." However, both "loyallest" (as grammatically questionable as that word is to our modern ears!) and "ever" are marked as elided, each decreased by 1 syllable. "E'er" is easy, but "loyall'st" can be quite a challenge to pronounce as it is marked in the text. The best way for the actor to think of saying it would probably be "loy'lest"—a fascinating word that also feels good in the mouth!

Now, try working with these multiple examples taken from a variety of the plays. All of them fit the criteria mentioned above: they have 11 syllables, but all of them end in stressed syllables, so none of them can have feminine endings. See if you can determine where there are potential elisions in them that work for the benefit of the line's flowing rhythm; after you've given them all a try, check your choices against the lines as I've scanned them, immediately following.

1. Whose misadventur'd piteous overthrows (*Romeo and Juliet*)
2. And the continuance of their parents' rage (*Romeo and Juliet*)
3. A heavier task could not have been impos'd (*The Comedy of Errors*)
4. Visit her face too roughly. Heaven and earth! (*Hamlet*)
5. But what my power might else exact, like one (*The Tempest*)
6. All liberal reason will I yield unto (*Love's Labour's Lost*)
7. He brings great news! The raven himself is hoarse (*Macbeth*)
8. I cannot do it; yet I'll hammer it out. (*Richard II*)

Finished? Here are the lines scanned, with probably the most acceptable and practical elisions for each line in italics that would help them keep their basic rhythm:

1. Whōse mís/ādvén/tūr'd pít/*eoūs* ó/vērthróws ("piteous" is pronounced as 2 syllables instead of 3, eliding the vowels)
2. Ānd thē/ cōntín/*uānce* óf/ thēir pár/ēnt's ráge ("continuance" is pronounced as 2 syllables instead of 3, eliding the vowels; note that the first foot is a pyrrhic)
3. Ā héa/*viēr* tásk/ coūld nót/ hāve béen/ īmpós'd ("vier" is elided, similarly to the previous lines)
4. Vísīt/ hēr fáce/ tōo roúgh/ lȳ. *Heá'en/* ānd eárth! ("Heaven" is elided, gliding over the "v"; note that the first foot is a trochee)
5. Būt whát/ mȳ *pów'r/* mīght élse/ ēxáct/ līke óne ("Power" is elided, gliding over the "w")
6. Áll *líb'/rāl* réa/sōn wíll/ Ī yiéld/ ūntó ("Liberal" is elided, losing the "e"; note the that the first foot is a spondee)
7. Hē bríngs/ grēat néws!/ Thē *rá'en/* hīmsélf/ īs hoárse ("Raven" is elided, gliding over the "v")
8. Ī cán/nōt dó/ īt; yét/ Ī'll hám/*mēr't* oút. ("Hammer it" is elided together, virtually losing the "i")

The more you work with Shakespeare's iambic rhythm, and its "heartbeat" works its way into your actor's soul, the more the obvious options for elisions will leap out at you. (In the same way, the more of his plays that you read consecutively within a short time period, the more natural and comprehensible his vocabulary and use of language will seem to you.)

So, this is how elision works. But what of the lines that you find that seem to be missing a syllable? Or sometimes, two? They might be termed a short line, and we'll deal with those next (as well as their counterpart, the shared line). But a short line is usually shorter than 8 or 9 syllables; generally they're 4 or 6 syllables, with 2 or 3 strong stresses in the iambic rhythm. For lines that at first seem shorted by only 1 or 2 syllables, a different thing might be happening with them.

Let's determine what it might be by looking at a few possible examples, starting with a section of Henry V's speech to his troops that we scanned earlier in the chapter:

> *Let it pry through the portage of the head*
> *Like the brass cannon; let the brow o'erwhelm it*
> *As fearfully as doth a galled rock*
> *O'erhang and jutty his confounded base,*
> *Swill'd with the wild and wasteful ocean.*

As already noted, there are author-directed elisions in the second and fourth lines quoted above; but what about the final line? It would appear to have 9 syllables. (Even with the notation of the apostrophe in "swill'd" the normal pronunciation of the word would be of 1 syllable.)

In this case, "ocean" should be given a 3-syllable pronunciation, instead of the usual 2 (o-she-en). Why? Well, not only does it regularize the iambic rhythm of the line, it makes the sound of the word itself onomatopoeic. (A word that sounds like what it denotes.) Henry conjures an image of a rock projecting over a wave-swept shoreline, with the surf surging in and around it, sloshing and swirling about it, "galling" the slab with its rough attacks. When the actor gives a full 3-syllable value to "ocean," it actually suggests the *sound* of the "swilling" waves against the rock.

Here's an interesting example extracted from Egeon's account of his search for his lost twin sons in the opening scene of *Comedy of Errors*:

> *We were encount'red by a mighty rock*
> *Which being violently borne upon*
> *Our helpful ship was splitted in the midst.*

(The context: Our ship was swept by the storm and waves onto a rock, which split it in two.)

The first and third lines scan quite regularly in iambic pentameter, with 10 clear syllables each. The second, however, might seem at first glance to have 9—until we remind ourselves that vi-o-lent is technically a 3-syllable word, even though in everyday speech we often naturally elide it to 2. By emphasizing the full 3 syllables in the context of the information that the line contains, the imaginative and deft actor can suggest the violence of the shipwreck by the rhythmic pronunciation of the word itself.

Here's another excerpt from Egeon's lengthy narrative:

> *Five summers have I spent in furthest Greece,*
> *Roaming clean through the bounds of Asia.*

Let's examine what the actor might communicate with the speaking of the line, combining analysis with his imagination and sensitivity to the "music" of the rhythm: "Five summers" opens the statement with a strong spondee, emphasizing the long, and thus far fruitless quest through which Egeon has suffered. A pyrrhic immediately follows that spondee, balancing the beat, before the line ends with three feet of regular iambs. The second line begins with a trochee—*rarely, if ever, will you find an "ing" syllable deserving a strong stress*—in which the actor can effectively use the full, open "o" of "roaming", followed by another possible spondee ("clean through"), which again emphatically describes, with both words and their sounds, the wearying length of his odyssey. Mirroring the previous line, this also ends in three iambs . . . or does it? Isn't it possible for the actor to *stretch* the normally 2-syllable word "Asia" to a full 3 syllables—A-si-a—making that faraway continent sound to our ears as exotic and mysterious as the lands that it holds? Yes, it is—and that's apparently what Shakespeare means the actor telling Egeon's story to do.

Here's a very subtle, yet extremely important example of how effective "stretching" can be, taken from another of Shakespeare's most famous speeches: Marc Antony's funeral oratory about the assassinated Julius Caesar in the play of that name. Here are the lines; try scanning them for yourself before reading on:

> *Friends, Romans, countrymen, lend me your ears!*
> *I come to bury Caesar, not to praise him.*
> *The evil that men do lives after them;*
> *The good is oft interred with their bones;*
> *So let it be with Caesar. The noble Brutus*

Hath told you Caesar was ambitious;
If it were so, it was a grievous fault,
And grievously hath Caesar answer'd it.
Here, under leave of Brutus and the rest
(For Brutus is an honorable man;
So are they all, all honorable men),
Come I to speak in Caesar's funeral.
He was my friend, faithful and just to me;
But Brutus says he was ambitious,
And Brutus is an honorable man.
He hath brought many captives home to Rome,
Whose ransoms did the general coffers fill;
Did this in Caesar seem ambitious?
When that the poor have cried, Caesar hath wept;
Ambition should be made of sterner stuff.
Yet Brutus says he was ambitious,
And Brutus is an honorable man.
You all did see that on the Lupercal
I thrice presented him a kingly crown,
Which he did thrice refuse. Was this ambition?
Yet Brutus says he was ambitious,
And sure he is an honorable man.

(*Julius Caesar*, Act III, ii)

Upon your initial attempt at scanning this oratory, what jumps out at you?

Well, the first line is pretty striking; it clearly begins with a spondee punch. Appropriate, since in the context of the play Antony has to quickly gain the attention of an unruly and somewhat hostile crowd in the Roman Forum. The line ends with the four strong monosyllables, the commanding imperative "Lend me your ears!" The single syllables demand a slower, powerful delivery, and both feet deserve spondees, which would bring 8 strong syllabic stresses to a 10-syllable line . . . quite a powerful beginning.

After getting "their ears," Antony's carefully planned funeral oratory then settles down into a smoother, more regular iambic rhythm. He must play his hand carefully; for his ultimate political (and personal) revenge on the conspirators to succeed, he must persuade the Roman mob (already inclined toward the assassin Brutus's perspective at this point) that Caesar's murder deserves their grief, their regret, and later, their outrage. He seems to be speaking against his murdered friend and mentor for a few moments:

> *I come to bury Caesar, not to praise him.*
> *The evil that men do lives after them;*
> *The good is oft interred with their bones.*
> *So let it be with Caesar.*

On a more general note, let's linger with that third line a moment. Young actors often raise the question early in their scansion work about "ed" endings (as in "in-ter-red" vs. "in-terred"): when should a past-tense "ed" ending on a word in Shakespeare receive full pronunciation, and when should it not? The answer depends entirely on the number of syllables in a given line, and how it scans. For instance, if Shakespeare had written the line

> *The good is oft interred beside their bones*

the line would scan like this:

> Thē góod/ īs óft/ īntérred/ bēsíde/ thēir bónes

In such a case, it's likely that Shakespeare himself would have guided the actor in his writing of the line, as we have already noted that he does in other places throughout the canon, by putting an apostrophe in "interred" (i.e., inter'd). Here, however, he does not, and he actually wrote the line to scan like this:

> Thē góod/īs óft/īntér/rēd wíth/thēir bónes.

And that, very simply, is how the actor is led by the rhythms themselves to the "ed" solution. To pronounce or not to pronounce; that is the question. The scansion is the answer.

But back to Marc Antony's intent in the scene, and how Shakespeare's cleverness with the verse lines' rhythm scansion can offer the actors valuable clues about that. The first strong indication for the actor of what Shakespeare may be up to—the subtle drama embedded in the verse itself—appears in the 10th and 11th lines of the oratory:

(For Brutus is an honorable man;
So are they all, all honorable men)

In order for the iambics to work as they should in both lines, "honorable" needs to receive 4 clearly pronounced syllables; it cannot be elided to 3, as we tend to do with the word in everyday speech (hon'-ra-ble). Shakespeare draws even more attention to the word by a carefully-placed spondee in the second line, right before the word reappears, thus scanning as follows:

(Fōr Brú/tūs ís/ ān hón/ōrá/blē mán;

Sō áre/ thēy áll,/áll hón/ōrá/blē mén)

But how Shakespeare follows this with full 4-syllable value given to another word over the next few lines reveals his (and Antony's) dramatic game:

He was my friend, faithful and just to me;
But Brutus says he was ambitious,
And Brutus is an honorable man.

Note the trochee in the middle of the first line, drawing the listener's attention to the word "faithful" that Antony uses to describe the murdered Caesar; again, it leaps out at you due to the abrupt change in rhythm. Immediately following in the next line, "ambitious" gets a full 4-syllable treatment: roughly pronounced "am-bi-shi-us." Then, once again, "honorable" gets the same 4 syllables it had before. Antony repeats this same two-line cadence thrice more in the course of his oratory, noting that Brutus deems Caesar "am-bi-shi-us", and therefore it must be true—mustn't it?—because Brutus is an "hon-or-a-ble" man.

This is not accidental or serendipitous on Antony's part—nor on Shakespeare's. We can see this because in two other lines that occur after Antony initiates these cadences, "ambition" is given its more normal, 3-syllable pronunciation:

Āmbí/tiōn shóuld/ bē máde/ ōf stérn/ēr stúff

and

Whīch hé/ dīd thríce/ rēfúse./ Wās thís/ āmbítioūs?

(Note the feminine ending in the second line, a 3-beat foot that ends the line with an unstressed syllable.)

Why might Shakespeare be doing this? In this instance, how might the rhythm be working in conjunction with the character's dramatic intent? Let's look at the context: Over the objections of Brutus's co-conspirators in Caesar's assassination, the murdered leader's friend, Marc Antony, has been granted a chance to speak at Caesar's public funeral. In a prior soliloquy from Antony in a previous scene in the play, delivered over Caesar's bloody corpse, the audience has heard clearly Antony's hatred for the assassins and his desire to exact vengeance. However, until he can effect his plans for that, Antony must work more subtly and indirectly to sway the Roman citizens to his viewpoint. He has one shot to achieve this: the public eulogy that Brutus has graciously—Cassius might say stupidly—allowed him to make. He dares not show his hand by speaking directly of his rage and grief to the populace; he has to persuade rather than exhort.

Marc Antony's clever manipulation of the syllables of the two contrasting words (Caesar was "am-bi-ti-ous" says the "hon-o-ra-ble" Brutus), coupled with the examples he gives of Caesar's political and military honors and the humble generosity Antony says Caesar offered the Roman people in past years, lays an effective foundation. The emphasis that the speaker gives to these two key words at pivotal moments in the speech—aided by the rhetorical device of careful repetition—drives home the irony behind Antony's words. The real message being delivered is precisely the opposite of what his words seem to be saying— and it starts to work as the speech progresses. It is absolutely masterful political oratory, masked at first behind supposedly neutral funeral oratory. By the conclusion of Antony's speech, the fickle Roman people have been stirred to riot against Brutus and his co-conspirators, all without any direct appeal of them to do so on Antony's part; and the actor's careful scansion and thoughtful use of the verse rhythms provided by Shakespeare himself help the character achieve this dramatically.

We should always assume that the rhythms Shakespeare provides in his verse offer a map for the thoughtful and imaginative actor that will lead toward the most effective line readings, the most interesting character choices, and the most striking performance choices possible. If he approaches his preparation from that initial premise, he will surely have the best chance to make the most of the opportunities that the heightened language offers him.

Before concluding this aspect of our discussion of line scansion and moving on to something else, let's look at one final example of character revelation which is perhaps a bit more direct than that of Marc Antony's oratory. In *Twelfth Night*, the shipwrecked Sebastian, a stranger in Illyria, has been mistaken for his twin sister Viola by the Countess Olivia. Viola has survived her own sojourn in this foreign land by disguising herself as a man; and in that disguise, she obviously resembles her brother. Olivia has fallen in love with Viola; consequently, upon first encountering the real male of the set in the streets of the town outside of her estate, Olivia takes Sebastian inside and lovingly entertains him. (What precisely that entertainment consists of is a choice that the actors and director have to make in the course of their rehearsals.) When the dazed Sebastian emerges from Olivia's house a bit later, he delivers a soliloquy that begins:

> *This is the air; that is the glorious sun;*
> *This pearl she gave me; I do feel't and see't,*
> *And though 'tis wonder that enwraps me thus,*
> *Yet 'tis not madness.*
>
> (*Twelfth Night*, Act IV, iii)

Although the elisions of *feel't* and *see't* in the second line, and *'tis* in the third, are certainly suggestive of the confused energy that drives Sebastian's vocal pace as the soliloquy progresses, let's look simply at the first line.

Over my years of teaching Shakespeare, I have found that young actors often tackle this soliloquy as one of their first serious audition pieces from the plays; and as such, it's a good choice. The age of the character is appropriate for them; the subject (young love), a good one; it's not one of the more iconic characters from the canon who carry with them lots of preconceptions from the auditors; there's the action of a significant problem to be worked out by the actor/character over the course of the speech; the language and imagery are direct and the rhythms are fairly regular, yet offer enough interesting anomalies to demonstrate the actor's knowledge and skill of scansion tools and techniques; and finally, the piece is one that several of the major audition-based university/conservatory programs in the country actually suggest or require for their applicants. All of these points represent good guidelines for young actors to follow when selecting a piece to work on early in their experience of Shakespeare.

In almost all initial passes at the soliloquy, I've found that most young actors scan the first line as follows:

Thís īs/ thē aír;/ thát īs/ thē glór/ī-oūs sún;

If indeed spoken with this scansion, an easy thing for a teacher to note first in coaching the actor about what to address would be the elision of *glor-i-ous* from its 3 syllables to the 2 of *glor-yus*, making the line 10 syllables with a stressed ending.

That done, direct your attention to the choice of making the first and third feet of the line trochaic. Is that necessary? Or desirable? I think neither; in fact, to scan the line in strict iambic pentameter, as thus,

Thīs ís/ thē aír;/ thāt ís/ thē glór/ioūs sún;

actually better serves the context of Sebastian's moment. He stresses *is* both times, instead of first *This*, then *that*. Both choices can work; but this latter option seems to more effectively reveal a Sebastian on the verge of questioning his own sanity. "This *is* the air," he seems to be verifying to himself, giving his psyche a figurative pinch; "that *is* the glorious sun." *I know both of these things to be true*, he affirms aloud, listening to his own voice to keep his hold on concrete reality. Going with Shakespeare's regular rhythm and avoiding the inessential anomalous choice in that first line, one could argue, even tells the story more clearly and with more humor.

It's a good point to keep in mind when starting to scan Shakespeare: *regular iambs can often tell your story more clearly than leaping to a choice of anomalies*. Scan with regular iambs first, and see if the words that are stressed in that rhythm teach you something about the moment, or even clarify it more effectively than what might be your first impression of the line. Very often, this will indeed be the case.

It seems that Shakespeare knew what he was doing!

SHORT LINES, SHARED LINES

There is another possibility the actor might consider when analyzing the scansion options of Marc Antony's speech. What if we don't "punch" the words *ambitious* and *honorable* by slightly (and ironically, as we have noted) drawing them out into a full 4 syllables? What if, instead, the lines simply lack the additional 2 syllables for a full pentameter, making them *short lines*?

What should we know, and what are we to do with short lines in Shakespearean verse?

Simply put, short lines imply a *pause* of some kind. It might be a pause that the character needs for thought or discovery. It might be a pause for action or activity of some kind. It might be a pause that occurs while the character notices something that the other character is doing—or not doing. Whatever the case, the actor should assume that when Shakespeare offers a short line of verse in the midst of a speech or dialogue sequence in regular pentameter rhythm, something significant is going on that is important—either in a small or large way—to the story being told.

If the actor playing Antony opts not to subtly extend the pronunciation of those two words for the ironic effect in performance, he may choose to offer a slight pause after each line, punctuated by some behavior (raised eyebrows? A grim smile?) which communicates to his listeners that he may not mean precisely what he is saying. Try it yourself, using both choices: first stretch the words a bit; then try the slight pauses after each. What works best for your vision of Marc Antony?

> *Yet Brutus says he was ambitious;*
> *And Brutus is an honorable man.*

If we do treat these as short lines, they would be rather unusual in the Shakespeare canon; as we touched on briefly earlier, most short lines that we find in the plays are 6 syllables or fewer. This makes them clearer and more notable for anyone in the audience tuned in—consciously or unconsciously—to the rhythms of speech, and therefore more dramatically effective.

Let's look at some examples. First, let's return to the balcony scene of *Romeo and Juliet*, specifically the following section of Romeo's passionate soliloquy; speaking of why Juliet should not follow the example of Diana, goddess of virginity (hmmm!), he charges:

> *Be not her maid, since she is envious;*
> *Her vestal livery is but sick and green,*
> *And none but fools do wear it; cast it off!*
> *It is my lady; O, it is my love!*
> *O that she knew she were!*
> *She speaks! Yet she says nothing; what of that?*
> *Her eye discourses; I will answer it.*

Upon the quickest scansion of this passage, we see immediately that the line "O that she knew she were!" is only 6 syllables, a short line. So what is going on there during the beats when Romeo doesn't continue speaking? The next line tells us: Juliet has made some inarticulate noise that interrupts his rhapsodizing. What that noise is—a wistful sigh, an expression of exasperation—the actress playing Juliet must discover for herself. But Romeo's attention is momentarily arrested, his flow of speech is interrupted, and the line is consequently cut short by 4 syllables.

In this soliloquy of Isabella's from *Measure for Measure*, the young novice has been physically and emotionally assaulted during the action of the scene (Act II, iv) that occurs right before she speaks. The supposedly virtuous Angelo, left in charge of the governance of Vienna by Duke Vincentio, has suggested to the religious young woman that he will release her brother Claudio from prison if she will submit to him sexually. Making the proposition even more outrageous is the fact that the puritan Angelo has sentenced Claudio to death for impregnating his own fiancé—execution for consensual sex (forbidden by the strict law of Vienna, albeit long unenforced)! This particular play is populated by troublesome characters, including Isabella herself, as shown by how she responds here; speaking of her brother, she says,

> *Though he hath fall'n by prompture of the blood,*
> *Yet hath he in him such a mind of honor*
> *That had he twenty heads to tender down*
> *On twenty bloody blocks, he'ld yield them up,*
> *Before his sister should her body stoop*
> *To such abhorr'd pollution.*
> *Then, Isabel, live chaste, and brother, die;*
> *More than our brother is our chastity!*

The sixth line is once again short by 2 syllables. During that brief moment in which she gathers herself, absorbs what has happened to her, and ponders her options, Isabella quickly makes a choice of priorities: her virginity is more valuable to her than her young brother's life! The short line indicates that moment of determined decision, however long the actress needs to take there in making it.

In Act I, iii of *Othello*, Iago lingers on the stage while all of the other characters have departed, sharing with us his intention of undermining and destroying his general, Othello.

> *The Moor is of a free and open nature,*
> *That thinks men honest that but seem to be so,*

> *And will as tenderly be led by th' nose*
> *As asses are.*
> *I have 't; it is engend'red. Hell and night*
> *Must bring this monstrous birth to the world's light.*

As the excited declarative "I have't" indicates, Iago has had a sudden inspiration about how he might proceed with his plot; the light bulb, as the saying goes, has turned on for him. Where does this happen? Right at that moment, during the short, 2-foot line that precedes it.

Or consider this section of Hamlet's soliloquy in Act II, ii of that play.

> *'Swounds, I should take it; for it cannot be*
> *But I am pigeon-livered and lack gall*
> *To make oppression bitter, or ere this*
> *I should 'a' fatted all the region kites*
> *With this slave's offal. Bloody, bawdy villain!*
> *Remorseless, treacherous, lecherous, kindless villain!*
> *O, vengeance!—*
> *Why, what an ass am I! This is most brave . . .*

and so on. Note that after the powerful, short line that comes at the height of his tortured passion, Hamlet turns himself around abruptly, realizing that he is being impotently self-indulgent. That realization happens in the absent beats of the short line.

So, to repeat: *short lines in Shakespeare's iambic pentameter indicate that something notable is* happening *during the missing beats of the line: the speaker is thinking, a discovery is occurring, or some physical activity is taking place in lieu of speech.*

We've just glanced at examples from Shakespearean soliloquies. Some lines in Shakespearean dialogue are short, too—but very often (although not always) they are completed to a full pentameter length by a different speaker. This is called a shared line, and they occur regularly and often throughout the plays of Shakespeare.

Here, from *Love's Labour's Lost*, is a section of a feisty exchange between Berowne and Rosalind. It seems that they met previously at a court function in Brabant (in Belgium), experienced some romantic chemistry together . . . and then, apparently, something went awry between them before the relationship progressed very far. Now, they encounter one another again, unexpectedly, at the court of the King of Navarre. Rosalind, in her pride, pretends not to recognize the cocky Berowne.

BEROWNE:Did not I dance with you in Brabant once?
ROSALIND:Did not I dance with you in Brabant once?
BEROWNE: I know you did.
ROSALIND: How needless was it then
            To ask?
BEROWNE: You must not be so quick.

And there, in Berowne's last line, lies the very information that the actor needs to know about shared lines in Shakespeare: *If two characters share a single line of iambic pentameter, then they need to pick up their cues even more quickly than they normally would—and as all professional actors know, cue pick-up is always an essential practice, even in prose plays when there is not a shared iambic pentameter verse line.*

Shared lines in Shakespeare always occur when the characters are most eager to engage with one another, or engage together with (or against) some immediately impending situation. Usually, the actors working on such a text can easily see from the context of the scene itself why the dialogue needs to be snappy and sharply paced; with shared lines, Shakespeare simply offers them yet another tool to encourage that choice.

Here's a brief section of a longer passage from Act I, iii of *Henry IV, Part 1*: the fiery-tempered, hot-headed young Harry Percy (aptly nicknamed "Hotspur") launches regularly into impatient tirades against perceived wrongs and slights. His uncle, the Earl of Worcester, attempts valiantly to calm him down—or even get a word in edgewise!

HOTSPUR: By heaven, methinks it were an easy leap,
        To pluck bright honor from the pale-fac'd moon,

> Or dive into the bottom of the deep,
> Where fadom-line could never touch the ground,
> And pluck up drowned honor by the locks,
> So he that doth redeem her thence might wear
> Without corrival all her dignities;
> But out upon this half-fac'd fellowhsip!
> WORCESTER: *(speaking to Northumberland, Hotspur's father)* He apprehends a world of figures here,
> But not the form of what he should attend.
> *(to Hotspur)* Good cousin, give me audience for awhile.
> HOTSPUR: I cry you mercy!
> WORCESTER: Those same noble Scots
> That are your prisoners—
> HOTSPUR: I'll keep them all!
> By God, he shall not have a Scot of them,
> No, if a Scot would save his soul, he shall not!
> I'll keep them, by this hand!
> WORCESTER: You start away,
> And lend no ear unto my purposes.
> Those prisoners you shall keep.
> HOTSPUR: Nay, I will! That's flat.

Notice that in the last shared line, Hotspur not only jumps quickly on Worcester's speech yet again, his insistent rhythms even spill over longer than the normal five stresses of the pentameter line. Even after Worcester's "*pris'ners*" has been elided into 2 syllables, the 11-syllable line that remains still demands 6 stresses. It appears that not even Shakespeare's standard iambic pentameters can stop Hotspur from having his full say!

The last example of shared lines at which we'll take a glance is actually a brilliantly effective combination of both shared and short lines. As Act II, ii of *Macbeth* commences, Macbeth, encouraged by his Lady, has just completed the murder of King Duncan, his guest and patron, as he slept in the guest quarters of their castle Dunsinane. Both husband and wife are understandably wound tight with tension, adrenaline, and horror at what they are doing; and as Lady Macbeth waits in apprehension in the dark castle courtyard, the dark figure of Macbeth appears, his hands soaked in his King's blood.

MACBETH: I have done the deed. Didst thou not hear a noise?
LADY MACBETH:: I heard the owl scream and the cricket cry.
    Did not you speak?
MACBETH: When?
LADY MACBETH: Now.
MACBETH: As I descended?
LADY MAB: Ay.
MACBETH: Hark!
        Who lies in the second chamber?
LADY MACBETH: Donalbain.
MACBETH: This is a sorry sight. *(Looking at his bloody hands)*
LADY MACBETH: A foolish thought to say a sorry sight.

(A quick note here: Remember the points we were making in Chapter II? That every serious Shakespearean actor should consult several reputable modern editions of the play, as well as the original Folio, or quartos of the play where they exist? Well, this scene provides a wonderful example of why that's important. Almost every edition of *Macbeth* presents a slightly different take on how these lines should be printed out, and thus scanned. The version above is my own take on it; so readers—and especially actors and directors—are highly encouraged to compare what I've suggested here with every other option that they can find to determine what would work best for them.)

    Macbeth's first line elides *I have* to *I've*; otherwise, the rhythm, although hurried, is regular. Lady Macbeth's responding line begins with two iambs, followed by a trochee, then concludes with bookending double iambs; slightly irregular, but still pretty rhythmical. After that, their dialogue involves a panicked, rapid-fire exchange that has four terse utterances inhabiting a single pentameter line. This is followed by another quick 2 syllables: Lady Macbeth's "Ay", with Macbeth's shushing "Hark!" coming hard on its heels. After a tense pause where both listen in the dead of night for any hint of their possible discovery, there is another hushed shared line, with Macbeth's hurried elision of "in the" into a single syllable: *"Who lies i'th' second chamber?"* To which Lady Macbeth responds, *"Donalbain."* After that, we're back to regular verse . . . but not for long. The short and shared lines will continue throughout the scene, until the Macbeths, changed forever—and not for the better!—stumble brokenly from the stage.

It is arguably the most harrowing scene in all of Shakespeare, excepting perhaps King Lear's death and Othello's realization of his murdered wife's innocence; and actors who make full use of Shakespeare's masterful verse rhythms contribute vitally in achieving the desired effect.

It's worth repeating: all of the various points we've touched upon regarding Shakespeare's scansion over the course of this chapter should be embraced as aids and resources for actors, not codes to trip them up, strict rules to follow, or tests that they must pass or fail. Once they are practiced and a certain level of comprehension and mastery achieved, they will provide fun, revelatory, and ultimately invaluable tools for unlocking effective techniques that reveal many intriguing facets of Shakespeare's rich characters; icons in the annals of dramatic literature. Remember: the questions that arise when engaging the text in this fashion become what is most important. Those questions spark thought, reflection and discussion; but your answers will never be right or wrong. They will simply be your own. And they will be *informed*.

Practice is the key to making all of these things work effectively together. With that in mind, let's take a look at a few more examples, try putting together all of what we've covered so far, and see what we might come up with.

PUTTING IT ALL TOGETHER

First, we'll glance at the final appearance of Malvolio in *Twelfth Night*. Poor Malvolio has had quite a time over the course of the story. As the head steward of Countess Olivia's household, he has been tricked into believing that his aristocratic mistress harbors a secret love for him, and encouraged to present himself before her in a ridiculous costume (mistakenly thinking she approves of it) to proclaim his love for her. Mistaken for a madman as a result of his absurd behavior, he is subsequently imprisoned in a dark cell. Belatedly learning of the cruel practical joke, perpetrated by her own uncle Toby Belch in partnership with her chambermaid Maria, Olivia immediately sends for Malvolio. As he appears before her, the director, actor and audience for each individual staging must determine how sympathetic he may appear to us; but let's examine a bit of what Shakespeare himself might be suggesting to us by the manner in which he structures the dialogue during the first moments of their encounter in Act V, Scene i:

OLIVIA: How now, Malvolio?
MALVOLIO: Madam, you have done me wrong,
     Notorious wrong!
OLIVIA: Have I, Malvolio? No.
MALVOLIO: Lady, you have! Pray you, peruse this letter.
     You must not now deny it is your hand;
     Write from it if you can, in hand or phrase,
     Or say 'tis not your seal, not your invention.
     You can say none of this. Well, grant it then,
     And tell me, in the modesty of honor,
     Why you have given me such clear lights of favor,
     Bade me come smiling and cross-garter'd to you,
     To put on yellow stockings, and to frown
     Upon Sir Toby and the lighter people;
     And acting this in an obedient hope,
     Why have you suffer'd me to be imprison'd,
     Kept in a dark house, visited by the priest,
     And made the most notorious geck and gull
     That e'er invention play'd on? Tell me why!

The first thing we notice, of course, are the shared iambic pentameter lines between Olivia and Malvolio, suggesting that their initial greeting occurs at a rapid, highly-charged pace. In fact, the first line of shared dialogue has 12 syllables, with 6 iambic beats (if Olivia elides Malvolio's name, making it 3 syllables—Mal-vo-lio—instead of 4). The actors' quick cues here are essential; one might even suggest that Olivia's spoken "Malvolio" and Malvolio's strong "Madam" are both spoken as an overlap, virtually simultaneously (with the first syllable of "Madam" spoken against the second syllable of "Malvolio"); indeed, if that is done, then the line may still function almost as a pentameter line. This rapid pace and strong force suggests the highest emotional content behind the words. This continues in the next shared line between the two, with elisions of "notorious" into 3 syllables again offset by Olivia's repeated elision of "Malvolio." Many actresses playing Olivia make the choice of emphasizing "Have" in her response; but the natural rhythms that Shakespeare's verse provides suggests that emphasizing "I" might be the more effective choice; it certainly underscores Olivia's bafflement at the accusation that she has been behind this malicious prank. Her single final "No!" is also quite strong.

And now, Malvolio launches into his impassioned accusation. Tellingly, it is the first and only use of verse that Shakespeare gives this normally repressed and resentful man in the entire play, and it flows out of him with the heightened passion that the context of his humiliating situation demands. Not unexpectedly under the circumstances, he begins not with iambs, but with a trochee followed by a spondee, emphasizing his rage: "LA-dy, YOU HAVE!" This is followed by another trochee ("PRAY you") before he begins to settle into a regular iambic rhythm again for the next 5 lines of verse. This regularity allows the words to flow out of the unfortunate man in a flood of emotion, which he tries to balance against his natural affinity for order and propriety.

(Note on the third line of his text, the words "Write from it if you can, in hand or phrase"; on first glance, the actor might naturally want to emphasize "Write" instead of "from"—it is a stronger word, after all. But in so doing, he runs the risk of muddying the meaning and intent. What Malvolio is saying is that Olivia cannot give a sample of her handwriting that would differ from what appears on the letter. [As Maria noted earlier in the play, she has mastered the ability to forge Olivia's signature.] *The actor must always consider the standard rhythmical choice first before leaping to depart from it.* If he doesn't, he runs the risk of missing key elements. Shakespeare knew what he was doing!)

However, notwithstanding the overall regularity of rhythm, the actor should take note of the large number of single syllable words, one following another in quick succession, that can be utilized to dramatically underscore the accusatory nature of the lines. As we've briefly noted earlier, monosyllabic words in the course of iambic pentameter verse tend to slow the rhythms for emphasis when the actor chooses to utilize them that way . . . such as with "YOU CAN SAY NONE OF THIS!", which caps his list of evidence against Olivia. After this series of strong monosyllables, one can imagine Malvolio drawing a breath to find a calmer demeanor before launching into the series of questions that follow, pleading almost desperately of his fantasized lover to explain why she would do such things to him after so cruelly setting him up. Now the rhythms become less regular, less flowing. So here is how it might sound, with emphasized syllables capitalized:

WHY you have GIVEN (*elided to 1 syllable*) me such CLEAR LIGHTS of FAVor,
BADE me COME SMILing, and CROSS-GARTer'd to you,
To PUT on YELlow STOCKings AND to FROWN,
UpON Sir TOby AND the LIGHTer PEOple,
And ACTing THIS in AN oBEDient (*elided to 3 syllables*) HOPE,
WHY have you SUFfered ME to BE imPRISon'd,
KEPT in a DARK HOUSE, VISited (*elided to 2 syllables*) by the PRIEST,
And MADE the MOST noTORious (*elided to 3 syllables*) GECK and GULL
That E'ER inVENtion PLAY'D on? TELL ME WHY!

5 of these 9 lines seem to best play as irregular lines for optimum theatrical effect, at least to my ear; and yet the iambic

engine hums regularly along underneath, like the bass and drums sustaining an improvised melody line. The final line concludes to wonderful dramatic effect with three successive monosyllables in summary demand: "Tell me why!"

Now let's return once more to Romeo's famous tribute to Juliet's beauty as he hides beneath her balcony, voyeuristically rhapsodizing on her appearance above, candlelit loveliness beneath the stars, and ponder some of the things that Shakespeare's verse might suggest to the actor preparing the role.

ROMEO: But soft! What light through yonder window breaks?
    It is the east, and Juliet is the sun.
    Arise fair sun, and kill the envious moon,
    Who is already sick and pale with grief
    That thou, her maid, art far more fair than she.
    Be not her maid, since she is envious;
    Her vestal livery is but sick and green,
    And none but fools do wear it; cast it off.
    It is my lady, O, it is my love!
    O that she knew she were!
    She speaks, yet she says nothing; what of that?
    Her eye discourses; I will answer it.
    I am too bold; 'tis not to me she speaks.
    Two of the fairest stars in all the heaven,
    Having some business, do entreat her eyes
    To twinkle in their spheres till they return.
    What if her eyes were there, they in her head?
    The brightness of her cheek would shame those stars,
    As daylight doth a lamp; her eyes in heaven
    Would through the airy region stream so bright
    That birds would sing and think it were not night.
    See how she leans her cheek upon that hand!
    O that I were a glove upon her hand,
    That I might touch that cheek!
JULIET: Ay me!
ROMEO: She speaks!
    O, speak again, bright angel! For thou art
    As glorious to this night, being o'er my head,

As is a winged messenger of heaven
Unto the white-upturned wond'ring eyes
Of mortals that fall back to gaze on him
When he bestrides the lazy puffing clouds,
And sails upon the bosom of the air!

As we've already taken some measure of Romeo's rampant romanticism in earlier sections of the book, let's focus here on several places in the text where Shakespeare emphasizes and guides the actor toward that very characterization. Here again is the context: Romeo, a young adolescent in his hormonal prime, has just come from crashing the Capulet party with his posse; while there, partaking freely of wine, music and dance, he encountered for the first time the girl who is to become the love of his brief life: Juliet. Totally enamored, he eludes his friends in the streets after the party by climbing a wall—where he finds himself in Capulet's orchard, overhung by Juliet's bedroom balcony. Upon seeing her there in her nightgown, enjoying the moonlight, he is struck once again to the heart—but certainly not struck dumb!—by her breathtaking beauty; and being inclined to poetic rhapsodizing (as we have already noted in his earlier scenes) he cannot here contain himself. The verse rhythms he speaks—fed by his passion, the beautiful night, and the alcohol he has sampled from the Capulet party casks—are fairly regularly iambic throughout, from first to last. In fact, they are so regularly rhythmical and lyrical in tone and image that they almost cry out to be sung! However, this inherent musical quality makes the anomalies that crop up here and there even more telling as clues to verbal and physical behavior. Let's take a look at some of them.

For the first 13 of these 31 lines, the actor need not depart at all from the iambic pentameter rhythm. Several words elide easily to fit this rhythm: "Juliet" (in the second line), "livery" (in the seventh line), and "envious" (in the third line)—however, we should take note that in the line "Be not her maid, since she is envious," the elision of this particular word does not happen; if it did, the line would lack a tenth syllable. So why the change from one line to another in how this word is handled?

Well, it's not just a matter of rhythm . . . the change clues the actor that at this point, Romeo is more carefully considering the implications of his initial personification of the moon by *examining what should come of the moon being envious*—and the implication suggests that Juliet should consequently behave in a way that would ultimately benefit him: since the Moon (personified by Diana, goddess and protector of virginity) is *envious* of Juliet's beauty, Juliet should refuse to follow her—therefore renouncing her virginity! As this idea occurs to Romeo—coming out of his own initial metaphor—the image that it conjures up slows him down, and the fact that the same word that was elided in an earlier line is not treated similarly here emphasizes this!

"O that she knew she were!" (line 10) is a short line . . . so what happens in the four syllables that are missing? As we noted earlier in the section on short lines, we find out in the next line: "She speaks, yet she says nothing; what of that?" In the beats that are absent, Juliet makes a sound; what that might be is left to the actress. A sigh? An impatient exclamation of her frustrated feelings? A groan? Whatever it is, it draws the dreamily poetic Romeo's attention immediately back to the present reality of his love's proximity, which leads in turn to a new string of poetic metaphors in the passages to come.

From this point on in Romeo's musings, the rhythms become a bit less easy, but not strikingly so. The born poet still possesses a flare for spontaneous lyricism, but now the he seems to be working slightly harder to find just the right imagery to match her stunning beauty. This is illuminated by the presence of several trochees in the next four lines, marked below by capitalizing the anomalous syllables:

> *TWO of the fairest stars in all the heavens,*
> *HAVing some business do entreat her eyes*
> *To twinkle in their spheres till they return.*
> *WHAT if her eyes were there, THEY in her head?*

In each of these instances, the normal iambics are interrupted by trochees; his thought isn't flowing as facilely as it did, and we experience him in the very act of poetic composition, finding a wonderful new image in the very moment, as he looks at her face in the candle's glow, that speaks to him strongly and personally. (Note also the elision of "business" into 2 syllables, just for the record. It appears to have been a common elision, even in Elizabethan times.) Having discovered this image and incorporated it into his spontaneous poetic tribute, the following lines then continue their easy iambic flow.

A quick word about the O's that crop up throughout impassioned Shakespearean verse: it is virtually impossible to deny an O a strong stress, wherever it may fall in the line. Thus, even when a line seems naturally iambic in its basic rhythm (such as "O that I were a glove upon that hand"), the "O" strongly suggests that the first foot of the line would work best as either a trochee, or even a spondee. The actor should think of it like this: a character often utters an "O" in the course of his line because his emotions are simply too strong at that moment to be adequately expressed in language. A sound must suffice; words fail.

The famous passage begins its final arc with a shared line between the two longing lovers: Juliet, ignorant of Romeo's clandestine presence in the garden below, sighs "Ay me!" hard upon Romeo's poetic impromptu ode to her bright cheek; excited further by the sudden sound of her voice, Romeo jumps in to finish the verse line with "She speaks!", followed immediately by several feet of verse comprising a spondee, an iamb, and another spondee ("O speak again, bright angel!"). His passion inflamed even further, his verse once again flows like a rushing river in regular iambic pentameter on to its conclusion. Finally, the actor should note that the last lines contain a couple of elisions that transform 3-syllable words into 2 syllables ("glorious" and "wondering", the latter noted for the actor in the written text itself), along with two words that merit the full syllabic value of the "ed" ending as dictated by the rhythm of the pentameter lines ("wing-ed" and "upturn-ed").

For our final example, let's scan and analyze an entire sonnet using some of the techniques we've covered in this chapter thus far. In the wonderful series of British videos entitled *Playing Shakespeare*, actor David Suchet gives a marvelously mischievous reading of Sonnet 138 that we will build upon here. He offers a very simple performance context for the piece, suggesting that it might be delivered by an older teacher to his younger students in an Ethics class, after he is asked if it is ever acceptable to misrepresent the truth in a given situation, or if the truth is always an absolute. He responds with the following sonnet, which we here offer with a possible scansion; as outlined earlier in the chapter, stressed syllables are marked as ´ , unstressed syllables as -. We will also mark phrasing caesurae with a /, and possible places for an actor to take breaths with a double //. Any anomalies that break the regularity of the iambic pentameter rhythm, we will note by italicizing the word or words where the anomalies occur.

With this system, we'll offer a beginning blueprint for the actor in effectively speaking the text aloud, a system of marking and analysis that can be applied to any Shakespearean verse.

Whēn mý lōve sweárs thāt shé īs máde ōf trúth,/

Ī dó bēliéve hēr,/ thóugh Ī knów shē líes;//

Thāt shé mīght thínk mē sóme ūntútōr'd yóuth,/

Ūnleárnēd ín thē wórld's fālse súbtlētiés.//

Thūs/ váinlȳ thínkīng thát shē thínks mē yoúng,/

Ālthoúgh shē knóws mȳ dáys āre pást thē bést;/

Símplȳ Ī crédīt hēr *fálse-speákīng* tóngue;//

Ōn bóth sīdes thús īs símplē trúth sūppréss'd.//

Būt whérefōre sáys shē nót shē ís ūnjúst?/

Ānd whérefōre sáy nōt Í thāt Í ām óld?//

Ó, lóve's bēst hábīt īs īn seémīng trúst,/

Ānd áge īn lóve/ lōves nót tō hāve *yeárs tóld.//*

Thērefóre/ Ī líe wīth hér,/ ānd shé wīth mé,/

Ānd ín oūr faúlts/ bȳ liés/ wē fláttēred bé.

And there is a beginning plan for the actor in bringing the verse to verbal life before an audience.

Now that it's initially scanned, let's look at Shakespeare's use of *metaphor* in the sonnet:

In line 1, the speaker suggests that his love has sworn to him that she is the very personification of Truth itself ("my love swears that she is *made* of truth")

In lines 3 and 4, the speaker compares himself directly to a naïve schoolboy (the "untutored youth/Unlearned in the world's false subtleties").

In line 11, the speaker suggests that Love wears a suitable costume for appropriate identification ("love's best *habit*").

In addition to metaphors, Shakespeare's writing also abounds in *double meanings* and *irony*. The former is when a word can successfully mean two things within a single context; the latter occurs when the speaker says one thing, but also could be suggesting something else entirely—even the very opposite of what it might first appear!

Let's look at some possibilities of these:

In line 5, the word "vainly" might mean "uselessly"; it might also mean "egotistically." Both work effectively within the sonnet's context.

In lines 7 and 8, the speaker's use of the words "simply" and "simple" might imply both "ignorantly/ignorant", as well as "fundamentally/fundamental." Try substituting both in place of the actual words used, and see for yourself.

In line 11, "habit" might mean "repetitive action"; but it might also mean "an identifiable mode of dress" (as we noted above: such as a nun's habit).

In lines 13 and 14—the most interesting "double" usage of all, that is key to the subtle humor of the sonnet's conclusion—a "lie" can mean both an untruth as well as an act of sexual intimacy (as in lying down *with* someone).

Shakespeare's love of language and its intricate possibilities is the most important tool at the actor's disposal for the effective portrayal of character and text. In the next chapter, we'll look at how he uses antithetical (that is, *opposite*) words, phrases and images for wonderful dramatic effect; but let's have a quick preview of that right now by identifying some examples of *antitheses* in the sonnet we've just examined. You can refer back to this after you've had a chance to read and think about the information covered in Chapter V.

In line 2, the phrase "I do believe her" is antithetically set against "I know she lies."

In lines 5 and 6, "thinks me young" is set against "knows my days are past the best."

And in line 7, the speaker claims to "credit" what he knows is her "false-speaking tongue" (that is, he chooses to believe what he actually knows to be lies).

But more about this anon!

So, to briefly review the primary components of an actor's scansion that we've covered in this chapter:

1. **Shakespeare wrote the vast majority of the verse contained in his plays in iambic pentameter, a structure that uses as its foundational norm a line containing 10 syllables with 5 feet (units) in each line; each foot contains 2 syllables, and the usual rhythm is comprised of an unstressed syllable followed by a stressed syllable—an *iamb*.**

2. **When an actor maps out the stresses in each line of iambic pentameter, the way Shakespeare has structured the verse rhythm itself will suggest what the most important words will be for understanding the meaning of the line and imparting that meaning to audiences.**

3. **Whenever a section of Shakespeare's verse departs from this basic rhythm, the resultant anomaly**

(the irregularity of rhythm) will usually point to something important that is happening with the character or situation at that moment in the play. The most common departures from iambs are *trochees* (stressed/unstressed), *spondees* (stressed/stressed), and *pyrrhics* (unstressed/unstressed).

4. Most of Shakespeare's iambic pentameter is in "blank verse" (that is, unrhymed lines); however, sometimes he writes in rhymed couplets, and when that occurs, the actor should consider the option of making the character aware of that, determining the psychology behind that choice. This will better embrace the style of writing instead of working against it by trying to act like you don't realize you're rhyming.

5. The actor should look for slight, pleasing variations within the format of the iambic rhythm, such as syncopations, feminine endings, etc., and explore how to utilize them for best dramatic effect.

6. Many lines of verse contain contractions and elisions of polysyllabic words that serve the rhythm of the line; the actor should analyze each line that seems to contain more than the normal number of syllables (10), and determine whether such an elision is called for. If such a line ends with a stressed syllable, there's usually an elision or contraction within the line to be found.

7. Conversely, some lines may appear to need "stretching." In those cases, the actor should look to see if the context of the character or moment might benefit from giving full value to syllables in words that normally might not be emphasized. This practice also leads the actor to words that benefit from pronouncing an "ed" ending as a separate syllable.

8. Short lines (that is, lines that contain fewer than 5 feet of verse) should suggest to the actor that some other dramatic activity is happening during the time of that line's beats which aren't filled with words to be spoken.

9. **Lines of iambic pentameter verse that are shared between two or more speaking characters suggest that the cues need to happen even faster between the actors.**

If a Shakespeare play is ultimately a blueprint for a stage performance, then the verse scansion represents the architect of that blueprint offering direct, helpful hints to the builder that can prove both thoughtfully illuminating and practically useful. And in this case, those hints are coming to us over four centuries! With his carefully crafted verse rhythms, Shakespeare is essentially directing us from beyond the grave. Young actors tackling a Shakespeare performance should eagerly attempt to apprehend that direction with an effective use of scansion and verse analysis skills.

However, perhaps the most important thing for the young actor to remember is this, and we'll emphasize it yet again: *There are no "right" or "wrong" answers in Shakespearean verse scansion. The methods are there for the actor to learn and use in order to more successfully bring these challenging texts to dramatic life. But it is not a test. Rather, it is a tool; and once learned well, a very helpful tool that enables Shakespearean actors to serve their audiences better.*

Keep remembering Hamlet's advice to the players: *Let your discretion be your tutor.*

CHAPTER V

"SET THE WORD AGAINST THE WORD":
THE VITAL ANTITHESIS

an tith' e sis: 1. Direct contrast; opposition. 2. The direct or exact opposite. 3. *Rhetoric.* **a. The juxtaposition of sharply contrasting ideas in balanced or parallel words, phrases or grammatical structures; b. The second and contrasting part of such a juxtaposition.**

William Shakespeare himself led a life full of antitheses. Indeed, it was the nature of the time in which he lived.

Imagine yourself for a moment living the circumstances of many British families of the Elizabethan era: you are born, raised and tutored in the religious faith of your forefathers, stretching back for generations. You believe in its precepts devotedly; the immortality of your very soul depends upon your unquestioning devotion to the teachings of the priests and your acceptance of their instruction in the Faith. The only path to your spiritual salvation lies in the long-established Roman Catholic doctrines. However, because of the personal and political turmoil surrounding the Tudors' personal lives (England's current royal line that occupies the throne), much of what you and your loved ones have held sacred and based your lives upon is suddenly deemed unacceptable, even illegal. In the decades just before Shakespeare was born, Henry VIII had engaged upon an all-out war with the Roman Catholic Church, its priests, its bishops, and its Pope. The conflict stemmed principally from his personal desire to divorce his first wife, Spain's Catherine of Aragorn, ostensibly due to the marriage's failure to produce a male heir to England's throne, and to then marry a second wife, Catherine's lady-in-waiting Anne Boleyn. However, this rivalry between Church and Crown was not entirely new to English monarchs, due to long-continuing political debates about the tax-exempt wealth held behind the walls of English cathedrals and monasteries, as well as the authority of the Pope over secular British and European monarchs.

So by 1564, the year that Shakespeare came into the world in the village of Stratford-upon-Avon in rural Warwickshire, the Tudors had ignited the fires of a religious civil war within the British populace: under Henry VIII and Chancellor Wolsey, many of the cherished icons and rituals of "the Pope's church" were systematically dismantled, and opponents of the newly established Church of England (whose leader was not the Pope, but God's anointed English King) were ostracized, penalized, fined, imprisoned, or executed.

In such a hostile climate, what is one to do with one's religious faith, the central pivot of worldly existence? Suddenly, your King (to whom you owe temporal loyalty under penalty of treason and death) declares your Pope, the earthly representative of God (to whom your owe spiritual loyalty under penalty of eternal damnation), to be wrong and heretical to the "true faith." Should you risk death by openly defying your monarch? Or risk the fires of Hell by abandoning your church?

Following Henry's reign, he was succeeded by a son and two daughters, all of whom brought their own "spin" to the raging conflict between the Catholic and Anglican churches. Queen Mary (also known as "Bloody Mary"), the daughter of Henry VIII's first wife Catherine, was perhaps the most extreme in her position: hoping to bring England back into the folds of devout Catholicism, she authorized the imprisonment and executions (usually by burning alive) of Anglican priests who, only a few years before under the reign of her father, had been on the "right" side of religious issues. When Elizabeth I (Anne Boleyn's daughter by Henry) finally came to the throne, the lines defining spiritual truth and heresy became even more blurred . . . and therefore, more dangerous for all.

Antithesis.

Or imagine yourself born a country boy, and raised among simple tradesmen and village farmers, weavers, glovers, tinkers, and blacksmiths. Your father's family are entrepreneurs, your mother's family landed country gentry. Your father's ambition serves him well, raising your family into well-respected members of their rural community; his hands are in several successful businesses, and the respect accorded him is such that he becomes an important office-holder in your bustling village, a highly regarded man of some wealth and power. Then—suddenly—your family's stature disappears, almost overnight. Family business ventures collapse, debts accrue, offices once held are lost, your mother's family lands are sold, and fines for non-compliance of community regulations are levied upon your once-esteemed father. In the space of years—perhaps months—your family's status as well as your own future hopes for similar success are compromised, perhaps forever.

This is essentially what happened to the young Shakespeare's family in Stratford. What was the cause? Surviving documents fail to provide certain answers, but some scholars believe that it might have resulted from the personal difficulties the Shakespeares had in reconciling the demands of England's new political realities with their devotion to the Catholic faith. Perhaps as a result of this new and dangerous social quicksand, the family suffered much financially; this sounds entirely possible—even likely—but the precise details appear to be lost to history.

From wealth and promise, to sudden loss of influence, comfort and stature; a young boy's first-hand experience of both sides of the social economic coin. More antithesis.

What of love and romance, important and defining factors in a young man's life? Evidence survives of a hurried marriage between a young 18-year-old Will Shakespeare and the 26-year-old surviving daughter of a recently deceased nearby farmer. Six months later, his new bride Anne Hathaway gave birth to their first daughter, Susannah, followed a few years later by twins, Hamnet and Judith. Soon thereafter (or even possibly prior to the latter births), Will departed Stratford to finally end up in London, pursuing the career as actor, playwright, and theatre entrepreneur that would make him commercially successful and artistically celebrated.

From young man sowing his wild oats to sudden husband and father. From poor rural household patriarch to urban bohemian artist in a few short years (with no television or social media to prepare you for the differences in lifestyle you will face). Antithesis after antithesis.

And then, there are the facts of Shakespeare's life itself after he arrived in London, the social circles in which he found himself as part and parcel of his professional career as actor, playwright and poet. There is strong evidence that he was personally associated with aristocracy, including the Earls of Southampton, Pembroke and Oxford. We know that the Lord Chamberlain's Men (his primary acting company of the 1590's, of which he later became partial owner/shareholder) performed at court before Queen Elizabeth on numerous occasions; moreover, it was later singled out as King James's (Elizabeth's successor to the throne) own "personal" company, receiving both the monarch's royal patronage as well as a prestigious name change to the King's Men. Yet, he lived and worked for many of his London years in the Southwark district, a neighborhood of the working classes populated by apprentices, tradesmen, innkeepers, actors, and prostitutes, all of whom gathered at the various taverns, brothels, and playhouses that lined the streets. His work as a playwright/actor gained him proximity to the Queen; his poetry was patronized by noblemen; and simultaneously, he lived among some of the wildest, most raucous denizens of London. The schizophrenic Jekyll/Hyde nature of his social and professional life clearly burdened him in many of his relationships, and he writes of it, implicitly and explicitly, in his Sonnets. Here, in Sonnet 36, we find more than a hint of his struggle to live with each foot in such different worlds:

Let me confess that we two must be twain,
Although our undivided loves are one;
So shall those blots that do with me remain,
Without thy help, by me be borne alone.

In our two loves, there is but one respect,
Though in our lives a separable spite,
Which though it alter not love's sole effect,
Yet doth it steal sweet hours from love's delight.
I may not evermore acknowledge thee,
Lest my bewailed guilt should do thee shame;
Nor thou, with public kindness honor me,
Unless thou take that honor from thy name.
But do not so; I love thee in such sort,
As thou being mine, mine is thy good report.

To "translate" this challenging language: here the poet (we'll assume Shakespeare, for the moment, as I suspect he writes from his heartfelt experience here more than from his imagination), speaking to his friend or lover, admits that they are of two distinct social strata, even while they maintain such affection for one another; and since those two worlds can never completely unite, the fact of their social differences must inevitably steal some of the joy of their feelings. He realizes that they can never publicly admit their closeness, and concludes the poem by consoling himself—along with his "other"—that he will be happy simply basking in the high regard in which his friend is held.

Thus, stark contrast and antithesis was a central theme of William Shakespeare's life, as indeed it was with many of his fellow countrymen of the time. To come down firmly on one side or the other of any issue was extremely dangerous, as the "winning side" was ever-changing. Moreover, life's circumstances in general—and particularly Shakespeare's—were evolving ever more rapidly as the English Renaissance (with the innovation of the printing press providing one of its most powerful engines) swept inexorably forward.

Shakespeare was fascinated with the ambiguities and ambivalences that were an integral part of the times in which he lived and created. Perhaps more than any other playwright, before or since, he found empathy with all viewpoints of a given issue, topic, or conflict. In doing so, he created epic histories that were powered not by mythologized heroes, but by flawed human beings, sometimes confused by their own urges and feelings, and often bewildered by the storm of events around them. He created comedies with strong shadings of melancholy that make the humor more poignant, more thoughtful . . . and surprisingly, funnier. And he created tragedies and romances that (in the right actors' and producers' hands) attain an almost supernatural dramatic power due to their multiply faceted and subtly nuanced "heroes" and "villains."

Take Hamlet: we empathize with him when we learn what has become of his father, we cheer for his passion for vengeance, we wonder at his hesitation to act in the light of what he has learned. But hold on . . . shouldn't we cheer his hesitation? (Look at our own multi-billion dollar war on Iraq and its citizens in the name of stopping what we subsequently discovered was a non-existent—or at least, non-immediate—threat.) After all, what is his source for the charge of Claudius's crime? A ghost's message. Well, what exactly is the nature of this ghost? Is it an hallucination born of an emotionally distraught mind? Or even, as Hamlet himself speculates, a demon sent from Satan himself to provoke the prince to wrongful murder of his uncle, the king? Thesis and antithesis.

Or Coriolanus, one of Shakespeare's most fascinating protagonists: Caius Martius, a renowned and incomparable Roman patrician warrior, capable of nearly singlehandedly defeating the forces of an entire rebellious town (Corioli, from whose conquest he is honored with his new name); and yet, at the same time, so very consumed with pleasing his mother, Volumnia. A lover of Rome, but also a despiser of all Romans who do not conform to his own rather narrow view of appropriate class and political behavior. As with most Shakespearean tragic protagonists, we are simultaneously fascinated and troubled by him.

The complex and unique world of Shakespeare's time—with London and all of its cultural turmoil as its microcosm—fed and informed the characters and situations in all of his plays. The stories themselves may have been borrowed from history, from past literature, from contemporary writers, even from fairy tales and legends told him as a child; but no other writers used the antithetical nature of the times to greater effect than William Shakespeare. That is what transforms his sometimes melodramatic plotlines into tales of tragic grandeur, what makes us recognize in the comedies familiar aspects of our own shortcomings, and what makes us ponder the complexities of history in an entirely new light; and it's also the single most important reason why his works have survived for four centuries losing little of their dramatic power, while others have faded.

If Shakespeare's use of the antitheses of Elizabethan life in his themes and characters provided his plays with much of their power, the actor's effective handling of his verse in performance depends just as strongly on the recognition, illumination, and technical use of the antithetical elements to be found there. In fact, it may be the single most important thing for a Shakespearean actor to understand and master in order to succeed at bringing a character and play to life for an audience.

Basically, the way antithesis works for the actor is as follows: one image, word, phrase, or perspective is presented by a character in his speech, soon thereafter followed by an image, word, phrase, or perspective presented either by that same character or by another in dialogue. They measure against one another as either directly antithetical to one another (that is, directly opposite in meaning), or indirectly antithetical to one another (suggesting a contrast that may not be directly opposite in meaning, but still eliciting a striking comparison).

In using antithesis, a character considers the two sides of an issue, and seeks exactly where, in the continuum existing between one side and the other, the point of discovery, or "truth", might live. By his active examination of both sides of the antithesis, and his spoken emphasis (subtle or pronounced) of those words or phrases that frame it, the actor leads the audience to ponder the balances and contrasts that Shakespeare endeavors to reveal.

So let's "ponder" a few of them from various Shakespearean passages together.

Once again, the most famous passage in Shakespeare's plays provides perhaps the most famous core antithesis, as well as the most basic antithesis of the human condition: Life and Death. As the soliloquy begins, Hamlet posits:

> *To be, or not to be: that is the question.*
> *Whether 'tis nobler in the mind to suffer*
> *The slings and arrows of outrageous fortune,*
> *Or to take up arms against a sea of troubles,*
> *And by opposing, end them. To die; to sleep,*
> *No more; and by a sleep to say we end*
> *The heartache and the thousand natural shocks*
> *That flesh is heir to; 'tis a consummation*
> *Devoutly to be wish'd. To die, to sleep—*
> *To sleep, perchance to dream. Ay, there's the rub.*

Let's look at the antithetical elements in this passage that the actor "speaking the speech" must be aware of and emphasize in his delivery in order to take the audience's thoughts and understanding with him on Hamlet's journey. First, the obvious beginning: *To be* is balanced directly against its opposite, *not to be*; a direct antithesis. He then asks himself (and us, by extension) whether it is better *to suffer the slings and arrows of outrageous fortune* (accept one's quota of mortal suffering along life's journey), or whether one should struggle against the inevitable tribulations of existence, *to take up arms against a sea of troubles*. These entire phrases are antithetical, one held up against the other in direct comparison; but let's narrow it down a bit and find the most direct antithetical words in these phrases, which would be *to suffer* against the option *to take up arms*—in other words, to passively bear the inevitable pain of life, or to actively struggle against it.

These are both examples of direct antitheses; words, phrases or images that are directly opposite to one another. What follows next, however, are two antitheses that are not quite opposite, but certainly contrasting. Examining the nature of death itself, Hamlet balances it against the experience of sleep, imagining both of them to be similar experiences when reduced to their essentials. *To die*, he suggests, is *to sleep— no more*. After examining that idea a bit further in the next few lines, he has a small epiphany: death itself may not be all that peaceful. For the peace of *sleep* is often interrupted by *dreams*, a kind of semblance of life that exists in this semblance of death. This is the pivot upon which the rest of the soliloquy turns, for "there's the rub." If we aren't sure what the afterlife may be like ("what dreams may come"), then we had better be prepared for the proposition that it might be more painful than life itself—and that's what keeps us (Hamlet suggests) from committing suicide every time things get rough.

Thus, in the first ten lines of Hamlet's famous soliloquy, we are shown four sets of antitheses, two very direct, and two more subtly framed (indirect). In truth, the line of Hamlet's reasoning here is entirely based on his opening antithesis.

Let's look at a few lines from Petruchio's soliloquy in Act II, i of *The Taming of the Shrew*, as he prepares to meet his new bride-to-be, the fiery Katherina:

> *Say that she rail; why then, I'll tell her plain*
> *She sings as sweetly as a nightingale.*
> *Say that she frown; I'll say she looks as clear*
> *As morning roses newly wash'd with dew.*
> *Say she be mute, and will not speak a word;*
> *Then I'll commend her volubility,*
> *And say she uttereth piercing eloquence.*
> *If she do bid me pack, I'll give her thanks,*
> *As though she bid me stay by her a week.*
> *If she deny to wed, I'll crave the day*
> *When I shall ask the banns, and when be married.*

Here is a series of direct antitheses, juxtapositions that work to great comic effect as Petruchio prepares and shares his plan with us for dealing with the "shrew" he has been contracted to marry. With every antithesis in Shakespeare, it's always good practice for the actor to try to narrow the key elements of it to the core words or phrases; this will give him the direction of what words require more emphasis or "punch" in the speaking of them. (In acting parlance, these are called *operative words*; the words that are most important in bringing out the sense or the action of any given line, verse or otherwise.) What are Petruchio's key words here, most vital for the antitheses he sets up? (All of them are pretty direct.)

Rail in line 1 is balanced antithetically against *sings* in line 2.

Frown in line 3 is measured against *looks as clear*, both in line 3.

There is a set of double antitheses in the next few lines, a technique that Shakespeare uses often and effectively to emphasize a point or a passage even more; *mute* (line 5) is antithetical to *volubility* (line 6), and *will not speak a word* (line 5) to *uttereth piercing eloquence* (line 7).

Bid me pack in line 8 is balanced against *bid me stay (by her)* in line 9.

Deny to wed in line 10 is set against *(ask the banns, and) when be married* in line 11.

Here's another passage to look at, this one from Act IV, iv of *The Two Gentlemen of Verona*, spoken by Julia. There are a few interesting variations here:

Alas, poor Proteus, thou hast entertain'd
A fox to be the shepherd of thy lambs.
Alas, poor fool, why do I pity him
That with his very heart despiseth me?
Because he loves her, he despiseth me;
Because I love him, I must pity him.
This ring I gave him when he parted from me,
To bind him to remember my good will;
And now am I (unhappy messenger)
To plead for that which I would not obtain,
To carry that which I would have refus'd,
To praise his faith which I would have disprais'd.
I am my master's true confirmed love;

> *But cannot be true servant to my master,*
> *Unless I prove false traitor to myself.*
> *Yet will I woo for him, but yet so coldly*
> *As, heaven it knows, I would not have him speed!*

Upon first glance, it might seem clear that *fox* would be an obvious antithesis to *lambs*, and you would not necessarily be incorrect to say so. But let's take a closer look: Is the real antithesis between *fox* and *shepherd*? A fox behaves as a predator on the lambs, a shepherd as their protector. Mightn't that be the true contrast that Shakespeare (or Julia) wants us to note?

The next four lines contain three antitheses that it's easy for actors to become entangled in; but let's sort them out. Line 3's *pity him* works antithetically against line 4's *despiseth me*. In line 5, the antithesis works both to contrast the verbs themselves, as well as the difference Julia perceives between the way Proteus feels about Silvia, and the way he feels about her: *loves her* measures against *despiseth me*. Finally, in line 6, Julia notes that because she *loves* Proteus, it follows that she must *pity* his unrequited love for Silvia, her rival; an antithetical balance, perhaps, but not quite a direct antithesis.

Lines 7 and 8 pits *parted from me* against *bind him to remember*; almost a direct antithesis, and certainly an antithetical balance that the actress must recognize and play in speaking the line.

Shakespeare loves to use lists and repetitive structure to hammer home a point, and lines 10 through 12 offer an example of three pretty direct antitheses that echo one another: *plead for* works against *would not obtain*, *carry* against *refus'd*, and *praise* against *disprais'd*.

At first, the actor might look for an antithesis that seems to be originated in line 13 with "I am my master's true confirmed love"; but upon closer examination, it would seem that the most workable (and direct) antitheses exist in lines 14 and 15, between *true servant* and *false traitor*, as well as *master* and *myself*.

Finally, the soliloquy ends with an antithesis that is almost—but not quite—direct. It is not direct because there is no pair of key words in the antithetical phrases that denote a precise opposite—yet, the contrast remains pretty clear. Julia will *woo for him*; yet she *would not have him speed* (lines 16 and 17).

Sometimes Shakespeare uses antitheses to emphasize the crackling exchanges and witty dialogue between two characters. Here are a few wonderful examples from the encounter between Richard of Gloucester and Lady Anne Neville in their famous "wooing" scene in *Richard III* (Act I, ii). We'll look at this scene in a bit more depth in a later chapter:

GLOUCESTER: Lady, you know no rules of charity,
    Which renders good for bad, blessings for curses.
ANNE: Villain, thou know'st no law of God nor man:
    No beast so fierce but knows some touch of pity.
GLOUCESTER: But I know none, and therefore am no beast.
ANNE: O wonderful, when devils tell the truth!
GLOUCESTER: More wonderful when angels are so angry.
    Vouchsafe, divine perfection of a woman,
    Of these supposed crimes, to give me leave
    By circumstance but to acquit myself.
ANNE: Vouchsafe, defus'd infection of a man,
    Of these known evils, but to give me leave
    By circumstance t'accuse thy cursed self.
GLOUCESTER: Fairer than tongue can name thee, let me have
    Some patient leisure to excuse myself.
ANNE: Fouler than heart can think thee, thou canst make
    No excuse current but to hang thyself!
GLOUCESTER: By such despair I should accuse myself.
ANNE: And by despairing shalt thou stand excused
    For doing worthy vengeance on thyself,
    That didst unworthy slaughter upon others.
GLOUCESTER: Say that I slew them not?
ANNE: Then say they were
    not slain.
    But dead they are, and, devilish slave, by thee.
GLOUCESTER: I did not kill your husband.
ANNE: Why then he is alive!

This is a piece of wonderfully exhilarating dialogue for two actors who have done their homework with scansion, rhythms and antitheses. The cues are fast (note the shared lines), and each character argues with passion and wit; and they use antitheses much as two skilled duelists use their sharpened rapiers on one another. Here are examples:

Internally, in Richard's first line, *good* and *bad*, and *blessings* and *curses* are both antithetical pairings. In her response to him, Lady Anne addresses him as *Villain*, indirectly antithetical to his address of her as *Lady*. She also juxtaposes the laws of *God* and *man*, as well as using *fierce* against *pity* immediately following.

In their next exchange, Richard counters Anne's "O wonderful, when *devils* tell the truth!" with the antithetical response, "More wonderful when *angels* are so angry." Not to be outdone, when she next speaks, Anne trumps Richard's flattering "Vouchsafe, *divine perfection of a woman*" with her own "Vouchsafe, *defus'd infection of a man*." She goes on to antithetically parry his "*supposed crimes*" with her preferred "*known evils*", and his "*acquit myself*" with "*accuse thy cursed self.*"

"*Fairer than tongue can name thee*", he tries next, only to be countered by her "*Fouler than heart can think thee*"; she also suggests that, instead of "*excusing myself*" (as he attempts to do), he should do better to "*hang thyself*!" When he responds by saying he should "*accuse himself*" in his despair if he were indeed guilty of her accusations (which he really is!), she answers that in such despair he should actually "*stand excused*" if he were to exert "*worthy vengeance*" on himself after doing "*unworthy slaughter*" on others—another antithesis, with a mix of direct and indirect contrast.

Two more antithetical dialogue exchanges complete this short excerpt: Anne retorts to his "*Say that I slew them not*" with her contemptuous "*Then say they were not slain*"; and, an even more sarcastic response follows his "*I did not kill your husband*"—"*Why then he is alive!*" she cries. A fine and exciting scene for two prepared and inspired young actors!

As we've noted at other places in this study, Shakespeare's sonnets are wonderful for actors to practice with if they want to be most effective in their work on the plays. Shakespeare's language here is his most carefully constructed, his images the most complex, and if the actor can speak the sonnets clearly for a hearer's understanding, passages from the plays will often seem quite easy by comparison. (After all, the latter were specifically written to be heard in performance, while the sonnets were composed primarily for readers.) So, let's take a couple of the sonnets and note any antitheses, direct or indirect, that they might contain. First, Sonnet 96:

> *Some say thy fault is youth, some wantonness,*
> *Some say thy grace is youth, and gentle sport;*
> *Both grace and faults are lov'd of more and less:*
> *Thou maks't faults graces that to thee resort.*
> *As on the finger of a throned queen*
> *The basest jewel will be well esteem'd,*
> *So are those errors that in thee are seen*
> *To truths translated, and for true things deem'd.*
> *How many lambs might the stern wolf betray,*
> *If like a lamb he could his looks translate!*
> *How many gazers mightst thou lead away,*
> *If thou wouldst use the strength of all thy state!*
> > *But do not so; I love thee in such sort,*
> > *As thou being mine, mine is thy good report.*

Interestingly, the word "youth," used twice in the first two lines, almost works antithetically one against the other; but the real antithesis is between the two words that describe how that youth is perceived by others, one of the major themes of the sonnet. Thus, *fault* in line 1 is juxtaposed against *grace* in line 2, and similarly *wantonness* contrasts with *gentle sport*. Both are pretty opposite to one another, so both are direct antitheses. The antithetical *graces* and *faults* are repeated in line 3, and *more* and *less* are also directly opposed in the same line; and *faults* and *graces* are used yet again in line 4. (He really wants to make this point!)

Line 6 sets up an antithesis between *basest* and *esteem'd*; *errors* and *truths* are measured against one another in lines 7 and 8, and in partnership with that, *errors seen* (line 7) become *true things deem'd* (line 8). Although *lambs* and *wolf* in line 9 are certainly antithetical, the image is more of a set-up for the metaphor to come in the following lines rather than a focus on the antithesis itself; still, it's worth the actor's attention.

The last line also suggests antithesis, although it's pretty indirect. A bargain is suggested by the speaker to his wayward lover/friend: If the lover/friend will commit to him solely, he will join those who speak well of their behavior (as noted in the second line).

Sonnet 66 is almost entirely built upon the use of antitheses; some are pretty direct, some less so. Let's take a look:

> *Tir'd with all these, for restful death I cry:*
> *As to behold desert a beggar born,*
> *And needy nothing trimm'd in jollity,*
> *And purest faith unhappily forsworn,*
> *And gilded honor shamefully misplac'd,*
> *And maiden virtue rudely strumpeted,*
> *And right perfection wrongfully disgrac'd,*
> *And strength by limping sway disabled,*
> *And art made tongue-tied by authority,*
> *And folly (doctor-like) controlling skill,*
> *And simple truth miscall'd simplicity,*
> *And captive good attending captain ill;*
> > *Tir'd with all these, from these would I be gone,*
> > *Save that to die, I leave my love alone.*

This is a fascinating example of antitheses that are . . . .well, not quite neatly structured. Once again, Shakespeare uses repetition for strong effect; indeed, the plodding rhythm of each line wears the hearer down in a manner that makes him immediately empathetic with the speaker's state of mind. (Much the same, it seems to me, as Hamlet's state of mind as he begins, "To be, or not to be . . . ") Each example the speaker lists as adding to his cynicism and melancholy seems clearly antithetical; yet none seem exactly direct. Why is this? Mainly because in direct antitheses, nouns tend to oppose nouns, and verbs tend to oppose other verbs. Or, in many cases, the antithesis is oxymoronic, an adjective or adverb that modifies or clarifies a noun while simultaneously seeming to suggest the opposite: for example, "open secret", "seriously funny", "deafening silence", etc. Here, however, the antithesis is contained in a somewhat fluid state; each state of being (described mostly as adjective and noun, such as "gilded honor" or "maiden virtue") is actually in the process of metamorphosing into something else, which *will be* (when the change is complete) a direct antithesis to what it was.

Follow that? In other words, a deserving soul is *being born* into poverty; *purest faith* is being betrayed by lies, *maiden virtue* is being prostituted, *art* is being censored, and so on. The speaker is implying that everything is *being transformed* into its opposite in this corrupt world, and watching it happen makes him depressed and despairing. Here, we seem to be walking a delicate and deliberate borderline between direct and indirect antitheses, all the way through the sonnet.

In his excellent book *Clues to Acting Shakespeare* (which I would recommend heartily to any young actor who wishes to pursue Shakespeare performance further), Wesley Van Tassel uses three examples of character speeches from the plays that contain within them perhaps the most numerous and clearly delineated examples of direct antitheses. I'm also going to use those speeches here as "workbook" examples that young actors can try tackling for themselves. All three are unusual in that they are founded almost entirely on antitheses, so there are plenty of examples to find in each. Try identifying all of the direct antitheses on your own first, writing them down in a list and noting each of the direct opposite words, one against the other. Then check your lists against the ones provided immediately following the three texts.

(It's worth noting that although Mr. Van Tassel and I agree on many of the antitheses in these pieces, we do have some differences. Remember what we've said all along about looking too hard for "right" answers; it's rarely as neatly concluded as a simple math problem!)

First, let's take a look at one of Romeo's angst-ridden speeches in the first scene of *Romeo and Juliet*, before his "better half" is introduced:

ROMEO: Alas that love, whose view is muffled still,
    Should, without eyes, see pathways to his will!

Where shall we dine? O me! What fray was here?
Yet tell me not, for I have heard it all:
Here's much to do with hate, but more with love.
Why then, O brawling love! O loving hate!
O any thing, of nothing first create!
O heavy lightness, serious vanity,
Misshapen chaos of well-seeming forms;
Feather of lead, bright smoke, cold fire, sick health,
Still-waking sleep, that is not what it is!
This love feel I, that feel no love in this.
Dost thou not laugh?

BENVOLIO: No, coz, I rather weep.

Next, let's glance once more at Richard's initial musings in his prison cell at the climax of *Richard II* (Act V, v).

RICHARD: I have been studying how I may compare
This prison where I live unto the world;
And for because the world is populous,
And here is not a creature but myself,
I cannot do it; yet I'll hammer it out.
My brain I'll prove the female to my soul,
My soul the father, and these two beget
A generation of still-breeding thoughts;
And these same thoughts people this little world,
In humors like the people of this world:
For no thought is contented. The better sort,
As thoughts of things divine, are intermix'd
With scruples and do set the word itself
Against the word;
As thus: "Come, little ones"; and then again,
"It is as hard to come as for a camel
To thread the postern of a small needle's eye."

Finally, my favorite example of all, a lengthy piece of comic text built almost entirely on the use of antithesis: Phebe's protestations of love/not love for another man, delivered to her hapless, hopeless suitor, Silvius, in *As You Like It* (Act III, v).

Rosalind, Phebe, Silvius from *As You Like It*

PHEBE: Think not I love him, though I ask for him;
    'Tis but a peevish boy—yet he talks well—
    But what care I for words? Yet words do well
    When he that speaks them pleases those that hear.
    It is a pretty youth—not very pretty—
    But sure he's proud—and yet his pride becomes him.
    He'll make a proper man. The best thing in him
    Is his complexion; and faster than his tongue
    Did make offense, his eye did heal it up.
    He is not very tall—yet for his years he's tall;
    His leg is but so so—and yet 'tis well;
    There was a pretty redness in his lip,
    A little riper and more lusty red
    Than that mix'd in his cheek; 'twas just the difference
    Between the constant red and mingled damask.
    There be some women, Silvius, had they mark'd him
    In parcels as I did, would have gone near
    To fall in love with him; but for my part,
    I love him not, nor hate him not; and yet
    I have more cause to hate him than to love him,
    For what had he to do to chide at me?
    He said mine eyes were black and my hair black,
    And, now I am rememb'red, scorn'd at me.

I marvel why I answer'd not again!
But that's all one; omittance is no quittance.
I'll write to him a very taunting letter,
And thou shalt bear it; wilt thou, Silvius?

Now, check your own list of antitheses you discovered against the lists below. Did you find more, or fewer? Did you note how each one worked? Did they use directly opposite words or phrases against one another, or did they merely draw contrasts between ideas or balancing phrases? Or did some utilize a deft combination of both?

For ROMEO:

"*without eyes*" is antithetical to "*see*" in line 2
"*tell me not*" is antithetical to "*heard it all*" in line 4
"*hate*" is directly antithetical to "*love*"
"*brawling love*" and "*loving hate*" are oxymorons, therefore antithetical (line 6)
"*any thing*" is antithetical to "*nothing*" in line 7
"*heavy lightness*" and "*serious vanity*" are oxymorons, therefore antithetical ((line 8)
"*Misshapen chaos*" is directly antithetical to "*well-seeming forms*" in line 9
"*Feather of lead*", "*bright smoke*", "*cold fire*", and "*sick health*" are all oxymorons, therefore antithetical (all in line 10!)
"*Still-waking sleep*" is an oxymoron, therefore antithetical; and "*is not*" is antithetical to "*what it is*" (line 11)
"*love*" is directly antithetical to "*no love*" (line 12)
"*laugh*" and "*weep*" are directly antithetical, with Benvolio supplying the second part of the antithesis in a shared line with Romeo (line 13)

For RICHARD:

"*prison*" is antithetical to "*world*" in line 2
"*the world is populous*" is antithetical to "*here is not a creature but myself*" in lines 3 and 4
"*cannot do it*" is antithetical to "*hammer it out*" in line 5
"*brain*" and "*soul*" are antithetical, as are "*female*" and

"*father*" in lines 6 and 7
(The images Richard uses in lines 6 through 11 are those
of succeeding generations of thoughts and humors—that
is, fancies—that people his mind in an ever-increasing
number, as humans themselves increase exponentially from
generation to generation; the balance that the image conjures
is antithetical, but indirectly so; its components aren't "neat",
but they are no less interesting for that.)
"*things divine*" is antithetical to "*scruples*" in lines 12 and 13
"*set the word itself*" is structurally antithetical to *"against
the word"* in lines 13 and 14
"*Come, little ones*" is antithetically balanced against "*It is
as hard to come as for a camel/To thread the postern of a
small needle's eye*" in lines 15-17

For PHEBE:
"*Think not I love him*" is antithetically balanced against
"*though I ask for him*" in line 1
"'*Tis but a peevish boy*" is antithetically balanced against
"*yet he talks well" in line"* 2
"*But what care I for words?*" is antithetically balanced
against *"Yet words do well"* in line 3
"*he that speaks them*" is antithetical to "*those that hear*" in
line 4
"*pretty*" is directly antithetical to "*not very pretty*" in line 5
"*he's proud*" is antithetical to "*pride becomes him*" in line 6
(NOTE that this antithesis only works if the actress realizes
that—at first—she thinks of Ganymede's pride as a flaw;
then realizes that it's really kind of attractive!)
"*his tongue did make offense*" is antithetical to "*his eye did
heal it up*" in lines 8 and 9
"not very tall" is directly antithetical to "*he's tall*" in line 10
"*so so*" is antithetical to " *'tis well*" in line 11
the red of "*his lip*" is antithetically contrasted with that of
"*his cheek*" in lines 12 and 14; similarly, "*constant red*" is
antithetically contrasted with "*mingled damask*" in line 15
Phebe contrasts "*some women*" against herself ("*I*") in lines
16 and 17

"*love him not*" is directly antithetical to "*hate him not*" in line 19; "*hate him*" and "*love him*" are again antithetically balanced in line 20

"*scorned at me*" is antithetically balanced against "*I answered not*" in lines 23 and 24

While not really strictly antithetical, Phebe's balancing of "*omittance*" against "*quittance*" in line 25 *feels* antithetical somehow, and the actress should pay attention to the contrast in her delivery

"*I'll write to him*" is antithetical to " *thou shalt bear it*" in lines 26 and 27

Altogether, Phebe's struggling denial of her "crush" on Ganymede (Rosalind in disguise) is a fun, but challenging monologue for young actresses; unless the antitheses are carefully mapped out, separated, and rehearsed, the piece suffers the peril of sounding like a chaotic jumble of words for audiences. The actress's textual homework is truly cut out for her here!

Before closing our discussion of antitheses and related matters, let's note one more thing that will help to introduce some of the points we'll be discussing more a bit later on, in Chapter VII.

This is a soliloquy given by Philip the Bastard from one of the less familiar Shakespeare history plays, *King John*. Here is the general context: Philip is the illegitimate son of the late Richard I (the Lion-Hearted), John's elder brother and the ruler that John succeeded to the English throne. John and his mother Eleanor, impressed with Philip the Bastard's straightforward personality, bravery and valor, take him under their royal wing as an important protégé. They believe he will prove useful for them, as currently they struggle to suppress a bid to seize John's crown through a rough-hewn alliance between Constance, John's elder brother Geoffrey's widow (who claims the throne—rightfully—for her young son, Arthur), King Philip of France, and various Catholic bishops who have often been at odds with John in the course of his reign. As both sides prepare for war, suddenly an unexpected peace is brokered between France and England. This leaves Constance and Arthur without their expected allies in revolt, King John without some of his kingly entitlements, and Philip the Bastard without his anticipated battle, a fight in which he hoped to achieve both honor and advancement. As the newly reconciled enemy factions leave the stage, Philip the Bastard shares his thoughts aloud:

> *Mad world, mad kings, mad composition!*
> *John, to stop Arthur's title in the whole,*
> *Hath willingly departed with a part,*
> *And France, whose armor conscience buckled on,*
> *Whom zeal and charity brought to the field*
> *As God's own soldier, rounded in the ear*
> *With that same purpose-changer, that sly devil,*
> *That broker that still breaks the pate of faith,*
> *That daily break-vow, he that wins of all,*
> *Of kings, of beggars, old men, young men, maids,*
> *Who having no external thing to lose*
> *But the word "maid," cheats the poor maid of that,*
> *This smooth-fac'd gentleman, tickling commodity!*
> *Commodity, the bias of the world—*
> *The world, who of itself is peized well,*
> *Made to run even upon even ground,*
> *Till this advantage, this vile-drawing bias,*
> *This sway of motion, this commodity,*
> *Makes it take head from all indifferency,*
> *From all direction, purpose, course, intent—*
> *And this same bias, this commodity,*
> *This bawd, this broker, this all-changing word,*
> *Clapp'd on the outward eye of fickle France,*
> *Hath drawn him from his own determin'd aid,*
> *From a resolv'd and honorable war*
> *To a most base and vile-concluded peace!*
> *And why rail I on this commodity?*
> *But for because he hath not woo'd me yet.*
> *Not that I have the power to clutch my hand*
> *When his fair angels would salute my palm;*

But for my hand, as unattempted yet,
Like a poor beggar, raileth on the rich.
Well, whiles I am a beggar, I will rail,
And say there is no sin but to be rich;
And being rich, my virtue then shall be
To say there is no vice but beggary.
Since kings break faith upon commodity,
Gain, be my lord, for I will worship thee.

Difficult language; but let's take a moment and summarize the basic thoughts that Philip evolves here.

His anger and frustrated disbelief at what he has just witnessed is obvious from his first words: the sudden compromise and jettisoning of the very principles that brought both sides to the edge of battle appears (to his rallied personal ambition) insane! King John has given up much ground to his enemies in order to hold onto what Philip perceives as only a "part" of his kingly rights; while France, who proclaimed themselves the righteous champions of England's legitimate king—young Arthur—have quickly decided to put down their arms in exchange for those aforementioned concessions from John. And, as Philip notes, all of this compromise has been induced by specific material gain, a "win-win" deal for both England and France, struck at the expense of the "legitimate" rulers who have suddenly become mere pawns, Arthur and his mother, Constance. Commodity, Philip reasons with barely contained frustration, has won the day again; he realizes now that all noble causes are ultimately sold for short-term political gain and profit.

What is this "commodity?" the Bastard asks himself; why, it is invariably the force that swamps all others, that turns the tide of every struggle for every ideal of Right and Wrong. It is a pimp, an amoral broker who only works every situation for personal profit. And why does he condemn it? Well . . . .because he has yet to benefit from it himself! This is the pivotal discovery of the soliloquy that the actor must focus upon; all turns upon it. Is it a realization that he makes in that precise moment? Or a conclusion that he has reached before he even launches into his speech? Again, there's no right answer; but even though

Philip's outrage about "commodity" must be leading him toward his realized conclusions from the very start (after all, he's anything but naïve), it's always more effective for the actor/character to make all the discoveries that he possibly can in the exact moment that he speaks—or as close to that moment as is rationally possible under the given circumstances. Or, as Patsy Rodenburg so effectively puts it, Shakespearean actors must speak themselves into being.

After Philip makes this discovery—that he primarily rails against the personal gains reached by both parties in the surrender of Arthur's legitimate claim to the English crown because he has not enjoyed a share of those gains himself—he proclaims that, from this moment on, he will join the cynical ranks of the rest of the world and be in the game only for his own personal gain. As a poor man, he will condemn the rich as immoral; and once he gains wealth, he will condemn the poor as morally undeserving of anything better than their poverty. "Since kings break faith upon commodity," he concludes, "Gain, be my lord, for I will worship thee." He thus congratulates himself upon his newfound wisdom with this cleverly rhyming couplet!

Although earlier in the chapter, we focused on the antithetical elements—the balances and opposites—that weave themselves throughout Shakespeare's writings, here we find a slightly broader vision of antithesis that can be found in the majority of his play's soliloquies: the character begins with one distinct position; then, in the course of his verbal explorations, he concludes with a perspective that is very often 180 degrees away from where he began.

Antithesis, for the Shakespearean actor, is the primary key for unlocking the dramatic journey of soliloquies—scenes as well. The actor must map that journey thoughtfully in preparation for bringing it to theatrical life. Philip's soliloquy divides fairly neatly into three sections; the first runs through line 13 ("This smooth-fac'd gentleman, tickling commodity!"). In this initial section, he focuses on sharing his astonishment—perhaps anger—at the self-centered compromises he has just witnessed happening between these two enemy factions, England and France, all resulting in their sacrifice of principles for personal gain (commodity). Then, in the second section of the soliloquy (running through line 26, "To a most vile and ill-concluded peace!"), Philip broadens his consideration of the current situation, likening it to common practices and actions he sees around him in the wider world, building the argument that there really exists no true honor in the world anymore, when push comes to shove.

Next, he brings himself up short with the genuine question: Why am I upset about all of this, if it's truly the way of the world? Well, he realizes, it's because I'm not getting my share of it all! In a wonderful piece of dramatic self-discovery, he embraces the idea that he is really not above it all; he just hasn't yet managed to gain the socio-political position that would allow him to take advantage of any available "commodity." These musings continue through line 32 ("Like a poor beggar, raileth on the rich"). And then, in lines 33-38, he finally arrives at the decision that reveals the destination of the soliloquy's journey: "Gain, be my lord, for I will worship thee." He vows future participation in the same materialistic maneuvers as everyone else around him—and (he implies), in so doing, he will exceed their results.

Most Shakepearean soliloquies can be better understood by the young actor after he clearly defines and articulates the antitheses that lie at their cores. This is often true of Shakespearean scenework as well. Like the soliloquies, each scene also tells a small story, a part of the larger narrative of the play, and each has at its heart a *basic human situation*. (We'll examine this idea more closely as it pertains to both scenes and entire plays in the final two chapters.) For Philip the Bastard, the basic human situation is this: A good soldier of illegitimate birth (yet noble lineage), ready to loyally fight for principle, is stunned upon discovery that the very people who enjoy and use his loyalty are prepared to drop their principles for the guarantee of their own personal gain; but since this is the way of the world, he will henceforth embrace it himself, and look after his own personal benefit from now on.

So to summarize this final point: When young actors sift through the scenes and soliloquies in Shakespeare with an eye toward mapping the basic human situation of their individual characters' personal journeys, what at first appears to be a torrent of thorny text can be successfully dissected, examined, simplified—and more easily approached in rehearsal and more clearly played in performance. And very often, clarifying the foundational antithesis of a soliloquy or scene is the place to begin that process.

As we saw in the earlier parts of this chapter, antithetical experiences and perspectives pervaded Shakespeare's life and times, his personal thoughts, and his writings; and once the actor learns to recognize, examine, and effectively express those experiences that interweave throughout the structures of both Shakespeare's scenes and verse, the stories and characters will begin to find a vibrant life. Dramatic contrast and balance have given Shakespeare's plays their unique power to thrill and involve us for over four centuries in theatres around the world. The antitheses of thoughts and images revealed within those texts provide the actor with a vital key for unlocking that powerful world of ideas on the stage.

CHAPTER VI

"MERE PRATTLE, WITHOUT PRACTICE":
EXERCISING WITH THE TEXT

Now that we've been introduced to the various mechanical aspects of scansion and antitheses, let's consider for a moment how we begin to practically cope with all of this on the stage, in our preparation, our rehearsals, and our actual performance.

One of the truths about our particular art form with which young actors struggle the most is this: *only a limited portion of the actor's essential work actually happens in the rehearsal room.* The common misconception of novices is that once we have been cast, we then attend scheduled rehearsals where we are "directed"—that is, we are told by an authority figure (the teacher/director/mentor/guru) what we should do in order to insure a good performance.

This is not the case. If you think it is, start making corrections in your approach to the creative process of acting *right now*. The truth is, the actor should begin laying a lot of the foundation for what he plans to do with the role he has been assigned well before the first read-through—if schedules of the casting allow that—and continue doing daily homework throughout the entire rehearsal process and into the performance run of the show. Think of it this way, again using the analogies of a blueprint (the play), the construction (the actor's work in rehearsals), and the finished house (the performance): once the responsible and knowledgeable builder has seen the blueprint, he would not show up at the construction site without bringing the tools that he thinks he will need for the build. He wouldn't simply appear, and expect the foreman (director) to tell him what tools to use, or pick them out and hand them to him at every stage; this would slow down the teamwork for everyone concerned, and lead to natural frustration for the members of the construction crew who have arrived prepared and equipped for the work. You are expected to pull your weight on the team, to fulfill your part of the creative bargain.

We should also put to rest the tired belief that some amateurs still hold of a rehearsal process that can "peak too early"; the idea being that if the actors do their work in rehearsals too quickly that they will be ready for performances too soon, and consequently, when opening night arrives, the cast members will be stale, bored, and no longer inspired by the story they're telling. In other words, the dinner was served before the diners reached the table, and now the food is cold.

The truth that all serious young artists should hold onto is this: *When bringing a character from a great play to life on stage, no matter how long you prepare and work, there is always more to do, more to discover, and another level of quality and depth to explore and achieve.* An actor's art is never finished. Even in the final performance of a long theatrical run, it's not unusual for a new discovery to be made by the seasoned professional; a moment when they exclaim to themselves: "How could I have missed that?!" Actors who fear "peaking too early" are not using the full range of their creative imagination and potential.

An actor who comes to rehearsal having not pored over his text for ideas to experiment with, for alternative options to try, for possible buried meanings in each line, for subtextual clues, has not yet advanced from amateur into professional methodology. An actor who comes to rehearsal waiting to be told what to do by the director is already wasting everyone's time. Theatre is a collaborative process involving writers, designers, directors and actors. When all engine cylinders are firing together, the sum of the whole exceeds the value of the individual parts. Any actor who doesn't prepare to his capacity, thus bringing his "best game" to the table—even at the very first read-through—wastes everyone else's creative time.

Simultaneously, in spite of his detailed and thoughtful preparation, he must also remain flexible and open to changing his mind, to adapting the choices he might have already made in order to more effectively work with and complement his fellow actors who have brought their own intriguing perspectives to the rehearsal. It's a tightrope act, this creative two-step with other artists; actors need to be impeccably prepared, and yet willing to drop their preconceptions to pursue a different path at the drop of a hat. The high-wire walker who performs risky work without a net has honed his instincts through years of preparation: he's not thinking consciously of the components of balance up on the wire; if he is, he will constantly be monitoring himself instead of simply doing what his instincts tell him to do in order to work effectively and well. Self-evaluations and self-judgments come either before or after the act of creation; not during.

An actor doing his homework *during* the rehearsal is invariably turned inward, a black hole sucking all of the energy out of the room and his fellow actors; while an actor who has done his share of thinking and imagining outside the rehearsal brings an assurance and an eagerness to *try it out* into the room which both energizes and inspires the people working on stage with him.

So what kind of homework are we talking about with Shakespeare? Text analysis, of course, of the kind we've been examining thus far. But how might we start to actually translate this analysis into physical and vocal *action*?

First, regular vocal exercises . . proper breath support, resonance, diction . . . are essential for all types of stage acting work. Although a comprehensive approach to technical exercises for the voice is not the focus of this book, there are some fine examples of such out there for the student to read and practice with, many of which are specifically tailored for work with Shakespeare. A few fine examples are: *Speaking Shakespeare* by Patsy Rodenburg; *The Actor and the Text* by Cicely Berry; and *Freeing Shakespeare's Voice: The Actor's Guide to Talking the Text* by Kristin Linklater. All three of these books offer invaluable workouts for keeping the vocal instrument "in tune" for young and old actors alike, and all three are well worth consulting.

As you work on your voice—a process that takes months or years for optimum results, and continues for as long as you continue your stage work—there are other simple and fundamental exercises that you can try to help you better grasp how Shakespeare's text works for the actor. Here are a few to begin with:

Working with operative words: As we've already mentioned, *operative words* are those words that spring out to the actor as the most vital for communicating the sense of what he is saying, or pursuing his action through text. All of your work with scansion and antitheses helps you clearly identify those operative words. So, go through your dialogue and soliloquies, and play this game with yourself: if the character you are playing were absolutely limited to one or two words he was allowed to say (instead of all the words that Shakespeare has given you), what would they be?

For example, take the sentence that we used in Chapter IV when we were introducing iambic pentameter: "I'll climb those stairs to get a candy bar." If you had to strip this sentence down to its most important word or words, what would it/they be? Mostly likely, it would be "candy," or "candy bar." The speaker's desire for that, after all, is what propels the action of this thought. But what would happen if we chose to stress "stairs" instead? Try it. The meaning implied with that emphasis—using "stairs" as the operative word instead of "candy bar"—would be subtly changed. By emphasizing "stairs," we would set up for the listener that there was an alternative place we might go to find that candy bar, and the choice of *where* we were going would become the focus—the *action*, as it were—of the sentence, instead of *what* we were going for.

(Another important thing to note here is that "candy bar"— our natural emphasis, our operative word(s)—comes *at the end* of the thought. Remember that . . . we'll come back to it in a moment.)

For the heck of it, let's add another brilliantly conceived line to the first: "Or would you rather have a ball of yarn?" So now, our iambic pentameter couplet (unrhymed) goes:

I'll climb those stairs to get a candy bar;
Or would you rather have a ball of yarn?

If you were forced to choose one word from the second line that communicated its essence, what would it be? Well, if you weren't allowed the three words "ball of yarn"—only one—it would probably be "yarn." But let's say you could have the full "ball of yarn," just as you were allowed the three syllables of "candy bar." What do you have?

An antithesis. Not a direct one (opposites, that is), but an either/or, a contrast, nonetheless.

These operative word choices not only distill the action/ intention of the couplet down to its most basic elements— "candy bar" or "ball of yarn"—the operative words here are re-enforced by the scansion itself, and the emphases further bring out the core words of the antithesis: "I'll CLIMB those STAIRS to GET a *CANdy BAR*;/Or WOULD you RAther HAVE a *BALL of YARN*?" Once again, even though "get" has an iambic emphasis, if you further stress it—making it an operative word in the line, instead of "ball of yarn"—it would subtly change the meaning of the sentence you're communicating. Again, try it and see. The problem with giving "get" the strongest emphasis is that the second line contains nothing that it can be directly contrasted with. Maybe if we were suggesting that we climb the stairs and steal a candy bar, then giving more emphasis to having the ball of yarn as the preferred prize would make slightly better sense to the ears. (Not much, though!) But that's not the language that you're given to speak.

So, as you begin working with the text and speaking it aloud on your own before rehearsals begin, read carefully for meaning and mark the operative words in your text that best illuminate that meaning by underlining them. Not too many— not every word that receives stress in the natural order of your speaking rhythms have equal importance. Identify and mark the ones that are most vital for the other character to whom you are speaking—or the audience—to receive from you. What do they have to hear to best understand *what you want most*?

The scansion of iambic pentameter will help you to find these key words and phrases; and the antitheses that you find and identify will also lead you to operative word choices in the lines. It all works together. Mark it all—but remember: you can always change your mind about first choices of operative words as the rehearsal work progresses and you discover more about the character you are bringing to life, and as you decide what you need to emphasize in order to properly respond to the choices thrown at you by your fellow actors. Ongoing creative collaboration is the key!

Laying down the beat: Anyone who has spent a period of time learning to play a musical instrument knows what the early stages are like: you become familiar with the clef notations on the page in order to "read" the music denoting what to play; you count out the rhythm, slowly and cleanly, in the time signature that is given as you follow the notes on the page (4/4, 3/4, 6/8, etc.); you painstakingly learn the fingering on the valves, the position of your hands on the keyboard, the most efficient way to hold the sticks or mallets; and finally, you plunk it out. Repetitively. Again, and again, and again. Way more slowly than the piece is meant to be played in performance, without feeling, without interpretation, without expression. For until your unconscious becomes free to take over the playing—which it only can after you've spent hours, days, months, even years, working your body into the pattern of muscle memories it requires in order to play the instrument without thinking about the technique of playing as you play—you can never hope to master the *art* of the instrument, or play it with even rudimentary skill or freedom.

You often hear skilled musicians talking of trying to reach that state in their work where the music plays *them* rather than they playing the music. This sounds wonderfully mystic and magical; but the plain truth behind this phrase is less romantic. What they're really saying is that they have practiced, practiced, practiced, mechanically, technically—often soullessly—until they can play without their minds, their doubts, their conscious preparation or their technique getting in the way of the art.

Konstantin Stanislavsky's famous system for actors was founded on this same premise: "unconscious creativeness through conscious technique." Only when the actor has committed himself to hours of research, study, script and character analysis, voice and movement work—and yes, directed daydreaming about the life of the character he is to play—can the true "art" of the performance commence.

Thus, the iambic pentameter of Shakespearean verse must be notated and "pounded out" by the actor as he begins homework on his role. In the early stages of work, it's important that the verse rhythm gets some attention from the actor, along with the meaning of the words themselves. Just as a novice drummer learns a rhythm slowly at first, then picks up the tempo as it becomes more familiar and comfortable, the Shakespearean actor needs to "lay down the beat," consciously, until it becomes second nature—until he "gets it in his soul," as a famous jazz musician used to say.

First, the lines should be scanned in strict iambics, disallowing any anomalies. Then, very slowly and with exaggerated emphasis on the stresses, the actor speaks the words aloud. (You might even try tapping the table in front of you as you work to help you emphasize the stresses more.) Take this example from the opening of *Richard III*:

Now IS the WIN-ter OF our DIS-con-TENT
Made GLOR-ious SUM-mer BY this SUN of YORK;
And ALL the CLOUDS that LOW-'red upON our HOUSE
In THE deep BOS-om OF the O-cean BUR-ied.

The young actor with good instincts and solid common sense should quickly realize that not all of the syllables emphasized above would represent the appropriate way to speak the lines in performance; for instance, with all of the strong options for emphasis in the fourth line above, why on earth would one choose to punch words like "the" and "of"? Put those good instincts aside for the moment; right now, your focus is on the backbone of the verse's *rhythm*, not its sense. You are the drummer, learning the beat. When the beat is firmly rooted within you, then the anomalies will begin to jump out spontaneously—and therefore work more effectively, as Shakespeare meant them to.

You must remember: the rhythms of iambic pentameter must be laid down in your vocal delivery at the earliest stages of your homework processes. That way, *you can forget about it when you get into actual rehearsals, and just let it flow.* Actors with an affinity for music and rhythms—many of them with natural skills in musical theatre—often discover a natural affinity with the "beat" of Shakespeare's verse. To repeat—like a musician learning a challenging piece of music, you carefully lay down the beat, then the notes, learn them—and then forget about them. (If you're thinking about your iambic rhythms in actual performance, you're in trouble; obviously, that's not what your character would be thinking in the midst of a dramatic crisis in the world of the play!) You let the music play itself . . . or play *you*, as it were. Early in your work, this may take a significant amount of preparation time; but like everything in life, the more you practice it the easier it will become, and the freer your work with it will be.

Incidentally, some Shakespearean historians have speculated that there are more than aesthetic reasons behind the Elizabethan playwrights' preference for iambic pentameter in their plays. These rhythms, they suggest, made it easier for the actors, who had to keep multiple plays in their active repertoire, to memorize their lines quickly. Their rehearsal periods, by today's standards, must have been extremely short . . . .and very much different than how our own rehearsals work. Even today, those actors who have worked regularly with Shakespearean plays will often claim that on the occasion of "drying up" (that is, forgetting their line), they find themselves capable of ad-libbing in iambic pentameter. Through their long practice with it, the rhythm has "gotten in their soul."

Once it has begun to lodge in yours, let your actor instincts and common sense start to sneak back in amongst the emphasized rhythms that you've practiced. You'll probably find that the important anomalies and natural departures from the rhythm that help give the verse both variety and sense will leap out of their own accord. The lines from *Richard III* quoted above will probably begin to settle down into something akin to this:

NOW is the WIN-ter of our DIS-con-TENT
Made GLOR-ious SUM-mer by this SUN of YORK;

And ALL the CLOUDS that LOW-'red upON our HOUSE
In the DEEP BOS-som of the O-cean BUR-ied.

You may notice that there are probably several minor stresses at work here too that I haven't marked: the "of" in line 1, the "by" in line 2, the "of" in line 4. If you've practiced the strict iambic rhythms by pounding them out before you let the variations start to come out of their own accord, those small words should naturally enjoy a small "punch" as a result of the beat that you've laid down and practiced. In other words, the rhythms will begin to play themselves; the heartbeat of the line is established, and the music of it flows on top, like a boat carried downstream on a strong current.

Playing the Music: Continuing the musical analogy, once the beat of the line is laid down, it's time to explore the potential melodies suggested by the thoughts expressed. When using antitheses in Shakespeare, the expressive pattern of the actor's voice becomes very important in bringing those contrasts and comparisons to life for the audience's ears and thoughts. The experienced actor's voice floats over the top of the iambic beats like the jazz soloist's improvisation is launched by the steady foundation of the bass and percussion.

The musicality of an actor's natural voice is often formed by the people that he heard about him as a young child when he was first learning to speak. Some actors seem naturally blessed with an expressive and impressive range; they do not shy from using all of the "highs" and "lows" of their voices in everyday conversation, so those habits transfer easily into their stage work. However, for those actors less fortunate, consciously working on the extension of their vocal expression becomes an essential daily discipline, particularly when tackling classical poetic drama. Singing lessons with a professional teacher—even for those who adamantly claim that they cannot sing well—can help virtually anyone learn more about how to find and utilize the full range of notes in their vocal instrument. For those who haven't the resources to study regularly with a voice teacher, there are other simple exercises to explore.

Pick up a book or magazine. (Even the phone book will do!) Without pushing for volume or force, simply read aloud whatever text you have. Again, don't try to project; read in a relaxed, conversational tone of voice. Don't read for meaning; don't even think too much about the words themselves—just explore the sounds, exaggerating their formation with your lips, your teeth, and your tongue. Relax your jaw regularly with gentle yawns, and breathe regularly (not too deeply). Now, as you read, begin to slowly and gently—not loudly—let your voice slide on the words up and down your own personal scale of vocal notes. Use your falsetto at the top end, sliding in and out of it as you move up and down your range. Push your bass range gently as low as you can comfortably go. As you play with this, note what vowel sounds are hardest to vocalize at the extreme ends, high and low, of your range. When you find the areas of your range that you feel you tend to use the least, stay with them awhile. For many men, this will probably be your higher notes; for women, it will probably be in your lower range. (Society influences how we develop our voices; men think they should speak in a lower, more masculine range, while women tend to strive for the higher, more lilting voices. Both tendencies are largely unconscious and come of adolescent socialization.)

If you can find someone with even the most basic knowledge of piano and music theory (assuming you don't have that knowledge yourself), have them help you with this experiment. Take a few moments to warm up your voice by vocalizing with each piano tone struck; then, work down the scale of keys until you reach the lowest note that you can sing comfortably, without straining or stressing your voice. Once you've identified that note, go up one "fifth" interval, striking that key. This will be your "optimum pitch"—the median note for you, where your speaking voice should be at its most effective and resonant. Sing on that pitch for a moment, then try to segue the singing into a speaking note. Is it higher than you're accustomed to speaking through most of the day? Or is it lower? Many people are quite surprised to find out that they may not be utilizing their voices as effectively as they might be in everyday speech. Learning to work with your natural voice in everyday life is the first step toward finding your most powerful, expressive and effective stage voice.

Building and Phrasing the Thought: Once you've begun to find your operative words, your rhythms (and how they support those operative words as well as the headlong pace of the text), and experimented with how the music in your voice can complement the iambic rhythms and emphasize the sense of the antitheses that are often at the very heart of the play, you can begin to make all of these technical choices more organic; that is, coming from you and your personality within the fictional circumstances instead of from some abstract critical idea of how the character should be played. You begin to find your own individual perspective about how each thought is best phrased and illuminated by the text you're given to speak.

Let's practice with this brief excerpt from a speech of Miranda's in *The Tempest* (Act III, i):

> *I do not know*
> *One of my sex; no woman's face remember,*
> *Save, from my glass, mine own; nor have I seen*
> *More that I may call men than you, good friend,*
> *And my dear father. How features are abroad,*
> *I am skilless of; but, by my modesty,*
> *The jewel in my dower, I would not wish*
> *Any companion in the world but you,*
> *Nor can imagination form a shape,*
> *Besides yourself, to like of.*

This is an exercise that both Patsy Rodenburg and Kelly McEvenue often use with their students in studios and universities on both sides of the Atlantic, as well as with professional actors in the British Royal Shakespeare Company and the National Theatre, and at the Stratford Shakespeare Festival in Ontario, Canada, where they have worked, respectively, as voice and movement teachers for many years. (Patsy has written numerous books for actors from *The Right to Speak* through *The Second Circle*, and Kelly is the author of *The Actor and the Alexander Technique*.) Start by repeating the first word of your text while you move randomly about the space in which you're working or warming up; for the speech above, this would be "I." After repeating it several times, add the second word, linking them together: "I do." Try to forget the words that you know are to follow, concentrating simply on the words that you have spoken thus far, their meaning, their implications. Add another: "I do not." Obviously, now the whole meaning has suddenly turned, from a positive to a negative. Keep repeating. "I do not know." Then, "I do not know one." "I do not know one of." Repeat. "I do not know one of my." "I do not know one of my sex." And so on, following the same process until you have come to the end of your text.

Working with this simple exercise, you will begin to discover nuances about the words themselves: how the sounds connect with their emotional and informational content, how the character's thoughts build throughout their sentences as they unfold, how the words are chosen in the moment, how they express the need for a specific action or intent. Simple, but quite effective in personalizing the content of the text Shakespeare has written for you. And as an additional bonus, it can help you memorize lines!

Another exercise to play with after trying this one is a tad more physical. Again, working with the text above, walk around the space speaking the lines aloud. Every time you find a shift in the text that reflects some change—it can be small, but still must be significant—stop; turn to face a different direction in the room; resume moving as you continue speaking the text; again, stop when you come to a shift; turn again; speak and move; and continue this until you come to the end of your speech.

Of course, actors working on the same text will find different places to stop, turn and move with this exercise (once again, there are no right answers!); but the physicalization of the text in this way will help you effectively discover how the phrasing works best for you, and how to best express the meanings in the text. Consequently, you start down the path of making specific and strong acting choices with the text that you will subsequently take into your rehearsals to try. For the speech above, the phrasing *might* work something like this, with the caesurae marked with a /:

> *I do not know*
> *One of my sex; / no woman's face remember,/*
> *Save, / from my glass, / mine own; / nor have I seen*
> *More that I may call men / than you, / good friend, /*
> *And my dear father. / How features are abroad, /*
> *I am skilless of; / but, / by my modesty, /*
> *The jewel in my dower, / I would not wish*
> *Any companion in the world / but you, /*
> *Nor can imagination form a shape, /*
> *Besides yourself, / to like of.*

Don't interpret all of these /'s to mean that the text should ultimately play this segmented or disjointed in its final form. Stanislavksy applies the analogy of cutting up a text like a meal of roasted chicken into bite-sized pieces in order to more carefully chew and digest it. When first working on a play, that's exactly what an actor must do. But once the thoughts become your own—a gift to you from the playwright—then the words will flow more easily, quickly and naturally. *But you can't skip these initial steps of breaking down the text so that it has specific meaning and resonance for you.* This initial work, slow and steady as it is, will also help clarify even better for you how the rhythms of the verse (and the antitheses contained therein) reveal exactly who the characters really are.

Supporting the Thought Through to its Conclusion: Next time you're with a group of friends—and not a principal contributor to the conversation going on—take a moment to really listen; not to *what* is being said, but to *how* it is being said. Listen to how people use their voices in casual conversation, what the music and rhythms sound like, without focusing too much (as we usually do) on the words. The pattern you will probably hear for many of the more casual exchanges is this: a low build from the beginning of the sentence or thought into a slight peak of vocal energy in the middle, then trailing off into a dying fall at the end. For most of us in American conversation, this is the common musical dynamic of our speech.

However, when our excitement and emotion is aroused, we tend to treat the beginnings and conclusions of our spoken sentences more emphatically. Our "attack" on our sentence's thought (or perhaps it would be more accurate to call it our attack on the *other's* thought by way of our rejoinder) becomes louder and more impassioned, and our "carry-through" on to the end of the point we are making becomes more fully sustained. We don't let it fade away; we plant our viewpoint firmly—or at least, we try to—into the person's mind whom we're addressing. Our instinct is then to sustain the percussive rhythms of our consonants and the expressive music of our vowels all the way through until the end, working harder for the hearer's acceptance of our perspective or, at the very least, their clearer understanding of it.

Onstage, both in rehearsal and performance, this vocal force—demonstrated by a strong attack on your text with sustained energy all the way until the end—should become the actor's norm. A strong vocal attack on your line indicates a passionate involvement in the interchange with the other character(s) you share the scene with, an eagerness to engage with the situation, the action that the words express. (And remember: intensity doesn't always mean volume, but volume—that is, a consistent vocal projection—is most often lacking in young, inexperienced actors; so it's a pretty good practice early in your work to try to always be louder without sacrificing your sense of truth.) But perhaps even more important to your work will be this cultivated vocal habit: the actor must have enough vocal force *to sustain the line of thought all the way to the end.* He must not let any sentence drift to a weak or inconclusive finish, unless it is for a specifically crafted and planned dramatic effect for a particular moment that might call for that choice (very rare).

In good dramatic writing—writing meant to be spoken aloud on a stage by dynamic and well-trained actors in a performance— the key words or phrases of a character's sentence most often are found at the beginning and at the end. This is especially true with Shakespeare. The actor must therefore launch into the line with power, then sustain the train of thought all the way through to its "punch" at its end.

What's most necessary for his success with this practice? Proper breathing, and sustained diaphragmatic support of his voice, from attack through to conclusion.

Lord Laurence Olivier, probably the most gifted, respected and influential Shakespearean actor of the 20th Century, once suggested that an actor should strive and practice until he is able to speak 16 lines of iambic pentameter verse on one sustained breath. This may be an ideal goal that most aspiring actors will never achieve, especially if they must also project those 16 lines to a 2000-seat house; but it is nonetheless a target worth aiming at. (Indeed, upon hearing Olivier's suggestion when I was a young actor, it inspired me to quit smoking in order to try achieving that goal; so, it had great benefit for me in more matters than just theatrical!)

No book that describes breathing exercises for an actor will adequately substitute for actual studio work with an able coach or teacher; but there are a few things that a young actor can try that might aid his awareness of how his breathing works.

First, lie on the floor facing upwards, with arms at your side (palms of your hands may be face up or face down). Slide your feet up toward your rear end, with soles flat on the floor and knees pointing up toward the ceiling. This position should allow the small of your back, just above the hips, to lie almost flat against the floor.

Relax, and breathe slowly and deeply. After you've taken a few minutes with this, lay one of your hands gently upon your stomach above your navel. As you breathe in, you should feel your belly expand against your hand, swelling downward and outward below your rib cage to accept the deep, relaxed, full breath. When you allow the air to slowly flow out (don't push it), you will feel your abdomen fall once more.

We all tend to breathe more shallowly in everyday life than an actor needs to do in order to support the vocal power necessary to fill an auditorium and supply the soaring vocal music and expressiveness that a play text requires—especially a play text comprised of poetic metaphor and rhythm; classical drama. Our chest expands with our breaths, but the inhalation very often doesn't expand completely down into our lower regions, pushing the diaphragmatic muscles downward as well as outward, to both sides and front. These full breaths, coupled with how we learn to control the expulsion of the air as we intone the words, are the key to projection, resonance, and expression. When we lie on our backs, feeling how the breath fills us when we are totally relaxed, we can begin to get a sense of what needs to happen with our breathing once we are on our feet.

So, now stand. Experiment for a moment with where to plant your feet in order to give you the most comfortable, relaxed stability of balance. If your feet are too close together, with a foundation not wide enough, you will easily tip, losing your balance; if they are too wide apart, you will need to adjust significantly before stepping forward. The distance between your feet will obviously vary depending upon your height; but what you are trying to find in this relaxed stance is *a state of constant readiness*—the ability to move, with assurance and balance, at the clap of hands.

Moving up from your feet, check in with your knees; make certain they are unlocked. When you "soften" those knees, you will find that your pelvis also tucks slightly forward, giving a better alignment and base to the vertebrae that stack up from the coccyx—the "tailbone", as we commonly call it. Let your shoulders relax down in their sockets, dangling at your sides; the hands and wrists should be loose, so if someone should come along and shake them lightly, they would show no tension resistance at all.

Finally, imagine that the brow of your head is encircled with a golden crown (a good image for Shakespeare!); and that crown holds your head firmly but comfortably. Imagine that it has anti-gravity qualities! It gently floats your head upward toward the sky, completely encircling it so that the entire upper portion of your skull wants to float, gently lengthening your neck, your spine, your entire upper abdomen. Imagine that your spine, your pelvis, your feet no longer need to bear the weight of your body; this "magic crown" takes much of your weight, pulling your entire being upward, working directly against the forces of gravity. Completely invest in this image, and see if your body begins to achieve that relaxed sense of alignment and "softness" that you found when lying on the floor. Raise one of your relaxed arms (imagine letting it "float" to this position), and place your palm against your abdomen, right between the rib cage and the navel. Is your abdomen beginning to naturally expand with the breath, as it did on the floor? As you do this, keep checking in with the rest of your skeletal and muscular structure to make certain everyday tensions aren't sneaking back in. Your feet and ankles, your soft knees, your tucked forward pelvis, your relaxed shoulders and arms, your magic crown gently tugging/ floating you skyward. Breath fully and gently. Think of allowing the air to flow in and flow out, without making an effort to pull it in or push it out. Don't hold your breath; let the cycles flow naturally.

After a few moments of this, start to gently vocalize, keeping your throat relaxed and open. (If tension begins to creep in anywhere in your body as you stand, send your awareness to that point and consciously relax the muscles that don't want to cooperate. Try to release the muscular tension in conjunction with the breath flowing out of you. Tension is often our natural state in specific areas of our bodies: the shoulders, neck, lower back, jaw, etc. . . . identify those places where they exist in you and focus in on them.) Use the five open vowel sounds: "Ahhhh", "Aaaay" (long "a" sound), "Eeeee" (long "e" sound), "Ohhhh" (long "o" sound), and "Ooooo" (as in "who"). Sustain the strong, supported resonant sound of each, as long as your breath allows you to, without strain. Try to ration your outgoing breath in order to keep each sound going as long as possible. Take note of how your throat, jaw and mouth work to produce each different sustained vowel. If you feel any scratchiness in your vocal folds, try making adjustments in volume or physiology to reduce that strain. The more you practice such vocal exercises, the more you will become aware of how your unique vocal mechanism works at its best; how to adjust your projection without undue tension; and how to make certain you retain enough breath to carry your lines, with full vocal energy, all the way to end of each thought. The books by Linklater, Berry and Rodenberg that I noted at the beginning of this section will provide you with many other daily exercises to add to your regimen.

Preparation and practice: Identifying the operative words in your lines, rehearsing the rhythms of the iambics, exploring the musical range of your speaking voice, building the sense of the textual thoughts with appropriate phrasing, and supporting those thoughts with the breath needed to project and clarify them for audiences—all of these tools are essential for bringing to vivid stage life the character passion, verse scansion and antitheses that we've examined in the past three chapters. For the Shakespearean actor, the preparation process always consists of striking the most effective balance between the head (analysis), the body (technique), and the heart (inspiration and passion). The experiments and tools are prepared in advance, tested in rehearsals, and ultimately proven in the presence of an audience.

CHAPTER VII

"THUS PLAY I, IN ONE PERSON, MANY PEOPLE":
CONTEXTS, ICONS, CONTRASTS, AND CONTRADICTIONS

There's a lot of bad Shakespeare being produced around the country nowadays, not only in schools and universities, but by prestigious professional companies as well; so much, in fact, that it prompted one critic a few years ago to call for a complete moratorium on the staging of Shakespeare plays for the next five years!

What's wrong with most of these poor productions has nothing to do with the relevance of Shakespeare's plays for modern audiences. I suspect that the same actors and directors who are producing them, would produce similarly flawed results were they working with any other playwright. They simply aren't doing the homework they need to do, nor finding personal and meaningful connections with the scripts and characters; instead, they rely on clichéd directorial choices borrowed from once-revolutionary, now decades-old stagings, design approaches that distract from the stories by bringing undue attention to themselves, "avant garde" gimmicks that have come to mean little or nothing (and that have long outlived their ability to provoke new thought or perspectives on the plays), arbitrary transgender casting which confuses the story rather than refreshes it . . . and on and on.

I don't want to be misunderstood here; I'm not a hidebound traditionalist when it comes to Shakespeare, and I'm not at all against subjecting his plays to innovative and surprising examinations, both critical and theatrical. But any such approach must facilitate the audience's path into the story of the play if it is to succeed. At its heart, it must serve, in very specific and thoughtful ways, the various elements that have given the works their power to excite and move us for over four centuries; and it must never seek to show audiences how clever or "original" the director is at the expense of the play itself.

How are the directors and actors to accomplish that? First, clarify the narrative for yourself; second, make whatever adaptations you might wish to try depending upon that clarification; third, determine very carefully and specifically how each character should work within your story's setting—plot the "backstory" of the play with great care (that is, what previous actions and events led into the play's beginning); and most importantly, make certain that all of the choices you make throughout your planning stages and rehearsal period are consistent with the context that you've settled upon. This context, and the details for it that you supply, both as actor and director, is crucial for the success of bringing to life your (that dreaded word!) theatrical *concept*. Concept without context will almost certainly lead to sterile and boring results in performance.

Very often, the era and society in which a play is first presented supplies a context that its audience intuitively understands. For example, Shakespeare's history plays were certainly not intended as dry chronicles of fact or schoolroom lessons upon their first presentations in London's public theatres. If that were all they were, and all Shakespeare meant them to be, the Elizabethan audiences would have avoided them like plague. (Just as many do such "dry" productions today.) After all, bear-baitings, brothels and torturous public executions provided stiff competition for the playhouses, and such bloodthirsty and lustful entertainments were great attractions for a decidedly large segment of the population—as indeed they are in every era, for better or for worse. Yet Shakespeare's plays held their ground against such competitors; indeed, they were the primary reason that Shakespeare's company of players were the most successful of their time, making their shareholders—including Shakespeare himself—wealthy men.

Yes, Shakespeare provided violent melodramas such as *Titus Andronicus*, providing enough rape, mutilation, murder, and cannibalism to compete with the bloodiest chapters of

Friday the 13th and similar cinematic examples today; and passionate, timeless romances, such as *Romeo and Juliet* to stir the imaginations of young and old lovers alike. But a good many of his works were grounded firmly in the events of the era in which he lived. Audiences viewed the battles of the Plantagenet cousins, the Lancasters and Yorks, for England's throne against the background of the uncertainty of their own aging sovereign's succession: What would happen if Elizabeth died without an obvious heir? Was the turmoil and civil war that Shakespeare depicted onstage in the *Henry VI* and *Henry IV* cycles—"history" plays—a portent of things to come to England once more upon Elizabeth's death? Was Hamlet a fictional echo of Lord Essex, a man whom many considered to be the proper candidate to join with Elizabeth, thereby providing a new lineage for English royalty? (Or was he more readily seen as Claudius, the lustful usurper?) And were the depictions of the fickle crowds of *Julius Caesar*, *Coriolanus* and *Sir Thomas More*, easily swayed by powerful oratory and unscrupulous political leaders, a little too familiar to those contemporary audiences, moving warily and anxiously toward a new, 17th Century?

A context, relevant and immediate to our own lives, is the lens through which we may focus upon the events of any play that we see upon the stage, whether it be the works of William Shakespeare, Anton Chekhov, or Neil LaBute. Thus, a production "concept" without a relevant context will likely distance us from any connection with or deeper understanding of the narrative, rather than inviting us into that world. It will be an impediment to the empathy necessary for our ultimate involvement and enjoyment.

Michel St. Denis was a brilliant theatre philosopher, teacher and thinker of the early 20th Century. In addition to directing and writing, he was also one of the original instructors for the Juilliard Drama program founded by John Houseman in the 1960's. His brief and profound book, entitled *The Rediscovery of Style*, speaks eloquently to the importance of establishing a context in the acting and the setting of a play's *mise en scene* (the fictional world and its visual details that tell its story which a director determines with designers before a play is cast or rehearsed). In sum, St. Denis posits that directors and actors must do their research and analysis in order to grasp the historical and social context in which a play was written and first presented: What cultural forces and realities instigated and inspired its composition, and how did they affect its initial audiences' acceptance and understanding of its story, its concerns, its themes? Once those things are fully determined, the challenge then follows to effectively translate the play's "forming principle" into a staging that will actively speak in a similar fashion to audiences of today. Actors and directors can never recreate the circumstances and methods of a play as it was first presented in earlier eras—nor should they! To do so would be to fashion a museum piece, and not a living, breathing, relevant theatre experience. What theatre artists must do—especially with the plays of Shakespeare that are so richly textured and surprisingly modern, potentially pertinent for every age in which they are staged—is determine the issues of today that directly relate to those matters which concerned the playwright when he first set pen and ink to paper.

By no means does this require that all Shakespeare plays be staged in modern era settings. But it does mean that audiences of today must be able to relate in a direct manner to whatever context is ultimately determined for its staging, and thus see its relevance to their current life experiences in today's world. As we've hopefully begun to grasp in prior chapters, the modern actor's effective path into Shakespeare lies in his ability to bring these texts forward into the spheres of his own personal history and imagination, accompanied by his understanding of the techniques of presenting heightened language and verse on stage; that is, *finding a naturalistic and organic reason why the character must use such language in the situation and context in which he finds himself.*

Let me offer an example of how a director, in creative collaboration with both actors and designers, might effectively define a concrete context for a Shakespeare play, a context in which the players can exercise their imaginations in a world that might successfully engage a modern audience. Several years ago, I staged a production of *Measure For Measure*, long categorized by critics and academics as one of Shakespeare's "problem" plays, and thus a difficult one for audiences to fully understand and enjoy. (Ironically, this category was primarily created by academic critics in order to describe those plays that seemed to elude the easier categories of Tragedy, Comedy, History, or Romance.) Here, in the following pages, I offer sections of an essay written for our production's actors and designers in which I endeavored to provide a firm and specific dramatic location for our unique version of "Vienna" that we were soon going to create together. Hopefully, this will provide a helpful example of how theatre artists, working in creative partnership, can together imagine a singular and vibrant fictional world in which a Shakespeare play written four centuries ago might live and breathe afresh on the modern stage.

(Note: You'll get much more out of the following pages if you first read Shakespeare's *Measure For Measure* in its entirety. In fact, I would suggest that you skip this section and return to it after you've had the opportunity to do that.)

SOME THOUGHTS ON *MEASURE FOR MEASURE*:

So, what's the "Problem" here?

I was having a conversation with a student several weeks ago; gently demonstrating his interest, he noted that *Measure for Measure* was one of Shakespeare's "problem" plays, according to a critical source he had read when he found that we were going to produce it this year. (The other two plays that most critics group into this category are *All's Well That Ends Well* and *Troilus and Cressida*, both written during the same period of Shakespeare's career as this one.) Genuinely curious, I asked him how he thought a "problem" play might be defined. He responded that he understood critics to say that these were the plays in which Shakespeare presented a distinctive "problem" in the characters' basic human situation, a dilemma which they were called upon to solve that would also intrigue and involve the audience; for *Measure*, it could be simply summed up (from Isabella's viewpoint) as: Is surrendering your virginity for your brother's life a worthwhile thing to do? Is saving a sinful transgressor's life—even if that transgressor is your blood relative—a defensible reason to sacrifice one's own virtue, or compromise one's own moral code?

Isabella and Claudio from *Measure for Measure*

So, I asked him, is *Hamlet* a "problem" play? (Should a possible murderer of your father be himself murdered in revenge, based upon the word of a ghost?) Is *Two Gentlemen of Verona* a "problem" play? (Should love/lust for a woman trump an established male friendship?) *Julius Caesar*? (Can a political assassination ever be considered noble and patriotic?) And on and on. My questions made him reconsider—as I have, of late—exactly what that passel of critics mean who keep referring to this triumvirate of plays as Shakespeare's "problem" plays.

Frankly, such categories are pretty meaningless, and are mostly there to provide unimaginative critics and teachers intellectual cover in dealing with dramatic works that don't fit neatly into specific and neat genres—which covers a majority of all the plays ever written in western literature, and most especially those of Shakespeare, our greatest western dramatist! In the First Folio, the player/editors chose to group the works by

Tragedies, Comedies and Histories. The 17th Century brought in a new name for some of these plays (tragicomedies), and the 19th Century brought in an even newer designation, the Romances; these re-defined genres helped a little in critical confrontations with *Cymbeline, Pericles, The Winter's Tale,* and *The Tempest,* but it still leaves in a troublesome purgatory a goodly number of Shakespeare plays. I would offer, in further theoretical generic additions, the following categories as well: farce (*Comedy of Errors*), romantic comedy (*Much Ado About Nothing*), fantastic comedy (*A Midsummer Night's Dream*), social satire (*Two Noble Kinsmen*), black comedy (*Timon of Athens*), political satire (*Troilus and Cressida*), horror story (*Macbeth*) . . . etc., etc.

Actually, the beauty and genius of Shakespeare is that he DEFIED category and genre . . . and too many critics want to stuff him back into those genres, and too many theatre practitioners are glad of the provided cover, and in fact use it to define—and limit—their production approaches to these fascinating and complex plays.

So . . . what, precisely, is the "problem" with *Measure for Measure*?

For me (if you want to deem it a problem), it is that not very many of the characters are very likeable. Interesting, yes. Compelling and fascinating in their behavior, definitely. Neurotic and anguished, certainly. Conniving, obviously. Funny, at times. But likeable? Sympathetic? People you might like to have over to your house for dinner? Not really. And that is at the crux of the "problem" of the play, as well as audiences' steady fascination with it over the years. We are intrigued and caught up in Isabella's situation, but have considerable difficulty relating to a woman who can affirm "More than my brother is my chastity!" We find Angelo's sudden submission to his overriding lust both frightening and comic, the latter primarily due to his clueless clumsiness with all things physical. We know that we should side with the Duke in his exposure of the hypocrisy of people in power (even though he himself put them in power!), but are troubled by his ethical cowardice and easy Machiavellian tactics. We know that we should feel ready to condemn Lucio's exaggerated portrayal of his licentious personal intimacy with the Duke's prurient exploits . . . .but, strangely, it ends up feeling more like truth than slander. We hear not a peep from Claudio about his regret at leaving a vulnerable, pregnant fiance behind him after death—only fear about his own coming death, and the leavetaking of his own sensual feast that will result (which, to judge by Juliet's condition and some of the comments of others in the play—including his sister—his life has clearly been). We feel a kinship with Poppy and Mistress Overdone—these are poor women trying to eke out a living in a corrupt social system—but we also recognize them as syphilitic prostitutes and bawds. We admire Escala's (note: *in our world, a female counselor, the name adapted from Shakespeare's Escalus*) dignity and reserve, but can also see her as a too-reticent prig—at least at times. We sympathize with the over-worked and under-trained constable Elbow, but also laugh at his ignorance and extremism. Who do we tend to like without serious reservation? The Provost, a character without a proper name, who is the real Everyman of the story: a simple, common man who does his job responsibly, but has no real power in this world, except to choose whom to follow. And that choice is clearly limited by the circumstances of the life around him.

This is a really troubling world, but dramatically fascinating nonetheless. It is Shakespeare a la Harold Pinter, in a way. An intricate, dark, yet blackly comic chamber play; certainly nothing close to an heroic epic or a light comedy. And, with that in mind, I've crafted a few adjustments in the text to bring these elements out.

SOME OF THOSE "TEXTUAL ADJUSTMENTS"

First off, I've done extensive cutting, and the current version that we'll be working with as we begin this design process is my sixth revision since beginning with the original Folio text (there are no extant Quartos, so there are no alternate versions of the play to consider). I estimate that I've cut at least one third of the play, perhaps more. Some of the cuts were fairly easy to make, as I believe that large portions of the play as it has come down to us do not represent Shakespeare's original version delivered to the King's Men sometime around the ascension of King James I. (The role of the Duke was probably meant to represent James himself—but as we'll come to see, if it was intended as a tribute to his leadership and judgment, the characterization is more than a bit problematical in that regard!) For instance, it sounds to my ear that another writer contributed significant portions to particular scenes in the play which present contemporary Jacobean satirical references, such as the beginning of Act I, Scene ii, with its nearly incomprehensible (to modern audiences) exchanges of bawdy jokes between the "Gentlemen." And the doggerel that the Duke spouts in Act III, Scene i . . . if it is Shakespeare, then it seems like a fairly low point in the quality of his writing. Exits and entrances of various characters are unmarked in some scenes, leaving the reader (and various editors) to decide for themselves if characters are present on stage or not; and these ambiguities sometimes occur at very crucial moments, such as the final revelatory scene of the play. (Some critics suggest that this usually points to the original source material for printing being "foul papers", or an author's manuscript . . . but the seeming interpolations from other authors throughout the play would seem to conflict with that idea, if we view those interpolations as revisions that occurred some time after the original production of the piece.) Moreover, the timeline of that action is, at points, so jumbled as to seem incomprehensible. The time of Claudio's appointed execution is more than a little fluid, and the final scenes are chaotic with "ghost" characters who are named, but never actually appear. A few plotlines remain unresolved (Pompey/ Poppy, Mistress Overdone, and Elbow, for one), and the overall tone of the writing seems very strange in many of the play's latter exchanges. Many scholars believe that Thomas Middleton had a hand in some of the writing, as it appears that he also did in *Macbeth* and *Timon of Athens*, two plays from roughly the same period of Shakespeare's writing. Nonetheless, many of the play's scenes have remarkable power, and the characters—

not always transparent in their motivations—have retained a dramatic fascination for audiences throughout the four centuries since its composition.

So . . . I've streamlined the progression of the scenes considerably, cut several minor characters and combined a few others, and made some significant gender changes of certain folks that I hope will prove not only workable for us, but also help to illuminate some of the suggested themes and thoughts that intrigue me the most. Pompey is no longer a pimp, but another prostitute, a "colleague" of Mistress Overdone—they run the brothel together. Overdone is older (forties?), but Poppy is also a bit past her prime. Although both are survivors, Poppy has the most resilient sense of humor and feels less sorry for herself than her partner, who tends to be on the hysterically weepy side. Master Froth is now Mistress Froth (making the strange affair of the conflict over the prunes in the brothel that Elbow tries to sort out even more bewildering—as it should be for maximum comic effect), and Escalus—the super-efficient and somewhat priggish aide to the Duke—is now a prim and proper woman we'll call Escala. These gender changes (I hope) will point out some major contrasts in the role options of the various women who operate in this society; instead of the exclusively female victims of Shakespeare's original story, we will now have a wider variety of the "fair sex" represented: a funny and tough street woman (still generous of heart), a quietly efficient bureaucrat with a conscience, a saucy chambermaid pressed into a new responsibility by the advancement of the Puritan Angelo to leadership office, etc. And since a major source of the conflict of *Measure for Measure* is centered around sexual tension, enforced (and unnatural) sexual repression, and sexual hypocrisy, I think that these gender shifts can simultaneously open up the themes of the play a bit more while also providing our Company's women with some very interesting acting opportunities that they would not otherwise enjoy in a more "traditional" production.

Truthfully, I've agonized a bit over some of the cuts I've made. (The Duke's long and striking philosophical speech to Claudio about the value [or lack thereof] of life in Act III, Scene i, for instance . . . I revisited that set piece several times, and gritted my teeth over each subsequent excision.) By making some of them, I confess that I have perhaps forced the play into areas that Shakespeare probably did not intend for it to go; yet at the same time, I think that the focus remains consistent with the issues that concerned him in his original composition: the problem with absolutism in any form balanced against the dangers of moral relativity; the natural tension between our highest spiritual ideals and the flesh and blood that we are; and the selfishness that is often cloaked beneath platitudes of moral superiority. In making the cuts and alterations here and there, I hope I have streamlined the story and brought out some unique potentials of the dramatic situation that will resonate with 21st Century audiences without completely derailing the original play as Shakespeare envisioned it. In whatever form the production of this play takes, one has to allow that it is not the most obvious and clear of Shakespeare's dramatic conflicts, even in its original textual form. We don't know how to feel about these people and what they do to one another—and that (again) is exactly what makes it a "problem" play for its audiences; and hopefully, what will also make it entertaining, thought-provoking, and at least slightly controversial for our audiences.

And at the heart of that potential controversy is how I intend to present the Duke; the mover and shaker at the heart of the play.

The Duke's "Political Play of the Week"

Many critics and performance theorists feel that a strong key for unlocking the story (and backstory) of *Measure for Measure* lies in the playing and behavior of the short, tersely spoken first scene of the play. The opening is decidedly unusual for Shakespeare; he must have had something very specific in mind. The Duke speaks to his aide and confidante: "Escalus." The aide responds, "My lord." And then the Duke proceeds to spring what must be the surprise of his life on Escalus: he is abdicating his office for an indefinite period of time and for an undisclosed reason—effective immediately—and wants to remind Escalus of how much wiser he (Escalus) is in the history and political theory of statescraft than is the Duke himself. Having done this in the first 25 or so lines of the play, the Duke then commands that an even younger political mentee be summoned and the reins of leadership of the city handed over to him. The audience can only imagine the turmoil roiling within Escalus: "What?! Why?! Who??? ANGELO?????? What the . . . ?!!" To Angelo's credit, when he enters to hear the news only a few lines later—begging the question of whether he's already been summoned and has been waiting in some bafflement to be admitted into chambers (with perhaps not a little apprehension) some time before the opening lines, just as Escalus presumably is awaiting the Duke in this inner office—he seems as taken aback and incredulous as Escalus. However, there is no time for further explanations; the Duke's business is pressing and suddenly he's gone, leaving Angelo and Escalus to tentatively begin the process of sorting all duties out carefully and diplomatically between them.

Is this a demonstration of admirable and thoughtful leadership? Well, that depends on the backstory, and it is the backstory that will shape how the scene (indeed, the entire drama) is played. Some productions take the Duke at his word when he explains to the Friar in the third scene (as he asks for his monkish disguise) that he is taking an expedient yet subtle means for addressing the increasingly extreme licentiousness of his community with stricter methodology, while at the same time testing the mettle, both moral and ethical, of his talented young protégé, Angelo. Indeed, for better or for worse, this may have been Shakespeare's intended premise for the action; he certainly writes several self-serving soliloquies and speeches for Duke Vincentio throughout the rest of the play that seem to reaffirm this purpose of "political education all around" (which I have either cut or severely edited to suit my own presentation of the character). Personally, I have never found this simple interpretation of the unusual scenario very convincing, or very theatrically interesting. It seems to me that with this approach, the Duke is either very naïve, dumb as a rock, or morally smug and simplistic—or perhaps all three. While this might be an interesting journey to explore in a different production, it makes (for me) the events of the concluding scene, orchestrated by the Duke as if he'd planned it all along, difficult to play, and ultimately very puzzling. It seems to suggest that the Duke is meant to be seen as a "good guy"—enlightened, or newly so—a Father Who Knows Best, fair and stern. But that image is difficult for me to reconcile with a man who claims that he must leave Angelo to clean up the mess in Vienna because it wouldn't be "right" for him (the Duke) to do it himself after he's let things go for so long. Huh??

So, I offer a different backstory, one that was first suggested by the somewhat menacing terseness of the opening scene, an atmosphere of things unspoken and a suggested danger that reminded me a bit of Harold Pinter's "comedies of menace": What if the Duke was quite licentious himself? A well-known playboy, a "Jack Kennedy" of Vienna who had a line of ladies in and out of his boudoir (with a particular taste for the classier brand of streetwalker), something that those in his inner circle were aware of but knew better than to talk much of. What if he were also adept at disguises, which allowed him to frequent seedier establishments with the power and money of the aristocracy at his command to help him fully enjoy the surroundings. (I recently re-read Stevenson's *Dr. Jekyll and Mr. Hyde*, and I suspect this "double life" story plays a strong part in my new reading of *Measure for Measure*.) To help bolster a necessary political image of the dashing and decisive leader that disguised this "secret life" to all but a very few in the upper levels of the government, Vincentio surrounded himself with pious supporters and aides: Escala (changed to a female in our version), a prim and proper (uncharitable people would say "priggish") middle-aged scholarly spinster, an asexual in practice with lesbian leanings, a woman who is a symbol of the repression of her time—whatever we ultimately decide that era is; and Angelo, a young, pious virgin aesthete, a sharp thinker and a sharper moralist. If these were his two most prominent aides, who of his political rivals could doubt the Duke's moral image? Or prove their stance if they did doubt it?

Unless the Duke, in his power and arrogant feelings of immunity from prosecution and security from slander, began to get sloppy in his sense of discretion; if common folk began to see through his slumming disguises, and were openly gossiping about it (like Lucio); if Escala herself began to witness different ladies in the Duke's private chambers, and the Duke worried little about it because of Escala's own dysfunctional social skills—after all, who would take the stories of such an eccentric spinster-type seriously, even if she were shocked and/or outraged enough to speak out? And Angelo—holier-than-thou Angelo, the man whose hobby of theology hides a suppressed variety of sexual obsessions—began to realize for himself what kind of man his political mentor was/is; and as a result, his ire—and perhaps, his envy and ambition—was aroused.

So, what is the Duke to do? The people believe he is a paper tiger when it comes to authoritative moral action now; the gossip about his own lifestyle is becoming more widespread. His top aides respect his wit, his political acumen, his cleverness and style—but are quietly (so far) disapproving of his moral lassitude. And certain well-known ne'er-do-wells of the city— such as the aforementioned rake, Lucio—have really got his number after seeing him in action in the taverns and brothels of the town over the past few months.

He devises what the CNN anchorman might call "the political play of the week"—or in his case, maybe the decade. An elaborate trap that enables him to address the increasingly out-of-control licentiousness of the city's lower classes, thus gaining political favor from the hypocritical upper classes (many of whom actively partake of the pleasures on Saturday nights that they condemn loudly on Sunday mornings); to re-establish some political respect from Escala; to put Angelo in his place by setting him up to fall (he may not know precisely how this might happen, but he recognizes powerful sexual repression when he sees it); to put out-of-control gossips like Lucio in his sway by revealing them; and—an unexpected fringe benefit, as it plays out—to find an incredibly respectable, yet desirable, trophy bride, the beautiful (and clearly virtuous) Isabella. Of course, the Duke doesn't have everything planned out perfectly when he initiates his venture—he's not prescient, after all—but he's a great political (and theatrical) improviser. He seizes unexpected opportunities throughout the play, and even though we may sometimes be repulsed by his Machiavellian behavior, we are in awe of it as well. He is, perhaps, what Richard Nixon might have been if he'd had some iota of personal charisma and charm.

ISABELLA: NUN, NOT A NUN?

For me, Isabella is one of the most difficult and complex female roles in Shakespeare; her psychology is as intriguing as it is often off-putting. Shakespeare is always very specific and careful about the way that he introduces his major characters: with Isabella, almost the first thing we hear from her is a complaining observation about her new lifestyle thus far in the nunnery, as she is being given an initial tour by one of the sisters (a cute little cameo role, a squeaky mouse of a sister who pops up only for this brief scene). The complaint, however, is not what we (or the sister) expects; instead of observing about how restrictive the lifestyle is which she is about to embark upon, Isabella observes stiffly that she wishes it were stricter! Moments later, bad news is delivered to her from Lucio, a friend of her brother, Claudio: Claudio is to be put to death (!) for getting his betrothed, Juliet, pregnant before they are legally wed. Isabella's reaction to the news seems somewhat emotionally muted: "I'll see what I can do," she says, planning to ask permission for leave from her Mother Superior. She seems a bit reluctant, however, claiming that she will surely prove incapable of doing Claudio or Juliet any real good in her proposed pleas to Angelo. Indeed, when she is finally brought before Angelo by Lucio, Lucio keeps pushing her to continue her pleading and reasoning long after she initially tries to surrender the attempt. "You are too cold!" he complains to her in a brief aside. Her arguments to Angelo are all quite intellectually-based, logical and careful. This does not appear to be a sister who is desperate to save her only brother, perhaps her only surviving family member. (Her mother is never mentioned in the text—except in a quick referential slur of "Heaven shield my mother played my father fair!" when she is angry at the way that Claudio is reacting to her refusal to sleep with Angelo in exchange for his pardon, thus by this exclamation implying that Claudio may be a bastard, which would explain his dishonorable behavior; and her father is dead. ["There my father's grave did utter forth a voice!" she says as a compliment to Claudio's apparent courage just a moment before delivering the implied insult to her mother!]) Probably the most perplexing thing that Isabella blurts out in a moment of heightened emotion, however, is her famous line, "More than my brother is my chastity!" Now, I certainly understand how a novice's chastity would be considered her most precious gift to Christ, her spiritual "husband"; but Isabella's complete lack of doubt in this proclamation (there is no sense of "What should I do? What is more important? My living brother or my virginity?") certainly gives one pause. No soul-searching here, no remorse or personal guilt about her proposed choice; she is as certain that she is "right" in this choice as is any moral crusader . . . and that stance is a little hard for most audiences to feel complete empathy for.

So what makes Isabella tick? What brought her to the nunnery in the first place (Shakespeare really doesn't give us any detailed personal background of the character—a very modern, existential expository approach, a la Pinter once again), and what makes her so completely obsessed with the value of her chastity? Isn't the sin of Pride one of the most deadly? Or has Isabella—obsessed with the anti-sensual accoutrements of Christian sin and redemption—conveniently forgotten that one? I think to simply dismiss Isabella as a woman who is "cold" emotionally and sexually disengaged is too uninteresting dramatically. Last year, students who were working on the scene in my Acting Shakespeare class advanced an intriguing notion: perhaps Isabella has a very high sexual drive . . . so high that it frightens her and sends her to the safety of a convent where she won't have to confront it, deal with it, live with it, make it a healthy part of her life. And perhaps, because of who she is and how she has been raised, that passion lays a tremendous burden of guilt on her. That certainly might explain her extremity of attitude when dealing with the questions that the play's situation raises for her: that is, if she fears her own unleashed libido, but cannot even begin to admit that truth to herself. It might also put into a somewhat uncomfortable Freudian perspective her obsession with the goodness and strength of her father; maybe Isabella is more akin to Electra than we (or she) initially realize(s). That would also support her apparently unquestioning faith in the mysterious male authority figure of the Duke (disguised as an all-knowing monk through most of the play). And it also allows some fascinating possibilities of stage behavior and business when the Duke steps forward at the close of the play—fairly surprisingly (and problematically), many feel—to claim her as his new bride. Isabella does not clearly respond with any words when this occurs: no protestation of her chastity, no reminder of her intended religious vows, nothing at all. How she behaves at that moment, however, is a vital acting choice in telling her story and clarifying the concerns of this "problem" play to an audience; and that will be an exciting exploration for actors and directors to have during the course of our rehearsals.

ANGELO: HE'S NO ANGEL

If Isabella is a complex young woman, sexually, morally, historically, Angelo seems to me to be a pretty straightforward young male . . . albeit, more than a little twisted, short-sighted, and therefore emotionally tortured. He is a man with absolutely no sexual self-confidence, no ease with the more biological side of his human nature; and as a result, he tries to "decide" to be asexual, and thus pursue more aesthetic and purely intellectual studies. Interestingly, Angelo is taken by all of the citizenry who know him to be a devout man, but in his soliloquies he really doesn't talk much about spirituality with any real passion; it seems, instead, a dryly reasoned faith rather than a devout one. Through rabid reading and study of history, politics and philosophy, he has carefully defined "the Good" as a category, and in his new (and surprising, for him) leadership role, he proceeds to divide the people of his community into black and white chess pieces on an abstract playing field. He really doesn't seem to deal at all with the personal implications of judging a human life and deciding to take it away; it's a political/social issue to make such judgments, and one does it better if one never—under any circumstances—bends any established rule. He is the quintessential emotionally repressed male, who as a result of that repression, never really had the chance to evolve out of adolescence into true adulthood. He still believes that the ideal world is—or should be—objectively fair.

Then, along comes Isabella, who combines for him the soulful ideal of spiritual womanhood with a clear sexual presence—a presence that even she is not fully aware of, or successfully in control of. And sure enough, what emerges from Angelo's tortured psyche is the age-old conflicting adolescent male's simultaneous desire and repugnance for the absolute madonna vs. the absolute whore—and the inability to deal with the realities of the more grey areas of human nature and sexual identity. His subsequent behavior displays all the cliches: a simmering pot that finally boils over, a volcano that smolders before violently erupting, etc., etc. However, what redeems Angelo somewhat as a human being—in spite of the despicable things that his long-repressed desires drive him to—is the clear suffering that he feels in the deeds. "This deed unshapes me quite," he notes; and "When once our graces we have forgot, nothing goes right! We would . . . and we would not." These thoughts rack him in the midnight hours after he has transgressed against everything he holds philosophically dear, when it is too late to undo the deeds. And yet, true to the complexity of play and characters here, Shakespeare decides not to have Angelo ever truly confront another major wrong that he has committed in his relatively young life: the blithe disposal of Mariana (clearly a loving, vulnerable and heartbroken woman) whom he had pledged troth to, simply because she was unable to furnish an agreed upon dowry due to an unforeseen personal misfortune. Mariana loves him dearly, and he clearly does not reciprocate; yet he is married off to her by the Duke's decree at the play's conclusion, in a travesty of traditional "comic style", along with Lucio to an unseen pock-marked prostitute from his own past, and—most startlingly—Isabella, the determined, would-be nun, to the Duke himself (!).

So once again, here's the core of this "problem" play, that is both its inherent weakness for some audiences, and its involving strength for many: we really, really don't like these main characters in any traditional, dramatic/comic fashion. We're not supposed to, I don't think, because feeling any depth of sentiment for them takes us away from the social satire of an entire society gone askew. Isabella is a morally judgmental young woman who puts her own chastity above her brother's life; the Duke wants to clean up his city, but doesn't want to get his own hands dirty and perhaps damage his own political image in so doing—and he also doesn't want to sacrifice his own secret pleasures; Angelo wants to correct the perceived moral hypocrisy of his society, but is all too ready to "give his own sensual race the rein" at the earliest opportunity in his governance; Claudio resolves not to beg his sister to give herself to Angelo in trade for his own life, but is too cowardly and weak to hold that resolve for more than a moment; and Mariana, who warmly loves Angelo, is all too ready and willing to forgive him for treating her like a doormat. Who are we to really like in this play? Interestingly, the characters I personally like the most are the ones that we might feel, by the traditional generic roles that they play in the plot, we are not really supposed to empathize with: Elbow, the ignorant, foolish constable who is only trying to do his job, a job that no one else will do and thus he feels it's his moral obligation to take it up; Poppy, a straightforwardly amoral (but amiable) bawd who wishes no personal harm to anyone—she just wants to continue making a living in prostitution; Lucio, a witty, busybody gadfly, who does more to help Claudio and Juliet at the story's outset (when no one else seems to care) than virtually anyone in the play—and whose biggest "sin" in the story is his condemnation of the Duke (who really morally deserves all the slander that Lucio lays upon him, whether its entirely factual or not); Escala, unostentatiously ethical throughout; and the Provost, a working man who wants to do his job well, do the right thing, while doing no one unjust harm if he can possibly avoid it.

So, here we are, full circle, back to the point I began this essay with: Quite a fascinating, yet ultimately troubling, cast of characters here!

VIENNA? OR WHITECHAPEL?

These are some images that have leapt out from my subconscious while I've been involved with *Measure for Measure* over the past year or so:

—A dark, glistening pool of water, reminiscent of a stone well, in a gloomy chamber; while light reflects flatly off the surface, nothing can be seen beneath. When something is dipped into the water, only a murky shape appears under the tepid surface.

—Old cathedral-like structures from an earlier Gothic era; stately and somberly impressive (and strongly forbidding) on the outside, but archways into the interior show only impenetrable darkness.

—Moisture shining on worn stone masonry on a foggy street corner.

—The famous Escher drawings with stairs to and from nowhere resulting in architecture with impossible geometry—all in black and white. And are there strange beings—suggested or obvious—lurking in the oddly angled corners and landings?

—A chessboard with austere kings, queens, bishops and knights—mixed with grotesque and twisted pawns and rooks.

The dichotomies and opposites of the play have clearly resonated with me: images of the Sacred against the Profane, a healthy-looking surface (illusory, of course) with syphilitic disease underneath ("Let all the poisons that lurk in the mud hatch out," says Derek Jacobi in the wonderful BBC TV series *I, Claudius*—another quote that keeps returning to my thoughts); Seeming vs. Being, a favorite theme in Shakespeare's writing as the aging Queen Elizabeth prepared to die, leaving her carefully built Protestant kingdom to a rather unlikely heir, the Catholic James of Scotland (see *Hamlet* and *Troilus and Cressida*, two contemporaneous pieces with *Measure for Measure*, for more references, insights and reflections on this state of British affairs); and, perhaps most blatant of all the contrasts, that of "class" and the hypocritical privileges that go along with those fortunate enough to be on the upper end of that stiff hierarchy: they seemed to be allowed their Saturday night licentiousness along with their donned Sunday morning piety and propriety.

I also keep remembering a favorite film of mine of the early 1980's—interestingly enough, with a clever screenplay (adapted from John Fowles's novel) by Harold Pinter, whose striking dramatic works *Measure for Measure* keeps bringing me back to. The actress, Anna, played by Meryl Streep (who is also playing this actress playing the title role of Sarah in *The French Lieutenant's Woman* in this movie of the same name—how's that for re-enforcing the duality theme outlined above?) reads her co-star Jeremy Irons (playing Mike/Charles) this passage of her research for her role: "In 1857 the *Lancet* (a contemporary newspaper) estimated that there were eighty thousand prostitutes in the County of London. Out of every sixty houses, one was a brothel. We reach the surprising conclusion that at a time when the male population of London of all ages was one and a quarter million, the prostitutes were receiving clients at a rate of two million per week."

That really boggles the mind, doesn't it?

This, to me, is the "Vienna" of Shakespeare's play; and it really isn't the image that usually comes to mind when one thinks of Vienna. Instead, it's what strikes me when I think of the seamiest side of Victorian London: the world of Jack the Ripper's Whitechapel, Dickens's Edwin Drood, Stevenson's Edward Hyde, the mad mass murderer Sweeney Todd . . . all of them representing the poisons lurking in the mud, waiting under the false social piety to "hatch out."

Another option that we have (of course) would be to set it more closely to Shakespeare's own time; although with the way that I've adapted the text and how I want to flesh out the characters and their motivations, I think the era of the civil war between the

Parliamentarians and the Royalty (1642-1660) would be a better option than the actual early Jacobean era, which is when the play was composed. Recall that this is also the time of the zealous Puritans with their holier-than-thou crusades . . . people such as Matthew Hopkins, the self-appointed Witchfinder General, who made a career for himself by traveling from location to location in the English countryside identifying troublesome "witches" (i.e., unpopular citizens of those communities) and providing a cleansing remedy (i.e., trial, torture and execution). Hopkins might be seen as a missing link between Shakespeare's Deputy Angelo and Salem's Judge Hathorne of the American Colony Witch Trials of 1692.

Music is usually a helpful key for me in finding my way definitively into the world that I think is most appropriate for how I'd like the play to be presented. This time, I'm finding this path more obscure, more elusive. I'm thinking of the coldness of Philip Glass. I like the austerity of a single keyboard; it needs to be spare, stark, forebodingly icy, like crystal; brittle. (Not stately, or very melodic.) Interestingly enough, I also keep hearing a scratchy gramophone recording of "Only a Bird in a Gilded Cage" when the needle sticks on a particular phrase and repeats . . . sticks and repeats . . . .sticks and repeats . . . .sticks and repeats . . . Or plays through the simpering and sentimental melody until the gramophone . . . winds . . . down . . . and . . . d..o..w..n . . . a . . . n . . . d . . . . . . .d . . . ..o . . . .

And there you have it; my own take on the contextual world of this very fascinating "problem" play of Shakespeare's; an interesting world to explore for actors and designers alike.

✧

Now . . . having dealt with imagining a playable foundation of an entire Shakespeare play—and not an easy one at that!—in a workable dramatic context, let's now have a go at applying some of the same ideas and principles to a few individual characters within several of the plays.

For example:

You are a graduate student, studying successfully at a university far from your home. You are, in the common critical parlance, a "perpetual graduate student"—you have always loved the classroom, the seminar discussion table, and the lecture podium (both sides of it). Put simply, you love to learn; the more you're exposed to new ideas and knowledge, the more you crave it . . . for you, it's a powerful, addictive drug. Although you're approaching thirty years of age, you have never forsaken your studies for more practical endeavors, much to your father's dismay. Your father, in fact, is a "doer" rather than a "thinker"; throughout your childhood, your doting mother has indulged and spoiled you (at least in the view of her often impatient husband), allowing you to pursue your never-ending study. You are an only child, gifted in intellect, sensitive by nature, yet also exposed to—and fairly proficient in—all of the athletic activities that young, upper-class "prep school" types enjoy.

You come from a wealthy and well-respected family. Your father is the CEO of a powerful corporate business—the stewardship of which has been a birthright of your family for many generations—and it has always been tacitly assumed that you will one day take the reins of that operation and continue your family's successful heritage. Your father would prefer that you take a more active interest in developing the foundational skills necessary to achieve that goal . . . .but nothing about the family business interests you nearly as much yet another enrollment in yet another university for yet another semester to study yet another scientific, historical or philosophical discipline, far from home.

For you, it is a good life. Your romantic interests are met by a relationship with the daughter of your father's closest advisor, a somewhat younger "girl next door" that you have known and been fond of for years. You see her every time you are home for a visit, and lately those visits have led to more intimacy between you, advancing the relationship to new levels of promise. Each new educational corridor leads you to yet another fascinating door, impossible to resist going through. You are admired and respected by all who know you, in spite of your father's mild frustration that you are frittering your life away in academia instead of fully embracing the challenges of life outside the "ivory tower." Your future seems filled with golden possibilities.

And then . . . the unthinkable happens.

You are suddenly and unexpectedly summoned home from your stimulating life at the university by the news that your father—a presumably healthy and vigorous man of late middle age—has suddenly died of an unexplained cause. Still dealing with the profound shock of this event, you arrive home to find that your mother has entered into a serious and intimate relationship with your uncle, your father's brother, who has always been a staple in the family business (which you have avoided any involvement in, to your father's deep chagrin). The surprising rapidity of this development disturbs you, adding to your deep mourning and grief over the loss of your father. You soon discover that the situation is even more pronounced than you imagined: your mother and uncle have moved quickly to seal their relationship with marriage, and your uncle has presumptuously stepped in to assume complete executive leadership of your father's corporation.

Unanswered questions haunt you: Precisely how did your father die? What was the cause of death, and why has it not been shared or discussed in detail with you? How long has this relationship between your beloved, indulgent mother and your uncle been gestating? Was it happening even before your father's death? How is it that your uncle could step in and assume complete control of your father's estate, apparently with your mother's complicit support? Why is there no talk of your own rights and heritage? Why have you been virtually excluded by your mother from all practical participation in the aftermath of these events? Dazed, depressed—and yes, angry—you prepare to return to your distant University home to reflect upon it all; but before you can depart, you are informed by your uncle—in a public forum—that your mother wishes you to remain at home for the indefinite future. You feel a prisoner in your own home!

Recognize this scenario? Substitute the kingdom of Denmark for "powerful corporate business", and you have the contextual setting that initiates the events of the most famous tragedy of Western literature, Shakespeare's *Hamlet*.

Such valid substitutions of dramatic context are important for all actors to make when preparing a role—but most especially for younger actors who are preparing for such an intimidating role as the Bard's Prince of Denmark. "I'm playing Hamlet?" the youthful actor exclaims. "How exciting! A dream role!" Followed rapidly by, "How in the name of Heaven am I ever going to pull this off?!"

The answer: step by step. Don't get distracted by the enormity of the big picture. Yes, the role has been played by the greatest actors that ever strode the stage over the past four centuries. *But none of them are you!* None of them have been inside your mind, have experienced your feelings, your unique perspective of life. Audiences will be coming to your performance, not to see the "perfect" Hamlet, but rather to see what *you* might do with the part. And the first thing you must do is re-define the character's given circumstances— the *personal context* in which the events of the story play out—in a manner that allows you to better embrace those circumstances in an imaginary setting which ignites your emotional life, with which you can relate. The scenario that I've outlined above is similar enough to the essence of the events that Shakespeare has laid out for his protagonist to offer the humbled actor a path into the life of an *icon*. With such a substitution, you will not focus on playing "one of the most challenging roles in dramatic literature"; instead, you will be playing a young man whose life could conceivably be your own.

That is how to use Stanislavsky's "magic if" in acting Shakespeare; very much like it is used in any contemporary play with more recognizable circumstances. If you have absolutely no idea what it would feel like to live the life of a royal European Prince, you seek a substitution that is closer to a life you can imagine that retains the same basic details. You *personalize* the role as much as your imagination allows. "What if" Stanislavsky says, "is the actor's doorway into 'living truthfully in imaginary circumstances.'"

And it is virtually impossible to live truthfully if you view the character you are playing as an icon.

Let's bring another Shakespearean icon "down to earth":

You are a young wife, married very happily to one of your country's most skilled, renowned and respected military leaders. Your husband is feared by his enemies, and celebrated by his allies. He seems to fear nothing on the battlefield; and yet he also has always treated you with the utmost love and respect. Your marriage is virtually ideal in all aspects . . . save one.

You are childless, although that was not always the case. Your son, the only offspring of your union, died in infancy. A sickly child, he struggled from birth; and in spite of your devotion to him and your best efforts at motherhood, he succumbed to his frail constitution, experiencing a scant few months of a harsh life. Although you know it is irrational to feel this way, you continue to blame yourself for his weakness and death. You and your husband rarely speak of it; less than a year in the past, it is still a trauma too intense for you both to accept. The unused milk for your child remains in your breasts. In some ways, your husband has been more fortunate in his distractions; civil rebellion within your country has necessitated his presence and participation in many battles over the past few months, far from your home. You have been left alone to confront your grief, in a house that is haunted by loss and memory. Your circumstances are made even more devastating by the knowledge that, because of your late child's difficult birth and its effect on your own body, you may never be able to conceive another child, even if you and your beloved husband chose to try.

After this devastating personal loss, all of the love and attention that you were prepared to lavish on your child must be directed elsewhere—and where more appropriate than your husband, his career and his welfare? From all reports, the current rebellion against the country's leadership is crumbling—due in large part to your husband's war-like prowess. He has the reputation of a human dynamo in conflict, a fighting machine; in action, his physical ability, tactical knowledge, and relentless determination to destroy his foes—not just defeat them—inspires an almost supernatural awe in friend and foe alike. Although his military career and its triumphs have thus far been unquestionably dedicated to benefiting his country's political leader, the question looms increasingly larger for you both as the years pass and his legend grows: Who really *deserves* to be leading your country? The weakened old man who currently holds the power with his spoiled and pampered sons, a man who relies on his stronger soldiers to preserve his decaying rule? Or the smartest, toughest, strongest, and arguably the most virile, powerful man currently in your country's landed hiearchy: your very own husband? In your mind and heart, he is the very best your country has to offer, and your country owes him the very best in return . . . .whatever it might take to achieve that. And with you at his side, believing in him and encouraging him, that position is finally within reach.

This is the context—personal and political—that sets the scene for Lady Macbeth at the outset of Shakespeare's darkest tragedy. She is not the devil incarnate—that approach defies actor empathy and playability; she is a devoted and loving wife, dealing with the devastating emotional loss of a child. She is a woman who loved her father dearly ("Had he not resembled my father as he slept, I'd have done it" she observes of the helpless, sleeping King Duncan, her husband's victim), a woman who will go to any length to secure her husband the honor and respect that she believes he truly deserves. She has enough vulnerability to be unnerved by the hoot of an owl in the night, and a sense of guilt that will ultimately not let her live with the violence that she has promulgated. From beneath the steely persona that she strives so hard to project, Shakespeare lets her fragility peak through, again and again. She is a living, breathing human being that any actress, younger or older, can relate to once they properly come to grips with her context. She need not be an icon.

One more:

You are an attractive young woman in your late teens, on the verge of adulthood. You're an only child. You've been raised in a very wealthy family, and throughout your life granted all of your needs and most of your desires from your very wealthy—but emotionally disengaged—parents. You live in near sequestration as a young socialite on a beautiful private estate, and yet your brief life has been filled with travel, attendance at the finest private schools, and publicized social events designed to show you (and your family) off to society with the greatest public relations advantages possible. It has been an extremely comfortable life, but it hasn't invested you with optimum "people skills."

Today, you experienced the first in a series of "coming out" parties arranged by your parents, planned for the purpose of introducing you to larger societal circles that herald a prelude to official adulthood; for you are now also officially of marriageable age. Present at the party were a number of young men from "proper" (read: wealthy and influential) families, especially identified as appropriate potential matches for a young lady of your particular assets. One of the drawbacks of the sheltered life you've led as a result of your class and wealth is a relative lack of social skills: you have virtually no close friends of your own age and, since you have attended only girls' schools during your adolescence, have limited experience with the opposite sex. You tend to cover the social insecurities brought on by this lack of experience with an assumed haughtiness, commonly found in nervous teenagers; you project to others that you are above the feelings of attraction and vulnerability that are felt by your less sophisticated and worldly peers. However, one constant companion that sees through your various protective emotional shields is one of your family's hired maids, personally assigned to see to your daily needs; a down-to-earth, friendly, no-nonsense young woman from a lower middle-class family, only a few years older than you are. She is fond of you, even while she often delights in bursting your bubbles of pretension; and although you would resist admitting it outright, she has been your closest friend and confidante for most of your later teenage life.

Today's party has been particularly stressful, as you have been paraded past a number of interested young men, all of whom your mother sees as appropriate suitors for you. None of them really interest you; all seem to you to be too aggressive, too immature, too unintelligent, or too boorish—save one. He interests and attracts you, and because you've never been comfortable with feeling even slightly out of control of your emotions, this disturbs you. Your best defense is that recognizable one of most teens: pretending that you don't care. ("Whatever.")

Your young maid, however, easily sees through your front, and astutely detects your true interest in this particular young man, as only another young woman who knows you well might. After this particularly wearing day, as you move into your private quarters to wind down from all of the soiree's activity, you begin to question your companion about her responses to these various young men—including the "special one"—with studied offhandedness, designed to cover your true interest. Your maid, however, will have none of this assumed neutrality of feeling on your part, for she has clearly perceived your attraction for this particular young lad.

And here we have the context that leads right into the scene introducing the protagonist Julia from *The Two Gentlemen of Verona*.

So context is always the entrance for any actor into the world of any play; a context suggested by the combination of the author's text and the actor's imagination. For our so-called "iconic" characters such as Hamlet or Lady Macbeth, defining the context in everyday terms with which you can identify helps you past an initial intimidation. For less familiar characters such as Julia—for whom Shakespeare supplies significantly less textual information and background for an actor to work with—defining context lends depth to their personality, making them more than simply "stock" characters when they walk upon the stage and journey through the story.

The world of the play, when it is thoroughly imagined and defined in detail by actors, directors and designers, becomes much more accessible for both artists and audiences in production. The individual characters, when placed within that context by an imaginative actor in terms that are recognizable and down-to-earth, live vitally and truthfully within that world's borders.

Always in acting, context is the cake. Text is the icing. But with Shakespeare, that's very tasty icing!

✧

Another aspect of fleshing out a character in rehearsal and performance that a young Shakespearean actor should fully embrace is that of discovering opposites. Most simply put: if you are playing a villain, search for his vulnerabilities; if you are playing a hero, find his character flaws. As people moving through our daily lives, we are amazing masses of contradictions. It is often the case that the more those contradictions become apparent, the more surprising, intriguing, and yes, attractive, people find us. It's no different with a dramatic character on the stage, in Shakespeare or in other plays; but Shakespeare is especially brilliant at leaving little clues and indications of those effective character "contradictions" throughout his plays. The Shakespearean actor must become a practiced detective at seeking those traces out, discovering their implications for the character he is playing, and giving them effective life on stage.

Literary critics examining the character of King Leontes in *The Winter's Tale* often complain of how "contrived" his inexplicable psychosis appears at the beginning of the play. Summarizing their concerns, these particular scholars conclude that Shakespeare simply needed a character personifying jealousy in order to begin the story's fairy tale journey from sin to redemption, from death to resurrection. The sensitive and attentive actor asked to portray Leontes, however, will find that the King's mad jealousy is not contrived nor mechanical, but carefully set up by the author both through the details of the play's opening situation as well as specifically revealed in a telling line of text which he speaks in his opening scene. It depicts the "opposite" side of this tyrannical, judgmental ruler of Sicily: a man who is still, in his secret heart, a small and insecure boy who has never really come to accept that he is either loved or loveable.

In the play's first public scene involving Leontes, his heavily pregnant wife Hermione, and a visitor to their court, King Polixenes of Bohemia, we learn the following circumstances: the two kings were fast boyhood friends (perhaps royal cousins) before geographical distance and regal responsibilities inevitably drew them apart. Polixenes is preparing to depart from Sicily for his own country after a long reunion (nine months, Shakespeare is careful to note in Polixenes's first line) with his old friend and his beloved queen. We will soon discover that it has been a rather emotionally exhaustive visit for all concerned: Polixenes misses his own son, family and court, Hermione copes with her second pregnancy, and Leontes . . . .well, we'll soon learn more about his private turmoil! As with all such reunions between old friends, they have discovered that much has changed between them in the ensuing years. Their experience is probably much like the middle school friends, once bonded so firmly, who encounter one another years later as virtual strangers. The mythos of their friendship and bonding still resonates in their memory . . . .but why does the relationship now seem so strained and foreign?

Leontes's energetic and insistent hospitality in the scene seems peculiarly hostile. He insists that Polixenes stay even longer as the kingdom's guest, and when Polixenes understandably demurs, he frames the invitation as something of a test of his friend's love. Leontes urges Hermione to second his invitation; a devoted and vivacious wife, she quickly accedes to the request. In fact, we soon learn that Leontes is greatly disturbed by how quickly Hermione steps in to issue her personal support to the invitation. ("Too hot!" Leontes exclaims in an aside, only moments after Hermione follows his wishes.) He is clearly disturbed by what he perceives as Hermione's eagerness for his friend to stay—even though she only speaks at her husband's instigation!

What's eating at Leontes? Well, clearly it has crossed his mind that Hermione conceived shortly after Polixenes arrived for his visit, nine months ago. (She will deliver her daughter, Perdita, only a few short scenes later in the play.) And Leontes interprets his wife's open, warm and generous manner with her guest as proof of her ulterior motives toward his old friend. However, another dialogue exchange moments later in the scene provides the clue to character that an actor seeks. Leontes recalls his courtship with Hermione, years before, in the following manner:

> *Three crabbed months had soured themselves to death*
> *Ere I could make thee open thy white hand*
> *And clap thyself my love.*

Not exactly the sound of a man who appears confident in the committed love of his wife, the mother of his children! At least in his own perspective, Leontes had to court his wife quite strenuously those many years ago; and ever since, he has apparently wondered if she indeed married him for love, or if she "settled" for him.

Here is an "opposite" that astute actors search for when building their character. Upon first reading of the play, by his actions, Leontes seems an irrational, unreasoning man, seemingly ready to condemn his wife and child to death presumably purely as a result of some unexplained psychosis. But if we more carefully examine the text, looking for an opposite facet to this apparently crazy tyrant, we soon might see him as a frightened, heartbroken little boy with inferiority and abandonment issues; and this opens up fascinating and inspiring vistas to explore for the eager and empathetic actor.

Many an actor playing Shylock, the Jewish moneylender, in *The Merchant of Venice* over the years have concluded that the predominant characteristic that drives him through the play toward his violently conceived revenge has been a white-hot anger that he harbors at the bigotry and anti-Semitism that has been leveled at him throughout his life by the Christians of Venice. However, the real key to a textured, multi-leveled portrayal of the "villainous" Jew lies in the clues about his family life that Shakespeare deftly slips into pivotal scenes.

For instance, let's take Shylock's one brief scene with his servant, Launce, and his daughter, Jessica (Act II, v): at first glance, the young actor will undoubtedly lock onto the haranguing tone that Shylock's lines seem to imply. He appears quite angry at Launce's decision to leave his service in favor of Bassanio (the young friend of his enemy, Antonio, and a recent recipient of a loan of three thousand ducats, provided by Shylock himself), and aggressively impatient with his daughter for little reason, worried about the possibility that she might sneak out to join the street revels in Venice. However, when the actor looks more closely at the circumstances, he finds the "opposite", as it were: Shylock's apparent anger grows out of a sense of pain and betrayal. He is hurt that his servant, Launce, whom he feels that he has sheltered well, fed well, and compensated fairly, has suddenly decided to leave his service in favor of a foe. Of course, he is abrupt and berating! It comes more of confusion and of isolation than of villainy; the petty lines he speaks, and the obvious, clichéd performance choices that they might lead to is a trap the actor must avoid at all costs in order to develop a layered, multi-dimensional character. Again, look for the opposite of what might initially seem to be the obvious choice.

And what of his ridiculously strict, overly reactive tirade against his teenaged daughter? Again, the actor should look beyond the text, focusing on the context. Shylock is a single father, and might have been so for a long time (precisely when his wife died is not specifically related in the text itself); he has raised his daughter single-handedly, while also working to provide well for her in the hostile, racist environment of the Venice depicted in the play. And why might he be so overly-protective of Jessica, to the point that he would attack her before she's even committed any transgression? Many reasons: he knows the prejudiced Christian community that surrounds his fellow Jews in Venice; his daughter (now a young lady) probably resembles his beloved lost wife (Leah); and he feels—as most men undoubtedly would when trying to find the right balance of discipline and love with an adolescent daughter, rapidly growing distant from him, even rebellious—lost and alone.

Shakespeare provides actors playing Shylock a brilliant revelatory moment of character and soul in Act III, i: upon hearing that his daughter has eloped with the young Christian, Lorenzo, abandoning him and her home and absconding with a good deal of money and family jewelry as well, he collapses in utter grief. His friend, Tubal, reports the rumor that she has given away a valuable ring in Genoa to a street mountebank in exchange for a pet monkey; to which he cries to his comrade, "It was my turquoise; I had it from Leah when I was a bachelor. I would not have given it for a wilderness of monkeys!" Not only has he lost his wife, his daughter, and the security of his home—he has also been robbed of an important sentimental remembrance of his youth and his lost soulmate. This could very well be the pivotal moment in which the jesting "pound of flesh" bond with Antonio turns, for him, deadly serious. He has lost everything, and he believes (perhaps correctly) that the world has done its worst against him. It is a searing moment that shows the opposite of the tight, disciplined, and often angry man that we see throughout most of his other scenes. If the actor fails to find the full import of this brief textual/contextual revelation in his characterization, his portrayal of Shylock will lose much.

More examples of key character "opposites": in *Coriolanus*, we are shown for four Acts a seemingly unsympathetic, hardened Roman warrior, a man who distrusts any emotion as a demonstration of weakness (he shows little for his wife and son), harbors very unattractive aristocratic snobbery toward those he deems lower-class "rabble," and repeatedly claims to be uninterested in any aspect of Roman society which is uninvolved with military honor and acclaim. All of this makes his "opposite" moment, when Shakespeare offers it in Act V,iii, all the more striking and dramatically effective. Leading a dangerous, but basically petulant attack upon the walls of his home city, Rome, he comes face-to-face with his own proud mother, Volumnia, clearly the cold, hard matron who has too strongly influenced her proud son's life and demeanor. The usually stoic Volumnia surprises us with a flow of pleas and tears, all directed at her "hard-hearted" son—who then, himself, at the forefront of the powerful Volscian army, surrenders completely to those tears. ("O mother, mother!/What have you done? Behold, the heavens do ope,/The gods look down, and this unnatural scene/They laugh at.") Both characters' true motivations and vulnerabilities are dramatically revealed to us in this, the climactic moment of Shakespeare's final tragedy: Volumnia is a mother unable to show affection and emotion, even toward her own son, and this has restricted and reduced her life substantially; while Caius Marcius (Coriolanus), raised by such an emotionally distant mother, has channeled all of his energy into gaining her approval by subsuming that unfulfilled love into battlefield violence. The entire play has been leading us toward this momentous "opposite."

Many a production of *Othello* has featured a Desdemona who only shows one facet: that of the naïve, innocent, virginal bride, thus setting her up to be seen by audiences as an archetypical victim. However, an analytically attentive actress preparing the role should see more depth, as Shakespeare has allowed her some very revealing moments that are, once again, somewhat "opposite" to that initial shallow image. In fact, this "opposite" is suggested before she even appears on the stage, as Othello describes the method by which he originally won her romantic interest: this "naïve innocent", hearing his personal history, has been totally enthralled and thrilled by the stories of adventure, violence, and exotic romance; so much so, in fact, that she initially approaches Othello with her romantic interest in him. ("She bade me," Othello says, "if I had a friend that loved her/I should but teach him how to tell my story/And that would woo her.") Rather a bold statement for such a shy lamb! Furthermore, she quite holds her own ground in some racy banter with Iago upon her arrival in Cyprus (Act II,i) which is full of obvious sexual innuendo; and in her later scenes with both Othello and Cassio, her text sometimes suggests a bit of exuberant flirtation on her part. And yet . . . .in her wonderfully effective private scene with Emilia in the play's climax (Act V,i), Desdemona seems genuinely horrified at the idea that a wife could ever bring herself to cheat on her husband with a lover . . . .even if she stood to gain the whole world by the act! Truly, this fascinating young woman is a study in potential contrasts.

Shakespeare uses these moments of contrast throughout his plays, both delighting and moving us in memorably key moments; thus, he uses "opposites" to great dramatic advantage in situation as well as character. (Although, as with most of the greatest playwrights, situation and character are rarely separable.) In Act I, v of *Twelfth Night*, the wayward jester Feste confronts the young Countess Olivia about her intention to remain in secluded mourning for seven years (!) after the death of her brother. (However, as we'll discuss in the next chapter, her reasons for doing so may extend beyond simple familial grief.)

FESTE: Good madonna, why mourn'st thou?
OLIVIA: Good fool, for my brother's death.
FESTE: I think his soul is in hell, madonna.

OLIVIA: I know his soul is in heaven, fool!
FESTE: The more fool, madonna, to mourn for your brother's
   soul, being in heaven.

The risk that Feste takes is fairly considerable: he calmly sets his mistress up for the ultimate point he desires to make to her, but he does so publicly, risking her wrath. The audible gasp that her attendants probably make in their response to Feste's assertion that the late beloved lord of the manor is in hell tells that story on the stage. In response to this outrageous statement, Olivia vents her anger forcefully; the attendants tensely await the consequences to Feste for this brash and tasteless jest. But then, with calm, gentle, almost fatherly wisdom, the "fool" quietly drives his point home. It can be a profoundly moving moment onstage, giving us a glimpse of both characters' hearts. Indeed, in many ways it sets a perfect tone of bittersweet humor, presenting the entire mood of the play in a single moment . . . .a moment of "opposites." In that instant, Olivia's indignant anger melts; and perhaps with tears glistening in her eyes, she asks her attendants, "Doth he not mend?"

A similarly striking dramatic moment occurs in Act II, i of *Much Ado About Nothing*. Beatrice (who has been involved in a "merry war" with Benedick for years, although it's pretty clear to everyone who knows them both that they are in love and destined for one another—if only they can negotiate the rocky journey from witty rivals to devoted partners) and her uncle Leonato have just paved the way for the young soldier Claudio to declare his love for Leonato's daughter and Beatrice's cousin, Hero. Don Pedro, Claudio's superior officer (and friend) in the army, has helped their efforts succeed. As the lovers embrace, Beatrice gives a theatrically melancholy sigh and initiates the following exchange:

BEATRICE: Good lord, for alliance! Thus goes every one to the
   world but I, and I am sunburnt! I may sit in a corner and cry
   "Heigh-ho for a husband!"
DON PEDRO: Lady Beatrice, I will get you one.
BEATRICE: I would rather have one of your father's getting.
   (meaning "begetting" in this joking context) Hath your

Grace ne'er a brother like you? Your father got excellent husbands, if a maid could come by them.

DON PEDRO: Will you have me, lady?

BEATRICE: No, my lord, unless I might have another for working days! Your grace is too costly to wear every day.

Although the text reads simply, it suggests what could be a beautiful and revealing moment for both characters in performance: what Beatrice hasn't noted in her joking public banter is that Don Pedro is making a serious offer for her hand. A moment later, looking in his kind eyes, she sees that her blithe dismissal has hurt and humiliated him. Quietly horrified, she adjusts her tone and continues:

BEATRICE: But I beseech your Grace pardon me; I was born to speak all mirth and no matter. *(An awkward pause is implied here.)*

DON PEDRO: Your silence most offends me; and to be merry best becomes you, for out a' question, you were born in a merry hour.
    (Perhaps with her eyes sparkling with tears, Beatrice continues, striving mightily to make light of it all:)

BEATRICE: No, sure, my lord, my mother cried; but then there was a star danc'd, and under that I was born. *(Turning from him to Hero and Claudio)* Cousins, God give you joy!

LEONATO: *(Gently helping her out of the awkward moment)* Niece, will you look to those things I told you of?

BEATRICE: I cry you mercy, uncle. By your Grace's pardon.
    (She exits)

DON PEDRO: By my troth, a pleasant-spirited lady.

Thus, in the midst of all the laughter and merry-making, a moment of slight heartbreak for both Don Pedro and Beatrice. It's another "opposite," the kind that abounds in our everyday lives. Joy gives over quite suddenly to melancholy, and vice versa. For the astute actor and director, these are small moments that crystallize Shakespeare's dramatic genius, and seem impressively sophisticated in their simple stage truthfulness, even in the midst of all the heightened language they employ. Three hundred years later, a Russian playwright named Anton Chekhov would perfect the use of this technique of situational "opposites" in theatrical moments, giving official birth to the psychological realism that dominated the Western stage throughout the 20th century.

For a final example of the importance of an actor uncovering effective contrasts and "opposites" when building strong characterizations and interesting interpretations, let's glance at one of the most famous of all Shakespeare's sonnets. Once young actors train themselves in text preparation to look beyond their first, more obvious perspectives and choices, they will begin to discover the real dramatic riches that lie just beneath the surface of all good dramatic writing.

Sonnet 116 holds the dubious honor of being the Shakespeare poem of choice for many young brides who wish a brief literary recitation as a part of their wedding ceremony. Here it is:

> *Let me not to the marriage of true minds*
> *Admit impediments; love is not love*
> *Which alters when it alteration finds,*
> *Or bends with the remover to remove.*
> *O no; it is an ever-fixed mark*
> *That looks on tempests and is never shaken;*
> *It is the star to every wand'ring bark,*
> *Whose worth's unknown, although his height be taken.*
> *Love's not Time's fool, though rosy lips and cheeks*
> *Within his bending sickle's compass come;*
> *Love alters not with his brief hours and weeks,*
> *But bears it out even to the edge of doom.*
> > *If this be error and upon me proved,*
> > *I never writ, nor no man ever loved.*

We've already touched on the iconic aspect of this particular piece of text: it's used regularly in wedding ceremonies throughout the country to symbolize the undying nature of marital devotion. In fact, most people who don't take the time to carefully examine the points that the poem actually makes (as opposed to just combing it for key phrases that support a preconception) might well conclude that this is a love poem that vows everlasting devotion for a potential lover or spouse.

But let's look more closely both at what we might deem the opposite of that first impression, as well as the apparent context of the piece as a whole. The first four lines seem to be a response to something, some "moment before" situation that the speaker feels begs for a strong reply. The strength of the reply is underscored by the use of monosyllables at key points in those initial lines: "Let me not", and "love is not love." (Monosyllabic words, as we recall, tend to slow the iambic rhythms down and add force to the speaker's words; and this adds to the impression that what the speaker has just heard has prompted an adamant response.)

So, let's play with the possible context here of that "cue for passion" that leads to this declamatory sonnet: suppose the speaker has just heard someone that he/she has cared strongly for say that "Our love was good . . . .once. I've cared for you, I still love you, but people sometimes outgrow each other. So, even though I still love you, I'm ready to move on. Sometimes love just isn't strong enough by itself to keep people together forever."

You are shocked. You are hurt. But you are also angry at what you see as the "convenient" way that your former lover justifies the choice to flush your relationship away so blithely. They don't seem to be truly taking full ownership of this decision, which is so emotionally devastating to you. *You have not really loved me at all*, you seem to be saying through the words of the sonnet. *In fact, you don't really understand what love is; so let me explain it to you:*

True love does not accept or succumb to obstacles (although life may deal us many along the way). It does not compromise in those struggles, or waver in the face of adversity; if it does, it is not true love. True love stands its ground. True love faces down storms. It is as constant as the Northern star. True love withstands the tests of time, and true love does not enslave itself to youth and physical beauty, as those things are transitory and fade all too quickly.

If it's *true* love, the speaker affirms (perhaps with an anger that is barely contained), it *endures*. If it's not, it will conveniently move on to the next shallow conquest. The speaker seems absolutely certain of that—or at least, he/she needs to project that in their argument; so certain, in fact, that if these assertions are not true, *then all love is illusion.*

A very powerful claim, that. One that seems to come almost from a place of aggression on the speaker's part, sparked by a passionate response to what he/she has just heard. His/her love has been true and faithful—and would have remained so—even if their partner's has not.

Sonnet 116 isn't quite the gentle, lovely poem that so many wedding presenters wish it to be. It is much more passionately resolute—and thus, perhaps even more appropriate for such a solemn ceremony. So, as an actor, always look beyond the accepted *iconic* interpretation which others—or a cursory first appraisal of the text on your own—might give you. Examine the text carefully for what it might suggest about the circumstances and *context*; and then explore the *opposites* and *contrasts* with imaginative gusto. If you do these things as regular steps in your acting preparation, Shakespeare will always surprise you. And reward you.

CHAPTER VIII

"As Thus":
Shakespeare Scenework: Plays in Miniature

Now, to work.

In this chapter, we'll attempt to combine much of the information covered in the previous sections in a practical manner. Here is where the creative collaboration between the actor and the Western world's greatest playwright really begins. Together, we'll work through several scenes from a few of the Bard's plays and explore behavioral options suggested and supported by the texts that will help bring the characters and dramatic situations to vibrant life on the stage. We'll use examples from all three of Shakespeare's Folio genres: Comedies, Histories and Tragedies. We'll take each scene in sections, printing the Shakespearean text first, followed by an examination of a possible performance approach. In all instances, we'll focus upon "translating" these plays and characters, particularly for younger actors, using the analytical techniques previously discussed.

Keep in mind, however, that all of these suggestions are simply possibilities for the actor to consider, not definitive answers. There are as many different potential characterizations and performance approaches as there are different actors. Don't feel limited by my suggestions here; instead, think of them as springboards that can lead you to your own individual perspectives and ideas. With a playwright as rich as William Shakespeare, there is never a final or a right conclusion.

Before we plunge in, a quick work about Shakespearean prose:

All of Shakespeare's plays contain passages in prose; often they are passages of comic banter, although not always. (One of the most beautiful passages in Hamlet—the one in Act II, ii that contains his famous observation, "What a piece of work is a man"—is prose.) Two of the most popular comedies—*Much Ado About Nothing* and *The Merry Wives of Windsor*—are predominantly prose throughout. In all of my Acting Shakespeare classes, as they begin their work and notice that a goodly amount of Shakespeare's plays are written in prose and not in iambic pentameter verse, students invariably ask: Do you scan prose?

The simple answer is no. However, that said, you may find that sometimes the rhythms of many prose passages in Shakespeare plays sound much like verse when they are spoken aloud. (In fact, many editors of the plays from the First Folio and Quartos have disagreed throughout the centuries on which prose passages might have been intended to be printed as verse, and which were not. Printing practices being what they were in the late 16th and early 17th Centuries, we should not always assume that the typesetters were slavishly following the layout of their source manuscripts— or even, for that matter, that such manuscripts were always entirely clear in their own delineation of verse vs. prose.) Not only do many modern editions disagree on whether certain passages were indeed originally intended by their author as verse; often, if they do agree that they should be verse, they do not agree on how that verse should be structured—that is, which phrase or word belongs in one line, and which would be more dramatically effective in the next. There is also significant disagreement between editions about which lines are meant as shared verse lines, and which were intended simply as short lines. As we've seen in Chapter IV, such decisions are fairly important for the actor when making choices that bring the character to life on the stage. The truth is, after consulting several editions of the play and considering the various editor/scholars' rationale, ultimately the actor may very well be left to make an informed, intuitive decision himself. That's a good thing, actually; it is one more vital step in the actor taking creative ownership in the role he's been charged with performing.

Verse or prose aside, it's most important for an actor to remember that virtually all of the other aspects of Shakespearean acting approach that we've covered thus far will apply as much to prose as it does to verse: Marking and using the antitheses;

finding the opposites and contrasts; noting the operative words in the text (although obviously the rhythms of verse will not be able to help you in denoting them in prose passages); identifying and imaginatively envisioning the metaphors and similes; expanding your passion and the importance of your fictional circumstances to support the heightened language. All of these things are as crucial in the prose passages of Shakespeare as they are in the verse.

(By the way: a common "rule" suggested by many literature teachers is that verse is spoken in the plays by the upper class characters, while prose is utilized by the plain-spoken middle and lower classes. Ignore this dictum; it can't be relied upon because it's simply not consistently supported by examples from the plays.)

We'll deal with the scenes in this chapter in the following manner: first, we'll outline the foundational circumstances and character contexts that inform the scenes; second, we'll take each scene section by section and examine what the text might be suggesting for possible acting behavior—where the important discoveries occur, and what dramatic responses these might elicit; and finally, a summary of the "journey" of each scene— the basic human situation that evolves, and how the characters have been changed by the revelations they've experienced.

Let's begin.

Twelfth Night, Act I, Scene v

The Characters:
Olivia, a Countess of Illyria
Viola, a woman from a foreign land, disguised as a boy
named Cesario
Maria, a gentlewoman attending Olivia (small speaking role in
the scene)
2 or 3 of Olivia's ladies-in-waiting (non-speaking)

The Context and Circumstances:
The Countess Olivia is a young woman, perhaps no more than 16 to 18 years of age. (While it's true that she has often

been played by actresses quite older than that, and there is no specific indication in the play text of her age, as we examine the scene more closely I believe that we'll find that her behavior and emotional state is significantly more explicable and justifiable with a younger actress playing the role.) Within the past few years, she has suffered two enormously devastating emotional losses: first, the death of her father, apparently the brother of her uncle, Sir Toby Belch; then, much more recently, the death of her older brother. (Olivia's mother is never mentioned; explicit mother/daughter relationships are curiously rare in Shakespeare's plays.) Upon her father's passing, we may assume that Olivia's brother assumed the supervision and management of the household, becoming his younger sister's guardian and surrogate parent; in such a role, he presumably would have stewarded her through her "coming of age" during her teenage years. He must have handled those emotionally turbulent years (made more so by their mutual grief for their father) fairly well, as the text makes it clear that Olivia actively grieves his recent death.

So as the play opens, Olivia is truly an orphan, alone, grief-stricken, and probably quite frightened, her situation even more complicated by several other factors. She longs for the comfort of a father figure to share her burdensome life, now denied her twice by unexpected deaths. Feste, her father's witty "fool" and confidante, has inexplicably disappeared, just when she needed him most. (We might explain this by considering that Feste's sojourn away—wherever it might have been—was prompted by his own grief; but that should be explored further by the actor playing Feste, as it will obviously illuminate the kind of man he is.) Her uncle, Toby Belch, instead of "stepping up" in her time of trial, has descended even further into alcoholism. (Toby is a "likeable drunk" for audiences in most productions of the play, but his humor and wit hints at a darker side beneath.) He wages constant battles with the ambitious and officious household steward, Malvolio—and whether Malvolio is played as a younger or an older man will determine much of the tone of the play as the story progresses. Olivia's gentlewoman, Maria, a slightly older woman who could ease her mistress's situation by helping to manage Toby's wild ways, is limited in her ability to do so by the fact that she and Toby have an ongoing romantic relationship; her loyalty seems to lie first with him, rather than with Olivia.

Olivia is now in charge of an aristocratic and wealthy household, complete with a staff of servants and a set of serious responsibilities, once managed by her two late male family members, and now under the sole command of an 18-year-old girl—a somewhat bewildered "Countess." But in addition to being bewildered, she is also besieged by an older man with obsessive romantic intentions, all directed toward her: the Duke Orsino. In today's legal system, Orsino's persistence would probably classify him as a stalker. He sends repeated and aggressively insistent letters to the young Countess, professing his passionate love for her and soliciting her hand in marriage. If there was a time when the young Olivia was ever flattered by this attention, that time has passed; she now seems quite exasperated by Orsino's obsession with her, and desires it to cease immediately. Perhaps it even frightens her. (After all, he is significantly older than she, and presumably more experienced in amorous matters.) With all of the matters currently demanding her emotional and intellectual attention, Orsino's daily—sometimes even hourly—messages of love are additional burdens which she does not need.

To put it in today's youthful parlance: Olivia is "stressed to the max." So, she decides to deal with her problems by *not* dealing with them; she announces to the world that she will be in mourning for her brother's death for seven years (!), during which time she will accept no visitors—and especially no suitors. Overwhelmed by it all, she is trying to dig a hole and pull it in after her.

Enter Viola into Olivia's Illyrian court; and she has her own problems, no less stressful than Olivia's. In fact, her problems aren't dissimilar: she's been washed exhausted onto the shores of Illyria after a terrible shipwreck in which she's also lost a brother—her beloved twin, Sebastian. (We'll find out soon that Sebastian has survived the shipwreck as well—but as far as Viola knows at this point, he's drowned.) No living parents for Viola are mentioned in the text, so we must assume that she, like Olivia, is an orphan.

Nevertheless, Viola presents a clear contrast to Olivia—she will not surrender to her tribulations, but will survive them in any way that she can. The particular way that she decides to go about this is readily recognizable to most Shakespeare audiences: in order to protect her life and chastity from predators in this strange land, she will disguise herself as a young adolescent boy and seek shelter and employment with the Duke Orsino, reputed far and wide (according to the ship's captain who survived the wreck along with her) to be a noble and honorable man. (She first considers seeking out Olivia to offer her service, but is prevented from that when she learns of the Countess's mourning seclusion.) Plucky and determined in the face of what could have been devastating grief, she asks the captain to escort her—in boyish disguise, and under the name of Cesario (the name referring to an "unnatural" birth)—to the court of Duke Orsino.

Shakespeare moves with characteristic rapidity to advance the story, for when we next see Viola/Cesario, she has already solidly ingratiated herself with Duke Orsino. Valentine, a fellow page, mildly complains that Orsino has precipitously (in only three days!) advanced Cesario higher in estimation and trust than the "old-timers" of the court. In other words, Orsino seems to feel a strange attraction to and trust of this boyish stranger—feelings that will develop with a beautiful mixture of poignancy and humor as the play unfolds. His feelings are clearly reciprocated by this new page, for Viola confesses in a solitary moment on stage that she has already fallen seriously in love with her new lord and protector.

Over the past few weeks, Orsino has been sending messenger after messenger to the young Countess Olivia with token gifts for her and vows of his everlasting love, begging her hand in marriage. Olivia has refused to even admit any of them into her presence. In sudden inspiration, Orsino decides that this charismatic new page is just the right courier to effectively win Olivia's ear—and heart—to his suits.

So, in Act V, scene v, the steward Malvolio informs his Lady Olivia that there is a new, insistent messenger from Orsino waiting at the gates of her villa; and this one says that he will not depart until Olivia grants him an audience. Buoyed in spirits by her reconciliation with the returning Feste (we examined that precise moment in Chapter VI), Olivia impulsively decides to receive this stubborn visitor; however, she will teach him a lesson for his rude persistence by playing a small practical joke on him. She instructs her attendant ladies—including Maria—to cover their faces with their ever-present mourning veils, always worn in honor of Olivia's formal grieving. Let this presumptuous messenger try to guess just which of the veiled faces belongs to the lady of the manor! Giggling with anticipation at the fun they will have at the hapless messenger's expense, the ladies await the entrance of Cesario—Viola in disguise—as the scene begins.

(Enter VIOLA to OLIVIA and her ladies)

VIOLA: The honorable lady of the house, which is she?
OLIVIA: Speak to me, I will answer for her. Your will?
VIOLA: Most radiant, exquisite, and unmatchable beauty—I pray you tell me if this be the lady of the house, for I never saw her. I would be loath to cast away my speech; for besides that it is excellently well penn'd, I have taken great pains to con it. Good beauties, let me sustain no scorn; I am very comptible, even to the least sinister usage.

Amazed and a bit exhilarated at winning the battle for an audience with the reclusive Countess, Viola enters the scene with determination and newfound confidence—and is immediately taken aback to find several ladies all looking pretty identical in their black dresses and veils. Recovering quickly, her first order of business is identifying the real Olivia from her ladies-in-waiting. Olivia mischievously evades Viola's direct question with her first line, and her attendants revel in the discomfiture of this forward "boy," Cesario.

Cesario plows ahead with the address that she has "conned" (memorized), commencing with the suitably grandiose greeting ("Most radiant, exquisite, and unmatchable beauty")—to which the ladies all respond with giggles at the inflated rhetoric. Viola/Cesario acknowledges their reaction by cutting to the business at hand. The moment is pivotal for the actress, as it allows her to show Viola's resilient sense of humor and self-deprecation, qualities that will allow her to survive and triumph over the many confusions and challenges that await her later in the play. We see that she is a good sport at her own expense. She once again asks for Olivia to identify herself, noting that she has worked hard to memorize and rehearse a perfect presentation of Orlando's missive, and that she would hate to waste such an excellent performance on the wrong person! The ladies again respond with laughter, this time mixed with some appreciation of Cesario's self-deprecating humor. Smiling at "himself", Cesario humbly asks the ladies to stop teasing her; she is too sensitive (comptible), even to the slightest of jokes. If the ladies continue to make jokes at her expense, they will almost certainly hurt her feelings!

OLIVIA: Whence came you, sir?
VIOLA: I can say little more than I have studied, and that question's out of my part. Good gentle one, give me modest assurance if you be the lady of the house, that I may proceed in my speech.
OLIVIA: Are you a comedian?
VIOLA: No, my profound heart; and yet (by the very fangs of malice I swear) I am not that I play.

Olivia is intrigued, in spite of herself. Orsino's previous messengers have all been painfully stiff, self-conscious, and humorless. This one seems different—he smiles, he laughs, he responds to teasing with teasing! He talks of his own sensitivity, even if in a joking manner! In fact, Olivia begins to realize, he doesn't seem to be fearful of his feminine side, as most testosterone-driven young men appear. (Small wonder, that; and the audience can begin to enjoy the irony of Olivia's growing interest, beginning in a small way with this moment.)

"Where are you from?" Olivia asks; and Cesario now has a chance to tease her in return. "I'm strictly charged to deliver one specific message," Viola/Cesario responds, "and it doesn't include the answer to that question." During this initial exchange, she has taken note of this one veiled lady's initiative in driving the encounter, and has concluded that she is, in fact, Olivia, the woman Orsino has sent her (as Cesario) to address; so once again, she asks directly. If the answer is yes, then she will continue with her prepared message.

"Are you an actor?" Olivia inquires, responding to Cesario's reference to resuming his performance. Again, her ladies laugh in enjoyment; after all, a "comedian" is so much more lowly and common than a "tragedian" in the acting hierarchy! Again, Cesario resists being put off her game. No, she says, calling Olivia a "profound heart" (a wise woman) in a slightly mocking return that hints at the truth beneath the disguise. Then, she delivers her own direct tease to her hostess, revealing slyly that, although she is not an actor, she is also not who Olivia thinks she is. This is, of course, true on several levels: in personality, in social rank, and in gender.

VIOLA *(continuing)*: Are you the lady of the house?

OLIVIA: If I do not usurp myself, I am.

VIOLA: Most certain, if you are she, you do usurp yourself; for what is yours to bestow is not yours to reserve. But this is from my commission; I will on with my speech in your praise, and then show you the heart of my message.

OLIVIA: Come to what is important in't. I forgive you the praise.

VIOLA: Alas, I took great pains to study it, and 'tis poetical.

OLIVIA: It is the more like to be feign'd; I pray you, keep it in. I heard you were saucy at my gates, and allow'd your approach rather to wonder at you than to hear you. If you be not mad, be gone. If you have reason, be brief. 'Tis not that time of moon with me to make one in so skipping a dialogue.

MARIA: Will you hoist sail, sir? Here lies your way.

VIOLA: No, good swabber, I am to hull here a while longer. Some mollification for your giant, sweet lady. Tell me your mind—I am a messenger.

OLIVIA: Sure you have some hideous matter to deliver, when the courtesy of it is so fearful. Speak your office.

VIOLA: It alone concerns your ear. I bring no overture of war, no taxation of homage; I hold the olive in my hand. My words are as full of peace as matter.

OLIVIA: Yet you began rudely. What are you? What would you?

VIOLA: The rudeness that hath appear'd in me have I learn'd from my entertainment. What I am, and what I would, are as secret as maidenhead: to your ears, divinity; to any other's, profanation.

OLIVIA: Give us the place alone; we will hear this divinity.
(MARIA and ladies exeunt)

Stubbornly determined, Viola again asks directly if the talkative veiled lady before her is truly Olivia. This time, Olivia admits it, but still a bit cagily: "If I've not overthrown my own title—that is, replaced (usurped) my self—I am she." Again demonstrating her sharp wit, Viola uses Olivia's own words against her to make a salient point: "If you are indeed the object of a good man's (Orsino's) love and devotion, you do depose yourself; as a woman, you have a responsibility to treat a serious and respectful suitor of your hand with equal respect—and acceptance." The audience already knows of Viola's own newfound love for Orsino, so they can perhaps forgive this somewhat impertinent statement. It appears that Viola herself quickly recognizes the bold bias of this opinion, for she immediately tries to steer the dialogue back to her prepared message.

Olivia, simultaneously fascinated and put off by this young boy's brashness, now speaks to him with clipped impatience: Skip the preliminaries and get to the point. "But I've worked so hard on crafting and memorizing the preliminary praise and greeting!" Viola protests; "Besides, it's nice poetry!" Olivia quickly parries Viola's thrust with a summary critique of poetry in general: It's untruthful by its very nature, and therefore, if her message is "poetical", it's almost certainly going to be an exaggeration or a lie. (A continuing critique of both poetry and acting by those of puritan natures which has been made through the centuries, and one that was particularly prevalent in Elizabethan England at the time of the play's writing.) This volley initiates a flood of irritation from Olivia: "You've been rude to my steward at the entrance to my villa, and refused to deliver your intentions to him as you were requested by me to do. Now again, get to the point! I'm no longer amused at you, and I'm in a bad mood today as it is." (The line referring to Olivia's "time of the moon" may also be a not-so-subtle indication of why she's more impatient than usual; although it seems quite unlikely to me that Olivia would share such an intimacy with a male stranger. Nonetheless, that choice is ultimately up to the boldness of an individual actress in the role.)

As if on cue, clearly understanding that her mistress wishes to terminate the audience, Maria steps forward to take Viola/Cesario's arm and usher "him" forcefully to the exit, using a nautical analogy: It's time to pull up anchor and sail away, she tells him. Viola cleverly continues the metaphor as she struggles to pull away from Maria's manhandling, stating that she means (as a ship) to stay in this harbor a while longer. She appeals to Olivia to call off her "giant" as the physical grappling continues. (Maria might indeed be a formidable physical presence; however, for a petite actress playing Maria, calling her a "giant" might be another attempt by Viola to use humor to defuse the situation.) "Talk to me," pleads Viola/Cesario to Olivia; "I'm a messenger, and I'm charged with taking your response back to my master." (It's interesting to note here that some modern editors give the line "Tell me your mind" to Olivia, not Viola; but the First Folio—there are no existing Quarto versions of the play—assigns it to Viola.) "You must have a frightening message to deliver," Olivia counters, "since your behavior is so aggressive." "I'm aggressive because it's a private message for you and not for anyone else!" Viola/Cesario responds: "I come to make peace between you and my master." "Then why have you been so rude?" Olivia retorts, and demands once again: "Who are you and what do you—or you master—want or expect from me?!" This meeting has clearly progressed from light fun to darker intensity in a matter of moments; emotions and stakes have heightened rapidly yet believably, a fine example of Shakespeare's dramatic skill.

Pulling free of Maria's clutches, Viola/Cesario, attempts a final, impulsive gambit. She reminds her hostess that if she has been as rude as charged, it has only been in response to the inhospitality that has been first served to her. Then comes the line that causes Olivia's maids to gasp in embarrassed astonishment at its complete inappropriateness. This cocky young "boy" claims that Orsino's message for her is as private as a virgin's hymen: to an intimate and respectful lover, a divine thing; but if heard by others, the figurative equivalent of a rape.

For a moment, the stage is silent as all the young ladies present absorb this incredibly impertinent statement from a male stranger who is well below the Countess Olivia in rank and status. What will the Lady do in response to this outrage? Call upon the steward Malvolio or her Uncle Toby to forcefully apprehend Cesario? Slap his face? Call for his imprisonment? Anything could happen. Then, after Olivia stares at Viola/Cesario for a long, suspense-filled pause, she draws a breath and issues her verdict: "All of you go away," she instructs Maria and her ladies; "I'll hear this man in private."

The ladies all exit . . . surprised? Worried? Slightly titillated? Who is this boy/man, anyway? He doesn't even have the beginnings of a beard yet; but look at the way he got what he wanted from the mistress, even when more mature and grounded emissaries from Duke Orsino had failed miserably. What can Lady Olivia be thinking?

The audience, however, is beginning to see what Olivia's thinking: no other young man has ever talked to her so directly, courageously, and wittily before, through all of her young, sheltered life. In spite of herself, she is intrigued . . . and more than a little attracted.

OLIVIA: Now, sir, what is your text?

VIOLA: Most sweet lady—

OLIVIA: A comfortable doctrine, and much may be said of it. Where lies your text?

VIOLA: In Orsino's bosom.

OLIVIA: In his bosom? In what chapter of his bosom?

VIOLA: To answer by the method, in the first of his heart.

OLIVIA: O, I have read it; it is heresy. Have you no more to
  say?
VIOLA: Good madam, let me see your face.
OLIVIA: Have you any commission from your lord to negotiate
  with my face? You are now out of your text! But we will
  draw the curtain, and show you the picture.
  (OLIVIA removes her veil)

The best defense is often a good offense; Olivia chooses
to deal with the confusion caused by her growing attraction
to this boy with aggression. In rapid-fire manner, she begins
to grill this forward messenger about his mission. When he
attempts to answer her first question, Olivia interrupts, using
the analogy of a clergyman who introduces his sermon with a
pre-summary of the lesson—or doctrine—that he intends to
address. His doctrine of compliments to her, she says, is a valid
one—but where lies the substance of the proposed "sermon"?
When the somewhat rattled Viola/Cesario responds that the
text of this "sermon" springs from Orsino's heart, the caustic
Olivia—continuing the analogy—wants to know from what
chapter of this book that supposedly lies in Orsino's heart.
"The opening chapter," Cesario responds; "the most important
one." Olivia dismisses it airily as containing a heretical theme.
Finally exasperated with the wordplay, as well as having to
talk to Olivia through her concealing veil, Viola/Cesario makes
a direct request for the young Countess to remove her veil.
Momentarily, Olivia seems nonplussed at Cesario's boldness;
then, her attraction prevails, and she uncovers her face. She
knows quite well how beautiful she is, and she obviously
wants Cesario to appreciate it!

OLIVIA *(continuing)*: Look you, sir, such a one I was this
  present. Is't not well done?
VIOLA: Excellently done . . . if God did all.
OLIVIA: 'Tis in grain, sir, 'twill endure wind and weather!
VIOLA: 'Tis beauty truly blent, whose red and white
  Nature's own sweet and cunning hand laid on.
  Lady, you are the cruell'st she alive

> If you will lead these graces to the grave,
> And leave the world no copy.

OLIVIA: O, sir, I will not be so hard-hearted; I will give out divers schedules of my beauty. It shall be inventoried, and every particle and utensil labell'd to my will, as: item, two lips, indifferent red; item, two grey eyes, with lids to them; item, one neck, one chin, and so forth. Were you sent hither to praise me?

VIOLA: I see you what you are, you are too proud!
> But if you were the devil, you are fair.

Revealing her beauty, Olivia adopts a haughty, indifferent attitude: "Here is my face," she says to Cesario. "Pretty nice, isn't it?" Clearly she's used to men reacting notably to her loveliness, and here tries to use that asset as a weapon to throw Cesario off balance, gaining the advantage in the encounter. And Viola is suitably impressed at this first sight of her gorgeous rival for Orsino's affection. Recovering quickly, she shows us an endearing humanity by throwing a somewhat catty remark back at Olivia: "Yes, you're beautiful . . . but how much of it is natural?" Olivia's temper flares at the implied insult, assuring this young male pup that everything he sees is truly hers, and not a painted mask. "How dare you suggest it!" we can hear in her tone.

Viola quickly backs away from her gibe, admitting with characteristic honesty that the young Countess is indeed exceedingly beautiful. And here the attentive actress playing Viola should take note of another significant shift: the prose briefly becomes verse, seemingly in an honest poetic tribute to her rival's assets. "You need to marry a man who loves you and have beautiful children," she pleads in this brief passage of fervent iambic pentameter, suggesting greater passion than before in the delivery; "You owe your beautiful genes to future generations." Noting Cesario's shift in tone and tactic, Olivia feels she has won the encounter; and she quickly resumes her studied haughty carelessness. "My features are just 'items' to be noted in inventory," she sighs, with (perhaps) a toss of her head. "Let me list them for you." And so she does, purposely drawing this strangely attractive young man's attention specifically to each and every one of them in a not-so-subtle manner: red lips, grey eyes, (lovely) neck and chin . . . "Are you here to praise them?" she asks in conclusion. (That's just so boring, she seems to imply.)

Amazed at what she sees as Olivia's blatant conceit about the gift of her own beauty, Viola cuts through all of the banter with one of the most astute and direct critical personal observations in all of Shakespeare, a precise slice that cuts into Olivia's immature and un-gracious pretensions like a scalpel: "I see you what you are, you are too proud!" Olivia barely has time to register this criticism before the ever-generous Viola softens it: "But even if you were the devil himself in your behavior, it can't rob you of your undeniable beauty."

Olivia is hooked. This young man is speaking to her as a human being, not treating her as an "object" as the other men in her life always have. Cesario's direct frankness is coupled with kindness and humor—a potent and attractive combination. From this point on, the scene appropriately transitions to full impassioned verse, even in the shared line dialogue exchanges.

VIOLA *(continuing)*: My lord and master loves you. O, such love
    Could be but recompens'd, though you were crown'd
    The nonpareil of beauty.
OLIVIA: How does he love me?
VIOLA: With adorations, fertile tears,
    With groans that thunder love, with sighs of fire.
OLIVIA: Your lord does know my mind, I cannot love him!
    Yet I suppose him virtuous, know him noble,
    Of great estate, of fresh and stainless youth;
    In voices well-divulg'd, free, learn'd, and valiant,
    And in dimension, and the shape of nature,
    A gracious person. But yet I cannot love him;
    He might have took his answer long ago.
VIOLA: If I did love you in my master's flame,
    With such a suff'ring, such a deadly life,
    In your denial I would find no sense,
    I would not understand it.

OLIVIA:Why, what would you?
VIOLA: Make me a willow cabin at your gate,
    And call upon my soul within the house;
    Write loyal cantons of contemned love,
    And sing them loud, even in the dead of night;
    Hallow your name to the reverberate hills,
    And make the babbling gossip of the air
    Cry out "Olivia!" O, you should not rest
    Between the elements of air and earth
    But you should pity me!
OLIVIA: You might do much.

Viola here launches into her final plea to Olivia: "Orsino loves you so much and with such an all-consuming love that he deserves to receive a little of that back . . . even if you were the most beautiful woman in the world!" Frustrated by this constant pressure of Orsino's love—now advocated by a young man that she is feeling a dawning attraction to herself—she cries out in anguished impatience: "How does he love me (if he continues to torment me with this unwanted courting)?" Viola details the deleterious effects that are resulting from Orsino's unrequited obsession; he cannot continue to live this way, she implies. Feeling both pressure and guilt (for she is far from heartless—only young), Olivia argues her position, hoping for understanding and empathy from Cesario. "I recognize that he has many gifts, and many things to offer the right woman," she declares, "but that woman is not me." Viola shakes her head in helplessness; it appears she has reached a dead end in her mission. "If I were doing and feeling for you all that Orsino is—and you refused to acknowledge it or respond—I would be absolutely bewildered by it," she says. This statement gives Olivia an unexpected opening; she asks Cesario what he would do to win her hand if he were in Orsino's place.

Much of Viola's strong feelings that have arisen in this initial encounter with Olivia are founded in her own secret love for Orsino, the very man for whom she pleads with Olivia. For a heart that burns like Viola's, with such an intense love and loyalty, this situation is both ironic and nightmarish. Out of that deep well now erupts the fountain of beautiful images that informs her response to Olivia's question, resulting in one of the most beautiful passages of poetry in the whole of Shakespeare's canon. Paraphrasing the passage would never begin to illuminate it further, and would certainly fail to do justice to the beauty of the portrait Viola paints of the hopeless lover who will slowly fade and die, singing the praises of the woman (or man, from Viola's perspective) who will never be his (or hers).

Its effect on Olivia is electric. She responds—tentatively? Breathlessly? With even a tender touch upon Viola/Cesario's arm (who has transported her own soul with her inspired and heartfelt response)? "You might do much," she breathes, and turning, Viola instantly understands the true—and unintended— effect of her spontaneous burst of poetry on the Lady Olivia. Olivia has fallen in love with the "character" of Cesario—Viola in disguise!

OLIVIA *(continuing)*: What is your parentage?
VIOLA: Above my fortunes, yet my state is well;
    I am a gentleman.
OLIVIA: Get you to your lord.
    I cannot love him; let him send no more—
    Unless (perchance) you come to me again
    To tell me how he takes it. Spend this for me.
    (Tries to give VIOLA a purse)
VIOLA: I am no fee'd post, lady; keep your purse.
    My master, not myself, lacks recompense.
    Love make his heart of flint that you shall love,
    And let your fervor, like my master's, be
    Plac'd in contempt! Farewell, fair cruelty.
    (Viola exits)

If all the groundwork has been appropriately laid, the comedic fuse of the play now begins to burn in earnest; as actors soon discover in their work on any such play, comedy is serious business. The more committed to their circumstances the actors are, and the less they worry about "playing" comedy, the more humor inevitably surfaces. As Olivia's newfound infatuation with this poetic messenger grows in strength—as it only can, perhaps, in the youngest and most inexperienced of lovers—so, simultaneously, does Viola's awareness of the spell that she has inadvertently cast upon the object of Orsino's love. Olivia advances—Viola evades. The audience, in on the joke, enjoys.

Recovering something of her emotional equilibrium—at least momentarily—Olivia tries to bestow the gift of a monetary "tip" to the subject of her amorous interest. At the same time, she asks that Cesario relate to the Duke Orsino that his love for her is hopeless, and that he should stop sending messengers to her villa; then, in a quick afterthought, she amends the directive slightly to say that she would be happy to have Cesario himself come again to her presence. Understanding the meaning behind that (and refusing the offered money), Viola/Cesario moves even more rapidly toward a graceful exit; but not before casting a mild "curse" on Olivia's heartlessness: "May you someday feel the frustration in love that you've caused my master." Like so many such pronouncements in Shakespeare's plays, this is destined to come true as the story evolves—at least until the comic situation is finally and fully resolved. Olivia, alone and charged with feelings both emotional and sexual—feelings that she's experiencing for the very first time—concludes the encounter with a confessional soliloquy that seems to gush from her at times.

OLIVIA: "What is your parentage?"
 "Above my fortunes, yet my state is well;
 I am a gentleman." I'll be sworn thou art!
 Thy tongue, thy face, thy limbs, action, and spirit
 Do give thee fivefold blazon! Not too fast! Soft, soft!
 Unless the master were the man. How now?
 Even so quickly may one catch the plague?
 Methinks I feel this youth's perfections
 With an invisible and subtle stealth
 To creep in at mine eyes! Well, let it be.

The primary question that young actresses playing Olivia struggle with is this: from where does this passionate love for Cesario—actually a woman in disguise—spring, and how does it come on so fast? In truth, the question becomes more problematical the older the character of Olivia is played. If Olivia is—as we have suggested earlier—a young lady still in her teens, saddled with frightening responsibilities and enjoying little help and comfort in dealing with them from the various men in her life (Toby, Malvolio, Feste), then she is undoubtedly in a state of high emotional vulnerability when the story begins. Completely inexperienced in amorous love, she's besieged by an experienced and obsessive older suitor. The messengers who have borne Orsino's prior messages have also perhaps been older comrades of the Duke, men like Valentine and Curio to whom we are introduced in the play's first scene.

Suddenly, this new messenger appears before her, a younger "boy/man" much closer in age to Olivia, with a manner both light, playful, and decidedly less intimidating. In every modern cultural age, for every generation, there usually appears a male "teen idol" in various media who becomes an iconic attraction, a first "crush" for young adolescent girls. The Beatles, Bobby Sherman, Justin Bieber, the Hansons, even Leonardo de Caprio in his earlier career. A young man, in other words, who is charismatic and attractive, yet who also projects an innocence that holds limited sexual threat for a young girl; a boy/man that they can feel both drawn to and secure with, while maintaining a sense of situational control. Someone, for Olivia, who is markedly different from the more sophisticated Duke Orsino. Details such as these might surely help young actresses encountering the play for the first time to find a foundation of truth in Olivia's given circumstances . . . a foundation that allows them to secure a solid degree of belief and faith in the rather unusual encounter between these two young ladies which we've just examined.

Viola departs Olivia's villa to deliver the disappointing news of her failure to win the Countess's love for her master; if anything, after seeing Olivia, she's now herself more in love with Orsino than ever before. Behind her, Olivia has already begun to pine for "Cesario" with an intensity that equals Orsino's obsession for her.

The comic circumstances have been expertly set up, and the play is off and running!

HAMLET, ACT III, SCENE I

THE CHARACTERS:

Hamlet, the Prince of Denmark

Ophelia, his former girlfriend, daughter of King Claudius's counselor Polonius

King Claudius and Polonius (in hiding and spying upon the scene; they do not appear or speak, but their suggested presence is rather important to the dynamics of the scene!)

THE CONTEXT AND CIRCUMSTANCES:

Apart from the balcony scene of *Romeo and Juliet*, this might be the most famous male/female scene in all of Shakespeare. That can make it extremely intimidating for young actors (for all actors, actually), so let's look at its basic human situation in fundamental terms:

We spoke a bit of Hamlet's context and circumstances in the last chapter, so we'll not go over the details of his initial situation again here. However, since the play's beginning, some fairly momentous events have occurred for the Prince, the most major being the appearance of the ghost of his murdered father, the elder King Hamlet, who has revealed to his son the treacherous details of his murder at the hands of his brother Claudius—with, perhaps (Hamlet has to wonder!), the complicity of his own mother (now Claudius's wife) in the deed. The revelation obviously affects Hamlet immensely—certainly driving him into a serious manic depression that perhaps borders on madness. The problems facing him are incredibly complex: having been absent for so long, he no longer knows who are his allies at the court of Elsinore, and who are his enemies. Whom can he trust? Not even his closest friend, Horatio; for the ghost of his father has sworn him to silence, forbidding him to share the accusation of regicide with anyone. His girlfriend, Ophelia, also happens to be the daughter of the man closest in confidence to Claudius, his counselor Polonius; so where can her loyalty really lie? And, perhaps driven by a guilty sense of personal responsibility (after all, the betrayal and murder happened while he was the perpetual college student, still studying at age 30 at the University of Wittenberg), Hamlet accepts the accusation of the ghost without question—at least, at first. Now, however, with more time to reflect upon the vision, he wonders how much faith and trust he can place in a message delivered in such an unearthly manner. After all, he muses in an earlier scene,

> *The spirit that I have seen*
> *May be a devil; and the devil hath power*
> *T' assume a pleasing shape; yea, and perhaps*
> *Out of my weakness and my melancholy,*
> *As he is very potent with such spirits,*
> *Abuses me to damn me.*

To top it all off, as a result of all of his university study (not to mention his own innate proclivity for the minute examination of all sides of an issue or theory) Hamlet is a reasonable young man, an intellectual, and a deep philosopher; thus, his nature isn't that of leaping into action impulsively. However, this is the murder of his father! Shouldn't he be moving more quickly toward some action, some confrontation with Claudius and his mother, some resolution? The brilliance of Hamlet's tragic situation lies in the sharp clarity of his personal conflict—and ours: normally, to move cautiously and slowly in assessing a serious situation is an admirable quality, showing mature restraint and judgment. But isn't that how he's conducted his entire life? As a watcher, rather than a doer? And what's been the result? If he had been more of a doer all along—like his heroic father, the late King— mightn't he have grown into the kind of son that could have prevented the murder of his own father, on the grounds of his own castle? If Claudius had perceived the young Hamlet as a manly threat—instead of a weak "egghead"—would he have dared to move so boldly against the king? And taken his widow to bed in the bargain? This is an enormous emotional burden that Hamlet carries!

But if Hamlet appears enmeshed in a complicated web of personal doubt and regret that "puzzles his will," Ophelia's situation seems no less devastating. In spite of the recent tragedy at the court of Elsinore, at the beginning of the play Ophelia seems fairly happy. And why should she not be? She has loved young Hamlet for some time; although younger than the Prince, she grew up at the court and has had her girlish eye on him for some time. Indeed, of late the relationship seems to have developed apace, perhaps because Hamlet has been more open to receiving the affection and comfort that Ophelia can offer him in his deep grief. In fact, the relationship has blossomed enough to catch the attentions of both her brother, Laertes, and of her father, Polonius. Concerned about her emotional vulnerability (and her chastity), both of the men in her family (again, like Olivia in *Twelfth Night*, no mother is spoken of in the play) warn her against allowing the relationship with Hamlet to develop any further. He is out of your reach, they advise her; a Prince will not—cannot, even—marry a "common" girl like Ophelia, even if she is the daughter of an important courtier like Polonius.

But does this advice come too late to preserve Ophelia's virginity? There is some reason to think so, based upon the intensity of the young lady's emotions revealed in later scenes when she descends into both melancholy and madness as the play's events unfold, death surrounds her, and her relationship with Hamlet slips away. Hamlet speaks lasciviously and with startling sexual innuendo to her—publicly, no less—in the "play within the play" event of Act III, scene ii (not to mention what is implied in the scene we're about to examine). In her famous and challenging "mad scene" in Act IV, scene v, Ophelia makes several references to sexual knowledge, romantic and practical, including carrying a flower whose herbal qualities were known by midwives to induce spontaneous abortions. Considering all of these textual clues, the actress should, at the very least, consider the dramatic possibilities inherent in a potential characterization of a young girl who has been impregnated by a Prince, whom she loves; then inexplicably abandoned by him; then physically and verbally abused by him; and finally, after all of this trauma, left heartbroken and alone when the Prince apparently loses his mind and murders her father during a confrontation in the Queen's own chambers!

So, in the present scene, here is our situation: Ophelia, in her early stages of pregnancy, is terrified and alone. Her father has forbidden her to see Hamlet privately, and Hamlet has avoided her as well, and behaved remarkably strangely whenever she does see him publicly. She can tell no one about her condition, and is desperate to seek comfort from her former lover. Meanwhile, her father Polonius has convinced himself that Hamlet's recent bizarre behavior has resulted from his enforced isolation from Ophelia; in other words, his unrequited (that's what he thinks!) love for the royal counselor's daughter has driven the young Prince to distraction. To prove this theory to King Claudius, he instructs Ophelia to confront Hamlet in a room of the palace and return to him all of the love-tokens that he has given her in their past courtship. While this happens, Polonius and Claudius will hide themselves in the room, eavesdrop upon the encounter, and witness Hamlet's reaction. Poor, distressed Ophelia; to whom does she owe the most loyalty? To her father? To the good of the state? To her estranged lover, possibly the father of an unborn child in her womb? In this scene, she will try to walk a fine line between reluctant obedience to her father and her king, and her desperate love for Hamlet.

To intensify the situation, Hamlet himself has apparently reached a low point in his musings and mood. What is he doing, he asks himself, wasting time and wit while his father's murderer revels in his power as well as in his bed—both of them his late father's, and the former rightfully his! Should he believe a ghost, and risk eternal damnation if he's mistaken? Should he act boldly now, or seek conclusive evidence first? Is he a coward, playing around with tricks and banter, when the situation demands assured and violent action? And what of Ophelia? Does he love her? Does love matter? Ultimately, does anything matter? Or is life simply a cruel joke that we all live out uselessly for the ultimate reward of eternal oblivion? Put bluntly, Hamlet is in the depths of a serious clinical depression which he begins to doubt that he can ever climb out of. As another Shakespeare character puts it (Hermione in *The Winter's Tale*), life now seems to him no commodity (no gift). And when one finally reaches that point, he muses, what is the best—the noblest—choice to make? It is at this crucial juncture that the two young lovers are brought face to face, after weeks of separation and loneliness. Claudius and Polonius hide, Ophelia waits reluctantly to play her part, and Hamlet enters.

HAMLET: To be, or not to be: that is the question!
    Whether 'tis nobler in the mind to suffer
    The slings and arrows of outrageous fortune,
    Or to take arms against a sea of troubles,
    And by opposing, end them. To die, to sleep—
    No more; and by a sleep to say we end
    The heartache and the thousand natural shocks
    That flesh is heir to; 'tis a consummation
    Devoutly to be wish'd. To die, to sleep—
    To sleep, perchance to dream—ay, there's the rub!
    For in that sleep of death, what dreams may come
    When we have shuffled off this mortal coil
    Must give us pause. There's the respect
    That makes calamity of so long life!
    For who would bear the whips and scorns of time,
    Th' oppressor's wrong, the proud man's contumely,
    The pangs of despis'd love, the law's delay,
    The insolence of office, and the spurns
    That patient merit of th' unworthy takes,
    When he himself might his quietus make
    With a bare bodkin? Who would fardels bear,
    To grunt and sweat under a weary life,
    But that the dread of something after death,
    Th' undiscover'd country from whose bourn
    No traveler returns, puzzles the will,
    And makes us rather bear those ills we have
    Than fly to others that we know not of?
    Thus conscience does make cowards of us all!
    And thus the native hue of resolution
    Is sicklied o'er with the pale case of thought,
    And enterprises of great pitch and moment
    With this regard their currents turn awry,
    And lose the name of action.

This most famous Shakespearean soliloquy from the most famous Shakespearean tragic hero comes at the nadir of his mood and fortunes. He has spent his time since the visitation of his father's ghost weighing the pros and cons of all options in addressing his situation, while brooding intensely about issues of personal betrayal, semblance vs. reality, and the existential aspects of life's brief journey. His love (Ophelia) is lost to him; for their mutual good, for better or for worse, he has chosen to break off the relationship. He has sworn to hide what he has learned about his father's murder from his dearest friend (Horatio). From his perspective, his own mother has chosen her lust for Claudius over her blood bond to her son. And now, when all circumstances seem to cry out for him to take action—some action, any action—he is discovering that, in spite of all his years of reading the great works of literature, philosophical study, and education at the best universities of Europe, he doesn't really know what to do, and thus feels cripplingly impotent and useless. He is dealing with the severest form of mental and emotional depression, feeling totally isolated, and the question is no longer what action to pursue, but whether or not it is even desirable, in his current state of feeling, to draw another breath. Life has become so painful and lonely for him that the central question has now become whether it is worthwhile continuing along any path. Is it nobler—as nobility has always been one of Hamlet's clear ideals—to fight all of the injustices he sees around him? Or should one simply surrender to oblivion, escaping all of the unbearable angst of questioning and determining what is right and what is wrong? If sleep brings some relief from the ever-present demons of his mind—and death is simply a permanent sleep—then what should prevent him from taking the simple step to insure that his next sleep is a permanent one? Hamlet truly stands upon a precipice in this moment: suicide is not an abstract consideration, it is an immediate and viable option that, in this present moment, he feels prepared for, even reconciled to.

But wait, he thinks; let's examine that analogy of sleep and death a bit more closely. Sleep isn't simple oblivion—for there are dreams; and those dreams can be lovely, horrifying, or even both. We are helpless in the face of them, helpless to control them. How would it be to find yourself—in the "sleep" of death—locked in an eternal nightmare, a literal hell from which there was no hope of ever awakening? It's a devastating vision for Hamlet, for it throws a fearful obstacle in the path of what he thinks might be his best, final hope of escape and release from deep depression and emotional pain: even death might bring no release! Indeed, it might bring on a new reality that would make his current reality seem like a paradise. If that were not true—if the devil that you know was often much better than the devil that you don't know—then why would people who suffer so much through life's bitter events ever choose to continue their pain? Wouldn't *nothing* be preferable? Ah, but what if it weren't nothing, but instead, something *much worse* than we could even imagine? That's what keeps us all here in this often unbearable world, he realizes, cowering in the face of what *might be* above what is. So in the course of this famous soliloquy, Hamlet comes to discover that even the comfort of suicide as a final resort is effectively denied him. "Nothing is neither good nor bad, but thinking makes it so," Hamlet observes a little earlier in the play to his comrades Rosencrantz and Guildenstern; and here, thinking has once again frozen his will to act. For someone as depressed as the Prince is in his current circumstances, this discovery seems devastating—and perhaps, simultaneously, bitterly funny in its absurdity.

HAMLET: *(continuing)* Soft you now,
  The fair Ophelia. Nymph, in thy orisons
  Be all my sins rememb'red.
OPHELIA:Good my lord,
  How does your honor for this many a day?
HAMLET: I humbly thank you, well; well, well.

As Hamlet comes to the conclusion of his rather dark inner journey, Ophelia uncomfortably makes her commanded appearance before him. She seems furtive, shy, frightened, and desperately needy. She wants to speak to Hamlet—after all, they have not had that opportunity in some time, and her early pregnancy (if my previously noted surmises on that issue are adopted by the actress) proceeds apace. Most of all, she loves and misses him, and—along with others in the court, but for different reasons—she is concerned about the changes she's observed in him; the distance, the coldness, the cynically mad wit. Is he all right? Has he missed her at all? Does he need her, as she knows she needs him? At the same time, she's ever aware that her father, along with King Claudius, listens from their hiding place to every word exchanged between her and her erstwhile lover.

To her great relief, Hamlet speaks to her first. Although relatively impersonal, his words still hold a touch of warmth and gentleness: he asks her to remember him in her prayers. Addressing him with somewhat awkward formality, she asks him how he's been, slipping in a slight reproach to him with "this many a day", thus noting that he's been absent from her for some time—perhaps avoiding her? Hamlet expresses "humble" appreciation for her concern (he seems to know that he's caused her pain); then replies with an interesting repetition of the word "well" three times. (NOTE: This repetition only occurs in the Folio version of the play, and neither of the two Quartos; as thus, it might be concluded that the repetition indicates stage business that was practiced in an early performance by Richard Burbage or one of his immediate successors in the King's Men.) There are many options for the inventive actor in dealing with this repetition: Is it a "throwaway"? (Not a good acting choice!) Does each "well" indicate a different feeling coming to the surface? Is Hamlet trying to tell Ophelia something deeper than any words can express? Are the words accompanied by some physical action? (A kiss on each cheek, for instance, or a touch to her hand, her face, her hair.) After a silent moment of gazing in one another's eyes and saying nothing further—for what else can he say under the current circumstances—Hamlet turns to leave.

OPHELIA: My lord, I have remembrances of yours
    That I have longed long to redeliver.
    I pray you now receive them.
HAMLET: No, not I;
    I never gave you aught.
OPHELIA: My honor'd lord, you know right well you did;
    And with them words of so sweet breath compos'd
    As made these things more rich. Their perfume lost,

Take these again; for to the noble mind
Rich gifts wax poor when givers prove unkind.
There, my lord.

Ophelia stops him with the words "My lord"; she then produces (from the bodice of her dress? Pressed in a prayerbook?) a ribbon-bound collection of letters, notes, poems, and small gifts—all that she has received from her lover during their better times together—and sadly, tentatively holds them out to him. (In scanning the line, actresses should note that Shakespeare has helped them deal with the coupling of "longed long"—"I've wanted to do this for some time," in other words—in their speech by the way the iambics are structured: "long-ed" is spoken as two syllables, making the pairing easier to speak and easier to hear and understand.) The sight of the small parcel in Ophelia's trembling hands must have a profound effect on Hamlet's heart, especially at the height of the vulnerability that we've seen revealed in his soliloquy. Why does he deny that he gave her these gifts? Is it to be "cruel, only to be kind," as later in the play he says to his mother? Is it because he truly sees himself as a different person now from the one who was involved with this girl in the past, as recent events have irrevocably changed him? Or is he telling her subtly to forget him—that their time together is over, and it can never be again?

Whatever his motivation may be for the denial, the heartbroken Ophelia will not accept it passively. Suppressing her tears and finding her strength, she stops Hamlet's attempt to turn away, perhaps physically, perhaps only with her voice. (Note Hamlet's short line "I never gave you aught"; during the silent beats is when such physical action might occur.) What is going on with you? her subtext seems to cry out. You gave me these things, and you did so with true feeling! Gathering herself with a shaky breath, she acknowledges that perhaps he has now lost those feelings for her that he once had; and if that is indeed the case, then it's even more appropriate that she return these physical tokens of an affection that he no longer feels for her. Slowly, hoping against hope that he will stop her, she gently and sadly puts the parcel in her lover's hand. He stares down at it as her fingers linger on the touch of his hand; but as the pause stretches out, she realizes that he's going to accept the return without further protestation. As her emotion wells up even further, she turns quickly away and starts to leave this excruciating encounter that her father has pushed her into.

HAMLET: Ha, ha! Are you honest?
OPHELIA: My lord?
HAMLET: Are you fair?
OPHELIA: What means your lordship?
HAMLET: That if you be honest and fair, your honesty should admit no discourse to your beauty.
OPHELIA: Could beauty, my lord, have better commerce than with honesty?
HAMLET: Ay, truly; for the power of beauty will sooner transform honesty from what it is to a bawd than the force of honesty can translate beauty into his likeness. This was sometime a paradox, but now the time gives it proof.

Hamlet's next words stop her dead in her tracks; and it's not so much what he says as the harsh whiplash sound of his words. Initiated with a humorless laugh, he rapidly questions in staccato syllables both her integrity and her beauty. His tone is cruel, probably in response to his own pain; here is a man absolutely pushed to his emotional limits. While this doesn't excuse the way he behaves toward Ophelia, perhaps we can at least understand it better in light of what he has shared with us in the earlier soliloquy about his current state of mind. It's also important to note that at this point in the scene, the iambic pentameter verse is dropped; instead of flowing or shared lines between the estranged lovers, the text itself becomes clipped and brittle prose.

Hamlet initiates the exchange with an aggressive int-errogation, hardly waiting for Ophelia's bewildered responses. "Are you honest?" is not only inquiring as to her truthfulness; it also touches upon her ability to be faithful in love as well as the state of her virginity (a particularly cruel question for him to ask her if we're indeed correct about the nature of their past relationship!). "Are you beautiful?" he asks her next—a question for which Ophelia can really give no "right" answer. That hardly matters, as Hamlet gives her no time to respond, verbally pushing her to the wall with a barrage of cynical observations, words that are less about Ophelia herself than about his own worldview. After all, if his own mother appears to him to behave as a harlot, then what must he conclude about womanhood in general?

He personifies "Beauty" and "Honesty" and asserts to Ophelia that if both of these "people" live within her, they should not have discourse (a sexual "discourse"/intercourse is subtly implied here, as that is close to Hamlet's mind). Why? Because the "better angel" (see Sonnet 144) will inevitably be corrupted and diseased by the worser one; superficial beauty and lust will conquer all that is good in the human soul with every encounter, he says. Taken aback by his sudden anger, Ophelia tries weakly to protest that view, but Hamlet will have none of it. Perhaps this corruption wasn't so pervasive in previous, more ethical eras, he says; but in the present state of the kingdom of Elsinore, it is now the norm.

HAMLET: *(continuing)* I did love you once.
OPHELIA: Indeed, my lord, you made me believe so.
HAMLET: You should not have believ'd me; for virtue cannot so inoculate our old stock but we shall relish of it. I lov'd you not.
OPHELIA: I was the more deceiv'd.
HAMLET: Get thee to a nunn'ry; why wouldst thou be a breeder of sinners? I am myself indifferent honest, but yet I could accuse me of such things that it were better my mother had not borne me! I am very proud, revengeful, ambitious, with more offenses at my beck than I have thoughts to put them in, imagination to give them shape, or time to act them in. What should such fellows as I do, crawling between earth and heaven? We are arrant knaves all; believe none of us. Go thy ways to a nunn'ry.

In the midst of his general tirade against the moral nature of the current times (of which his personal situation is a microcosm), Hamlet's agitated attention suddenly centers on his stricken lover's eyes. "I did love you once," he says to her. Is this the truth, at least as he sees it now? Does he really no longer love her? Is he discovering that he did truly love her, even as he speaks the words? Is he trying to push her away from caring for him in these dangerous times, for her own personal welfare, out of his love for her? All of these are valid options for the actor playing Hamlet to explore; but whatever motivates the statement, we can almost hear Ophelia's heart break upon hearing the words. "I believed you did," she says, much like a lost little girl; to which Hamlet bluntly responds, "You shouldn't have."—for he, like all of those who people the court of Elsinore and the world that surrounds it, is so corrupted in his nature that even a young innocent spirit like Ophelia's cannot heal him. (By the horticultural metaphor he uses here, the "stock" of his own ills cannot be bettered by grafting the stock of Ophelia's purer nature onto his line—it will not "take.") He chooses to be even harsher, ripping the bandage off the wound in one sweep: "I lov'd you not," he now tells her—not even in their past times together. Crumbling before him, yet still trying to hold onto some shred of her emotional dignity, Ophelia says simply, "I was the more deceiv'd"; perhaps she even starts to leave.

But whatever drives him, Hamlet isn't finished with her yet. He gives her a last piece of cutting advice: "Get thee to a nunnery." In Tudor times, this held a double meaning: the literal one (a spiritual haven for the Church's brides of Christ), as well as being a slang reference for a brothel, a whorehouse. Which does he mean for Ophelia? Either—and both. Why would you want to live a so-called moral life, bringing more children into this corrupt world? he challenges her. (The "breeder of sinners" reference is another cruel touch, referring to her in animalistic terms.) Even I, he points out, who am not a particularly evil person—even I have so many faults and sins in my nature that they can't even be listed or named. (It's quite fascinating that he notes here that "revengeful" is one of his sins, since he seems so very reluctant to take the violent action against Claudius that he feels is deserved!) Vile humanity doesn't need to be propagated any further, he asserts to her; therefore, a nunnery (of either kind) is where any "honest" woman belongs in this tattered and decadent world.

HAMLET: *(continuing)* Where's your father?

OPHELIA: At home, my lord.

HAMLET: Let the doors be shut upon him, that he may play the fool nowhere but in his own house! Farewell.

OPHELIA: O, help him, you sweet heavens!

HAMLET: If thou dost marry, I'll give thee this plague for thy dowry: be thou as chaste as ice, as pure as snow, thou shalt not escape calumny! Get thee to a nunn'ry, farewell. Or if thou wilt needs marry, marry a fool, for wise men know well enough what monsters you make of them. To a nunn'ry go, and quickly too. Farewell!

OPHELIA: Heavenly powers, restore him!

HAMLET: I have heard of your paintings well enough: God hath given you one face, and you make yourselves another. You jig, you amble, and you lisp, you nickname God's creatures and make your wantonness your ignorance. Go to, I'll no more on't!

Even as he moves to leave her, something happens to prompt Hamlet's suspicion. Is it a sound from Claudius's and Polonius's hiding place? A quick glance by Ophelia their way? Or perhaps a pure intuitive response on his part? Whatever it may be, Hamlet suddenly seems fully aware for the first time of what is truly going on here: he's being spied upon by his enemies, who are using Ophelia as "bait" for him to reveal more of himself and his intentions. He asks her directly of her father's whereabouts, seemingly already knowing the answer; for when, both frightened and distraught, she chooses to lie in response, he flies into a rage at what he perceives as her betrayal. Not content to simply leave the scene, he attacks her even more directly and cruelly: he curses her—always a more serious action in Elizabethan times than we tend to hold it today. Whomever she marries—if she marries (that it won't ever be him is clearly implied)—however chastely she behaves, she will still be seen as the whore that she is by all around her. In fact, only a fool would ever believe that she is anything but corrupt.

Ophelia, scared and broken by his words, still prays aloud and desperately for God—or some emissary from Heaven—to come to the aid of her seemingly mad lover. Still raging at her deception, Hamlet continues to abuse her verbally—and now perhaps physically as well. He spills out a litany of misogynistic charges against women in general, for he now feels that both of the important women in his life have proven irredeemably treacherous. He rails on women painting their faces to "fool" their lovers—a very symbol of duplicity itself—and using their bodies to entice ("jigging" and "ambling"), and "lisping" like little girls to pretend innocence that they no longer possess. They are the embodiment of affectation and deceit, cooing over animals, giving them pet names, acting naïve—while all along plotting and conniving to get what they want from those around them. "I'll have no more to do with them!" Hamlet asserts, resembling in that moment nothing so much as a hurt child abandoned by his mother. Then, at the very height of his fury, as if awakening from a dream, he again sees and hears the "fair Ophelia", shivering and sobbing in the sudden silence.

HAMLET: *(continuing)* It hath made me mad. I say we will have no more marriages. Those that are married already, all but one shall live; the rest will keep as they are. To a nunn'ry, go.
    (Hamlet exits)
OPHELIA: O, what a noble mind is here o'erthrown!
    The courtier's, soldier's, scholar's eye, tongue, sword,
    Th' expectation and rose of the fair state,
    The glass of fashion and the mould of form,
    Th' observ'd of all observers, quite, quite down!
    And I, of ladies most deject and wretched,
    That suck'd the honey of his music vows,
    Now see that noble and most sovereign reason
    Like sweet bells jangled, out of tune and harsh;
    That unmatch'd form and stature of blown youth
    Blasted with ecstasy. O, woe is me
    T'have seen what I have seen, see what I see.

The actor playing Hamlet has multiple choices to make in this scene; and all of my suggestions are just that: suggestions. They are not the *right* choices, only options. However, using the idea of finding "opposites" in key stage moments to achieve striking and memorable effects, an opportunity presents itself here. Instead of continuing to climb the heights of rage, Hamlet could make a present-tense discovery about both himself and Ophelia at this point in the scene: he could truly realize that his depression and resultant rage has taken him somewhat "'round the bend", and that his feigned madness no longer seems so feigned, but dangerously real; and he could also realize the full extent of what all of this has cost the young woman whom he truly loves, in spite of the awful situation in which they now find themselves. He takes Ophelia in his arms, sadly, tenderly and almost whispers in realization: "It hath made me mad!"

The proclamation about marriages is uttered for the benefit of the eavesdroppers that Hamlet now knows are present in the room, a coded threat against his enemy and his father's murderer, Claudius. Then, in one final private moment between them, Hamlet kisses Ophelia, looks deeply into her eyes—as they once did in happier times together—and tells her again to leave this place and, in effect, save both herself and her honor: "To a nunn'ry go." Then, releasing her, he is gone.

For Ophelia's final brief soliloquy, Shakespeare returns from prose to verse as the young girl struggles to make sense of all that has just occurred. Notably for the actress, the primary focus of her concerned response seems to be Hamlet's mental and emotional welfare, not her own very significant problems that have arisen as a direct result of that "madness." She lists all of his attributes, as she sees them: he is an indisputable scholar, knows all the manners and behaviors required of the best courtier, he speaks well, knows the weaponry and tactics of war (does he?) . . . he holds a physical form everyone admires, and all look to him as the symbolic hope of Denmark's future. (We might wonder if her talk of his "form" is the subjective view of a lover—after all, Gertrude in Act V, scene ii says of her son that "he's fat, and scant of breath"—although "fat" in this context, at least according to the Riverside Shakespeare notes, might mean "sweaty." Hmmm.) Only in the latter half of her brief soliloquy does she begin to note just how awful an effect all of his current deterioration has had on her own psyche and physical well-being. Just in the prime of his manhood—just when they should be finding the most happiness together—his "ecstasy" (madness) has dashed it all to pieces. "Oh woe is me/ T'have seen what I have seen, see what I see."

Those last four words present an interesting possibility for the actress playing Ophelia. They seem a bit redundant—unless they represent the initial stirrings of a new discovery on Ophelia's part. We know what she has just seen—we've been witness to it ourselves, after all—but what does she suddenly see? The hint of some method behind Hamlet's supposed madness (to paraphrase an earlier observation from Polonius)? A word or bit of behavior he's just exhibited that has now taken on some significance for her? Some clue to what's really going on at Elsinore, some epiphany about the politics that's suddenly clarified by her father's and Claudius's re-entrance? It's a repetitive phrase that moves to present from past tense "seen what I have seen, see what I see." It's very important that the actress choose exactly what prompts these particular words in this particular moment, for it's her creative job to make Shakespeare's text spring from her own very specific imaginary circumstances. So . . . what precisely does she now see?

We're not allowed very much time for it to sink in, however; for Claudius and Polonius quickly stride back onto the stage, evaluating what they have just witnessed, and pondering what next to do with their "mad" Prince. This is the first time in the play—Act III, midway through—that Shakespeare has allowed us to see these two characters, Hamlet and Ophelia, so pivotal to the play's action, together. We will only see them together once more, in the very next scene during the moments before the Players present "The Mousetrap" before the guilty King; and once again, Hamlet treats her less than sensitively. However, the fact that it is a "public" scene in which he is once again "performing" his antic madness for the court at large, clearly affects his behavior.

He will live to regret his treatment of the girl that meant so much to him before murder, incest and usurpation arrived at the

Danish court; for the next time he sees her, she will be dead and in her grave.

OTHELLO, ACT IV, SCENE III

This scene presents a good example of why a comparison of available texts of a Shakespeare play—quartos, Folio, and modern edited versions—is a vital preparatory step for actors and directors. *Othello*, like *King Lear*, *Hamlet*, *Romeo and Juliet*, and several others we've already touched upon in an earlier chapter, is a multiple-text play; that is, a Shakespeare play whose variants between source texts published in the era in which its author worked (*Othello*'s First Quarto was published six years after Shakespeare's death, and one year before the First Folio) contain enough significant differences between them that a careful consideration of both becomes both essential and enlightening.

As it so happens, some of the most pronounced differences between the two texts of *Othello* are found in this very scene. The Folio version contains about 170 lines that are not found in Q1, and Q1 has many variations of words, phrases and punctuation from the Folio. There are different academic theories about the reasons for this, and they provide thought-provoking reading for interested young artists and scholars. Whatever stage history may lurk behind the variations, it is indisputable that the loss of those 170 lines of text harms the depth of characterization that the Folio's additions provide for the two main female characters of the play, Desdemona and Emilia. For instance, in this scene in Q1, Desdemona only mentions the haunting, death-laden Willow song that won't "go from her mind" this night; she doesn't sing it as Emilia prepares her for bed; and Emilia loses completely her spirited and liberating defense of sexual equality for women which closes the scene that we are about to examine. Consequently, we will use the Folio version for this scene, as it provides much more insight and challenge for the two actresses than does the Quarto. However, those staging the play should consider all their options when preparing a working script; for although this particular scene loses a lot of its individual dramatic texture in Q1, it's also true that the play as a whole moves more rapidly and inexorably toward its powerful climax if the cuts in this scene are utilized.

THE CHARACTERS:

Desdemona, the new bride of Othello, Venetian general and military governor of Cypress

Emilia, her maid and companion—and the wife of Iago, Othello's army ensign and aide

THE CONTEXT AND CIRCUMSTANCES:

Othello is a particularly rich play for imaginative actors and directors; with a tighter focus than the other tragedies and a plot concerned primarily with domestic issues, the psychologies of the main characters are open to a variety of interpretations and subtle nuances. Different creative choices for Othello, Iago, Desdemona and Emilia have yielded effective and memorable characterizations over the span of the four centuries since its composition. In fact, Othello has proven to be a perennial favorite with audiences; one of the most immediately accessible of Shakespeare's tragedies, *Othello* has enjoyed a more consistent stage life than has perhaps any other of the major plays apart from *Romeo and Juliet*. Perhaps that has to do with its primary theme—love and jealousy (racism is only one facet of its complicated mosaic). Othello's feelings—albeit extreme, and artificially fed by Iago—are ones that we've all experienced in the course of our lives, to one degree or another, and with which we can all identify.

Desdemona is a young woman (generally played as aged 18-22) who has come to physical maturity in a wealthy household, the daughter of a Venetian politician/aristocrat, Signior Brabantio (again, no mother is mentioned!). As a part of his life and work—a senator in a city/state that's involved in an ongoing war with Moslem Turkey—Brabantio maintains strong and friendly relationships with Venice's military leaders.

One of those generals—the exotic foreigner, Othello, a dark-skinned Moor who has proven himself one of the city's most valiant soldiers in its recent battles—Brabantio has hosted regularly in his home, encouraging him to share exciting tales of his adventurous past in after-dinner conversations. He has apparently been oblivious to the fact that his impressionable daughter has also been enthralled by Othello's stories—as well as his strength, restrained passion, and quietly charismatic personality. Although young in years (and practical life experience), Desdemona appears intelligent, confident, and assertive; enough so that she very forwardly invites Othello's proposal of marriage, then weds him secretly, without seeking permission or blessing from her stunned father.

Little does Othello know that he harbors a viper close to his heart—and it's not the devoted Desdemona. Iago, a career soldier in Othello's unit reveals in the play's first scene how angry he is as a result of a rival soldier's (Cassio's) promotion to lieutenant over him. One has the sense that Othello's appointment as General with the division has occurred relatively recently, perhaps as a reward for his past valor in the service of Venice; thus, he and Iago are still in the process of learning to work together, although Othello clearly trusts his enlisted men implicitly—to his misfortune, as it turns out. Not only is Iago dissatisfied with what he perceives as the unfairness of Cassio's preferment over him, he assures his befuddled and rather unsophisticated civilian acquaintance, Roderigo, that he's determined to do something about it—starting with surreptitiously causing problems between his dark-skinned superior officer and his new father-in-law.

When Brabantio finds out from Roderigo (at Othello's direction) that his daughter has eloped with black Othello, he's instantly enraged; one senses that his feeling of betrayal is based largely on deep-seated racism, an aspect of Venetian society that will permeate all of Othello's and Desdemona's experiences in the events to come. He appeals to the Senate to have Othello arrested; unfortunately for him, the Senate is more concerned with a new Turkish assault on the island of Cyprus, a Venetian territory. Venice's urgent need for Othello's military prowess undermines Brabantio's demand that the Moor be apprehended and punished for what amounts to the abduction and "rape" of his daughter. Desdemona also directly disputes her father's charge; summoned before the Senate during their emergency nighttime session by her new husband, she unhesitatingly affirms her love for Othello. Devastated, Brabantio publicly disowns his daughter. Having settled this domestic dispute, the Senate immediately dispatches Othello to Cyprus to engage the invading Turkish army. His troops prepare to accompany him there (which include Iago and his rival, Cassio), as does Desdemona; she really has no choice, as she can no longer stay with her heartbroken father until her husband's return.

Upon their arrival in Cyprus, the Venetian troops are greeted with very good news: the Turkish fleet has foundered in a storm at sea in their attempt to land on the Cypriot shore. The battle is over before it really began! As the landed Venetian army anxiously awaits the arrival of their general (also struggling against the rough tides), we are introduced to Iago's wife for the first time. Emilia, an army wife of a career soldier, has been assigned as the young Desdemona's companion and maid; the ensign's wife thus waits upon the general's wife, much as the ensign attends the general himself. How must she feel about that? Well, perhaps she would feel better about it if she were happier in her own marriage to Iago; but it becomes quickly apparent that they are not a happy couple. Their harsher feelings about one another even creep into their public behavior together, as we can infer from their very first scene together of the play.

Othello's ship finally docks in the harbor, and he and Desdemona reunite in a touching moment that Iago mocks in asides to us. That evening, Othello (the new acting governor of Cyprus during their occupation) declares a public celebration; then he retires to finally have some time alone with his young bride. Iago's conspiracy to supplant Cassio as Othello's lieutenant, however, interrupts the festivities; he and Roderigo (who has also followed the army to Cyprus, being rather sappily and hopelessly in love with Desdemona himself) stir up a drunken brawl in the nighttime street that results in Cassio's wounding of Montano, the official governor of Cyprus whom Othello has temporarily replaced. As a consequence of this incident, the impetuous (but sincere) Cassio is demoted and, in the void left by his displacement, Iago gains more favor with the too-trusting Othello.

Even the success of this treachery fails to satisfy Iago. (Actors assaying the role will have hours of creative fun determining just what motivates this darkest of all Shakespearean villains!) He now determines to unmercifully destroy the lives of Othello and his bride Desdemona, along with Cassio. Using a skillful manipulation of acts and behavior of Desdemona which are actually quite innocent, Iago ultimately convinces the emotionally vulnerable Othello that his young bride is generally promiscuous, and specifically (at present) bedding Cassio. Why? Racism? Sociopathic or psychotic urges? Misogyny? Jealousy? Lust for Desdemona? A homo-erotic attraction to Othello? All these possibilities (and more) have been explored by critics, scholars, directors and actors over the past four centuries. Whatever the motivation, watching the process happen proves absolutely riveting in the theatre with imaginative and creative performances. Iago convinces Othello that the devoted young girl/woman who has literally given her life to him is actually lascivious and adulterous; and as a result of Iago's skilled duplicity, Othello physically abuses his bewildered wife before ultimately murdering her in the play's final scene, while the horrified audience looks on, helplessly.

Throughout this tragic progression, we also see the two army wives bond together, presumably in genuine friendship— one both experienced in the realities of military life, but also desperately unhappy in her marriage (Emilia); the other, Desdemona, naïve, lively, and unerringly dedicated to her husband. Perhaps Emilia, like other Venetians, instinctively distrusts Othello because of her own innate racism; or perhaps she has come to distrust men and love in general as a direct result of her own failing relationship. Whatever the actress determines of her inmost thoughts, Emilia comes to behave with almost parental protection toward her charge, the young wife whom she sees publicly abused by the Moorish general.

This scene begins shortly after Othello has violently slapped Desdemona and verbally abused her before a public audience consisting of political emissaries from Venice, including Desdemona's own uncle and cousin. Immediately after that terrible incident, Othello conducts her to their lodging and, with an angry and distraught Emilia locked outside the room, he furiously (and seemingly madly) accuses his wife of sexual betrayal. After his departure, Desdemona looks to Iago and Emilia for help and understanding. The comfort Emilia offers is heartfelt; Iago's, of course, is not. Later that evening, Desdemona retires to her bedchamber, nervously awaiting the return of her husband, yet passionately determined to convince him—however she can—of the purity and conviction of her heart's love for him. As she tries to make sense of all that has gone wrong so quickly in her marriage, Emilia enters to help her prepare for bed. As the scene between them progresses, it seems clear that Emilia also has some strong thoughts about men and marriage that she's ready to share with her young friend and mistress should circumstances invite her to do so.

EMILIA: How goes it now? He looks gentler than he did.
DESDEMONA: He says he will return incontinent
    And hath commanded me to go to bed;
    And bid me to dismiss you.
EMILIA: Dismiss me?
DESDEMONA: It was his bidding; therefore, good Emilia,
    Give me my nightly wearing, and adieu.
    We must not now displease him.
EMILIA: I would you had never seen him!
DESDEMONA: So would not I! My love doth so approve him,
    That even his stubbornness, his checks, his frowns—
    Prithee, unpin me—have grace and favor in them.

As Othello and Lodovico (the newly appointed governor of Cyprus) depart Othello's quarters, Desdemona is left to brood about what has changed her husband's feelings toward her so drastically in so short a time. As the men exit, Emilia enters the dimly-lit room. Sensitive about what her new young friend must be going through, Emilia attempts a positive note. "Things seem better with him now," she observes, trying to open up a conversation with Desdemona about what's been going on. Desdemona doesn't take the bait; instead, loyal to her husband (whatever may be troubling him), she relays his wish that Emilia be dismissed immediately after helping prepare her mistress for bed. Emilia seems apprehensive at this direction; Desdemona senses this, and tries to stifle any protest from her maid and companion before it can be expressed.

However, Emilia will not be discouraged. Always rather blunt, she expresses aloud what some others (including members of the audience by now) must be thinking: this marriage should not have happened, especially not so quickly. Immediately defensive of her husband as well as her own feelings, Desdemona shows a glimpse of her strength of will, shutting Emilia down with equal bluntness. "I'll hear nothing against my husband," her words make clear, "because I love him." Following that, she not-so-subtly reminds Emilia of her place by directing that she proceed in helping her undress, as a chambermaid should.

Note that the dialogue between the women begins in verse, reflecting both its formality and its quiet dramatic tension. The shared verse line between the two of them that concludes with Emilia's quick cue "Dismiss me?" underscores her concern for Desdemona that lurks barely underneath the surface of their interaction.

Desdemona and Emilia from *Othello*

EMILIA: I have laid those sheets you bade me on the bed.
DESDEMONA: All's one. Good faith, how foolish are our
    minds!
    If I do die before thee, prithee shroud me
    In one of these same sheets.
EMILIA: Come, come, you talk!
DESDEMONA: My mother had a maid call'd Barbary;
    She was in love, and he she lov'd prov'd mad
    And did forsake her. She had a song of "Willow."
    An old thing 'twas, but it express'd her fortune,
    And she died singing it. That song tonight
    Will not go from my mind; I have much to do
    But to go hang my head all at one side
    And sing it like poor Barbary.

Choosing not to pursue an argument with the distraught young wife, Emilia turns to more mundane housekeeping matters: she has readied their wedding night sheets for the bed, as Desdemona has directed her to do. Desdemona's wish is significant: she lost her virginity to her husband when they consummated their marriage, and perhaps the sheets themselves will serve to remind her inexplicably jealous husband of that fact.

Desdemona realizes that she has responded to Emilia's genuine concern for her somewhat curtly, so she attempts to defuse any hard feelings with some slight self-depracation. "How foolish are our minds," she says; which leads her into a thought that's been bothering her, a request that her nervous feelings tonight are prompting her to broach: if something should happen to her—if she should, in fact, die before Emilia (by whatever cause), she would wish herself buried in those same sheets that symbolize her devotion to Othello. Emilia again comes in with a quick shared-line cue, dismissing Desdemona's morbid thought with superstitious rapidity.

As Emilia busies herself helping her lady (brushing her hair? Lighting candles? Arranging the bedclothes?), Desdemona confesses an obsessive memory that haunts her this evening: she has suddenly recalled another maid from her childhood, a young woman by the name of Barbary who was abandoned by a man she loved dearly. As a result, she wasted away in melancholy, then died. (Psychologically, it's interesting to note that the name "Barbary" also conjures images of the African coast, another connection with Othello.) The song of the "Willow" that this Barbary used to sing in her sadness obviously had a profound impact on the child Desdemona; and tonight, she cannot seem to get the tune of it out of her mind. Barbary's life ended in broken-hearted despair; will hers as well, she wonders?

DESDEMONA: *(continuing)* Prithee, dispatch.
EMILIA: Shall I go fetch your nightgown?
DESDEMONA:No, unpin me here.
    This Lodovico is a proper man.
EMILIA: A very handsome man.
DESDEMONA: He speaks well.
EMILIA: I know a lady in Venice would have walk'd barefoot
    to Palestine for a touch of his nether lip.

Valiantly attempting to shake her sadness from her, Desdemona pulls her thoughts back to the mundane business at hand. She gently encourages Emilia to hurry; she anticipates that her husband may return at any moment, and she wants to be alone with him. Emilia helps her change into her nightgown as Desdemona tries to lighten the mood with a little "girl talk" about the handsome visitor from Venice who was just in her husband's company, Lodovico. The two women agree that he is quite a "catch," although it seems mildly significant that Desdemona focuses on complimenting his proper manners and speech, while her older, more earthy and worldly companion speaks of his physical charms. Indeed, who is the "lady from Venice" who would have walked barefoot across continents for a kiss from this man? Might it be Emilia herself?

DESDEMONA: *(Singing)*
    "The poor soul sat sighing by a sycamore tree,
    Sing all a green willow;

Her hand on her bosom, her head on her knee,
Sing willow, willow, willow.
The fresh streams ran by her, and murmur'd her moans,
Sing willow, willow, willow;
Her salt tears fell from her, and soft'ned the stones,
Sing willow"—
(To EMILIA) Lay by these—
(Singing) "—willow, willow"—
(To EMILIA) Prithee, hie thee; he'll come anon—
(Singing)
"Let nobody blame him, his scorn I approve"—
Nay, that's not next. Hark, who is't that knocks?
EMILIA: It's the wind.
DESDEMONA: *(Singing)*
"I called my love false love; but what said he then?
Sing willow, willow, willow;
If I court more women, you'll couch with more men."—
(To EMILIA) So, get thee gone; good night.

As Emilia continues her preparation of both Desdemona and the bedchamber, the "Willow" song creeps once again into the young woman's mind. She sings it softly, almost under her breath, and certainly not in any presentational manner. (This song passage, as noted earlier, doesn't appear in the Quarto version of the scene, leaving some scholars to theorize that the Q script indicates the scene as it was played when the boy actor playing Desdemona could not sing well. Perhaps; but we'll never know. Whatever the reason for its absence there, the longer Folio version—with song—more effectively re-enforces the brooding atmosphere of the scene for the actresses.) The sad, distracted singing affects the already worried Emilia; nonetheless, she keeps her peace for the time being, perhaps determining that Desdemona needs to be comforted rather than stirred with further forebodings. Throughout this passage, Shakespeare adds marvelously naturalistic behavioral moments: Desdemona's direction to "Unpin me here," followed shortly by her enjoining Emilia to hurry up, finish what she's doing, and leave, as her husband should be here at any moment.

Quite abruptly, the "Willow" lyrics that are flowing from her subconscious mind stop Desdemona short: "Let nobody blame him, his scorn I approve," she sings. Apparently realizing the lyric's connection to her own situation with Othello's "scorn" and her docile acceptance of it, she frowns and decides that it's not the correct line. Simultaneously, a sound from outside the room startles her disproportionately. Noting the apparent extremity of Desdemona's response (she's clearly on edge, to say the least), Emilia brushes it off. After a moment, Desdemona tries to pick up the thread of her memory of Barbary's song, but almost immediately another lyric makes her catch her breath at its seeming relevance to her own situation: "If I court more women, you'll couch with more men—" In the quick, charged pause that follows this realization, Desdemona directs Emilia to leave her.

DESDEMONA: *(continuing)* Mine eyes do itch.
Doth that bode weeping?
EMILIA: 'Tis neither here nor there.
DESDEMONA: I have heard it said so. O, these men, these men!

Before Emilia can depart, however, Desdemona stops her with a question that seems charged with a desperate, child-like need for reassurance: Should she read such simple signs as her itching eyes to be bad omens? she asks Emilia. Clearly, she's afraid, although she's trying not to be. After all, why should she fear her own husband? She loves him. And why should she fear for her well-being? She's innocent, and deserves no ill treatment from anyone, especially Othello. Emilia, sensing Desdemona's vulnerability, comes back to her side, perhaps kneeling or touching her in comfort as she dismisses the worry as superstition. Desdemona's determination to maintain her emotional equilibrium almost collapses entirely at Emilia's words. "O, these men, these men!" she nearly sobs in her frustration, sadness and fear. Then, turning to Emilia as the mother that she lacks and longs for—perhaps taking her hands fervently—she asks the more experienced woman:

DESDEMONA: *(continuing)* Dost thou in conscience think—
    tell me, Emilia—
  That there be women do abuse their husbands
  In such gross kind?
EMILIA: There be some such, no question.
DESDEMONA: Wouldst thou do such a deed for all the
    world?
EMILIA: Why, would not you?
DESDEMONA: No, by this heavenly light!
EMILIA: Nor I neither, by this heavenly light;
  I might do't as well in the dark!
DESDEMONA: Wouldst thou do such a deed for all the
    world?
EMILIA: The world's a huge thing; it is a great price
  For a small vice.
DESDEMONA: Troth, I think thou wouldst not.
EMILIA: By my troth, I think I should, and undo't when I had
  done't. Marry, I would not do such a thing for a joint-ring,
  nor for measures of lawn, nor for gowns, petticoats, nor
  caps, nor any petty exhibition; but for all the whole world!—
  God's pity, who would not make her husband a cuckold to
  make him a monarch? I should venture purgatory for't.
DESDEMONA: Beshrew me if I would do such a wrong for the
  whole world!
EMILIA: Why, the wrong is but a wrong i' th' world; and having
  the world for your labor, 'tis a wrong in your own world,
  and you might quickly make it right!
DESDEMONA: I do not think there is any such woman.
EMILIA: Yes, a dozen; and as many to th' vantage as would
  store the world they play'd for.

Initially, Emilia seems to evade Desdemona's question. Is she embarrassed by it? Amused by it? Even irritated? Does she view it as too personal? These are all key questions that actresses must confront in building their individual characterizations. Whatever the reason might be, Emilia avoids voicing any valuative opinion on the subject of adultery initiated by the wife in a marriage; she gives a figurative shrug by response of "There be some such, no question." In her current state of mind however, Desdemona won't be put off so easily; she asks Emilia pointedly if she would ever cheat on her husband with another man "for all the world?" Still elusive in response, Emilia turns the question coyly (and literally) back on Desdemona; but there is nothing equivocal about Desdemona's shocked answer. She even accompanies it with a mild oath ("by this heavenly light"), which indicates how shocked the young woman is by even the consideration of such a betrayal of her beloved Othello. Emilia turns her friend's impassioned vow into a slightly bawdy joke; such a tryst would be more suited to the dark, not "heavenly light." The shared verse exchange delineates the differences between a long-married woman, unhappy in that matrimony, who has become somewhat cynical about the romantic relationship between husbands and wives, and a new bride who still holds such a relationship in rather breathless reverence.

Emila is nothing if not practical; as such, she translates Desdemona's figurative proposition into down-to-earth terms. (The actresses should take note that as the conversation moves more in such a direction, the textual dialogue moves from verse to prose.) If a woman could gain "all the world" by a quick "roll in the hay" with a man other than her husband, why (in such a world) would she hesitate? She would personally gain by the act, and her husband would gain even more, becoming the hypothetical king of the world! All that for a simple sexual act? Why not? Shocked—yet slightly amused, in spite of herself, perhaps?— Desdemona calls what she believes is her companion's bluff: "Troth (in truth), I think thou wouldst not!" Emilia, increasingly bemused by Desdemona's devotion to a husband who is clearly abusive to her, takes her lady's proposal to its natural conclusion: "If I could gain the rule of the world by such a 'small vice'" (that is, one that she clearly believes is common in lots of marriages), she says, "then I would be in charge of what is considered sin and what is not—so I would declare it no sin at all!" It's a clever conceit, and one designed to both make light of Desdemona's original question as well as instill some courage and self-respect in the young lady, so enthralled (in Emilia's view) to a man who clearly is not as appreciative of her as he should be. Disturbed by Emilia's flippancy about a subject she feels so strongly about, Desdemona attempts to end the conversation by denying that her maid/companion is really serious about all of this.

But Emilia decides not to let the subject go so easily. She feels that it's time to help Desdemona regain her self-respect and independence as a woman. Her voice and demeanor begin to take on a new tone as she shares a more direct and personal philosophy with her naïve and inexperienced mistress. Does she now sit beside her on the bed? Take her hands? Whatever the actresses' choice, the scene becomes more personal and revealing for Emilia as she frankly shares a bit of her own pain in this "teaching moment":

EMILIA: *(continuing)* But I do think it is their husbands'
    faults
  If wives do fall. Say that they slack their duties,
  And pour our treasures into foreign laps;
  Or else break out in peevish jealousies,
  Throwing restraint upon us; or say they strike us,
  Or scant our former having in despite:
  Why, we have galls; and though we have some grace,
  Yet have we some revenge. Let husbands know
  Their wives have sense like them; they see, and smell,
  And have their palates both for sweet and sour,
  As husbands have. What is it that they do
  When they change us for others? Is it sport?
  I think it is. And doth affection breed it?
  I think it doth. Is't frailty that thus errs?
  It is so too. And have not we affections,
  Desires for sport, and frailty, as men have?
  Then let them use us well; else let them know,
  The ills we do, their ills instruct us so!

Here, the verse returns. It is one of the wisest, most lyrical defenses of equality between the sexes in all of Shakespeare—and it is entirely absent from the First Quarto! Whether its absence in Q was the result of a later authorial addition or a theatrical cut, it's undeniable that the play as a whole, and certainly the character of Emilia, suffers a substantial loss with its absence. Audiences for *Othello* through the centuries have wondered at the motivation for Iago's evil actions, at the life of the character offstage that would contribute to such conscienceless acts on his part. The insight into a troubled marriage that these words of Emilia's reveal gives us perhaps one of the play's few clear revelations of what might lie behind Iago's psychotic jealousy of others' happiness. A helpful modern analogy for young actresses might be this: a woman with significantly more experience in sex, love and marriage offers some no-bull counseling to a younger woman whom she knows is currently in an abusive relationship, and who (like many domestic abuse victims) seems to blame herself for the mistreatment she's receiving. "Don't do that to yourself, honey," Emilia says to her. "Here's how you should look at it:

"We're all human, and in any human relationship, we respond as we are treated. If a husband neglects his duties, physical and emotional, to his wife; if he pursues relationships outside of their marriage; if he's overly controlling, or physically violent towards her—then he should be prepared to receive the same treatment from her that he's dishing out. Women have temptations; they have desires and appetites; they have feelings, they have rights—just like men do. If men want love, respect and devotion from their wives—and a happy, peaceful home—then they must contribute 50/50 to the conditions that will lead to those results. Otherwise, they should prepare for the same pain and betrayal that they give to their mates."

One wonders what the Elizabethan and Jacobean audiences must have thought of this startlingly modern and well-articulated defense of equality between the sexes in relationships. And this, from the same playwright who, fifteen years earlier in his career, had at least a hand in the writing of *The Taming of the Shrew*!

DESDEMONA: Good night; good night. God me such uses
    send,
Not to pick bad from bad, but by bad mend.

The power of such a beautifully considered and passionately spoken position on the rights of wives in marriage has a profound effect on Desdemona. For a moment, she lets the words resonate within her; then she expresses her gratitude for her newfound friend's thoughtfulness and personal support. However, true to her unwavering devotion to the love of her life—whatever might be troubling him at present—she utters a simple prayer that God will give her the strength to patiently endure her trials and ultimately respond to her husband with love, however unfair his behavior might seem to her. Emilia bows to Desdemona's will and leaves the bedchamber with misgivings, still worried about the young woman's welfare in the hands of the inexplicably changed Othello.

Within moments, Desdemona will lie dead in that same bedchamber, murdered by the husband she adores.

The Two Gentlemen of Verona, Act I, Scene II

Here's another scene for two women, one very different in tone.

THE CHARACTERS:
Julia, a young girl of comfortable circumstances
Lucetta, her maid and companion; although she can be played as an almost parental figure for Julia, for our purposes we'll treat her as only a few years older. This seems very much to me a play by a young playwright about youth; the few adults that appear, although important to the action, don't receive equal emphasis.

THE CONTEXT AND CIRCUMSTANCES:
The Two Gentlemen is one of Shakespeare's earliest comedies. As such, young actors will find it simpler to grasp upon first reading; but problematical insofar as the insufficiency of texture, background, and motivation that's offered for the various characters. Some of the poetry clearly shows the beauty and potential that its author achieved more fully in the later plays (such as the prior three that we've examined in this chapter).

What light is light, if Silvia be not seen?
What joy is joy, if Silvia be not by?
Unless it be to think that she is by,
And feed upon the shadow of perfection.

Julia and Lucetta from *The Two Gentleman of Verona*

Such lines as these show the path toward the beauty yet to come.

On the other hand, directors and actors will find some significant challenges to address in the play as well, not least of which is the attempted rape of Silvia in the climax of the play, weirdly (by our modern tastes, at least) played for comedy. In the appendix of this book, I deal with a possible approach to working with this—as well as other issues—confronting actors and directors staging the play in the essay, "Some Thoughts on *The Two Gentlemen of Verona*." Reading that section might offer further initial inspiration for actresses preparing to work on this scene.

Shakespeare offers little specific background detail for Julia's home life; but certain conclusions may be reasonably drawn by what information he does offer. Although neither of her parents appear in the play, Julia apparently lives the life of a rather pampered debutante: she is attended by a private maid, she has been receiving courtship offers from a variety of suitors, at least one being a knight and another being a man of some wealth . . . and, judging by her behavior in this first scene of the play in which she appears, Julia seems a bit spoiled and pretentious. She pretends to be indifferent to the flattery of her suitors, she won't admit to her attraction to Proteus (even when it must seem pretty obvious to those around her), and she treats Lucetta with the assumed haughtiness of a young lady who hasn't yet earned the respect from either peers or servants that she believes that she deserves. Nonetheless, there's still something quite likeable about Julia; and that's primarily due to the excited vulnerability that gushes out of her later in this scene when she realizes fully that the young man for whom she harbors a secret crush reciprocates her romantic interest. Like most of Shakespeare's comic heroines, she will mature a great deal over the course of her adventures throughout the play, and we can see that potential in her in this scene. She's intelligent, vivacious, and really quite enjoyable; she's just young.

Lucetta represents one of Shakespeare's earliest depictions of the practical, rather saucy, common-sense serving lady that would evolve into similar characters of somewhat greater depth or age in several of his later plays: Maria in *Twelfth Night*, Emilia in *Othello* (both of whom we've met in the earlier scenes of this chapter), the Nurse in *Romeo and Juliet*, the Old Lady in *Henry VIII (All Is True)*, and Paulina in *The Winter's Tale*. She obviously knows the psychology of her young mistress, and teasingly plays upon it very effectively in the course of this encounter: like Olivia in *Twelfth Night*, Julia is too proud about showing her true feelings and longings—even to those who know her and love her—and Lucetta, who has perhaps mostly grown up alongside Julia in the same household (although "below stairs," as the aristocratic term for the servant class puts it), seems determined not to let her get away with it. She seems to truly enjoy Julia's personality and have a genuine fondness for her in spite of the girl's pretensions, and one has the sense watching them together that the only thing that separates these two young ladies from being the best of friends and confidantes on all levels is their difference in social and economic class.

As this scene begins (only the second in the play; in the first, we have encountered young Proteus, whose budding interest in Julia becomes the primary focus of the girls' discussion in this scene), Julia enters with a sigh, feigning with characteristically "above it all" exasperation her impatience about the incessant suits with which several young men are currently besieging her. Perhaps she is entering the stage after attending the equivalent of her societal coming out party, affecting boredom with how frustrating it is to be unceasingly adored by all of these men! However, underneath her act, Lucetta (and the audience) can quickly perceive that the "gentle Proteus" has truly captured Julia's romantic interest. What she doesn't know is that Lucetta has already received a secret love letter meant for Julia and written by Proteus; it was delivered to her earlier in the day by Speed, a manservant of Proteus's friend Valentine. Why didn't Proteus send his own servant, Launce? Well, once we've been introduced to the affably buffoonish Launce in a subsequent scene, the reason he wasn't entrusted with such a sensitive message becomes quite clear. Moreover, it seems entirely possible that the rakish Speed and the fun-loving Lucetta have had their own prior romantic history; if so, then Proteus would see Speed as the obvious choice for carrying his letter of love to Julia.

As we'll learn a bit later in the scene, it takes place outside, probably in an inner courtyard of her sizeable house; we know this because towards the end of the scene, Julia notes that a wind is blowing—which obviously wouldn't happen were the scene an interior one!

JULIA: But say, Lucetta, now we are alone,
    Wouldst thou then counsel me to fall in love?
LUCETTA: Ay, madam, so you stumble not unheedfully.
JULIA: Of all the fair resort of gentlemen
    That every day with parle encounter me,
    In thy opinion, which is worthiest love?

LUCETTA: Please you repeat their names, I'll show my mind
According to my shallow simple skill.

With their first entrances into the play, Shakespeare skillfully establishes our sense of them within their initial lines. Julia, sighing with affected frustration, asks her companion if it's the right "time" for her to fall in love. Suppressing her amusement at her lady's affectation, Lucetta—ever practical, and sophisticated beyond Julia's realization in her wry humor—responds affirmatively; if, she cautions with mock seriousness, Julia doesn't decide to love just anybody. Encouraged in her conceit by Lucetta's willingness to go along with this conversation, Julia suggests that she list all of the many men who have expressed interest in her (almost suppressing a feigned yawn—it can be boring to be so adored!), and Lucetta can then "rate" them for good qualities and bad. Suppressing outright laughter, Lucetta agrees; although she warns Julia that, as an unsophisticated maidservant (nothing could be further from the truth), her opinions may be hampered, and Julia should review them from that perspective. Pleased that Lucetta will play along, Julia begins to go down the list.

JULIA: What think'st thou of the fair Sir Eglamour?
LUCETTA: As of a knight well-spoken, neat, and fine;
But were I you, he never would be mine.
JULIA: What think'st thou of the rich Mercatio?
LUCETTA: Well of his wealth, but of himself, so, so.
JULIA: What think'st thou of the gentle Proteus?

The first two suitors Julia names are neither one the focus of her true interest, and Lucetta knows this. She responds to the names with characteristic wit, although she's a bit kinder to the first candidate than she is the second. Finding no specific fault with Sir Eglamour—particularly in the honor of his knighthood—she still dismisses him as not particularly attractive, at least in her own view. Julia offers no protest to that assessment, moving on to the next name on the list: the rich Mercatio. Again demonstrating her sly humor, Lucetta notes that she wouldn't mind spending his money; but as a man, he's not the most attractive guy around either. Believing too much in her own subtlety (which Lucetta, knowing Julia well, easily sees through), Julia throws out the name of the young man in whom she's truly interested—an offhand third on her list, so as not to be too obvious. Notably, she speaks of Proteus not in terms of his social status or his wealth, but of his gentleness. Lucetta has clearly been waiting for her to get to the real candidate here, and she responds to the name with open glee.

LUCETTA: Lord, Lord! To see what folly reigns in us!
JULIA: How now? What means this passion at his name?
LUCETTA: Pardon, dear madam, 'tis a passing shame
    That I (unworthy body as I am)
    Should censure thus on lovely gentlemen.
JULIA: Why not on Proteus, as of all the rest?
LUCETTA: Then thus: of many good I think him best.
JULIA: Your reason?
LUCETTA: I have no other but a woman's reason:
    I think him so because I think him so.
JULIA: And wouldst thou have me cast my love on him?
LUCETTA: Ay—if you thought your love not cast away.
JULIA: Why he, of all the rest, hath never mov'd me.
LUCETTA: Yet he, of all the rest, I think best loves ye.
JULIA: His little speaking shows his love but small.
LUCETTA: Fire that's closest kept burns most of all.
JULIA: They do not love that do not show their love.
LUCETTA: O, they love least that let men know their love.
JULIA: I would I knew his mind.
LUCETTA: Peruse this paper, madam.

Julia immediately raises her defenses, much as a teenage girl would do when being teased by a parent or older sibling about a first '"crush"; indeed, if the actress playing her identifies strongly enough with the character's life that her own autonomic systems engage, then surely a blush here would be absolutely appropriate. "Why do you react like this to his name?" she demands of Lucetta, rather indignantly. Suppressing a smile, Lucetta acts the lowly servant to her mistress for a moment, asking Julia's pardon for her boldness at passing judgment on the gentlemen Julia listed.

But Julia won't be distracted from her primary interest: why did Lucetta respond so differently to Proteus's name? Lucetta responds directly: "I like him the best of the three." When Julia pursues this further, Lucetta becomes coy about exactly why she thinks better of Proteus. Perhaps realizing that her interest in the lad is transparent to Lucetta—thus embarrassing her more acutely—Julia assumes a mask of disinterest in Proteus. She spars with Lucetta, who cleverly over the next few lines spars with antithetical phrases in rejoinder (and in teasing rhyme, no less!). Julia's assertion that Proteus has "never moved me" is countered with Lucetta's reply that he "best loves ye"; her fear that his love is "but small" prompts Lucetta to assure her that such a quiet lover's heart "burns most of all." Impatient, frustrated, and genuinely worried that Proteus may not be interested, Julia complains that lovers don't really love who "do not show their love." Again, Lucetta cleverly trumps her, noting that those "love least who let men know their love." The actresses tackling this scene should relish the witty back and forth of the antitheses, choosing as operative words those that best emphasize the joust.

Almost crying out in adolescent frustration that Proteus has revealed nothing thus far about his feelings for her, Julia is both surprised and intrigued when Lucetta draws a final hidden "weapon" from the bodice of her dress: a note that promises some new information pertinent to this very discussion! Julia reads the salutation of the note as Lucetta waves it teasingly before her eyes:

JULIA: "To Julia"—say, from whom?
LUCETTA: That the contents will show.
JULIA: Say, say; who gave it thee?
LUCETTA: Sir Valentine's page; and sent, I think, from
    Proteus.
    He would have given it you, but I, being in the way,
    Did in your name receive it; pardon the fault, I pray.

As it's addressed to her, Julia probably reaches to snatch it from her maid's hand; but Lucetta, having fun with her mistress, withholds it. (Note the several short lines of verse in these last two sections of text that imply some stage business or character behavior accompanying the lines.) Showing excitement in spite of her determination to hide any attraction for Proteus she might harbor, Julia demands to know from whom its sent. Lucetta happily relents, confessing that its author is Proteus, delivered to her by his best friend Valentine's page. Smiling, she finally hands the note to Julia. Lucetta fully expects Julia's response to this revelation to be joyous excitement, as she clearly senses her lady's "secret" love for Proteus; but instead of celebrating what promises to be the confessed reciprocation of her amorous feelings for the young man, Julia's young pride overcomes her candidness. Without even unsealing it, or looking beyond its simple written salutation, she turns vehemently on the surprised Lucetta.

JULIA: Now, by my modesty, a goodly broker!
    Dare you presume to harbor wanton lines?
    To whisper and conspire against my youth?
    Now trust me, 'tis an office of great worth,
    And you an officer fit for the place.
    There! Take the paper; see it be return'd,
    Or else return no more into my sight.
LUCETTA: To plead for love deserves more love than hate.
JULIA: Will ye be gone?
LUCETTA: That you may ruminate.
       (LUCETTA exits)

Now we see the young Julia overcome by her childish ego; it's humiliating for her that her vulnerability be revealed—and in front of her servant, too! (Never mind that her "servant" has quite often been more of a big sister to her as she's grown through her teenage years.) What's even worse, she realizes that Speed must know what's going on between her and Proteus as well; and that is truly intolerable. Should everyone know everything about her love life?! She explodes at the well-meaning Lucetta, likening her to a "broker" (a bawd, or pimp) who passes "wanton lines" (messages implying sexual content) that conspire against her propriety and virginity. She calls Lucetta "fit" for such a purpose, a pretty insulting thing to say. With that, she thrusts the unread letter back at her maid, ordering her to either return it to whomever gave it to her, or else return no more to her—thus, petulantly threatening her very employment simply for trying to do her mistress a good turn!

Taking the silly tantrum in stride, Lucetta primly receives the note from Julia, while admonishing her mistress that this behavior reflects poorly on her; she, Speed—and especially Proteus—deserve better treatment for their efforts on her behalf and their genuine wishes for her happiness. Julia's pride still dominates; she orders Lucetta to leave her immediately. Lucetta complies, but as she departs she advises Julia to think things over more carefully; for she's being way too impulsive and irrational in her reactions to the situation.

JULIA: And yet I would I had o'erlook'd the letter;
    It were a shame to call her back again,
    And pray her to a fault for which I chid her.
    What fool is she, that knows I am a maid,
    And would not force the letter to my view!
    Since maids, in modesty, say "no" to that
    Which they would have the profferer construe "ay."
    Fie, fie! How wayward is this foolish love,
    That (like a testy babe) will scratch the nurse
    And presently, all humbled, kiss the rod!
    How churlishly I chid Lucetta hence,
    When willingly I would have had her here!
    How angerly I taught my brow to frown,
    When inward joy enforc'd my heart to smile!
    My penance is to call Lucetta back
    And ask remission for my folly past.
    What ho! Lucetta!

Lucetta's assessment of the situation appears to be correct. As soon as she departs the stage, Julia confesses in a soliloquy that she really wanted to read the letter from Proteus, however she might have pretended otherwise. (Not that this should be any surprise for audiences.) Some of her more childish initial remarks berating Lucetta for not "forcing" her to read the letter may prove troubling to actresses with more modern sensibilities, for she seems to be saying that, very often, when young girls say "no," they really mean "yes." This outmoded way of viewing female sensibilities is quite similar to the challenges that contemporary actresses must struggle with in dealing with Shakespeare's *The Taming of the Shrew*. He was, after all, a product of his times, however much we might think of his writing being "for all time" (as his fellow author and erstwhile admirer, Ben Jonson, described him in the preface to the First Folio). Significantly, *Shrew* and *Two Gentlemen* were both written very early in Shakespeare's career; arguably, his sense of female rights and consciousness became more progressive as he grew older, and that's reflected in his later women characters (Viola in *Twelfth Night*, Rosalind in *As You Like It*, Volumnia in *Coriolanus*, and Paulina in *The Winter's Tale* to name but a few examples of that). Also, we should remember that Julia begins the play as a pretty spoiled, immature young girl, and one of the important facets of the play involves us watching her grow up a bit.

Shakespeare once again makes repeated use of antitheses in these lines, and the actress must pay particular attention to that. "Scratch the nurse" and "kiss the rod" are antithetical; "churlishly I chid Lucetta hence" is juxtaposed against "willingly I would have had her here", as is "How angerly I taught my brow to frown/When inward joy enforc'd my heart to smile!" The back-and-forth of these phrases and images reveal that Julia hasn't yet reconciled her true feelings with her senseless pride enough to be comfortable admitting her love for Proteus to Lucetta (or even entirely to herself). However, her attraction for Proteus quickly triumphs, and she determines to call Lucetta back and find a face-saving way to receive the letter after all.

(LUCETTA enters.)
LUCETTA: What would your ladyship?
JULIA: Is it near dinner time?
LUCETTA: I would it were,
    That you might kill your stomach on your meat,
    And not upon your maid.

JULIA: What is't that you
   Took up so gingerly?
LUCETTA: Nothing.
JULIA: Why didst thou stoop then?
LUCETTA: To take a paper up that I let fall.
JULIA: And is that paper nothing?
LUCETTA: Nothing concerning me.
JULIA: Then let it lie for those that it concerns.
LUCETTA: Madam, it will not lie where it concerns
   Unless it have a false interpreter.
JULIA: Some love of yours hath writ to you in rhyme.
LUCETTA: That I might sing it, madam, to a tune:
   Give me a note, your ladyship can set.
JULIA: As little by such toys as may be possible:
   Best sing it to the tune of "Light O' Love."
LUCETTA: It is too heavy for so light a tune.
JULIA: Heavy? Belike it hath some burden then?
LUCETTA: Ay, and melodious were it—would you sing it.
JULIA: And why not you?
LUCETTA: I cannot reach so high.
JULIA: Let's see your song.

The fact that Lucetta has been lingering just offstage—
undoubtedly knowing that Julia will be calling her back right
away!—is probably underscored by the fact that her first line upon
returning finishes an iambic verse line that Julia began with "What ho!
Lucetta!" In fact, it's so much of a shared line that the rhythms work
best when Lucetta speaks her first word—"What"—simultaneously
with the last, unstressed syllable of "Lucetta!" Her quick re-entrance
must take Julia momentarily aback; is Lucetta playing with her?

   Tactically, Julia chooses to ask an offhand question about
dinner. Lucetta pointedly turns that question back on her
with a joke about hoping that Julia will satisfy her frustrated
hunger with food instead of satisfying it with berating her
maidservant. Ignoring that retort, Julia again jumps in (finishing
a verse line with a fast cue) asking a direct question about the
letter that Lucetta ostentatiously drops, then picks up with
exaggerated theatricality. Julia walks a fine line during the next

bit of dialogue, pretending to still care nothing about the letter personally while at the same time trying to get Lucetta to drop it again and leave—so she can then pick it up herself and read it in private. But Lucetta will not go along with Julia's game, and continues to tantalize her with hints of what the letter's contents might reveal. When Julia observes that the letter is probably a note written in rhyme to Lucetta by a suitor of her own, Lucetta plays along. The banter might be paraphrased like this:

JULIA: I'll bet it's a love letter to you from your own boyfriend, written in verse!

LUCETTA: Oh, well then I'll try improvising my own music to sing it to; give me a note to start on.

JULIA: Well, it should be to the tune of "Unserious Love", because such love notes are stupid, and yours are probably more stupid than most!

LUCETTA: Oh, I think it's too serious for "Unserious Love."

JULIA: *(suddenly a little worried)*: Why? Is there something in there I need to worry about?

LUCETTA: Oh, no, not at all. It's just meant for you; so any tune *I* could put to it wouldn't be appropriate.

JULIA: Why not?

LUCETTA: I couldn't do its passionate poetry justice!

At that, Julia tires of the teasing exchange and makes a grab for the letter. Laughing at the game, Lucetta holds it out of her reach.

JULIA: How now, minion!

LUCETTA: Keep tune there still, so you will sing it out.
    And yet methinks I do not like this tune.

JULIA: You do not?

LUCETTA: No, madam, 'tis too sharp.

JULIA: You, minion, are too saucy.

LUCETTA: Nay, now you are too flat,
    And mar the concord with too harsh a descant:
    There wanteth but a mean to fill your song.

JULIA: The mean is drown'd with your unruly bass.

LUCETTA: Indeed, I bid the base for Proteus.

JULIA: This babble shall not henceforth trouble me!
  Here is a coil with protestation!
    (JULIA seizes the letter and tears it into pieces.)
  Go, get you gone; and let the papers lie:
  You would be fing'ring them to anger me!
LUCETTA: She makes it strange, but she would be best
    pleas'd
  To be so ang'red with another letter.

Julia, frustrated, now drops all of her pretensions of indifference toward the letter; as she and Julia continue to try to top each other's wit—still stretching the "song" metaphor for all it's worth—Julia pursues Lucetta around the stage, trying all the while to snatch the note from her. Both actresses can have great fun with this section, energetically physicalizing the dialogue for added emphasis. The more frustration the chase causes Julia, the more amused Lucetta becomes. Julia has now dropped all her former "coolness" toward the letter—she wants it, and wants it desperately. Her embarrassment at now being so obvious about that desire makes her even more indignantly angry at the boisterous Lucetta; and as a result, when she finally grabs the letter from her saucy servant's hand, she impulsively tears it to pieces, trying to demonstrate that she "wins" on all points: she won the tug-of-war, but she actually cares so little about it that she will destroy what she was struggling so much to procure. She does this completely without thinking, caught up in the breathless moment. Lucetta, surprised, starts to gather the pieces of the torn letter; but Julia, still flushed, orders her to leave them alone and GO!

After a beat, amazed at the intensity of Julia's silliness over the matter, Lucetta starts offstage. As she goes, she shares an observation about Julia, referring to her in the third person. The actress might make this a direct aside to the audience; or she might make it an observation to herself, albeit meant to be overheard by her mistress. It works well either way.

An important thing to note here: the one "original" version of the play, as printed in the First Folio, does not designate an actual exit for Lucetta at this point nor does it show an entrance for her again after the upcoming speech of Julia's. I believe that this might indicate that Shakespeare doesn't intend for Lucetta to actually leave the scene, although Julia—focused primarily upon the letter—believes that she has. Instead, Lucetta creeps back again once Julia begins to gather the pieces of the torn letter. Much of the fun of these next moments comes from our knowledge that Lucetta is overhearing all that Julia—thinking she's alone—finally reveals about her true feelings toward the lovelorn Proteus.

JULIA: Nay, would I were so ang'red with the same.
    O hateful hands, to tear such loving words!
    Injurious wasps, to feed on such sweet honey,
    And kill the bees that yield it with your stings!
    I'll kiss each several paper for amends.
    Look: here is writ "kind Julia." Unkind Julia,
    As in revenge of thy ingratitude,
    I throw thy name against the bruising stones,
    Trampling contemptuously on thy disdain!
    And here is writ "love-wounded Proteus."
    Poor wounded name! My bosom as a bed
    Shall lodge thee till thy wound be throughly heal'd;
    And thus I search it with a sovereign kiss.
    But twice or thrice was "Proteus" written down:
    Be calm, good wind, blow not a word away
    Till I have found each letter in the letter,
    Except mine own name; that, some whirlwind bear
    Unto a ragged, fearful, hanging rock,
    And throw it thence into the raging sea.
    Lo, here in one line is his name twice writ:
    "Poor forlorn Proteus"; "passionate Proteus
    To the sweet Julia"—that I'll tear away—
    And yet I will not, sith so prettily
    He couples it to his complaining name.
    Thus will I fold them one upon another;
    Now kiss, embrace, contend, do what you will.

    The moment that Julia believes Lucetta gone, Julia's "cool" demeanor breaks suddenly into a desperate scramble for the many pieces of Proteus's letter that she has torn and scattered on the ground. (Actresses should take note that the more pieces she has torn the letter into, the more effort it will take to sort them out; consequently, even more comic energy will be infused into the scene.) She likens her hands to "injurious wasps" that raid and steal sweet honey from beehives; as she expresses the metaphor, she probably slaps her own hands in overwrought, child-like punishment. Pulling the scraps together in a pile, she begins to kiss each piece of paper in passionate atonement, imagining each one to be her beloved Proteus's lips.

As she does, she sees that her name is written on one of the pieces that describes her as "kind." In a fit of pique, she tries to hurl the paper away from her, perhaps even stamping on it, grinding it even further against the "bruising stones" of the floor. Another torn section catches her eye with the words "love-wounded Proteus." In maternal fashion (although certainly not without sexual overtones!), she cradles the tiny paper against her breast, giving it too a lingering kiss. Even as she does this, the breeze seems to freshen around her; suddenly the papers are all in danger of being blown away before she can assemble them! Desperately she sweeps the pieces up, crawling on her hands and knees to find every last one before they disappear. Nonetheless, she does note that all of the scraps of the letter that carry her name deserve to be blown away, over a rocky precipice and into a turbulent ocean!

She finds one that carries both her own name as well as "passionate Proteus"; taking her cue, she begins to play with the paper as if it were a doll, folding the two names together in her fingers, allowing them to cuddle, pet, and kiss, undoubtedly speaking to the crumpled pieces in cooing, playful tones. "Do what you will" takes on a charged, adolescently erotic overtone in her imagination, a very personal moment for Julia; which, to her surprised chagrin, she learns that Lucetta has been witnessing behind her all the while when the amused maidservant suddenly steps forward and speaks her name—right at her shoulder!

LUCETTA: Madam,
    Dinner is ready, and your father stays.
JULIA: Well, let us go.
LUCETTA: What, shall these papers lie like tell-tales here?
JULIA: If you respect them, best to take them up.
LUCETTA: Nay, I was taken up for laying them down;
    Yet here they shall not lie, for catching cold.
JULIA: I see you have a month's mind to them.

Julia's startled reaction, and her attempts to physically re-gather her composure and her wits after Lucetta's "Madam", fills the rest of the four beats of the iambic pentameter line. After giving her a moment to do this, Lucetta continues, telling her it's time for dinner. Julia takes a long breath, and delivers another short line of verse, during which she begins her desperately dignified exit. Lucetta lingers, expressing concern about leaving the pile of torn papers behind. (Perhaps she even mocks Julia's earlier loving tones to the inanimate objects for a bit of extra fun.) Julia, still vainly trying to pretend they mean nothing to her, says that if Lucetta cares so much about them, she can gather them up. Still having fun with what she has overheard from Julia, Lucetta notes (a bit smugly?) that she was reprimanded earlier in the scene for dropping the note on the ground; nevertheless, she will go ahead and pick the poor babies up so that they won't "catch cold" by lying on the chilly stone (acknowledging the human characteristics that Julia herself endowed them with in her soliloquy).

Knowing for certain now that everything she said to the scraps of paper have been overheard by her companion, Julia finally grows up enough to laugh a bit at herself, accepting her own silly behavior. Smiling at the whole situation, she notes that Lucetta has a "month's mind" for caring about the papers. Various editors disagree about the precise meaning of this phrase, but the gist of it is something like this: "I see you care about them too!" A "month's mind" could mean a sustained care; or, it could even refer to the idea that Lucetta—being a woman too, whose monthly menstrual cycle is also connected to her passions, both maternal and romantic, would naturally take a similar care of the poor torn letter, representing the "wounded" Proteus. (Shakespeare makes a similar reference in the earlier scene we looked at in *Twelfth Night*, when he has Olivia say to Viola "'Tis not that time of moon with me to make one in so skipping a dialogue.")

LUCETTA: Ay, madam; you may say what sights you see.
I see things too, although you judge I wink.
JULIA: Come, come, will't please you go?
(They exit.)

Whatever the precise meaning of Julia's words, they bring a knowing smile to Lucetta's face. She uses their moment of shared good humor to tell Julia that her feelings about Proteus are obvious to someone who knows her as well as Lucetta does; after all, in spite of their "class differences" they are also companions who know one another very well. So, Julia should drop the silly pride and embarrassment, and embrace her own feelings, especially with her friend. It's a nice moment between the two of them, and the audience can see that Julia actually matures a bit by accepting Lucetta's wisdom. She laughs—both at her own silliness as well as in delighted happiness over this new and certain revelation of Proteus's love for her.

And with that, the two young ladies run happily off to dinner—and probably further, excited conversation about the merits of young Proteus!

MACBETH, ACT I, SCENE VII

THE CHARACTERS:
Macbeth, Thane of Glamis, a province of Scotland. (A "thane" was a freeman granted control of land and territory in exchange for military service.) After the civil insurrection that opens the play, Macbeth is also named Thane of Cawdor, gaining the title of the rebellious soldier he's defeated in battle.
Lady Macbeth, his wife.

THE CONTEXT AND CIRCUMSTANCES:

Some years ago, I attended a talk given by the late David William at the Stratford, Ontario Shakespeare Festival. Then Artistic Director of that operation, he had just finished staging *Macbeth* with Brian Bedford, Goldie Semple, and Scott Wentworth (Macduff) in the main roles, and he offered his listeners a very important and concise insight about this challenging play.

"There are two things one has to accept and remember when bringing Macbeth to life," he said: "The first is that Macbeth is a very good soldier, the best there is in his time. The second is that the Macbeths have an extremely good marriage; they're deeply devoted to one another."

As simple as those observations may sound, most productions of the play take them too much for granted, to the point where often the driving mechanism of Shakespeare's tragedy becomes murky, or even lost altogether. Aristotle's "tragic flaw"—a term rising from the concept of *hamartia*, introduced in the *Poetics*—is misunderstood and misused when teachers, actors, and unimaginative directors attempt to bring the play to life. Macbeth isn't a noble soldier simply brought down by his wife's selfishness and his own ambition (an idea I recall delivered many years ago in an undergraduate English course). The Greeks were not developing their philosophical world-view out of a Judeo-Christian mentality of man's guilt and original sin; Aristotle's "tragic flaw" is not a tragic flaw in a character's personality; i.e., Hamlet is too indecisive, Romeo too impulsive, Othello too jealous. All of these things may indeed be true, but to believe that they alone set the tragic wheels in motion is way too simplistic a view of Aristotle's premise. *Hamartia* is better seen as a flaw in the very universe itself, a spoke in its wheels as it were, that can bring down men and women who are trying to do the right thing—or at least the thing that they have been applauded for in the past, and that has led to their overall success—at the wrong time, or under the wrong circumstances. This perspective is the real key to the dark and awful journey of the Macbeths, and fully understanding their unique context and personal perspective will prove vital for any actors taking on those roles.

We first hear of Macbeth through a wounded soldier's report of his actions in the midst of a bloody battle, led by the Scottish king Duncan to put down the rebellious Thane of Cawdor. When all other men and tactics have failed, and the outcome of the civil insurrection teeters in the balance, enter the warrior superman, "brave Macbeth," who inspires wonder and awe in all who witness his prowess. Reports the wounded Scottish soldier of the final encounter between Macbeth, Thane of Glamis, and Macdonwald, Thane of Cawdor:

> *For brave Macbeth (well he deserves that name)*
> *Disdaining Fortune, with his brandish'd steel,*
> *Which smok'd with bloody execution,*
> *(Like Valor's minion) carv'd out his passage*
> *Till he fac'd the slave;*
> *Which ne'er shook hands, nor bade farewell to him,*
> *Till he unseam'd him from the nave to the chops,*
> *And fix'd his head upon our battlements.*

Wow. That's quite an introduction to the play's protagonist, even if it happens offstage, and we only hear of it in report. The image sears our imagination: a brave and brutal Scot, with daunting and bloody death all around him and defeat a distinct possibility, wades through the melee until he faces the opposing leader; then, without a word, plunges his broadsword into the pit of the man's stomach and rips it up through his body, splitting Macdonwald up to his chin. Heaving the blade out, he swings it again through the air, blood and entrails flying, and strikes off his armored enemy's head with one powerful stroke. No wonder this man inspires such awe; his battle prowess, here described, appears almost supernatural in its intensity and skill.

Indeed, a truly supernatural element has appeared prior to this, in the play's first scene; so we have already been briefly introduced to the three "Weird Sisters" that Macbeth and his fellow soldier and friend Banquo encounter in the drama's third scene. They don't linger for long; after prophesying that Macbeth will soon become both Thane of Cawdor (assuming the title of the man he's just "unseam'd")—and shortly thereafter

King of Scotland!—the bearded women vanish. (However, not before also predicting that Banquo will beget kings for future generations.) Both men are filled with wonder—and perhaps not a little fear—at the apparitions, but Macbeth also feels the stirrings of exciting possibility. To be King of Scotland! As we'll learn later in the play, it's not the first time he's allowed himself to fantasize about this "what if" scenario.

When Duncan, King of Scotland, arrives shortly thereafter, he commends Macbeth's unmatched victories by naming him Thane of Cawdor, just as the Sisters foretold; but at the same time, he also proclaims Malcolm, his elder son, the official royal heir, and thus next in line for the throne . . . .not the valorous Macbeth, who is clearly disappointed. Additionally, Duncan announces that he intends to visit Macbeth's castle immediately for the purpose of bestowing honor upon his chief soldier and his wife; so Macbeth sends instructions to his wife to prepare for the King's visit.

The scene shifts to Glamis Castle, where Macbeth's young wife awaits his return with both anxiety and eagerness. She first appears reading the letter that her husband has sent in advance of his arrival home, wherein he describes to her the strange appearance of the Weird Sisters, with their even stranger prophecy. Lady Macbeth can scarcely contain her excitement. Completely devoted to her husband, she knows that he is the biggest, baddest soldier that Scotland has; if he hadn't supported King Duncan and opposed Macdonwald's revolt, Duncan wouldn't have prevailed—she's sure of that. Moreover, Duncan has passed his prime; he's an old, weak man, and his son, Malcolm, is way too young and inexperienced to hold the throne in these turbulent times. In her view, it's time for her husband to finally receive the honors to which his past valor has entitled him. He's the best there is, and he deserves the highest prize.

In youthful and naïve exuberance, Lady Macbeth decides to conduct a spontaneous ritual prayer to all of the spirits of Darkness, entreating their support in building her into the strong, unwavering partner that her husband will need for his efforts to take the crown. It has always seemed to me that this moment for Lady Macbeth is equivalent to a young teenage girl experimenting with a Ouija Board; she plays with dark and mystical powers that may truly be dangerous beyond her youthful understanding. She's not an older, embittered, cynically ambitious crone; later in the play, Shakespeare offers several important moments that depict the Lady as rather youthful and increasingly frightened by the bloody path she has encouraged her husband to pursue: she's startled by the cry of an owl in the night; she talks of being unable to visualize murdering Duncan herself, because he reminds her of her own father; she faints as she feels suspicions closing in on her husband right after the murder is discovered (some believe that this is an act on her part to divert attention, which is indeed possible, but not with the Lady Macbeth that I feel the text suggests); and finally, of course, there is the famous sleepwalking scene, which shows a young woman so devastated by guilt and horror that she has descended into a state of madness.

As she completes her invocation, asking the demons of Hell to lend her strength to aid her husband, the primary human devil in the action to come enters behind her: Macbeth himself. She runs to his arms, and he sweeps her passionately up. Between kisses and caresses, the young couple hurriedly share with one another the excitement of all that has recently occurred: Macbeth's "promotion," Duncan's impending visit (he's within hours of arrival), and most of all, the promises of the supernatural sisters for their glorious future. Eager to demonstrate that she's a worthy wife for such a strong, sexy man, Lady Macbeth broadly hints to him that she knows that he's tempted to dispose of Duncan, and now that opportunity has arrived. Moreover, she's ready to help him: Offer Duncan your clearest face and "leave all the rest to me," she says breathlessly, as they exit the scene in one another's arms.

Thus, Aristotle's "flaw" is set. Celebrated all of his life as the most successful soldier in the Scottish kingdom, praised for his intelligence, cunning and ruthlessness, Macbeth has impressively fulfilled the destiny that he has been lauded for. As a result, he's become a cold and calculating killer, fascinated with violence, with a soul both poetic and amoral. (In a way, he's kind of a medieval James Bond, only his state-sanctioned killing is done openly rather than clandestinely.) And Lady Macbeth's love and devotion for her heroic and glorious husband would, under normal circumstances, garner our admiration rather than our horror. An honored soldier and his loyal, loving wife—with a push from convenient political circumstances (as well as mysterious and supernatural prophecies)—are all too ready to take the terrible path that Fate has set for them.

This scene opens the very evening that King Duncan has arrived at Glamis Castle, hours after the Macbeths' reunion described above. A celebratory dinner is heard in the Great Hall, just offstage. As the darkness of the night gathers around the Scottish countryside, Macbeth leaves his place at the dining table, walks alone onto the stage, and begins to share his thoughts about the cold-blooded murder that he and his wife are considering for later that night.

MACBETH: If it were done when 'tis done, then 'twere well
    It were done quickly. If th' assassination
    Could trammel up the consequence, and catch
    With his surcease, success; that but this blow
    Might be the be-all and the end-all here,
    But here, upon this bank and shoal of time,
    We'd jump the life to come. But in these cases
    We still have judgment here, that we but teach
    Bloody instructions, which, being taught, return
    To plague the inventor. This even-handed justice
    Commends th' ingredients of our poison'd chalice
    To our own lips. He's here in double trust:
    First, as I am his kinsman and his subject,
    Strong both against the deed; then, as his host,
    Who should against his murderer shut the door,
    Not bear the knife myself. Besides, this Duncan
    Hath borne his faculties so meek, hath been
    So clear in his great office, that his virtues
    Will plead like angels, trumpet-tongu'd, against
    The deep damnation of his taking-off;

And pity, like a naked new-born babe,
Striding the blast, or heaven's cherubin, hors'd
Upon the sightless couriers of the air,
Shall blow the horrid deed in every eye,
That tears shall drown the wind. I have no spur
To prick the sides of my intent, but only
Vaulting ambition, which o'erleaps itself
And falls on th' other—

Macbeth's first lines of the soliloquy seem a key indicator of his character: note that he isn't brooding about the moral question of whether or not he should be pursuing the murder of his King—while the monarch is a guest in his own house, no less—but instead, he's perturbed about the possible political consequences of the act. "If the deed were actually finished once the murder had been committed," he muses throughout the initial seven lines, "I'd do it without hesitation; I have no moral qualms, and no concern about the consequences of going to hell." That's certainly the "life to come" he speaks of: the hypothetical afterlife that, with the appearance of the witches, must have moved more into the realm of reality for him. Even then, he's willing to risk that for the gain of becoming King of Scotland. This man fears little!

Nonetheless, he does express great concern about the practical ramifications of the deed. The examples of murder and usurpation which his deed will set will almost surely come back to haunt him in a variety of ways. The only time in the soliloquy that Macbeth touches solidly upon the moral aspects of the deed comes when he notes that the murder of a guest by his host seems particularly heinous. But then, almost immediately, he returns to considering the political costs, how he will be perceived by his fellows rather than whether or not he will be damned by any God. For me, this seems a strong argument against those critics and scholars who want to view Macbeth as a solidly moral man who has been tempted into immorality by pure greed, either his wife's or his own. For this professional soldier/killer, the idea of Duncan's murder appears more of a tactical issue than a matter of good and evil. Duncan's demeanor as a ruler has been so generous, so "meek" (Macbeth's word here doesn't seem to indicate a high degree of respect) that his removal from office—especially by clandestine murder—could stir up both civilians and military to open revolt against its perpetrator. Macbeth even uses a celestial metaphor to underscore how pronounced the public reaction could be, an image of angels, cherubins, and innocent babies' souls condemning the deed to all mankind in the form of a nearly apocalyptic, Book of Revelations-type series of heavenly apparitions. The peoples' response to such a regicide will be so pronounced, both physically and spiritually, that "tears shall drown the wind"—a pretty powerful cautionary image for Macbeth, it would seem. Furthermore, he has no political reason for usurping the crown from Duncan that could be viewed as justifiable—only "vaulting ambition." Here, in a nice piece of naturalistic writing within the formality of the verse, Shakespeare has Macbeth begin a visual metaphor of that "vault" that any soldier would understand: it's like an overly eager young recruit who brashly tries to leap onto the back of a horse, overshoots his mark, and tumbles ignobly off the other side. However, before he can completely speak the metaphor aloud, he's surprised by the hurried entrance of his wife. Understandably on edge as their plot unfolds, she wonders why her husband has suddenly—and obviously to all present—departed the banquet that is being given in his honor!

> *(LADY MACBETH enters)*
> MACBETH: *(continuing)*   How now? What news?
> LADY MACBETH: He hath almost supp'd. Why have you left the chamber?
> MACBETH: Hath he ask'd for me?
> LADY MACBETH: Know you not he has?

Macbeth completes his iambic line with a curt greeting/inquiry to his wife; yet he must certainly understand why she has followed him from the Great Hall, and why she's wound up. Although the reasons for her bewilderment at his behavior are clear, he anticipates that her response to his assessment of their political situation isn't going to be calm and compliant, especially as close as they've come to successfully realizing their shared ambitions. Her questions are rapid and breathless;

she knows that his absence will be noted and wondered at by their guests—and they certainly don't need anything tonight that might focus any suspicion their way! When Macbeth tries momentarily to avoid directly confronting the issue by delaying with an obvious question, his Lady almost hisses her frustration back at him. Knowing that matters need to be settled before another moment passes, Macbeth turns to bluntly share with her the decision he's come to:

MACBETH: We will proceed no further in this business.
    He hath honor'd me of late, and I have bought
    Golden opinions from all sorts of people,
    Which would be worn now in their newest gloss,
    Not cast aside so soon.
LADY MACBETH: Was the hope drunk
    Wherein you dress'd yourself? Hath it slept since?
    And wakes it now to look so green and pale
    At what it did so freely? From this time
    Such I account thy love. Art thou afeard
    To be the same in thine own act and valor
    As thou art in desire? Wouldst thou have that
    Which thou esteems't the ornament of life,
    And live a coward in thine own esteem,
    Letting "I dare not" wait upon "I would,"
    Like the poor cat i' th' adage?
MACBETH: Prithee, peace!
    I dare do all that may become a man;
    Who dares do more is none!

Macbeth's first line elicits a shocked silence from his wife; the warrior can see the stunned disappointment on his devoted wife's face, and he feels immediately guilty and defensive at his betrayal of their mutual agreement—and perhaps a bit cowardly, something unfamiliar to him. He tries to explain his reasoning to her. They have been awarded important honors by the King that they should both fully embrace and celebrate; why risk it all by seeking more? The argument shows Macbeth's innate tactical intelligence: a smaller, secure victory at this point should supersede the temptation to risk and (possibly) lose all. We should be smart and count ourselves lucky in what we have, he says.

(It's worth noting that Shakespeare uses a style of verse structure with this scene and others in the play that is characteristic of his later plays: there are very few "end stopped" lines, with pauses for breath or meaning that parallel the exact iambic pentameter rhythm; instead, the lines flow on, with important punctuation or caesurae occurring in the middle of lines rather than at the end of them. In the previous chapter covering scansion and verse analysis, we noted that this technique was called "enjambed" lines. It's an innovation of dramatic verse of which Shakespeare led the way in his plays written during the early 17th Century, and he became a master at using it to make his dialogue sound more natural, less formal and artificial. The exchanges in this scene as well as many others in the play have a headlong, urgent sense of tempo to them without sacrificing our sense of the poetry's beauty. The dramatic pace is enhanced, and the actors are better able to find a grounded sense of naturalism that's more difficult to achieve in the earlier plays which have more end-stopped lines—such as the scene we just examined from *The Two Gentlemen of Verona*.)

Lady Macbeth accepts none of this spirit of retreat from her husband. Although the hurried plan to murder Duncan began for her as a means of gaining all the respect, power and glory for her husband that she believes he truly deserves—why should a weak old man rule Scotland while its strongest and most virile warrior looks on?—now her own ambition and adrenaline have kicked in. They are so close to achieving all of their biggest dreams! Knowing her husband all too well, this young wife now goes for his most tender vulnerabilities—the pride he has in his own manhood, and his love for her. She links them together with cutting effectiveness. "You're behaving like a timid coward," she accuses him, "especially when everything we desire waits right here to be seized; and since a coward is not the man I thought you were, then perhaps your so-called 'love' for me is also suspect." She knows that they are both at a tipping point; if either one of them back down, such an opportunity as now presents itself for the taking will likely never come again. Her desperate, accusatory tirade spills out with no thought of caution.

Interrupting the flow of her words, and in the midst of an iambic line, Macbeth physically seizes her, perhaps even grabbing her jaw as if she were a disobedient child. The power of this action and his accompanying "Prithee, peace!" shuts his wife down quite effectively. His anger comes from knowing that she's aware of what he truly feels all too well, and that she can "push his buttons" to get the response that she wants. As David William noted, they have a very close marriage; they know how to manipulate one another very effectively. But Lady Macbeth won't be stifled so easily. After a very brief silence in response to the power of his rebuke—presuming that Macbeth's order and his Lady's answer are two short lines rather than a shared line, as they are arranged by some editors—she speaks once again . . . although now a bit more quietly and cautiously. She knows that she has baited the bear with some risk, so now she tactically puts the matter in more personal, more wifely terms:

LADY MACBETH: What beast was't then
    That made you break this enterprise to me?
    When you durst do it, then you were a man;
    And to be more than what you were, you would
    Be so much more the man. Nor time, nor place
    Did then adhere, and yet you would make both:
    They have made themselves, and that their fitness now
    Does unmake you. I have given suck, and know
    How tender 'tis to love the babe that milks me;
    I would, while it was smiling in my face,
    Have pluck'd my nipple from his boneless gums,
    And dash'd the brains out, had I so sworn as you
    Have done to this.
MACBETH: If we should fail?
LADY MACBETH: We fail?
    But screw your courage to the sticking place
    And we'll not fail!

The Lady suddenly becomes the injured little girl, bewildered that she has somehow angered her greatest love. She believes it's a tactic that will surely work. Her words reveal some interesting information as well: Macbeth has apparently spoken to his wife before today about his fantasies of removing the obstacle of Duncan from his path to the Scottish throne. Lady Macbeth here indicates that when Macbeth spoke of it in days past, there was then no opportunity for them to actually put an effective plan into place to make it a reality; now, however, all the pieces are arranged, seemingly by Fate and without them lifting a finger to make it happen! All they have to do now is muster the courage to pull the trigger, as it were. A small thing, she thinks.

Some scholars have believed for years that these references to things happening that we don't see on stage, scattered as they are throughout the play, give some indication that the version of the text we have in the First Folio represents a version significantly cut from Shakespeare's original, probably by the players who staged it. So, when it came time to assemble the Folio, this was the only version left for them to use. Such academicians cite the play's short length (when compared with his other great tragedies) as further support for this idea. Personally, I think the references to offstage occurrences to which we aren't witness add immensely to the mysterious ambience that infuses the story, helping to achieve an effect that matches the subject matter. It also makes it seem quite modern—and again, naturalistic, in spite of its supernatural subject and tone—in a manner that sets it apart from other plays of the period. It's a strength of the piece, not a flaw, giving us a stronger sense of an offstage psychological life that is ongoing, something rather unusual in most examples of Elizabethan and Jacobean drama.

After softening her husband with her child-like retreat from his anger, Lady Macbeth offers a final underscoring of her strength of devotion to this man who means the world to her. I have suckled a baby at my breast, she says to him; and I would have torn it away and smashed it on the floor at my feet before I would ever have broken a vow to you! This image obviously shocks both Macbeth and the audience, and it also reveals very telling background information about the couple: they have had a child and lost it, presumably to death in infancy, a shattering experience for any marriage, one which psychologists note will often either break it apart or bond it even closer. Perhaps the latter seems more the case with the Macbeths, but the subsequent events of the story may prove that assertion questionable. Nevertheless, this information provides given circumstances that are pivotal for actors to consider and to flesh out in some detail when preparing to embody these characters.

This statement, stunning at it is coming from a young mother who loved her lost child and still grieves for its absence, proves the turning point in Lady Macbeth's desperate attempt to get her hesitant husband back on track in their plans. It elicits the open question from him that's truly been troubling him all along, as we know from his soliloquy. "If we should fail?" he asks her with quick intensity, continuing her verse line. Without any pause whatsoever, she finishes the shared line with a mocking repeat of his question: "We fail?" (How could we? its tone seems to suggest: Together, we're an invincible team!) She's got him! If he only keeps his courage—which they both know he has more of than any man in Scotland—they can't lose. And here, she goes on to suggest, is where she can personally offer some further help for their mutual success:

LADY MACBETH: *(continuing)* When Duncan is asleep
   (Whereto the rather shall his day's hard journey
   Soundly invite him), his two chamberlains
   Will I with wine and wassail so convince,
   That memory, the warder of the brain,
   Shall be a fume, and the receipt of reason
   A limbeck only. When in swinish sleep
   Their drenched natures lie as in a death,
   What cannot you and I perform upon
   Th' unguarded Duncan? What not put upon
   His spongy officers, who shall bear the guilt
   Of our great quell?
MACBETH: Bring forth men children only!
   For thy undaunted mettle should compose
   Nothing but males. Will it not be receiv'd,
   When we have mark'd with blood those sleepy two
   Of his own chamber, and us'd their very daggers,
   That they have done't?

LADY MACBETH: Who dares receive it other,
    As we shall make our griefs and clamor roar
    Upon his death?
MACBETH: I am settled, and bend up
    Each corporal agent to this terrible feat.
    Away, and mock the time with fairest show:
    False face must hide what the false heart doth know.
    (They exit together)

Macbeth and Lady Macbeth in *Macbeth*

Offering further assurance to her apparently waffling husband, Lady Macbeth describes in some detail her planned initiative to personally aid their joint endeavor: Macbeth will (appropriately) wield the murder weapon, but his wife will pave the path for a smooth aftermath to the deed. Duncan is an old man; this day of battles won, hard journeying, and celebratory banqueting will inevitably bring on a sound sleep. To insure that he's not alone in that, the Lady will drug the evening drinks she serves to his guards and chamberlins so that they will sleep as deeply as their inebriated and weary King. The drug she has in mind for them will also blur their memory of the evening in general, thereby providing an additional benefit: they will be entirely unable to articulate any alibi that could preserve them from direct blame for the murder; consequently, they will be the logical suspects!

Macbeth's response to his wife's seemingly cold and calculating plans could be played in a variety of ways: admiring of her courage? Pleased—even delighted—at her forethought and planning? Or perhaps a bit horrified at her ruthlessness? I suspect it's a heady mixture of all of those elements, and it prompts the testosterone-driven soldier to offer his wife the best compliment he can devise: because of her obvious (and unfeminine—or unnatural) courage, she should, in future years, only conceive and give birth to male children. For him, it's a great compliment, and she almost certainly takes it as such, perhaps even giggling delightedly. His mind racing with newly ignited excitement, Macbeth suggests the next logical step of the plot: why not smear Duncan's blood on those same unconscious servants to further focus suspicion of the murder on them, consequently sealing their fate? Her enthusiasm bubbling over, Lady Macbeth concurs; their energy together is so headlong that they finish one another's verse lines, as if they are reading one another's thoughts. Embracing his wife, Macbeth assures her that his indecision has now passed; she has successfully convinced him that any political pitfalls or consequences from their plans going awry may now be avoided—if they both keep their wits about them, that is. For now, they will return to the banquet together, all smiles and hospitality, awaiting the bloody adventure that the night will bring.

What Lady Macbeth cannot know is that, like Dr. Frankenstein, she has created a monster in trying to help her husband become the perfect man, the perfect future King. While she would be more than satisfied with achieving this one daring leap together, as the play progresses she will learn—to her horror—that for Macbeth, they "are but young in deed." Murder after murder will soon bring a reign of paranoia and terror to Scotland, and the young wife—who wanted only great things for the husband she loves—unable to cope with it all, will descend inexorably into madness and suicide.

RICHARD III, ACT I, SCENE II

THE CHARACTERS:

Richard, Duke of Gloucester; youngest son of the trio of the late Duke of York's male heirs who now control the English throne after their overthrow of the Lancaster king, Henry VI. (Richard himself murdered Henry VI in his prison cell in *Henry VI, Part 3*.) Richard's older brother, Edward IV, currently sits on the throne, with his two young sons as his natural heirs. However, Richard has other plans: he intends to seize rule for himself upon Edward's death, by whatever means necessary.

Lady Anne Neville, daughter of Warwick, and young widow of another Edward, this one the son of the late King Henry VI, whom Richard killed in a battle of the War of the Roses. ("I stabbed in my angry mood at Tewksbury," he says in the scene we will examine) Thus, if the Lancasters had prevailed against the Yorks, she would have been in line to become Queen of England after Henry VI's death.

THE CONTEXT AND CIRCUMSTANCES:

(NOTE: As might be apparent just by the description of the characters above, one of the most confusing things for young actors about studying Shakespeare's history plays is the abundance of characters bearing the same name! For instance, we have Richard, Duke of York, the father of Richard, Duke of

Gloucester—and then, we also have yet another Richard, Duke of York, King Edward's youngest son. Also Elizabeth [Edward's wife], who has a daughter of the same name. Most modern editions of the plays provide complex charts to help readers and actors keep track of it all—but a certain amount of confusion is to be anticipated. Shakespeare often refers to his protagonist in this play as simply Gloucester to avoid confusion—until he's actually crowned, and then he becomes "King Richard."

It's also worth mentioning here that Shakespeare's history plays succeed as drama because of their deft compression of historical events; thus, precision and accuracy is often sacrificed for the purpose of more effective theatre. Actors doing appropriate historical research before embarking on rehearsals may find—to their understandable confusion and occasional frustration—that Shakespeare sometimes plays fast and loose with facts, time lines, and characters. However, the linked plays mainly have internal consistency with one another; and actors working on this scene will greatly benefit from a careful reading of the historical trilogy of plays that precede its action: *Henry VI, Parts 1, 2*, and *3*.

One final note before we begin to delve into the scene's context: in a previous chapter, we spent some time looking at the variations in the texts—some major, some minor—of Shakespeare's plays that were published in several forms during his lifetime, or shortly thereafter. We looked at the rather profound differences between Quarto and Folio versions of famous plays that we often treat in classrooms as if they have a single, indisputable, sacrosanct version, classic texts such as *Hamlet, Romeo and Juliet*, and *King Lear*. Well, for Elizabethan theatre audiences, there was no more popular play written by the Bard than *Richard III*. In today's vocabulary, it was a true blockbuster; it enjoyed multiple revivals during his lifetime and immediately thereafter. Its protagonist proves hypnotically fascinating in his Machiavellian efforts to usurp the English throne, while simultaneously displaying the blackest sense of warped humor: an irresistibly theatrical combination. In addition to its durability in stage revivals, this particular play also saw the most publications in Quarto form before its inclusion in the 1623 First Folio—no less than six separate Quartos from 1597 to 1622! The Folio version of the play is substantially longer than the most complete extant Quarto version that preceded it, and there are many variations in text, both large and small. The version that I use for our scenework here is a personal compilation using both Quartos and Folio, but creative and ambitious young actors shouldn't just rely on my choices; they should check a modern edition that offers reliable comparisons [such as those we mentioned earlier, the Arden, the Oxford, the New Cambridge, or the standard early 20th Century Variorum edition by H. H. Furness]. In doing so, they will immerse themselves further in the historical world they are to depict on the stage, while also arriving at their own informed and imaginative choices about what textual variations will work best for them in performance.)

Now, for the dramatic circumstances that begin the scene:

The long, contentious British civil war known as the War of the Roses has drawn to a close. The two family factions of the Yorks and Lancasters, both claiming a more direct descendance from the original Plantagenet line of English kings, have battled for years to control the throne, and the Yorks have prevailed. The weak and indecisive King Henry VI has been deposed, imprisoned, and murdered (by Richard, Duke of Gloucester) in his cell; Richard's older brother, Edward (IV of that title), has been crowned as the first Yorkist king. His two younger brothers, Clarence and Richard, envious of his power, also view his marriage to the widow Lady Elizabeth Gray with some disdain. Nonetheless, the marriage has been a fruitful one, producing two young male heirs, the Princes Edward and Richard, and a daughter, Elizabeth.

We learn from Richard's initial soliloquy in this play that bears his name three essential facts about him: 1. He wants the crown for himself. 2. He is willing to remove whatever people and obstacles are in his way—by whatever means necessary, including duplicity and murder. 3. He has lived his entire life under the shadow of congenital deformities, including a clubbed foot, a humped and twisted spine, and a withered arm. He displays a bitter sense of humor about all of the above, and feels that his physical impediments provide personal justification for the violent usurpations upon which he's about to embark. For readers or playgoers who have experienced his presence in *Henry VI, Part 3*, none of these things will be surprising; he lays the groundwork for all of this in that play.

So, Richard wants the crown, but these people stand in his way (in descending order): Edward IV (himself ailing as the play begins); Edward's two small sons, Edward and Richard; Clarence, Richard's elder brother, next in line after the two princes; and Clarence's son. Edward's own ill health will do him in; before that happens however, Richard convinces the King that their brother, Clarence, is plotting against him. True to form, Richard doesn't achieve this with direct accusation—that would be too crass, too obvious. Instead, he endeavors to plant rumors and gossip within King Edward's hearing that imply Clarence's personal aspirations for the throne, to be achieved through a plotted fratricide/regicide. The paranoid Edward immediately imprisons Clarence in the Tower of London; and Richard, in a bold turnaround, accuses Edward's wife, Elizabeth Gray, of being the motivator of this action!

Disgraced by the suspicion of treason, Clarence asks Richard to intervene with their brother, little suspecting that Richard will do just that—but not in the manner that Clarence hopes for. Richard tricks Edward into sanctioning Clarence's death in his Tower cell, drowned in a barrel of wine by two of Richard's cronies. Shortly thereafter, Edward meets with his own demise, killed by disease and remorse in equal parts. Clarence and his family—declared traitors—are now out of the line of succession; so with Edward dead, the late King's oldest son, the child Edward (Prince of Wales), is now in line to be crowned—with Richard of Gloucester, his last remaining uncle, as his official Regent and "Lord Protector." Before too much time elapses, Richard assumes this responsibility—by imprisoning his two young nephews in the Tower . . . .for their own protection, of course. There, they will disappear, and their skeletons will be discovered entombed within a Tower wall centuries later. Was Richard, Duke of Gloucester, their murderer? Or rather, did he order their clandestine execution? Shakespeare depicts it so, using as his source the official Tudor account written by Henry

VIII's Chancellor, Sir Thomas More. Other historians continue to wonder about the true circumstances of the Princes' death. (All of this speculation, however, is beyond the boundaries of Shakespeare's version of the play.)

Before all of these events involving the murder of the princes actually occur in the play, the Duke of Gloucester determines to better pave his path to the throne by marrying a wife whom he believes will further solidify his future claim to the crown: the Lady Anne Neville. This proposed courtship provides an extraordinary challenge for Richard, as Anne is freshly a widow, and her late husband, as previously noted, was none other than the deposed Henry VI's son, the young Prince Edward. (Yes, yet another Edward!) This Edward was also killed by Richard—her would-be suitor!—in a battle between the York and Lancaster forces at Tewksbury. (These events occur in *Henry VI, Part 3*.) As already summarized, Richard will shortly follow this battlefield action with the cold-blooded murder of King Henry himself—the Lady Anne's royal father-in-law. Nonetheless, he now sets out to woo and wed the lady whom he has bereft of husband, father-in-law, and a future crown.

What motivates him toward this audacious endeavor? Historically, Anne's marriage to the Lancastrian Prince Edward came as a result of a deal her father, the Earl of Warwick, brokered with the Lancaster faction in the civil wars. Agreeing to switch sides in the conflict (he had previously supported the Yorks), he gave the Lancasters a temporary advantage in the ongoing conflict—thus earning him the short-lived appellation of "Warwick, the King-Maker." The substantive reward for his commitment of resources to Henry VI was the marriage of his daughter to Henry's son, theoretically insuring her place as the next Queen of England. (As we shall see during the course of events in *Richard III*, Anne indeed becomes Queen for a brief time—but not as the wife of the prince she originally married!)

On a political level, Richard sees an opportunity to reconcile the Yorks with the Warwick factions by taking the young widow as his bride. This proposal will "reach out" to his family's former enemies, and if successful, further solidify a power base in his quest for the throne of England. On a personal level, Richard's ego craves the affirmation that such a conquest would bring. A "deformed, unfinished" lump of a man, marrying the beautiful widow of his rival—whom he killed? Against all odds, rationality, or natural feelings? It's a challenge that greatly appeals to this charismatic cobra, Shakespeare's dramatic version of the man who will soon become Richard III. In his own mind and heart, he must feel: If I can win Lady Anne under such circumstances, *I can do anything!*

As the scene we're going to work on begins, Lady Anne kneels in mourning over the corpse of her father-in-law Henry VI. (In the scene as Shakespeare composed it, there are attendants present who are bearing the corpse toward its final interment, and the exchange between Richard and Lady Anne is played out "in public" as it were, before these silent guards. While this adds a unique dynamic to the circumstances that would differ from a strictly private encounter between the two, I don't think that eliminating these supernumeraries, as well as the lines that refer to them, for the purposes of our scenework alters the scene's fundamental acting challenges.) Although her words initially express her grief over the deaths of King Henry and his son Edward, her thoughts quickly segue into a rage directed at the perpetrator of these violent deeds that have led to her current losses of both royal in-laws and stature.

(Lady Anne, before the bier of King Henry's corpse;
At some time during her soliloquy, Richard enters quietly
behind her.)

ANNE: Poor key-cold figure of a holy king,
    Pale ashes of the house of Lancaster;
    Thou bloodless remnant of that royal blood,
    Be it lawful that I invoke thy ghost
    To hear the lamentations of poor Anne,
    Wife to thy Edward, to thy slaught'red son,
    Stabbed by the selfsame hands that made these wounds!
    Lo, in these windows that let forth thy life
    I pour the helpless balm of my poor eyes.
    O, cursed be the hand that made these holes!

Cursed the heart that had the heart to do it!
Cursed the blood that let this blood from hence!
More direful hap betide that hated wretch
That makes us wretched by the death of thee
Then I can wish to wolves, to spiders, toads,
Or any creeping venom'd thing that lives!
If ever he have child, abortive be it,
Prodigious, and untimely brought to light,
Whose ugly and unnatural aspect
May fright the hopeful mother at the view,
And that be heir to his unhappiness!
If ever he have wife, let her be made
More miserable by the life of him
Than I am made by my young lord and thee!
(Richard makes his presence known to her.)

In preparing this scene, the actress playing Lady Anne must recognize first that, for the Elizabethans, cursing was serious business. The litany of dire wishes she lists for Richard within this eulogy to her father-in-law—and *in absentia* to her husband—isn't rhetoric; it's specific and literal. She wants these precise things to happen to Richard, and it's important that the actress visualize them clearly in her imagination so that the language comes to full life.

Anne begins her speech in a very low-key manner; the actress has a lot to say, and much of it quite violent. She must pace herself, building her distress and anger step by step, line by line, image by image. First, she pays appropriate and rather formal homage to the late King of England; even though he was her father-in-law, the words here seem a bit distanced from the open emotion that will follow. Although she recognizes the monumental import of this act of regicide to the state, it's only when she brings her grief for her husband forward that her personal feelings begin to overwhelm the formality. Her efforts at self-control crumble, and her tears ("the helpless balm of [her] poor eyes") begin to flow; and, quickly following, her invocation that God wreak a terrible vengeance upon this misshapen man who has brought so much pain and sorrow onto her family and her nation.

Perhaps she begins this part of her speech on the border of hysteria; if she does, she brings that quickly under rigid and furious control. After wishing more harm fall upon Richard than she could wish "to wolves, to spiders, toads/Or any creeping venom'd thing that lives", she moves from the general to the specific—and in doing so, she makes the arguable moral error of wishing ill upon the innocent. She asks that God not only curse the murderer himself, but also any of his offspring, begging that all of his children's births be "abortive" resulting in the same suffering deformity (or worse!) that Richard himself bears. She then prays that any future wife he may have be drowned in the same sorrow in which she now finds herself immersed.

Shakespeare loved irony, and he often depended upon his audience's knowledge of their own nation's relatively recent history to achieve its full dramatic effect; and here is just such an instance. The Globe playhouse audiences would have known that Anne was fated to wed Richard, the killer of her first husband; their suspense primarily lay in wondering just how Shakespeare was going to depict the journey to that event. They also would have recognized the (understandable) transgression made, in her grief, by Anne against God's law in wishing for suffering to be laid upon the innocent—i.e., any future wife of Richard, as well as any future children. They would have thus appreciated the terrible irony of Anne's own curse—one that would play out against Anne herself in the events to come!

As Anne builds her emotional intensity, piling scourge upon scourge, a lone figure appears on the stage, out of her line of sight. As she proceeds in her litany of his evils, Richard slowly creeps forward, much like one of the "venom'd things" to which Anne refers in her text, until finally he reveals his presence to her in a suitably dramatic fashion: a touch upon her shoulder, perhaps, or a light caress of her hair. Startled thus from her "prayers", Anne turns and sees their target standing before her.

ANNE: Avaunt, thou dreadful minister of hell!
    Thou hadst but power over his mortal body,
    His soul thou canst not have. Therefore, be gone!
RICHARD: Sweet saint, for charity be not so curst.

ANNE: Foul devil, for God's sake hence, and trouble us not,
    For thou hast made the happy earth thy hell,
    Fill'd it with cursing cries and deep exclaims.
    If thou delight to view thy heinous deeds,
    Behold this pattern of thy butcheries.
       (She uncovers the body, revealing it to Richard.)
    O see, see dead Henry's wounds
    Open their congeal'd mouths and bleed afresh!
    Blush, blush, thou lump of foul deformity;
    For 'tis thy presence that exhales this blood
    From cold and empty veins where no blood dwells.
    Thy deeds inhuman and unnatural
    Provokes this deluge most unnatural.
    O God, which this blood mad'st, revenge his death!
    O earth, which this blood drink'st, revenge his death!
    Either heav'n with lightning strike the murd'rer dead,
    Or earth gape open wide and eat him quick,
    As thou dost swallow up this good king's blood,
    Which his hell-govern'd arm hath butchered!

Anne's astonishment at discovering the object of her ill wishes standing before her must be profound. Recoiling from his touch as she would from a spider suddenly found crawling on her shoulder, she demands that he leave this place of her grief in which his very presence seems blasphemous. Richard responds to her with unexpected gentleness of tone; he asks that her sense of charity overcome her instinct to heap curses upon him, calling her a "sweet saint."

And here begins the thesis/antithesis device that Shakespeare will use to striking effect throughout their subsequent exchanges: Lady Anne parries Richard's phrases with an almost ebullient satisfaction, giving the audience the impression of an expert fencer with impregnable defensive moves. The language crackles with rapid pace and passion. "Sweet saint" is answered with "Foul devil"; and to justify her point, Anne charges that, like a genuine demon, Richard has turned her heaven on earth into a tormenting hell. Remembering that evidence of his sins lies lifeless between them, she impulsively raises the mourning sheet that respectfully hides the dead King Henry's corpse from living eyes, forcing the murderer to view the full results of his deeds. What is revealed takes her by surprise, and sends a thrill of the supernatural through the audience: the corpse, dead for some days, begins to bleed again! True to superstition and folk belief, the murdered victim's body thus points a finger of accusation in the presence of its killer. It's worth emphasizing again to modern actors that Shakespeare did not intend these evidences of ghostly intervention into mortal affairs to be seen by audiences as rhetorical or symbolic. *They are happening*, and as such, promise for Anne some Divine judgment upon Richard's evil actions and character.

Feeling as if God or His avenging angels must actually be hovering in the air above the murdered body, Anne begins to pray even more earnestly to the Deity, His earth, and/or His heavenly forces, pleading that they wreak sudden and unnatural vengeance upon Richard. This final exhortation must further exhaust her already frayed emotional state, and perhaps Richard can see how fragile she is underneath the fury, for he once more attempts to undercut her rage with a calm reason.

RICHARD: Lady, you know no rules of charity
    Which renders good for bad, blessings for curses.
ANNE: Villain, thou know'st no law of God nor man:
    No beast so fierce but knows some touch of pity.
RICHARD: But I know none, and therefore am no beast.
ANNE: O wonderful, when devils tell the truth!
RICHARD: More wonderful when angels are so angry.

Anne, however, again rejects his attempts to reach out to her in her grief; and again, she uses antithesis to strong dramatic effect. Richard's "Lady" is countered by Anne's "Villain"; "rules of charity" is balanced against "law of God." Moreover, both Richard and Anne use antithetical contrasts within their own arguments: Richard with "good for bad, blessings for curses", and Anne with "so fierce" against "some touch of pity." These rhetorical devices are followed hard upon by still more; and this time, Richard takes up Anne's own initial debate tactics, countering her "O wonderful, when devils tell the truth!" with his own "More wonderful when angels are so angry." But just as he begins to take up her thrown gauntlet in earnest, using her own weapons as effectively as she, he pivots skillfully to lay the groundwork for his most powerful central argument:

RICHARD: Vouchsafe, divine perfection of a woman,
Of these supposed crimes to give me leave
By circumstance but to acquit myself.
ANNE: Vouchsafe, diffus'd infection of a man,
Of these known evils, but to give me leave
By circumstance t'accuse thy cursed self.
RICHARD: Fairer than tongue can name thee, let me have
Some patient leisure to excuse myself.
ANNE: Fouler than heart can think thee, thou canst make
No excuse current but to hang thyself.
RICHARD: By such despair I should accuse myself.
ANNE: And by despairing shalt thou stand excused
For doing worthy vengeance on thyself,
That didst unworthy slaughter upon others.
RICHARD: Say that I slew them not?
ANNE: Then say they were not slain;
But dead they are, and devilish slave, by thee!
RICHARD: I did not kill thy husband.
ANNE: Why then he is alive!
RICHARD: Nay, he is dead, and slain by Edward's hands.
ANNE: In thy foul throat thou lie'st! Queen Margaret saw
Thy murderous falchion smoking in his blood;
The which thou once didst bend against her breast,
But that thy brothers beat aside the point.
RICHARD: I was provoked by her sland'rous tongue,
That laid their guilt upon my guiltless shoulders.
ANNE: Thou was provoked by thy bloody mind,
That never dream'st on aught but butcheries!
Didst thou not kill this king?
RICHARD: I grant ye.

Before he can make that argument, however, Richard finds himself besieged by still more of Anne's effective antithetical parries; they seem to mock all that he attempts to say even before he can find the words he wants to use. It's a tactic that Anne continues to utilize to full advantage, undoubtedly because she begins to see the frustration that is building in Richard as its result. Let's look for a moment at Anne's powerful use of antitheses in this section, for they are the actors' primary tools here. With their use, Anne's sense of triumph over her tormentor begins to soar; and Richard's impatience grows more pronounced as he tries to make his point. It seems that Anne might actually beat him at his own game of cleverness!

Here are the antitheses to note and emphasize; the actors must be on top of them all, for they come as fast and furious as a game of ping pong:

Divine perfection of a woman (Richard) against *diffus'd infection of a man* (Anne)

Suppos'd crimes (Richard) against *known evils* (Anne)

To acquit myself (Richard) against *t'accuse thy cursed self* (Anne)

Fairer than tongue can name thee (Richard) against *Fouler than heart can think thee* (Anne)

Excuse myself (Richard) against *hang thyself* (Anne)

By such despair I should accuse myself (Richard) against *And by despairing shalt thou stand excused* (Anne)

Worthy vengeance on thyself against *unworthy slaughter upon others* (Anne's own internal antithesis, used to make her point even more strongly)

Say that I slew them not (Richard) against *Then say they were not slain* (Anne)

I did not kill thy husband (Richard) against *Why then he is alive!* (Anne)

I was provoked by her sland'rous tongue (Richard) against *Thou was provoked by thy bloody mind* (Anne)

Anne is, as the saying goes, "on a tear", and her passion here lends her both clarity and strength of argument, much to Richard's annoyance. She seems to beat him on every point, and antithesis is her most potent weapon, building the scene wonderfully. It's little wonder that a thwarted Richard finally seems to give in and "grant" her what he denied previously: that he is indeed the slayer of King Henry and his princely son, Anne's late husband. However, his admission does nothing to dampen Anne's emotion; if anything, it brings it to a powerful climax, as she hurls the following epithet at the deformed Gloucester.

ANNE: Dost grant me, hedgedhog? Then God grant me too
    Thou mayst be damned for that wicked deed!
    O, he was gentle, mild, and virtuous.
RICHARD: The better for the King of Heaven that hath him.
ANNE: He is in heaven, where thou shalt never come.
RICHARD: Let him thank me that holp to send him thither;
    For he was fitter for that place than earth.
ANNE: And thou unfit for any place but hell.
RICHARD: Yes, one place else, if you will hear me name it.
ANNE: Some dungeon.
RICHARD: Your bedchamber.
ANNE: Ill rest betide the chamber where thou liest!
RICHARD: So will it madam, till I lie with you.
ANNE: I hope so.
RICHARD: I know so.

We sense a weary deflation of Anne as this exchange between them proceeds. Her rage has found a powerful expression through the prior antithetical match-up, and she has effectively achieved a rhetorical victory over the destroyer of her happiness and comfort. It must seem a hollow victory for her, nonetheless; her husband, her King, and her future hopes all still lie in ashes. We can feel the despairing resignation in her words "O, he was gentle, mild, and virtuous."

Re-assessing his approach to the problem of winning the lady to his will, Richard momentarily lapses into an almost absent-minded ironic flippancy. If King Henry was as "gentle, mild, and virtuous" as Anne describes him, then he's clearly better off in Heaven, Richard observes. Her anger apparently rekindled by this off-handed attempt at ironic humor, Anne says that Richard will never know personally whether this is the case or not, because he's "unfit for any place but hell." Sparked by her challenging words, he pertly claims that there may be one other place that suits him. When Anne sharply surmises that this could only be a dungeon, Richard stuns her by his response: "Your bedchamber." Both are short lines, with space left for the appropriate physical reactions from the actors, particularly from Anne; the same device occurs with "I hope so."/"I know so."

Anne is speechless. Richard lets the resulting pause linger for a brief moment before pursuing this seemingly outrageous proposal further.

RICHARD: But gentle Lady Anne,
 To leave this keen encounter of our wits
 And fall something into a slower method:
 Is not the causer of the timeless deaths
 Of these Plantagenets, Henry and Edward,
 As blameful as the executioner?
ANNE: Thou wast the cause, and most accurs'd effect.
RICHARD: Your beauty was the cause of that effect—
 Your beauty, that did haunt me in my sleep
 To undertake the death of all the world,
 So I might live one hour in your sweet bosom.
ANNE: If I thought that, I tell thee, homicide,
 These nails should rent that beauty from my cheeks.
RICHARD: These eyes could not endure that beauty's wrack;
 You should not blemish it, if I stood by:
 As all the world is cheered by the sun,
 So I by that; it is my day, my life!
ANNE: Black night o'ershade thy day, and death thy life!
RICHARD: Curse not thyself, fair creature—thou art both.
ANNE: I would I were, to be reveng'd on thee.
RICHARD: It is a quarrel most unnatural,
 To be reveng'd on him that loveth thee.
ANNE: It is a quarrel just and reasonable,
 To be reveng'd on him that killed my husband!
RICHARD: He that bereft thee, lady, of thy husband,
 Did it to help thee to a better husband.

ANNE: His better doth not breathe upon the earth.
RICHARD: He lives, that loves thee better than he could.
ANNE: Name him.
RICHARD: Plantagenet.
ANNE: Why, that was he.
RICHARD: The self-same name, but one of better nature.
ANNE: Where is he?
RICHARD: Here.
      (Anne spits in his face.)

As Anne struggles to come to grips with what Richard has just suggested (that he belongs in her bed as a lover), Richard presses his advantage in her surprise. "Let's slow down here," he suggests, "and put our clever verbal jousting aside for a moment." He then suggests that, although he held the actual weapons that ended the lives of her husband and father-in-law, what drove the weapons home deserves as much responsibility for the killings as he. Confused, Anne retorts that no one but Richard bears the blame; to which he counters that all that he has done, he executed for the purpose of pursuing his secret love for her. "Your beauty was the cause," he asserts; and as, shocked by this, she raises her nails to gouge at her own cheeks in horrified response, Richard passionately grips her wrists. This physical contact sends a shock through the vulnerable young woman; in spite of what he has done to her new family, in spite of his physical impediments, there's something powerful . . . assured . . . and yes, sexy, about this intense warrior's confession of adoration for her. You are everything to me, he proclaims: "My day, my life!" Wrestling with this new and shocking development—specifically, the idea of her own guilt and ignorant complacency in the final downfall of the Lancasters, even though her conscious hopes and dreams were to the contrary (or were they?)—Anne seems, in spite of a continuing (although perceptibly weaker) defiance, somewhat bewildered and off balance. *Could she really have brought all of this death and grief on herself, however unintentionally? All because of her beauty, irresistible to Richard?* Although on the surface this is a horrible thought, might it also appeal to her vanity? A fascinating and important possibility for any actress playing Anne to explore!

Anne still attempts to counter Richard by clever verbal fencing, but her antithetical rejoinders are fewer now, and lack a bit of the adamancy on display moments before. To Richard's observation that her quarrel with he who loves her is now "most unnatural," she responds that it is instead "just and reasonable." Richard presses through her weakening rejoinders to come to his point more boldly. "I killed your husband so that you would be free to marry a better match for you," he asserts. How can Anne, intelligent as she is and with all that she has already heard, not know where this is leading? Nonetheless, she doesn't turn away from it, but actually appears to push him into declaring it directly. (Again, does vanity play any role in that?) "Where is this better husband?" she demands; to which Richard replies simply: "Here."

Once again, a pause hangs momentarily; and the audience should also hang with breathless suspense for Anne's anticipated response. After a tense beat, pregnant with many possibilities— does Richard believe she's coming around?—she gives him her non-verbal answer: she spits directly in his face.

RICHARD: Why dost thou spit at me?
ANNE: Would it were mortal poison for thy sake!
RICHARD: Never came poison from so sweet a place.
ANNE: Never hung poison on a fouler toad.
    Out of my sight, thou dost infect mine eyes!
RICHARD: Thine eyes, sweet lady, have infected mine.
ANNE: Would they were basilisks, to strike thee dead!

Many modern editions of Richard III make this exchange between Richard and Anne a single shared line, thus encouraging actors to speed rapidly through the "spit." (A: Where is he? R: Here. Why dost thou spit at me?) Considering all that is happening here, however, I tend to feel it would be much more effectively played with two short lines, utilizing appropriate pauses. (A: Where is he? R: Here./Why dost thou spit at me?) During the pause after the spit, we are left to wonder: Just how will Richard react to this indignity? Violently? Even murderously? We already know that he's capable of it, and that he most likely doesn't have deep feelings for Anne beyond potential political gain and (perhaps) physical lust.

But true to form, Richard's calculating nature gives him the necessary restraint. With a patient release of breath, Richard wipes the spittle from his face. Does he actually taste it on the line "Never came poison from so sweet a place"? That certainly would be an interesting and theatrically striking choice. (One among many possibilities here for the actor to experiment with.) Once again, during their brief subsequent exchange of lines, Richard and Anne spar with antitheses, until Anne breaks it with the expressed wish that her eyes were "basilisks" (mythological dragon-creatures capable of killing mortals with a glance) that could strike Richard dead upon the instant.

Their bickering has reached its climactic turning point: Richard has tried his own brand of reason, feigned compassion for her mourning, attempted ironic humor, and offered flattery; and none of these tactics has gained him a firm foothold with her. It's time to improvise—a skill which Richard has learned to master through a lifetime filled with challenging events. It's all or nothing.

RICHARD: I would they were, that I might die at once;
    For now they kill me with a living death!
    Those eyes of thine from mine have drawn salt tears,
    Sham'd their aspects with store of childish drops:
    These eyes, which never shed remorseful tear—
    No, when my father York and Edward wept
    To hear the piteous moan that Rutland made
    When black-fac'd Clifford shook his sword at him;
    Nor when thy warlike father, like a child,
    Told the sad story of my father's death,
    And twenty times made pause to sob and weep,
    That all the standers-by had wet their cheeks
    Like trees bedash'd with rain—in that sad time
    My manly eyes did scorn an humble tear;
    And what these sorrows could not then exhale,
    Thy beauty hath, and made them blind with weeping.
    I never sued to friend nor enemy;
    My tongue could never learn sweet smoothing word;
    But now thy beauty is propos'd my fee,
    My proud heart sues, and prompts my tongue to speak!

Teach not thy lip such scorn; for it was made
For kissing, lady, not for such contempt.
If thy revengeful heart cannot forgive,
Lo, here I lend thee this sharp-pointed sword,
Which if thou please to hid in this true breast,
And let the soul forth that adoreth thee,
I lay it naked to the deadly stroke,
And humbly beg the death upon my knee.
(Richard hands her his weapon and lays bare his breast)
Nay, do not pause: for I did kill King Henry—
But 'twas thy beauty that provoked me.
Nay, now dispatch: 'twas I that stabbed young Edward—
But 'twas thy heavenly face that set me on.
(Anne drops the weapon.)
Take up the sword again, or take up me.
ANNE: Arise, dissembler! Though I wish thy death,
  I will not be thy executioner.
RICHARD: Then bid me kill myself and I will do it.
ANNE: I have already.
RICHARD: That was in thy rage.
  Speak it again, and even with the word
  This hand, which for thy love did kill thy love,
  Shall for thy love kill a far truer love;
  To both their deaths shalt thou be accessory.
ANNE: I would I knew thy heart.
RICHARD: 'Tis figur'd in my tongue.
ANNE: I fear me both are false.
RICHARD: Then never man was true.
ANNE: Well, well, put up your sword.
RICHARD: Say then my peace is made.
ANNE: That shalt thou know hereafter.
RICHARD: But shall I live in hope?
ANNE: All men, I hope, live so.

The one tactic that Richard hasn't tried thus far is vulnerability; it's foreign to his nature. Yet his instincts—and they have proven to be good in the past—lead him to seize on her words, launching him into a brilliant and spontaneous effort to bypass all of her strongest defenses. Anne resists what she perceives to be Richard's cold-blooded ruthlessness—even though a part of her (coming, as she does, from a family of powerful aristocratic politicians and warriors) responds to his charismatic self-confidence and power in spite of herself. In this section, Richard gambles all by switching directions, revealing his "true feelings" to her: his helpless, unmanly love and devotion that has driven him to do violence to her family in order to eliminate his rivals for her affection.

The importance of his tactic to the success of this problematical scene cannot be overstressed. Many are the actors who have struggled vainly to make this encounter credible to audiences. How can Richard possibly win Anne under such circumstances, and in such a brief time? Is she that naïve? Superficial? Is she as much of a Machiavellian, in her own way, as Richard himself, surrendering to his propositions for her own long-term political gain? Surely she cannot truly believe all of what he says to her of his love, young actresses will protest; and young actors playing Richard too often make the dire mistake of playing his villainous nature at the forefront of their characterization instead of playing against it. If Richard is obviously relishing his villainy in his public encounters as well as in his private confessions to us in soliloquy, then how dreadfully stupid all of the rest of the characters in the play must be!

So, Richard must *convince*—first himself and then us—with his fictions. In this, he follows the similar path of all good actors: one part of himself knows that what he says is pretence, not reality; while the other creative and imaginative part of himself appears able to believe it 100%. Anything less than this, and Richard would never have progressed as far as he has to this point—nor would he enjoy the successes he will realize over the course of the rest of this play.

As for Lady Anne's journey, what happens to her is akin to what happens to Belle in the old story of *Beauty and the Beast*. She has every reason to dread and despise Richard as the epitome of the heartless Beast—until she catches a glimmer of what appears to be a true and suffering heart beneath the ugliness, a heart that longs for the same love and fulfillment from another of which we all dream. The Beast is no different from any other man, Beauty discovers; he has simply built strong emotional shields to protect him from the pain that life has dealt him. Often, these shields have incited him to inflict similar pain on others. It's not because he is evil, but rather because he is hurt. Underneath the man is yet another little boy, needing compassion from others. It's a story old as time, as the Disney song goes. It's archetypal. And it's what Richard intuitively pursues in this last-ditch, cards-on-the-table effort to overcome Anne's own shields. If the actor playing Richard fully comprehends this concept and fully commits to it, it works—both for Anne and for his audiences (even though we know even better than Anne at this point what he's really all about). I'm convinced that this is the only tactic that will make the scene play successfully; the actor portraying Richard must be both vulnerable and *sincere*.

"I would they were that I might die at once;/For now they kill me with a living death!" Richard cries out in anguish in response to Anne's wish that her eyes could shoot death rays at him. The line must be infused with a tone from him that neither we, nor Anne, have heard before. All hints of the verbal trickery and smugness that he's used earlier in the scene vanish; after all, they were just masks to cover up his pain. His obsession with her beauty, and his long-held secret love for her has unmanned him, he confesses in a voice echoing with shame and self-loathing. He has never been a crybaby—even when faced with the many deaths of loyal friend and allies; even the death of his own father—but he has cried uncontrollably, alone and miserable, over his inability to win the woman he adores, Lady Anne Neville of Warwick. Indeed, his grief and anger over her family's ultimate alliance with his enemies, the Lancasters, finally broke his heart and pushed him over the edge, leading him (as he's already admitted to her) "to undertake the death of all the world/That I might live one hour in (her) sweet bosom." Finally, he uses Anne's own perceptions of him to support his claim: I've never been any good at courting women, or offering the "sweet smoothing word" that others around him are so facile with. Now—perhaps after it's too late, and he's already gone too far—his heart "prompts his tongue to speak", because it simply must.

He can see in Anne's eyes (perhaps so can we), that this new tactic has promise; so, to use a gambling analogy, he pushes even more chips onto the betting table. If she cannot believe and forgive him for his prior deeds—all prompted by his secret love for her—then he'd rather not live. Indeed, it would be only fitting and just for him to die by her hands. In the riskiest wager thus far, he pulls his own sword from its scabbard and forces it into the Lady's hands. Tearing the shirt open at his breast, he passionately exhorts her to go ahead and execute him there on the spot if she cannot ever find it in her heart to understand and forgive him for his actions. It's a brilliant psychological maneuver: at a time when Lady Anne feels the most powerless in her young life, Richard offers her the power of life and death over him whom she perceives to be her direst enemy. Go ahead and do it, he cries, kneeling before her; for if he has no hope of her love, then he has no hope for any happiness in his life. A distressed and confused Anne raises the blade twice, preparing to plunge it into his heart and finally avenge her husband and his kingly father. The audience holds its collective breath. But each time, Richard stops her before the point can descend and end his life by reminding her that *all that he has done, he has done for love of her.* For these moments to work as dynamically as they should in performance, the actors playing Richard and Anne must truly embrace the notion that the entire play could end here. It's a real possibility that Anne could choose to use that sword. If the characters—and we, the audience—don't believe in that potential, then the scene will not work as it should. Richard must risk it all to win it all. In that moment, there is no Plan B.

For Anne, it's all so overwhelming. As much as she has dreamed of such an opportunity, as much as she believe that she could kill him without hesitation if given the chance, his revelations of anguish and motivation seem more than she can emotionally process in such a compressed period of time. She drops the sword, and turns away, her heart and conscience both in turmoil. At that moment, Richard knows the outcome, and it exhilarates him. He's risked it all and won it all. She's his. "Take up the sword again . . . or take up me," he dares her.

Still Anne tries to walk a tightrope, buying time. "Even though I wish you dead, I don't want to be the one to do it," she claims. Tasting full victory, Richard refuses to let her take that escape route. He picks up the sword himself, placing the business end of it against his breast. "Say the word and I'll do it myself," he offers. When Anne responds that she has already said as much, Richard counters with "That was in thy rage." All she has to do (he says) is find it in herself to demand it again—now, after hearing and considering all that he has revealed of his deepest feelings—and he'll truly carry out her wishes. However, he warns her that in doing so she will be an accessory to the death of a "far truer love" than her late husband could ever have been for her.

For the first time thus far in this powerful scene, Anne shows her own uncertainty and weakness: "I wish I knew how you really felt," she agonizes. When Richard again tries to assure her that he means what he says, she again expresses her fear that she's being gulled. "Then never man was true," Richard responds; a line that must surely provoke knowing chuckles from some of the more cynically experienced members of the play's audiences. Sighing heavily, Anne tells him to put the sword away. Richard replies that he will do so only when he receives her forgiveness. When she counters that she needs more time to think about it all, Richard presses her to assure him that he has grounds to hope for it still; to which she responds that all men should live in hope for their future. Richard then sheathes his sword, knowing that he has beaten the enormous odds against him: she will be his wife.

Actors will note that Shakespeare has written Richard and Anne's lines in the final section of this scene in iambic trimeter rather than pentameter: 6-syllable instead of 10-syllable lines, each with three iambic feet. Although again there are no hard and fast "rules" about these things, I don't sense that these lines should work as normal short lines do; that is, with pauses or actions that fill the time left by the missing syllables. Rather, I think that these lines play best in performance when done very rapidly, almost as if each character's response virtually interrupts the other's ventured thought. It's an unusual verse technique for Shakespeare to use, and it merits both examination and experimentation with it during the scene's rehearsals.

RICHARD: Vouchsafe to wear this ring.
ANNE: To take is not to give.
        (Richard puts a ring upon her finger)
RICHARD: Look how my ring encompasseth thy finger;
        Even so thy breast encloseth my poor heart:
        Wear both of them, for both of them are thine.
        And if thy poor devoted servant may
        But beg one favor at thy gracious hand,
        Thou dost confirm his happiness forever.
ANNE: What is it?
RICHARD: That it may please you leave these sad designs
        To him that hath most cause to be a mourner,
        And presently repair to Crosby House;
        Where (after I have solemnly interr'd
        At Chertsey monast'ry this noble king,
        And wet his grave with my repentant tears)
        I will with all expedient duty see you.
        For diverse unknown reasons, I beseech you,
        Grant me this boon.
ANNE: With all my heart; and much it joys me too,
        To see you are become so penitent.
        (She starts to leave; Richard stops her)
RICHARD: Bid me farewell.
ANNE: 'Tis more than you deserve;
        But since you teach me how to flatter you,
        Imagine I have said farewell already.
        (She exits)

Believing that he has won the Lady's interest and inclination, if not yet fully her heart, Richard clearly knows that he who hesitates is lost; so, in an effort to "seal the deal" with her, he takes her hand gently and slips a ring upon it—probably one that is bejeweled and lovely, very much of the quality she would have expected had she eventually become the late Prince Edward Lancaster's queen. Still reluctant to completely surrender to

Richard's whirlwind (and rather bizarre) "courtship"—after all, Henry VI's corpse still remains as a palpable presence only a few feet away from them!—Anne coyly notes that although she will accept the gift, she does not yet feel obliged to give him anything in return.

After briefly rhapsodizing about the proposed union between them symbolized by his gift of the ring, Richard asks a final favor that he hopes will entirely convince her of his sincerity: he requests that he be given some time to privately confess before God the impetuous and sinful deeds that resulted in the death of King Henry VI, and indeed to personally grieve for Henry himself. Immediately following that appropriate ritual of mourning, he will seek her out again. Apparently impressed with this expression of regret and piety, the Lady Anne gently compliments him on the sincerity of his repentance, and makes to depart.

In a final bold move, with equally gentle firmness Richard takes Anne's hand and asks—perhaps with a balance of ardency and shyness—for a farewell kiss, one that assures him finally of her forgiveness and acceptance. No fool, Anne's suspicion of his motivation seems to quickly return in response to this request. ("Tis more than you deserve," she says.) However, perhaps in response to some behavior she notes from him—his downcast eyes, a slumping of his shoulders?—she appears to soften toward him almost immediately. "Since you've persuaded me to look somewhat differently at you, you may imagine what the experience of my kiss will be like for you." There seems to be more than a hint of encouragement and flirtation in this response. Anne appears to believe that she has the upper hand; Beauty has tamed the Beast.

RICHARD: Was ever woman in this humor woo'd?
    Was ever woman in this humor won?
    I'll have her; but I will not keep her long.
    What? I, that kill'd her husband and his father,
    To take her in her heart's extremest hate,
    With curses in her mouth, tears in her eyes,
    The bleeding witness of my hatred by,
    Having God, her conscience, and these bars against me,

And I no friends to back my suit withal
But the plain devil and dissembling looks?
And yet to win her! All the world to nothing!
Ha!
Hath she forgot already that brave prince,
Edward, her lord, whom I, some three months since,
Stabb'd in my angry mood at Tewksbury?
A sweeter and a lovelier gentleman,
Fram'd in the prodigality of nature—
Young, valiant, wise, and (no doubt) right royal—
The spacious world cannot again afford.
And will she yet abase her eyes on me,
That cropp'd the golden prime of this sweet prince
And made her widow to a woeful bed?
On me, whose all not equals Edward's moi'ty?
On me, that halts and am misshapen thus?
My dukedom to a beggarly denier,
I do mistake my person all this while!
Upon my life, she finds (although I cannot)
Myself to be a marv'llous proper man.
I'll be at charges for a looking glass,
And entertain a score or two of tailors
To study fashions to adorn my body:
Since I am crept in favor with myself,
I will maintain it with some little cost.
But first I'll turn yon fellow in his grave,
And then return lamenting to my love.
Shine out, fair sun, till I have bought a glass,
That I may see my shadow as I pass!
(He exits)

A successful characterization of Richard III calls upon the actor to portray a character who is himself a consummate performer. The clearest trap for an actor in the role lies in trying too hard to demonstrate the villainy and the duplicity, as if the audience needs to be regularly reminded that Richard is tricking all of those around him. Well, in a way, that's true: the audience should need to be periodically reminded through the course of the performance that Richard is always engaged in using and manipulating both situations and people; but the reason that they should need these reminders—in spite of what they know (because they've heard the truth from Richard's own mouth)— is because he's so darned *convincing*.

The goal of the actor in the scene with Lady Anne should be to completely persuade her of the truth in everything he tells her; if he's mostly successful in that effort, the audience should find themselves almost persuaded as well, even while knowing information about his true intentions that Anne does not. Actors succeed in their craft by being the best pretenders that they can be within the fictional circumstances and context in which they are given; and to achieve this, there must be a part of them that finds some quantity and quality of belief in those circumstances. Richard III and Iago are probably the best actors of all the characters we meet in the Shakespeare canon. While they are pursuing their duplicitous plots during the course of their plays' stories, their challenge is to make the other characters believe unwaveringly in their sincerity; and simultaneously, the actors playing them must make audiences believe the seeming evidence of integrity in their various dealings, even above what they actually know to be the truth as revealed by their private soliloquies.

So once Anne leaves the stage, we wait in some suspense to hear from Richard directly once again. After all, the emotional confession we've just seen him make to Lady Anne about the "real" reasons behind his seemingly villainous acts rang so true! Did some aspect of his personality reveal itself unplanned? Even though he confessed his manipulative intentions toward her earlier in the play, did his true feelings come out in the course of his encounter with her in spite of himself? In other words, does he truly love her after all? Has he discovered something profound about himself that he didn't know before while dealing with her in this encounter? Is he now going to reveal that discovery to us in another soliloquy?

Raising these questions in the spectators' minds should be the goal of the actor playing Richard; whether or not that is fully and practically achievable given the restrictions of the script's familiarity isn't really important. The actor's attempt to do so is what's vital. If he succeeds in this, his first moments in addressing the audience directly once again will be marvelously theatrical. We will almost want to applaud his unethical achievements in spite of our own feelings that *we* would never be so blatantly disingenuous, regardless of the potential gain. In brief, the actor portraying Richard needs to fool us almost as effectively as he fools Lady Anne.

If he does, then this final soliloquy becomes celebratory and triumphant, inviting us to be a willing cheerleader for his heartless deception. And if he's charismatic and charming enough, he will be difficult for us to resist. He begins with characteristic humor: his first two questions are posed as if he can hardly believe his success himself. What undercuts our initial delight in his jester-like delivery, however, is the terrifying coldness heard in the line: "I'll have her; but I will not keep her long." These passages emphasize the conflicting responses audiences have for Richard: a bad boy whom we can't help but admire in spite of our own moral misgivings about the violence he deals out to all around him.

He continues sharing his delight, reminding us of all of the odds that he overcame in winning thus much of Anne's trust: he killed her new husband in battle, thus robbing her of her hopes of being Queen of England some day; he murdered her father-in-law and her King in cold blood; he didn't even wait to let the pain of these wounds heal before attempting to seduce her; he won her in spite of her morality, her religion, and her ethics all telling her that what he had done was unforgivably evil; and he wooed her thus while further burdened with all of his obvious deformities and ugliness. And yet . . . he won her! "All the world to nothing!" he gleefully cries. Then Richard tops this list of handicaps with a wonderfully effective one syllable line of verse which says it all: "Ha!"

Then, reveling in his undeniable triumph, Richard struts the stage, utilizing his irresistible black humor to bask in the success, inviting us all to celebrate along with him. The soliloquy is full of horrifyingly funny lines and phrases: "stabb'd in my angry mood at Tewksbury"; "young, valiant, wise, and (no doubt) right royal." Here is a natural-born comedian, taking stage, his humor formed (as the funniest humor usually is) from the pain of living.

His manic wit actually seems almost to spin beyond his control as the soliloquy reaches its climax. Since he's obviously such a handsome man (he says), then it's time to pay more attention to his grooming: he'll hire "a score or two of tailors" to fashion the best wardrobe for him, and learn to admire the perfection of his (obviously deformed) shadow in the sun. And once he's dumped Henry's body off without further undue ceremony at Chertsey Abbey, he'll return "lamenting" (said with obvious scorn and sarcasm at her abject ignorance) to his Lady Anne. (Stupid girl, to think he really loves her!) The soliloquy shows Shakespeare's powerful dramatic potential, yet still very early in his playwriting career. Even the characters that people his later, more mature plays will rarely exceed Richard III's stage popularity with audiences. Horror and comedy prove a potent combination.

The dramatic irony of Lady Anne's initial curse invoked upon Richard over the corpse of King Henry VI now becomes all too apparent for audiences, both Elizabethan and modern:

> *If ever he have wife, let her be made*
> *More miserable by the life of him*
> *Than I am made by my young lord, and thee.*

From my own experiences in studios and rehearsals halls, once serious young actors gets bitten by the Shakespeare "bug" they're likely to develop a lifelong interest—if not an outright passion—for working with the Bard on stage. The language and verse that, at first exposure, seemed so incomprehensible and impenetrable evolve into an important component of their artistic life—for reading, for studying, for seeing in the theatre, for acting, for directing. The very things that initially seemed intimidating and daunting are sorely missed when absent—as they certainly are in so many modern plays.

The stories Shakespeare draws upon are timeless in their interest for us. They're not original in themselves—but after thousands of years of human storytelling, what stories really are? It's not the story itself, after all, which provides the real pleasure; it's how that story is presented: the analogies, the images, the very sounds of the spoken words. Of course, the latter component only moves to the forefront when the story begins to fulfill its intended life on the stage.

How many times in your daily existence do you walk away from a personal encounter with a loved one, a foe, a casual acquaintance, a teacher or other authority figure, a parent, etc., that has proven frustrating or unsatisfactory in its outcome—and then, suddenly, it flashes into your head what you *should* have said? What would have given the other person joy, what would have clarified their understanding further, what would have sealed your request for their loyalty and support, what would have effectively put them in their proper place? The *right words*

. . . the ones you wish you'd thought of at just the appropriate moment in the conversation.

Shakespeare always seems to give his characters the right words at just the right time. The most moving images. The most expressive descriptions. The most precise arguments. The ones that most surely evoke the strongest feelings and responses from listeners, be they those that stride the stage or those who hear them from the darkened auditorium beyond.

Some teachers are fond of proposing that there is no subtext in Shakespeare; everything to be found, every secret, motivation, or emotion of the characters, is to be found in the text itself. I think this view is a bit too simplistic; after all, it's human nature to purposely hold things back, to hide from too much revelation, or to struggle (and sometimes fail) to discover what you feel about a given situation when you're immersed in it—or maybe how you should feel. Every person, whether they are living an actual life, living within the pages of a novel or short story, or living as a dramatic character on the stage in front of spectators, has a subtext.

On the other hand, Shakespearean actors soon find that they can rely more directly upon the language spoken in his plays to tell a clear narrative and to deliver an emotionally satisfying and intellectually edifying experience for their audiences than they can with any other Western playwright. Shakespeare loved language—both written and spoken—and, in the mouths of able actors, that shines through every moment of his works. In fact, as we've noted earlier, Shakespeare loved the English language so much that he regularly contributed to it, inventing words, phrases, and metaphors that would assume common usage with many generations over the next four centuries. As former Royal Shakespeare Company director John Barton once put it, Shakespeare was truly *word intoxicated.*

So, to do him full service, the Shakespearean actor must become word intoxicated as well. For many, that's not so difficult; for once their first nervous experimentation with it has passed, Shakespeare's language can very well become a lifetime addiction.

✧

The purpose of this book has been to provide a non-threatening—hopefully even inviting—introduction for younger actors to the basic principles of performing Shakespeare. Obviously, no book on this subject can ever be comprehensive, and there are many fascinating aspects of the life and works of this greatest of all English playwrights that I have only briefly touched upon in these pages—or not covered at all. Some of the fundamentals that I've written of in the preceding chapters can be delved into more deeply if interest has been sparked in my readers (and I hope it has!) by consulting some of the following highly recommended books.

SHAKESPEARE'S LIFE AND TIMES:

New Shakespeare biographies appear in book stores on a regular basis; in recent years, as the controversy has gathered more steam about whether or not a man named Will Shakespeare actually wrote all of the plays attributed to him, this trend has only increased. There have been many of excellent quality published just in the last couple of decades, but one of the most engaging I've found has been Michael Wood's simply titled *Shakespeare* (New York: Basic Books, 2003), a volume intended as a textual companion to his excellent 4-hour BBC/PBS television series, *In Search of Shakespeare*. In addition to covering much about Shakespeare himself, Wood provides an excellent historical and social overview of the late Tudor and early Stuart historical eras in which Shakespeare lived. Both the book and the video will richly reward your time, and the ebullient author/host Michael Wood is a treat both to read and to watch.

A more basic biographical overview of William Shakespeare, as well as of his various major biographers and scholarly critics through the ages, can be found in what has become a standard reference work by Samuel Schoenbaum entitled *Shakespeare's Lives* (Oxford: Clarendon Press, 1970). This massive 800-page volume covers virtually all of the reliable accounts of and informational sources for the Bard's life from the 16th through the 20th Centuries. It even examines the various candidates who have been suggested since the 19th Century (even by such eminent personages as Mark Twain and Sigmund Freud) as the actual authors of Shakespeare's plays, from Sir Francis Bacon to Edward de Vere, Earl of Oxford. The writing style might prove a tad dry for younger readers, but it's a solid source for finding further, perhaps more accessible books on the subject.

Speaking of alternative candidates for the authorship of the plays (a subject that always seems peculiarly fascinating for the students who have taken my Acting Shakespeare classes and workshops over the past three decades), there are two recent books that examine the questions and inconsistencies posed by these theorists that largely avoid taking personal stands behind specific candidates. *Who Wrote Shakespeare* by John Michell (London and New York: Thames and Hudson, 1999) covers all the major proposals and the "evidence" supporting them in something of a survey form, while a brand new book called *The Apocryphal Shakespeare: Book One of a "Third Way" Shakespeare Authorship Scenario* by NASA physicist (!) Sabrina Feldman (Dog Ear Publishing, 2011) provides a wonderfully comprehensive examination of all of the Elizabethan data that have sparked these arguments over the years. (It should be noted that Feldman plans to argue for a specific candidate of her own choice in the forthcoming *Book Two*, and that may prove more problematical reading for those inclined to be skeptical of the entire matter; but *Book One* is quite entertaining and hugely informative.)

In the early part of the 20th century, the renowned English Renaissance theatre scholar E. K. Chambers published a two-volume compilation of all surviving references and documents to William Shakespeare that survive from the 16th and 17th Centuries (although a few more discoveries have been put forth for evaluation since that time). *William Shakespeare: A Study of Facts and Problems in Two Volumes* (London: Oxford University Press, 1930) provides a virtually comprehensive collection of source materials that scholars of all ages can enjoyably return to for enlightenment time and gain throughout their lifetimes. It is a substantive and standard academic study of Shakespeare that has never been bettered to the present day.

Finally, 2007 saw the publication of an informative, involving, and moving novel that envisions the events of Shakespeare's life within the structure of a first-person narrative of William's reflections upon the occasion of the writing of his last will and testament on his deathbed. It is entitled *Will* by Christopher Rush (New York: Overlook Press, 2007); and although ostensibly fiction, it serves as both a useful and entertaining (and reasonably accurate, as far as we might surmise from the limited evidence that has come down to us) account of what the life of William Shakespeare was probably like in a form that should prove attractive for a more general readership.

TEXTS OF SHAKESPEARE'S PLAYS:

In an earlier chapter I suggested some of the more reliable and informative modern edited texts of the plays that are easily available in bookstores or online, such as the individual Arden editions, the Oxfords, the New Cambridges, and the Folgers. However, after a certain point in your preparation process, there's really no substitute for a personal consultation of the source material itself; or at least the closest an average reader can come to that without personally perusing a surviving volume from the 17th Century under lock and key in some major library or archive.

For this purpose, the best available photographic facsimile of *Mr. William Shakespeare's Comedies, Histories, & Tragedies. Published According to the True Originall Copies* (the 1623 First Folio) exists in the form of *The Norton Facsimile* prepared by Charlton Hinman (New York: W. W. Norton, 1968). Unlike other photo facsimiles of the Folio that have been published, Hinman compiled his tome using the best surviving pages of multiple copies he collated from the original printing. It has yet to be surpassed since its publication, and has thus enjoyed many subsequent printings without significant internal revisions. It's a bit on the pricey side for the general readership, but not prohibitively so when a young actor considers that its usefulness should last for a lifetime in the theatre.

Quartos aren't quite as simple to track down in a comprehensive, collected form. The closest one can come to this would be *Shakespeare's Plays in Quarto*, a photographic "facsimile edition of copies primarily from the Henry E. Huntington Library" in California, edited by Michael J. B. Allen and Kenneth Muir (Los Angeles: University of California, 1981). Even pricier than the Norton Folio facsimile (and much harder to find), the collection nonetheless contains facsimiles of all the original First Quarto printings of the plays that were so issued before the 1623 Folio, as well as two "corrected" Second Quartos (*Hamlet* and *Romeo and Juliet*). It also contains original Quartos of two accepted instances of Shakespeare's collaborations with other writers that are not included in the First Folio: *Pericles* (with George Wilkins) and *The Two Noble Kinsmen* (with John Fletcher). It does not, however, contain facsimiles of surviving Elizabethan Quartos of *The Taming of A Shrew*, *The Troublesome Reign of John*, *King of England*, *The Famous Victories of Henry V*, and *The True Chronicle History of King Leir*, all source plays for Shakespeare's final versions that some scholars suggest Shakespeare himself might have had a hand in composing. It's difficult to draw definitive lines in such matters, however, and I think that in this case the editors have made justified choices of which texts to include and which to exclude.

In recent years, the New Cambridge Shakespeare series (mostly available in paperback) has issued some modern language editions of some of these original Quartos; tracked down separately, these should be easier to locate and less expensive for a general reader/actor. Also, many of the Third Series Arden paperback editions of certain plays include modern language editions of the original Quartos themselves, or (in some cases) even facsimiles of the original Quarto versions of such source plays listed above.

ACTING APPROACHES TO SHAKESPEARE:

Hopefully, this book will ignite enough interest in the young actor to lead him to seek out more detailed and specialized studies on performance approaches to Shakespeare. As with the Shakespeare biographies, there have been numerous books published on the subject, particularly over the past several decades. Many of them are very worthwhile, but perhaps better suited for a readership already somewhat knowledgeable of the fundamental techniques of Shakespearean acting, such as John Barton's *Playing Shakespeare* (New York: Anchor Books, 2001) and Peter Hall's *Shakespeare's Advice to the Players* (New York: Theatre Communications Group, 2003). Barton's book is basically an expanded transcript of the series of staged television workshops utilizing past and present RSC actors (Ian McKellan, Judi Dench, Ben Kingsley, Patrick Stewart, David Suchet, and Jane LaPoitaire among other luminaries). Your money is better spent on a purchase of those videos themselves, I think, all currently available on DVD.

Additionally, there are numerous so-called "how to" books on acting in Shakespeare plays currently on the market. (One goes so far as to imply a mastery of their particular approach in three short weeks. Good luck with that!) Although all of these books offer some valuable insights into the kinds of things we've examined throughout this study, there are two in particular that offer significant practical guidance for the more advanced actor, and I would recommend them to the reader who desires further exploration in the subject after this. They are: *Thinking Shakespeare* by Barry Edelstein (Spark Pub Group, 2007), and *Clues to Acting Shakespeare* by Wesley Van Tassel (New York: Allworth Press, 2000).

I've found that it's almost always interesting to hear teaching colleagues, fellow actors, directors and artists who personally inspire you share their individual views and experiences with acting Shakespeare. With that in mind, I'd draw your attention to the following books of that type: *Actors Talk About Shakespeare* with interviews by Mary Z. Maher (New York: Limelight Editions, 2009), and *On Acting* by Laurence Olivier (New York:

Simon and Schuster, 1987). For those readers too young to have yet discovered Olivier, he remains the indisputable master of the Bard on stage in the 20th Century. There's also a series of books that are worth searching for, although many of them are now hard to find and somewhat expensive when they are found: *Players of Shakespeare*, edited by Robert Smallwood and Russell Jackson (all published by the Cambridge University Press over several years). These volumes are comprised of essays and interviews with individual actors focused on specific characters in the Canon, and all make for fascinating reading.

PRODUCING SHAKESPEARE:

In recent years, the publishers of the Arden series and the New Cambridge editions of Shakespeare's plays have also issued a limited series of books focused specifically on "Performance Criticism," something that was virtually ignored by most Shakespeare academics and scholars until the mid-20th Century. (Before then, most critical scholarship rested on the premise that actual productions of Shakespeare's plays degraded their "purity" for serious study; and that the plays should be primarily valued as works of literature meant for reading in the privacy of one's study rather than experiencing on the stage.) These volumes vary in quality, of course, dependant upon their individual authors/editors; but most are worth reading for anyone preparing to stage one of the titles so examined. Both of these publishers also follow a policy of summarizing a given play's production history (along with its critical reception) in the editorial introductions of their individual play editions. The Oxford series adopts this practice as well. In addition to these publications, individual authors have regularly issued books over the years that narrowly focus on specific plays or characters: most particularly stage and literary icons such as Hamlet, Shylock, or Lear. Such books might prove a bit more challenging to track down than the readily available editions of the plays themselves, and they tend to be more for a specialized readership, and thus more expensive. But anyone embarking on acting or directing Shakespeare almost always benefits from the knowledge of what has gone before.

In my own directing and acting of Shakespeare's plays over the years, there is one series of essays in particular that I've found especially inspiring. They represent some of the first examples of an organized attempt to apply Performance Criticism to Shakespeare's plays, and they first appeared in individual essays in the early 20th Century before they were collected in two weighty volumes, along with one slim "addendum" volume that gathered the several essays (some unfinished) that remained unpublished after their author's death. Written by the insightful British director/scholar Harley Granville-Barker, these are the *Prefaces to Shakespeare* (New Jersey: Princeton University Press, 1946 [Vol. I], 1947 [Vol. II], and 1974 [*More Prefaces to Shakespeare*]). Although some young readers might find them steep going at first, keep trying . . . they're worth your time and thought. His preface to Hamlet alone (235 pages!) is one of the most enlightening revelations of that play's essence of any I've encountered in a lifetime of reading about Shakespeare's plays.

NOW, A LAST WORD.

During my doctoral studies in college, I had a particularly brilliant, challenging, inspiring—and often, quite infuriating—professor by the name of Robert Findlay. Bob had written numerous critical and scholarly articles over the course of his career, many of which dealt with Jerzy Grotowski's work with the Polish Laboratory Theatre, and he co-authored with Oscar Brockett what became for a time a standard text in many college courses covering theatre history in the late 19th and early 20th Centuries, *A Century of Innovation*. There were several pronouncements that he handed down in the early days of my first graduate seminar with him that have stayed with me throughout my acting, directing and teaching career. Here are three of the strongest:

1. Everything I'm going to tell you (about theatre) is a lie.
2. Every reading of a play (or any work of art, I've come to believe) is a misreading; but some misreadings are better than others!
3. There is only one ironclad rule in the theatre: DON'T BE BORING!

How do these maxims apply to what you've just read?

The first emphasizes the subjectivity of any artistic direction or evaluation. In the theatre, we're never dealing with a mathematical problem, one that has specific solutions that are either right or wrong. A theatrical experience that is forever memorable and sublime for one audience member often proves to be sublimely boring and uninteresting for the person sitting next to them. This might have to do with a variety of factors that have absolutely nothing to do with the play: how difficult (or not) it was to find a parking place, how good (or not) your dinner was, how well (or badly) you were treated by the box office staff and the house ushers. In other words, we bring the individuality of *who we are that at the moment in time* to every artistic experience we have. We're not simply responding passively to the plays we witness—we're collaborating in its creation; and even the same play changes from performance to performance, as do we. What is true for us today may not be tomorrow.

Often during rehearsals for a show I'm directing, the young actors—all seeking (in vain, they will eventually discover) for the *right* way of presenting a moment, of making a movement, of speaking a line—will confront me, saying: "But yesterday you told me something completely different!" To which I usually reply with words to this effect: "Well, yesterday that was the truth; today, this is." As a director, collaborating with actors to find the most effective way of telling a story, I can only respond (as they should be doing)—*in that moment*. What works one day may seem entirely stale and contrived the next. We're always searching together, moving forward hand in hand toward the unknown. There are some principles of acting—and acting Shakespeare—that remain pretty consistently dependable; but there are never any absolutes. Good actors learn to embrace the exhilarating creative terror of that reality; for that's the only way toward possible brilliance. Certain stage techniques and methods have been proven to usually work well; but never cling to anything doggedly, simply because you think it's supposed to be right.

The second quote from Bob somewhat echoes the first. There are no perfect interpretations of any character, line, or play that you are striving to accomplish. Instead, you're collaborating with the words that the playwright has given you in an effort to tell a story that's meaningful and personal for you—and that hopefully will prove so for others as well. Some playwrights give you better words to work with than others—and no one I've found in my forty years in the theatre is better with words than Shakespeare. So, take the pressure off of yourself to find the mythical "right" reading, the reading that critics, well-meaning colleagues, or directors may hint (or outright say) that they're waiting for. Give them *your* reading instead, as truthfully as you are able. No one else will see things in just the same way you do, and the audience is there to hear what *you* have to say about the characters you're playing. Even Shakespeare himself almost certainly changed his mind as his life progressed through its tumultuous decades about just what he was really trying to say with his own plays!

However, this isn't meant to undervalue the meticulous research and dedicated critical analysis that any actor—especially any actor of Shakespeare—should undertake with their role. It's no artistic sin to create and present something from your soul that "misses" with some audience members and critics; but it is a problem if this happens simply because you haven't done the research, or given the imaginative thought and disciplined creative time that the role and the play deserve from you. That's when your own particular "misreading" will almost certainly be significantly weakened, for yourself and for others.

Bob's final dictum has resonated most with me over the course of my artistic career. We might be able to demonstrate our voluminous research and preparation in our productions in a variety of ways; we might have spent months reading and thinking about our "concept" of the play; we might congratulate ourselves smugly about our "cutting edge" willingness to present "gender blind" casting, or other such directing choices; and we may be able to justify it all with the most impressively articulate written program note imaginable. But if what is happening *on the stage* fails to arrest the onlookers' attention and remind them of what it is to be *alive—in this moment*—then little else matters. Even if you've faithfully followed all the so-called "rules" that you've read and absorbed about what makes Shakespeare work on the stage. In fact, you might sometimes discover that you've followed these rules so closely that it becomes difficult to be anything *but* boring.

The German philosopher/artist Johann Wolfgang von Goethe once proposed that a theatre artist should have three goals, to be achieved in the following order: first and foremost, they must *entertain*—if they fail at that, anything else becomes impossible due to lack of interest on the part of the audience. Once they achieve something entertaining, then they might use it as a vehicle to *educate*, hoping that the audience will be edified when it leaves the theatre, knowing something about themselves or the world that they didn't know before the play began. Finally, if the collaboration between playwright, actor, director, and designers finds that effective combination of entertainment and edification, then the possibility exists that all those involved—particularly the audience—might be *exalted*; that is, spiritually changed as a human being in some profound way. And isn't this, ambitious as it might sound, what we all dream of? What we're all in the theatre *to do*?

Think of the techniques and approaches that we've discussed in this book as a road map that you're consulting in preparation for a trip that promises to be both exciting as well as a little scary. There are different routes that you might take. Even though all of the ones you've considered will eventually lead you to your destination, some will take your travels through many states, some only a few. Some paths will take longer to get there, but will show you more along the way. There are Interstate highways that will zip you through miles of uninteresting countryside; there are side roads that will take you to attractions off the most direct path that might change your perspectives while slowing you down; and there are pathways that aren't even found on some maps that could offer discoveries and insights that you've never even dreamed of. You know where you want to go, but how you eventually get there may reward your willingness to improvise a bit on the way. As the old proverb goes, the destination is not nearly as interesting or as important as the journey itself.

There are no hard and fast "rules" for acting Shakespeare. But there are proven techniques and previously travelled roads that you should know about. Tools to go in your creative toolbox, to be chosen when you need them, when the particular challenge to be addressed in the text demands them. Your intellect is important, your experience valuable. Your research and grasp of what has gone before, rewarding. And your imagination, all-important; so exercise it constantly.

But to return almost to where we began—and to what we've been reminding ourselves of throughout: when preparing to act Shakespeare, always keep returning to Hamlet's most important bit of advice to his players. I think you can never hear it too many times.

Let your own discretion be your tutor. Your *informed* discretion.

EXAMPLES OF DRAMATIC CONTEXT
FOR SHAKESPEAREAN PRODUCTION

In Chapter VII, when discussing the importance of finding a context for Shakespeare's plays in character and setting with which both actor and audience might effectively identify, I offered a lengthy section on the play *Measure for Measure* as one example of a text that offers some unusual challenges for the producing artist.

In these two appendices that follow, I offer additional short essays that explore two other Shakespeare plays that have often presented some interpretive and staging difficulties for critics, directors and actors alike. Both approaches outlined here proved successful with audiences in their eventual realization on the stage, thanks largely to some very talented student actors as well as my imaginative and skilled design colleagues (for whom the essays were originally composed).

I hope that the thoughts they contain, however rambling at times, might encourage prospective educational producers less familiar with the entire Shakespeare canon to take a chance on more "minor" titles from the Bard. They, like others—such as *Pericles*, *All's Well That Ends Well*, *Cymbeline*, etc.—offer hidden treasures that rival even the great titles with which we may be more familiar.

SOME THOUGHTS ON *THE TWO GENTLEMEN OF VERONA*:

"The weakest of all Shakespeare's comedies . . . Directors and actors would do well to stage the *Two Gentlemen* as travesty or parody . . . (And yet) I uneasily sense that we have yet to understand *The Two Gentlemen of Verona*, a very experimental comedy."

—Harold Bloom

"We must eliminate all parts of a dramatic text with which we cannot strongly agree or disagree."

—Jerzy Grotowski

"In love, who respects friend?"

—Proteus, Act V, Scene iv

LUST IN ACTION:

For most of the years of my familiarity with the Shakespeare canon, I found myself in complete agreement with the first part of Harold Bloom's assessment. And yet like Bloom, of late I've begun to feel that there are road signs and clues in this script for potential producers that many scholars and critics have missed, or even openly dismissed. Upon re-reading the play rather carefully over the past year—as well as seeing two different productions in the summer of 2003—I have been surprised and impressed with the passion and lingering imagery of some of the language and verse. Moreover, the structure of the play, with its alternation of scenes between comic or devious servants with fervent or hypocritical lovers (not to mention the relatively daring effect of presenting leading characters with whom we are asked to identify who are ethically or morally challenged), along with its bizarre ending (for modern tastes, anyway) is ultimately . . . well, intriguing. It seems to be a web of apparent contradictions and ambiguities, sewn up in a text with surprisingly tight structure; particularly when we consider that it could very well be Shakespeare's first extant play.

In spite of its undeniable challenges, *Two Gentlemen* seems to me an almost perfect production for staging with young actors. Although the male characters' behavior seems quite distasteful at many moments (and the females' too, at least in some instances), it also seems very naturally and understandably adolescent. It is, in fact, behavior that I see all around me virtually every day in my teaching . . . although affirming that so bluntly would undoubtedly upset a lot of my students, who aspire to be better human beings than either Proteus or Silvia often appear to be. For better or worse, the age of the play's main characters is a stage of life in which Lust Conquers All. In many, it overrides morality, loyalty, friendship, dignity, judgment. The instinct to secure a mate and procreate—to have that first sexual experience, or to find reciprocal love—is strong. Shakespeare, still a young man at the writing of this play—and yet also a husband and father—clearly retains full understanding of that instinct and drive. After all, his own marriage to Anne Hathaway (a young man of 18 with a presumably more sexually experienced woman of 26) was, to all evidence, a shotgun marriage, with Anne already several months pregnant by Will. Was Will unhappy in the marriage (as many have conjectured from their separate lives, she in Stratford, he in London)? Or was it a strongly private bond, with the conditions of Will's professional life apart from his wife and children accepted by both spouses? Save the discovery of a secret packet of love letters between the two in future years, we will never know. Whatever the truth, Will was almost certainly still strongly in touch (either ruefully or happily) with "the heaven that leads men to this hell." In fact, Sonnet 129—which some believe may have been composed in the early 1590's, within a few years of *Two Gentlemen's* writing—is worth quoting in its entirety. It is a more mature and wistfully moving perspective on the driving force of *2G*, (and thus better "art" to my taste), but it nonetheless taps into the same vein.

Th' expense of spirit in a waste of shame
Is lust in action; and till action, lust
Is perjur'd, murd'rous, bloody, full of blame,

Savage, extreme, rude, cruel, not to trust,
Enjoyed no sooner but despised straight,
Past reason hunted, and no sooner had,
Past reason hated as a swallowed bait,
On purpose laid to make the taker mad;
Mad in pursuit, and in possession so,
Had, having, and in quest to have, extreme,
A bliss in proof, and proved, a very woe,
Before, a joy proposed, behind, a dream.
  All this the world well knows, yet none knows well
  To shun the heav'n that leads men to this hell.

Whether all young students can yet appreciate fully the beauty and expressive form of sentiment displayed in this verse, they will certainly understand the content. And watching the throes of agony and tenderness that Proteus, Julia, Silvia and Valentine endure over the course of their story's journey, most adults will feel twinges of both relief and regret that such extreme physical passion is no longer the dominant force in their own lives.

INSPIRATION AND CONTEXT:

Several elements have been playing around in my consciousness as I begin to plan how *Two Gentlemen* could work for modern audiences, particularly young audiences.

The first is a relatively low-key character comedy film from the late 90's called *Swingers*. This film is a must-see for all of our design team, I think, and probably for the cast as well. The story involves a group of young men in their 20's, all from East Coast middle-America, who have migrated to L.A. in hopes of establishing themselves as actors, comedians, writers, etc. When Mike, the protagonist, picks up roots to move West, he leaves behind a less-than-faithful girl friend, and the separation has thrown him into a despondent, broken-hearted tailspin; he has no confidence with women, no confidence in himself, and no faith in his talent or his future. He has, however, a loyal best buddy (Trent) who is committed to bringing Mike out of his funk. He takes Mike to Vegas to cheap casinos and pick-up bars, trying to convince him that he is "money" in their vernacular: that he has everything it takes to make the ladies fall down in front of him, if he could only regain his confidence. The film is a surprisingly sensitive and truthful look at young male bonding, and the way guys deal with being loyal to one another above all other ties (like romantic connections with young women); also, it shows the way they care about one another while avoiding emotional sentimentality—something they obviously fear.

This film which I saw several years ago kept popping into my head while reading and re-reading Shakespeare's text. If our goal in the staging of the piece is to explore all facets and fallout, positive and negative, of post-adolescent male bonding (with sexual themes always lurking below the surface), while at the same time bringing it out of the Medieval Renaissance into a more modern and meaningful context, this film is a keystone. The behavior of actors Vince Vaughn (the Proteus character) and Jon Favreau (the Valentine character . . . sort of) together is what I hope to achieve in the behavior of my two actors in the Shakespearean roles. While the plotline of *Swingers* is much different than that of *Two Gentlemen*, I could see the guys in that film behaving much the same way with one another if put in the context of Shakespeare's story. So, the precept would be: what if an extremely sexy and sophisticated girl—a challenge for both, and a prize for both—came between these two young men, stretching the limits of their commitment to one another? Seeing that film will, I hope, bring the situation of Proteus and Valentine into a more familiar perspective for our youthful actors.

The second inspiration for much of my thinking about *Two Gentlemen* came from a new biography of Frank Sinatra I read recently: *Sinatra, The Life* by Anthony Summers and Robbyn Swan. While not going into greatly lurid detail about Sinatra, it points up the inherent contradictions in his persona that both attracted and repulsed admirers and detractors alike throughout his career. Without a doubt, here was one of the most sensitive and lovely singer of ballads and torch songs that American pop music has ever produced. Additionally, he could be abundantly generous with his fortune and his wealth: stories abound of his endeavoring to put down-and-out musicians that he admired back on their feet, of his giving large sums of money and time to both individuals and charities on the barest of whims. He was an outspoken civil-rights-for-minorities advocate before it was "cool" to be so; and yet at the same time, he uttered racial epithets regularly from the stage, and often treated his so-called friend, Sammy Davis Jr., with patronizing condescension. Similarly with women: he could break your heart with the male sensitivity of "One For My Baby" or "Only the Lonely," yet also be involved in distasteful private and public scenes with women that included violence, abuse, and even an accusation of rape.

Thus, the famously over-indulgent Rat Pack of the 1950's and 1960's became a dominant image for me in visualizing the behavior of Proteus and Valentine (and their surrounding society) in *Two Gentlemen of Verona*). I also think that our un-utilized idea of placing last season's *Romeo and Juliet* in the realm of the New Jersey *Sopranos* culture also was still resonating in my imagination; an idea that I never really wanted to let go of, even though I couldn't quite see it working for that play in its final outcome. *Two Gentlemen* is about potentially sensitive, intelligent and attractive Boys Behaving Badly. Why do they do so? How can they still engage our attention and sympathies with such compromised ethical centers? What ramifications will their unattractive behavior have for their chances of future happiness? And ultimately, are all young men (and women, for that matter) always fated to be governed by their hearts (and genitalia) instead of their heads and souls? And can we—or should we—judge them too harshly for that? Or is it something that we all fall victim to, in our own various ways? Can loyalty ever triumph over strong lust in young people? These are the primary questions that I believe the play is suited to explore . . . and the answers may not prove very attractive. Nevertheless, Shakespeare's strength as a playwright lies in the fact that he rarely, if ever, shies away from unattractive suggestions or conclusions. Paradoxically, it is often in his brutal honesty about human failings that his most beautiful imagery and verse may be found.

The last element that fed my interest in this "lesser" play by Shakespeare is the fact that it will be cast, rehearsed and performed in an arts school. I find much to admire and to be amazed at in the students that I have taught here over the past 17 years; for the most part, their souls are already rich and complex in ways that most young people, lacking their love of art and their life opportunities and experiences, are not. Yet at the same time, I am very often stopped dead in my tracks at their youthful callousness, their selfishness, and their outright dismissal of anything that does not fit into their limited spectrum of interest. The pure gold of their artistic sensitivity, insights, and sudden generosities, both with friends and teachers, makes their egocentric and self-indulgent behavior, when it is revealed in certain circumstances, even more stark. Their strong passions too, fed in the crucible of an arts boarding school with its structures and daily experiences of strict discipline and surprising freedoms, all combine to make their behavioral patterns dramatically intense.

It's safe to say that even the best and most attractive of our students are capable of the most heart-melting grace juxtaposed with the most insensitive cruelty . . . very often within seconds of one another. This is also the behavior of Proteus, Valentine, Sylvia and Julia in Shakespeare's darkly comic vision of the casual passions of youth, *The Two Gentlemen of Verona*.

SEXUAL POLITICS . . . AND SYLVIA:

The two most troubling aspects of producing *The Two Gentlemen of Verona* in the 21st Century occur in the final scene: Proteus's attempted rape of Sylvia, followed by Valentine's offer of her to his newly reconciled friend, who was only moments before the attempting rapist from whom he rescued her. Upon first perusal of this scene, a modern reader can only shake his head in amazement. How in the bloody hell can this scene ever play satisfactorily, particularly in a comic vein? How is an audience supposed to forgive a leading character that resorts to forcible rape to gain the girl? How is Valentine supposed to forgive him?

How are we to forgive Valentine once he offers his girl friend to his friend as a reward for the rapist's supposed remorse? How is Syliva supposed to go off happily with Valentine after he has just offered her as a gift to the rapist he saved her from moments before? How can Julia reconcile herself to a lover who has left her at the slightest temptation offered by his sight of another beauty, presumably going off with him to be married, happily ever after, at the play's conclusion? The mind boggles . . . .

However . . . might it be possible that this "mind boggling" is what Shakespeare, the brash, young, "upstart crow" playwright was intending all along, even at this relatively early stage of his long and revolutionary career? Critics have always treated *Two Gentlemen* as an early, unsophisticated play, unencumbered by the mature complexities of, say, an *All's Well That Ends Well*, a *Measure for Measure*, or a *Troilus and Cressida*. But what if this accepted critical categorization of youthful superficiality on Shakespeare's part is misguided? What if a darker, satirical aspect of the play is exactly what Harold Bloom fears that we have failed to fully understand, and that (in fact) *The Two Gentlemen of Verona* is a subversively experimental comedy by the "in-your-face" young Bard, a black social satire of "gentlemanly" mores, much like *The Merchant of Venice* could be seen (through our modern eyes, at least) as a black social satire of racism and religious intolerance, and *The Taming of the Shrew* as a black domestic satire of the chauvinistic violence commonly utilized to maintain an image of marital bliss to outside eyes? Whether or not this was Shakespeare's actual intention in the context of his times is ultimately beside the point. Our challenge is to find a way for the play to be revealed anew to the eyes and ears of our times, to break the accepted view of the play as an outdated comedy with questionable ethos. Trust the art, not the artist. Whatever Shakespeare's original intention, it seems to me that *The Two Gentlemen of Verona* takes a very hard look at the nature of male and female friendship, sexual competition, and betrayal during the primary "mating" years of youth. And although the comic slant of the vision is apparent overall, for us it will not be an innocent and romantic comedy, but instead a cynical comedy of the manners and mores of young courtship and lust.

The key to making the final scene play palatably in this more modern context obviously lies in the attempted rape and its aftermath. There have been many and varied modern approaches to the problem, even including productions that make the rape actual rather than attempted. (What this accomplishes in terms of making the play more cohesive, I haven't a clue.) For a nice summary description of some of these approaches, I recommend the wonderful introduction to the play by William C. Carroll in the Third Series Arden Edition, published in 2004, an essay that actually re-kindled my interest in producing the text on stage. Many years ago, when first pondering how the scene might possibly work onstage, I toyed with the idea of making the attempted rape "comic" by making Proteus a slight young man, posing no serious sexual threat to any physically fit female. In fact, I have seen that very approach attempted in the majority of the play's stagings that I have personally witnessed. Although it does work somewhat to defuse any suggestion of actual violence in the attack, it still fails to address the challenge of making the entire situation acceptable in its intent; nor does it clarify at all the inexplicable compliance of Sylvia and Julia with the plot's distasteful conclusion. Finally, upon contemplating an approach for our production, the realization dawned on me that the context for the audience's view of the attempted sexual assault depends less upon what the director does with the characters of Proteus and Valentine than it does upon what is done with the character of Sylvia, the "victim" of the assault.

There are a couple of interesting things to contemplate about Sylvia: first, after an exclamation of "O heaven!" after Proteus announces his intent to force her to comply to his advances in the final scene, she never speaks again before the play's conclusion; these are the very last words she utters, although the play proceeds along through several more discoveries, confrontations, revelations and reversals. Why the silence, and how is that dramatically justified with everything that is happening around her? Sylvia does not seem at such a loss for words at other times in the play. Is she in shock? In a faint? Or is there a more subtle reason for her keeping a low profile?

A second incident that puzzled me about Sylvia is her behavior in Act IV of the play. She has continued to ostentatiously rebuff and reprimand Proteus for his overt and professed attraction to her; she knows of his history of avowals to Julia back home, and challenges him on his apparent hypocrisy exhibited in wooing her simultaneously. And yet . . . .she acquiesces to Proteus's request for a picture of her, and tells him that if he returns again on the morrow, she will grant his request. Hmmm. This surely seems an unlikely feminine tactic for unequivocally denying a suit from an undesirable male admirer . . . doesn't it?

Considering both of these things, it seemed to me that their proper exploitation in staged behavior and characterization might contain a dramatic solution whereby the play's attempted "rape" would be rendered less offensive and more acceptable in the given situation, even if it still doesn't leave the best taste in one's mouth. What if the rape isn't a rape at all?

Sylvia is introduced early in the play as an only daughter of a powerful father; there is no mother in the picture. She is surrounded by suitors, some of whom are also aides of her father. She is pampered with attention, attended by servants, and indulged as only a father's "princess" can be. She is first seen openly flirting with a rather dull-witted (sexually, at least) but good-looking Valentine (much like Mike in *Swingers*; attractive enough, but an un-confident and inexperienced klutz when it comes to women). When he doesn't respond suavely to her open come-ons (obvious even to Valentine's servant, Speed), she becomes exasperated. Valentine appears to be mainly attractive to Sylvia because she has all of Daddy's other men eating out of her hand, and Valentine is slower to respond to her charms, and thus more of a challenge for her . . . at first, at least. One gets the impression that his naivete will only prove charming for her up to a point; once he is hers—or proves too obtuse to even be slightly interesting—her attention may soon fade, like it might in all pretty, shallow, spoiled young girls.

Later in the play, her fervent desire to pursue Valentine into his exile by running away from the authority of Daddy would seem to belie this view of the superficiality of Sylvia's love for Valentine. Yet, does it? If we already have been presented a clear portrait of an over-indulged, stubborn, vivacious young girl—a chip off of her bullish, headstrong father—is it inconceivable that she would be thrilled with the adventure of running away from home into the sexy danger of the deep, dark woods, and into the arms of a man to whom she has been forbidden to see? And that, in the company of another poor schmuck (Sir Eglamour) who serves her father, who is already perhaps enamored with her as well, wrapped around her pretty little finger? In other words, the idea of chasing a man into romantic adventure, a man whom her father disapproves of as a potential mate for her, may in fact be more attractive to someone like Sylvia than the man himself.

So how does Proteus fit into this adolescent *menage a trois*? Our words rarely reflect our actual feelings, and that is particularly true in matters of immature love. I would suggest that Sylvia is very attracted to Proteus from their first meeting; he has a rough sexual confidence that Valentine does not, and she senses that he is the "bad boy" to which all young girls like Sylvia are inevitably attracted. Perhaps, subconsciously, in Proteus she senses a self-centeredness and reckless conceit matched only by her own, something she finds extremely stimulating, yet cannot admit either to him or to herself. Using this subtext, how would the play's encounters between Sylvia and Proteus play? Extremely well, I think. It would give them a spark of amorous chemistry behind the "hard to get" role that Sylvia projects ("He's so conceited thinking he could hope to have me," Sylvia thinks, as she verbally puts him down; "Yet at the same time, he's terribly cute . . . !"). Indeed, perhaps the only reason that Sylvia would initially stay aloof at all from Proteus might be that she perceives that he is not of the established economic level of her own family and Valentine's . . . even though it seems clear from our brief glance of Proteus's family life in Act I, Scene iii that they would like to be seen as such.

Thus, when Proteus finally catches up with Sylvia in the forest, and grows increasingly frustrated with the mixed signals that she is sending him (non-verbal challenging flirtatiousness, verbal put-downs), he threatens to take her by force. To which she responds, "O heaven!" before he takes her in his arms and kisses her . . . and then, to the disguised Julia's horror, the hidden Valentine's outrage, and the attacking Proteus's delight, she begins to reciprocate his advances . . . by kissing him back! If this is obviously apparent to the audience, as well as the onlooking characters, it might do a lot to explain Sylvia's embarrassed and uncomfortable silence for the rest of the play (*Busted!*), Valentine's impulsive willingness to "give" her to Proteus, and Julia's final despair of the whole relationship (more about that later). It also will serve to somewhat defuse the audience's distaste for Proteus's attempted "rape", instead focusing their discomfiture upon all of the adolescent sexual game-playing taking place at the core of the play's primary romantic relationships . . . a discomfiture that, in one form or another, I believe Shakespeare perhaps intended all along.

THE TWO GENTLEMEN:

Harold Bloom suggests that the successful producers of this text will be those who interpret the play as a "travesty or parody." From what I've personally seen on stages, most directors tend to try to follow his advice: Valentine is a hapless buffoon, Proteus a sometimes witless and sometimes clever romantic, Sylvia a beautiful and icily virtuous young lady, and Julia a long-suffering martyr who stands by her man through all his adorable weaknesses (amongst which, apparently, are latent sex offender tendencies). All are stock classic comic figures. In the end, the girls teach the guys the true meaning of love and gentleness, the guys' better natures (there all along) are brought out, clowns have some clever banter and play around with dogs (always good for a laugh), and all are forgiven for their unintentional maliciousness, going offstage to presumably live happily ever after.

This approach indeed parodies the entire genre of romantic comedy, and thus gives the audience a comfortable distance from the play's most distasteful events. But the target of this particular parody seems a rather safe one to me. I believe that what Shakespeare may really be parodying here is not a prevalent comic genre, but a segment of society itself and its hypocritical attention to external decorum whilst decaying underneath. There is nothing particularly "gentle" about either

Valentine or Proteus, nor the social background from which they
seem to grow. Although they spend some time discussing (in
varying ways and in different levels of seriousness) how young
"gentlemen" such as themselves should behave, they mainly do
what they want to do, with little thought for their behavior's
potential effect upon others. Even Valentine, the "better" of the
two, is prepared to steal away the daughter of his patron/boss/
sponsor/protector, the Duke. And as for Proteus's moral regard
for others' feelings and rights, they are virtually non-existent.
These are gentlemen in name only, and already Shakespeare is
making a point about the travesty of some people's ideas of social
manners by parodying them. Brooks has the correct descriptive
words, but a blurred perspective (I think) of Shakespeare's true
satirical target.

Creating a context in which the characters' behavior plays
effectively is, of course, the primary challenge for director and
actors. The rivalry and competition between Valentine and
Proteus needs emphasis right from the beginning. I envision the
first scene between them, as they quarrel about the propriety
and potential of the paths that they have separately chosen for
themselves (Love vs. Making Something Of Oneself In The
World), to contain more than a bit of roughhousing. In fact, I
see the scene opening as both of them come in from a jog, or a
tennis game, wiping sweat, flush with the animal aspect of the
physical competition between them—perhaps being aided both
by Country Club servants, who offer them drinks, towels, etc.,
while members of the elite Club membership converse (in vogue)
in the background. From this earliest scene, I believe that we
should sense that Valentine's position in society is more secure,
more established. Interestingly, Shakespeare never allows us to
meet Valentine's family, only the young man's own manservant,
Speed (who is sharply sarcastic and sneeringly clever, as opposed
to Launce [Proteus's servant] who is simple and blunt). In my
view, the difference in the servants subtly mirrors the difference
in the families. While both young "gentlemen" are rich, both
come from significantly different kinds of money. Valentine's
family is of older wealth: local politicians, directors of
government agencies, CEO's of questionably ethical companies

(like Haliburton or Enron, perhaps?). Like many families of inherited wealth, their hands are figuratively dirty and bloody, but most of that questionable activity is several generations in the past. They have become "legitimate." Proteus's family, on the other hand, is of newer wealth, and seen in that light (by some, at least) as somehow less honorable. We might see Proteus's father Antonio (whom we get to meet briefly) as a self-made multi-millionaire, a car dealer/distributor or construction contractor blessed with extraordinary cleverness and ambition, but with little formal education or "class"—at least as that would be deemed in Valentine's family circle.

Why is Valentine departing at the first of the play? To learn a little about life, as his father might stuffily say from the smoking room of his most private club; to "learn the ropes" of where much of the family's wealth originally came from several generations past: the gambling casinos, perhaps, or the Teamsters? Either way, it would be fun to have the Duke as a powerful middle-aged Don of sorts, a Paul Sorvino or Danny Aiello type, who takes Valentine, his distant cousin, on as a sort of "apprentice" . . . a personal favor to his father. The dull Valentine is a little apprehensive about it, but mostly clueless. He's also jealous of Proteus's passion for Julia; as most young men, he doesn't particularly feel good about his friend possibly bedding a young woman while he is not.

Proteus, on the other hand, is mainly in love with the idea of a sexual relationship with Julia rather than a long-term romance, although he has convinced himself otherwise. Even so, perhaps he is rather envious of the possible adventures that loom on the horizon for his departing friend, adventures of a decidedly sophisticated and probably amorous nature. After all, in our world the Duke's Milan should be much like a modern Corleone's or Gotti's Atlantic City or Las Vegas. Those immature passions, curiosities and envies, fueled by an over-active and erotic imagination, helps to explain how Proteus, this second would-be "gentleman", might potentially behave as badly as he does in the course of the play and still retain a comprehensible, and perhaps even forgivable (?), motivation for his misdeeds. I suppose forgiveness might depend on the age of the observer of

Proteus's actions over the course of the story; yet young people also tend to be the sternest judges of one another's behavior . . .So, we make the circumstances of these two boys' different backgrounds clear to the two actors cast in the roles, wind up the unbridled lust for *amore* that drives both them and the play, and watch what happens as our young actors explore their roles. It is the perfect companion piece to *Romeo and Juliet*; the very fact that the two plays share identical locations for much of their settings (and even Friar Laurence is mentioned briefly in *2G*!), is strong evidence that Shakespeare himself saw connections between them as well. One of my struggles in directing *Romeo and Juliet* last year is that too often my frustration and aged annoyance with the perpetually short-sighted, arrogant and impulsive behavior of many of the young heroes of that play occasionally undercut my purest sense of the romantic tragedy. *The Two Gentlemen of Verona* appears a likely vehicle for working that out of my system and putting an apt coda to my more cynical perspectives about that most famous of Shakespearean tragedies. Thus, it will be a bit of "That was the Hollywood version of young love, kiddos; here's what, all too often, it's really like."

And once again, in reference to the play's title and Bloom's suggestion of "travesty" and/or "parody": the "gentlemen" aren't gentlemen at all. And that, I think, will be this production's central point.

JULIA'S JOURNEY:

The character of Julia is certainly an important key to the heart of *Two Gentlemen's* story, but in a different way than most of Shakespeare's other famous young heroines.

She doesn't have quite the same drive as *All's Well's* Helena, or *Cymbeline's* Imogen; she lacks the spirit of *Shrew's* Kate, or *Winter's Tale's* mother and daughter; she is weaker in personality than Marina, Beatrice, or Portia, and she doesn't have the intriguing neurosis of Isabella. She is not nearly as comfortable with her sexuality as a Cressida, or even a Juliet, and she certainly is not blessed with the serene assuredness of Viola. In most ways, she is as adolescent as the two males with which she shares the central story of the play, and not nearly as sophisticated as Sylvia. What she does have is a good heart.

But is that enough to see her through? Not without an inherently interesting and likeable actress in the role who will shape Julia to her own personality. In the world of this particular version of *Two Gentlemen*, how our modern audience perceives Julia's evolution through the course of the narrative will be essential to whether the play works at all.

When we first see her, she is filled with the naivete, insecurities and adolescent angst of all young girls: she has a desperate crush on Proteus, but is too proud and embarrassed to confess as much, even to her friendly confidante Lucetta. (Her servant? Best friend? In our world, probably a bit of both . . .) In fact, she carries this false haughtiness to an extreme, tearing up Proteus's love letter, delivered in a clumsy manner to her through a series of snoopy messengers; then, in an adorably immature moment, she desperately tries to piece the letter together again, treating it like an injured Proteus itself as she cradles it against her breast like a lover. Caught in this endearing act of silliness by Lucetta, she again tries to regain her dignity, but is largely unsuccessful in her efforts. Like most adolescents in love, she takes herself very seriously, and cannot relax with her feelings; she must futilely attempt to retain control by seeming "above love" . . . in front of others, anyway.

The next time we see her, things between her and Proteus have obviously progressed. They have proclaimed their passion for one another, although a physical consummation seems doubtful, given her innocence and pride. But puppy love is perhaps the strongest love we ever know, and we never really forget our first infatuation, do we? She is so stricken that she is speechless at Proteus's departure, even though he clearly is hoping for an articulate confession of her heartbreak and is upset at her grief-stricken and mute departure. The fact that he is completely clueless about the truth of her heart's feelings, and is expecting specific behavior from his beloved should be the audience's first indication that this is something of an immature romantic mis-match.

Not in Julia's eyes . . . at least, not yet. In her next scene, she resolves to follow him to Milan, disguising herself as a young man in order to protect her womanly virtue on the journey, the first time this familiar device is ever used in the Shakespeare canon. (One can clearly see the young Shakespeare's pride in delving into the mechanics of this disguise, mainly by his undue glee over codpiece jokes—all of which we will be excising from the text for our production, as modern wardrobes will render the dialogue senseless.) Interestingly, Lucetta issues her final piece of mature and womanly advice to Julia in this scene, warning her that many men don't fancy being pursued by women, even if they first seemed attracted to them. In her innocence, Julia either ignores this sage counsel or simply cannot yet understand it. Refuted, Lucetta departs the play—and yet, in only two scenes she has established a choral role that is a vital lens through which the audience can see the mis-steps that Julia (like all puppy-lovers) seems bound to make as she suffers through the growing pangs of first love.

A goodly amount of text passes before we next encounter Julia, in disguise and already arrived in Milan, seeking to be in the service of her lover, Proteus. She is in for a shock, however, soon discovering that the man she has risked so much to follow is deep in lust with the vivacious and youthfully sophisticated Sylvia, daughter of the man in whose employ both Proteus and Valentine now are. The scene contains some surprisingly poignant moments in this story of mainly superficial people and behavior; Shakespeare skillfully makes us feel Julia's silent heartbreak, Proteus's agonizing unfulfilled lust for Sylvia, and Sylvia's inner confusion beneath the pretentiously aloof exterior—for although rejecting Proteus, she invites him to drop by for her picture later on! And against it all, the simple, good-natured landlady of the inn (gender-switched in our production), an over-worked woman who, if she could get a good night's sleep, might occasionally remember with some fondness what it was like to be young and in love.

Julia's scene with Sylvia is a pivotal one for them both. In it, Julia discovers that she cannot hate Sylvia, much as she'd like to. They are sisters, they are trying to live in a world of men (both resenting and needing that at the same time) . . . and when young men behave badly, as these men are doing (either by Proteus's disloyalty or Valentine's self-centeredness), young women do well to try remaining unswamped in their wake. In a surprisingly real picture of a teenage girl's world, Shakespeare gives us the torment of Julia comparing herself to Sylvia's portrait . . . a poignant scene that still admits aesthetic distance and humor.

The final important scene in Julia's journey is the climax in the woods. After an offstage encounter with the Outlaws (more about them later) that has the trio's adrenaline pumping, Julia watches her first love express a willingness to rape Sylvia, and in fact begin the attempt. Frozen and helpless in her disguise, she watches in more horror as Sylvia responds to Proteus—which perhaps surprises Proteus as much as anyone. Suddenly onto the scene comes Valentine, who like the self-absorbed, self-congratulating dumbbell that such a privileged, good-looking young man of society tends to be, thinks it good sportsmanship to offer Sylvia to Proteus . . . or perhaps it's more likely due to the fact that he witnessed the chemistry between them too, and is . . . angry? Philosophical? Who knows but Valentine, and maybe it's even too complex for him to figure out entirely! This is too much for Julia, who faints, and when revived reveals herself and finally lets fly . . . a bit . . . at Proteus. He listens sheepishly—*busted!*—and then, rather theatrically, re-discovers his love for Julia.

Here's where things get interesting. The faces of the four young people must be a study in repressed emotions: the perpetually seductive Sylvia wondering who she really should be departing the stage with, Valentine also more than a bit befuddled by it all, Proteus already planning his next potential move with either Julia and/or Sylvia, and Julia in near shock over the incredibly unacceptable behavior of the boy she has loved and followed into danger.

It will be fascinating to see how our young actress playing Julia will explore in rehearsals what her feelings might be in such a real-life situation. Frankly, I see or hear of similarly outrageous things happening between young people all the time in their relationships, and I seem to recall a bit of what amoral idiocy I was up to at their age as well. Will she leave the stage with Proteus? Will she just stand there, leaving the audience in suspense? Or will she slap him across the face and stride out the opposite direction? Or . . . most intriguingly and perversely . . . might she slap him—and mean it—and then kiss him—and mean it?

If we don't try to "yuck up" the harshness of the situation . . . if we don't feel the need to be comfortably comic at the play's conclusion . . . what might happen? I'm fascinated to learn.

THE REST OF THE ILK:

None of the characters in *Two Gentlemen* are particularly well-behaved; and although they are intriguing in their actions and (some, anyway) complex in their desires and motivations, few seem the kind whom we would want to have a long-term relationship with, or who would be particularly easy (or suitable) to trust . . . at least in the contextual world that I would like to explore. Launce is probably the most likeable and trustworthy of all, but even that is somewhat compromised by his naivete and downright ignorance. Nonetheless, his loyalty to Crab, his dog, is commendable and endearing, and set as a very clever and enlightening counterpart to his master's devious egotism. (Proteus—even the name implies an ever-changing nature.) Shakespeare skillfully alternates scenes between the "gentlemen" and their servants throughout the play, primarily to point up the worst behavior of the upper classes. He does this by not only showing the good-hearted and uneducated Launce contrasting with his selfish master, but also the clever, cynical and sarcastic Speed against the often wooden and unimaginative Valentine, his own master. Speed seems to me much akin to Jean in August Strindberg's *Miss Julie*, but in a comic vein: an ambitious and quick-witted member of the lower economic class who has managed to latch himself onto a young upper class twit on whom he can figuratively feed, while mixing socially with his "betters." More experienced with women, he is much more initially attuned to Sylvia's flirtations and advances than is his master, Valentine, and even coaches the poor sod about what he should do to pursue the sexy young daughter of his new employer. Likewise, Launce also shows a sharp comprehension of what is actually going on around him in all the supposedly subtle intrigues involved with Proteus's intended betrayal of his "best friend" Valentine: "I am but a fool," he notes in Act III, scene i, "and yet I have the wit to think my master is a kind of knave."

Lucetta, as noted earlier, seems a nice combination of the better qualities of her male counterparts: she shows Launce's compassion and loyalty both in her playful teasing of her mistress as well as her street-wise counsel. She is a young lady already moderately experienced in love and relationships (no waiting on a debutante ball for a girl of her socio-economic class!), but she still has a sweetness that redeems her from the cynicism and social-climbing machinations of Speed. The Innkeeper/Hostess also seems a very sentimental, jovial and likeable sort, although she has clearly seen better days; I see her as a hard-bitten saloon owner, probably married and divorced several times, who now most often seeks dependable companionship in the bottle. Nonetheless, she still remembers what it was like to be young and innocently in love for the first time, and her presence as Julia is forced to initially witness her lover's betrayal is again an effective dramatic contrast between the fresh-faced and the world-weary.

Beyond these folks (not including Speed), the sincerity quotient drops rather steeply. I envision Proteus's father, Antonio, to be an aging divorced playboy CEO of a less than admirable corporate venture with rich political connections, sipping martinis by his pool much of the time and aspiring to be part of the "old money" society that he has fought tooth and nail to join all of his street-wise life. There is no mention of Proteus's mother at all—which is perhaps a significant reason for the boy's bad behavior with women. We should make it clear in Antonio's brief scene that he is a poor (and emotionally distant) role model for his teenage son, focusing primarily on what a potential apprenticeship for his son with Milan's Duke might do for the family fortunes and connections . . . particularly once he is reminded by his paramour at poolside that Valentine—the boy from the "old money" family that he believes his own son should have a firm connection with—is himself off to apprentice with the Duke in his "business." Antonio's mistress, Patina (the meddling uncle Pantino in Shakespeare's text, gender-switched in our version), bringing her sugar daddy his afternoon cocktail in Act I, scene iii, re-enforces his thought along that line; after all, if she can convince her aging, middle-aged lover to send his son across country after Valentine, then she can have more control of the estate, Antonio's time . . . and his bank accounts. Proteus is a constant reminder of her lover's previous marriage; it is past time to be rid of him hanging about the mansion all the time. Once that's accomplished, she can establish her domestic beachhead more firmly.

And what of the Duke of Milan, for whose realm Valentine is journeying at the play's beginning? In this world, I see him as a rather ruthless and cold old-world Don; once a punk, albeit with sophisticated tastes and business acumen, who runs a posh gambling and nightclub empire akin to Las Vegas or Atlantic City. He was a "made man" long ago, and now is firmly ensconced, like a Gotti, atop his amoral and shady empire. Valentine's father (patriarch of a political family along the lines of the Kennedys or the Bushs) has longtime ties to the Duke, and believes his spoiled and pampered son has much to learn in preparation for his future success by getting his fingernails dirty in the next couple of years in such a world. Yet in spite of its Vegas-y glitter and glamour, it is also a dangerous world, and we should have the sense that when the Duke banishes Valentine for daring to covet his daughter (whom he intends for Turio, a favorite "cousin" and *capo* in training), he's dealing much more lightly with the upstart boy than he might deal with a similar transgression done by someone who was not the son of a family friend. Again, with some careful cutting of clownish dialogue, I hope to present Turio as a character who is somewhat thick and stupidly macho, but not the flailing dolt that most productions make him. (Otherwise, one would wonder why the Duke would have bestowed so much favor upon him in the first place.) And Eglamour, in his brief spoken appearance in the latter part of the play, shows himself as a type that we know too well from any level of society: a man who talks a good game, and wants to be the noble, dashing rescuer of Sylvia (perhaps another of the Duke's "lieutenants," helplessly enamored with his daughter), but finally simply lacks the guts to face down real adversity when the chips are down.

In addition to these "named" characters, I also envision an Ensemble of approximately 8-10 actors, 4-5 men and 4-5 women, who will represent the three worlds of the play that we see during its course: they will portray rich business associates and household servants in the high society of Verona that we glimpse at the first of the play; then, the lounge/club women and "button men" of the Duke's operation in Milan; and finally, the exiled "outlaws" of the wilderness in the close of the play, a loose-knit conglomerate of leather-clad punks and motorcycle-gang types . . . albeit all a bit inept. If desirable, we could fill these necessary roles with individual performers, but it would probably be a much more fulfilling performance experience for the students involved to utilize doubling.

POSSIBLE SETTINGS:

As I preliminarily plan for our production, I am doing a fair amount of textual cutting to best present that world and those characters whose stories I am most interested in telling with this particular staging, and highlighting the themes that I see in the text which fascinate me the most. Frankly, I am not at all certain, using this approach, the play will turn out to be the outright "comedy" it is reputed to be; but since I don't find much of what happens in the play particularly funny, I am not too worried about that. We will tell the story that I see in the blueprint, and let the chips fall where they may. Much of what occurs is amusing, undoubtedly; but the circumstances actually seem painful more often than not. True comedy requires surprise, anger and emotional depth; in this production of *The Two Gentlemen of Verona*, we'll do our best to commit fully to that. We will present the events of the play as truthfully as possible, we will tap the emotional perspective, honesty and experiences that our young cast will offer us, and we will do our best to avoid the familiar comic pandering that I've seen far too much of in earlier productions of the piece. I'm not entirely certain how our audiences will react to this approach, but it will be exciting to find out.

In addition to the textual cuts I am making, in the interest of dramatic unity in the narrative and better integrity of the scenic design, I am experimenting with the sequencing of scenes in the play. To avoid a constant switching back and forth between physical locations in the play's initial half, I am re-assembling the play's scenes in the following order:

Act I, scenes 1-3;
Act II, scenes 2-3
Act II, scene 7
Act II, scene 1
Act II, scenes 4-6

Intermission

Act III, scenes 1-2
Act IV, scene 2 (jumbled and re-assembled a bit)
Act IV, scene 1
Act IV, scene 3
Act IV, scene 4
Act V, scenes 1-4

I believe that this sequencing might allow us to have the scenic elements follow this pattern:

I. Verona: an adaptable suggested location that reflects affluence, high society, the perpetual "cocktail hour", a la Newport, Rhode Island, Cape Cod, Massachusetts, or Kennebunkport, Maine. An elaborate estate patio? Health and Racquet Club with wetbar? An exclusive country club? Lots of sunlight and perpetually "perfect" weather (during the correct seasons, of course).
II. Milan: A dark, sexy, after-hours nightclub, with tables? Jukebox? Suggestions of gambling? Mostly posh, but with

a hint of sleaze? A piano bar or stage? Lots of possibilities
. . . a "mob" location.
III. A rather more vague, more general "all-purpose"
functional location that must eventually serve as the "woods"
(a suburban or urban wilderness surrounding Milan): a
cultivated garden with hedges? A wall, or walls, with ivy? Or
something more harsh and suggestively dangerous, such as an
urban landscape with chain-linked fences, concrete, burning
trash barrels, and graffiti? The latter, I think.

SOME TUNES:

As with many of my shows, music has played a decidedly
large part in my preparations for inhabiting this imagined universe.
Although of course all of this is subject to change, the following
songs have proven useful in stimulating the emotional context of
my vision for this incarnation of *The Two Gentlemen of Verona*:

You Don't Know Me (I've always loved this number, both
in versions by Ray Charles and Kenny Loggins, and the
lyrics very much fit the teenage angst of the characters)

*I Wanna Be Around To Pick Up the Pieces (When
Somebody Breaks Your Heart)* —Tony Bennett

Come Fly With Me—Frank Sinatra

The Good Life —Tony Bennett

Italian Mambo—Dean Martin

It All Depends On You—Frank Sinatra

You're Nobody Till Somebody Loves You—Dean Martin

One For My Baby (And One More For the Road)
                                        —Frank Sinatra

Young At Heart—Frank Sinatra

Smile—Tony Bennett

and finally,

My Way—by Sid Vicious

Do your creative self a favor while preparing your thoughts for our design/discussion process: curl up with your favorite catalyst for relaxation, put these songs on your favorite listening medium, watch the films *Swingers*, *Goodfellas*, or a couple of episodes of *The Sopranos*—and let your imagination roam.

I look forward to discussing the results.

Love's Labours Lost

SOME THOUGHTS ON *LOVE'S LABOURS LOST*

THE PLAY AND ITS TITLE:

The title of the play is interesting in itself: the first thing to note is the self-conscious alliteration that perfectly reflects the self-consciously literary "conceit" of the men who are its protagonists, and the age of courtiers from which it sprang. This fluffy meringue is juxtaposed against the melancholy fall of the order of the words, with love's labours (a curious way to look at love) being ultimately "lost." Thus, in the title we have a nearly perfect summation of the story's content, as well as its form.

A few more interesting facts: the play is the earliest in the canon to feature a story (such as it is) that is original, rather than one cribbed by Shakespeare from an existing play, poem, or myth—or in the case of the histories, from chronicles of past events. However, as it turns out, there really was a King of Navarre (a region in Spain) with Dukes Biron, Du Maine, and Longaville, and they did indeed aspire to create an admired academe, renowned for artistry and study. Beyond that, the incidents of the play, along with its minor characters and its depictions of their characteristics, are largely Shakespeare's, undoubtedly based in gentle satire on some contemporaneous members of the London aristocracy and court. *Love's Labours Lost* was the first published play in quarto (1598) to bear Shakespeare's name on the title page, presumably as a draw to potential buyers. And, most fascinating of all, according to Francis Meres's treatise on the current drama of London (also published in 1598), *LLL* had a sequel that has evidently been lost called *Love's Labours Won*.

There are various scholarly theories as to what might have happened with *Love's Labours Won*. Some believe that *LLL* has an ending that clearly cries out for a legitimate sequel, so that there was indeed such a play that related what became of these various couples when they reunited after a year's separation. However, there are no additional references about the plot of this lost play extant from the era, so there is no way of knowing (short of a copy of the play being discovered, perhaps along with *Cardenio*, another "lost" play by Shakespeare and Fletcher from the later stages of his writing career) if that theory is true. Others suggest that *Love's Labours Won* might be known to us under a different title (like *Twelfth Night* and *Henry VIII*, and *Henry VI, Parts 2* and *3* all have alternate titles). Candidates for this (for various reasons that I won't go into here) are *Much Ado About Nothing*, *The Taming of the Shrew*, and *All's Well That Ends Well*. Another possibility that occurs to me that I have not seen suggested elsewhere is that *Love's Labours Won* was a collaboration by Shakespeare with another playwright, a common practice in the early years of the public theatres and rival companies, a collaboration that wasn't ultimately included in the 1623 Folio because it contained too much material by the collaborator, rather than Shakespeare (other examples of this may include *Pericles*, *The Two Noble Kinsmen*, *Sir Thomas More*, and *Edward III*). Whatever the truth of the matter, it remains one of the more intriguing of many mysteries surrounding Shakespeare's works. One would love to know what happened to Rosaline and Berowne, and the Princess and the Duke/King after the sudden death and their subsequent separation at the end of *LLL*.

For many years now, I have been avoiding the challenge of producing *Love's Labours Lost*. The play has its fans, both theatrical and academic, but I fear that I've never been counted among them. Anne Barton calls the play Shakespeare's "most relentlessly Elizabethan" piece, and I find long passages of the unedited play impenetrable and tedious. The first scene is always enjoyable upon every reading, but confusion creeps in with the entrance of Don Armado and Moth, with incomprehensible jokes and puns piling one upon the other. It picks up again when the Princess and her ladies first encounter the men, and then starts to meander about for scene after scene, relying on in-jokes and references that only scholars related to Holoferness could decipher. The play-within-the-play at the conclusion of Act V seems a pale predecessor of that in *A Midsummer Night's Dream*. But then, out of the blue (like life itself) comes the startling announcement of death and loss that concludes the play with shocking and unexpected suddenness. And it is here, intimated by the dying fall inherent in the play's title, where I find the play's most interesting (and very Shakespearean) possibility and potential. Behind the determinedly lighthearted emphasis on love and the promised pleasures of the flesh lurks the Reaper. Always, the scythe awaits the blooming rose, a theme often explored in the Shakespearean sonnets, many of which are surely contemporaneous with this early and deceptively complex play.

"A DYING FALL":

I have yet to experience a satisfying staging of *Love's Labours Lost*. Even those produced by professional companies, featuring actors that I very much respect, have failed to illuminate fully (for me) the potential strengths of the play. Most recently, I saw the London Globe Theatre's production that toured the United States, concluding its run on Broadway. In spite of the rave reviews it collected in its travels, I found the show to be long on shallow, cheap comic "bits" and short on depth of character and texture. The audience around me on the University of Michigan Ann Arbor campus chortled and guffawed through over three hours of pratfalls, farting jokes, and food fights, concluding the play (after hearing of the Princess's father's sudden demise!) with a comical song and an exuberant jig. My distinct impression was that, for the majority of the people in the house, the play was a genuine "snob hit"; they believed that intelligent, sophisticated people should find the Globe's staging amusing, so they were doggedly determined to prove themselves "in the know" by laughing loudly whenever the actors signaled that they should do so. Needless to say, I found the experience extremely irritating.

I suspect that many directors and actors, like me, find the play a daunting challenge. Rather than taking any risks with a comedy that might succeed in getting smiles rather than chortles—and might, in fact, puzzle the hearers upon occasion—they impose farce and slapstick on a text that will simply not support it; not, at least, in the quantities that they wish. Our approach will be to ignore playing to a particular genre with this play, recognizing that the genius of the best Shakespearean texts lies in the constant juxtaposition of dark and light. So, while there are many obvious comic elements inherent in the play, they are consistently contrasted with the gentle melancholy that runs like a distant tune, only partially heard, throughout the play's slight action. It reminds me very much of the famous "breaking string", heard at a distance, in Act II of Chekhov's *The Cherry Orchard*: a symbol for the oncoming change that all of the characters will soon find inescapable. As Francis Fergusson notes, the Chekhov play is a "tone poem on the suffering of change." While that will not be the primary theme of *Love's Labours Lost* in our incarnation, it will certainly be the counterpoint melody throughout.

Although I don't wish to set the play in a specifically detailed actual period of western history, the era that I find the most appropriate place to begin is that of Europe in its "dying fall" of 19th Century empire, standing on the brink of the first great World War. *The Proud Tower* by Barbara Tuchman paints an involving picture of the increasing contrasts and conflicts between the conservative social orders of the early 20th Century and the rising tide of utopian socialism and outright anarchy that was threatening to engulf established political hierarchies. This particular world model seems a perfect canvas for the microcosm of the court of Navarre. The aristocratic men occupy a world of fantasy and ivory-tower academia that they (unrealistically) hope to protect from the plebeian world outside of their gates; and the Duke plans to accomplish this in a manner that is completely antithetical to the human needs of everyday society. There is no seeking of a proper balance here, nor any recognition that their feet touch the earth as all other biological beings' do. Instead, they intend to live only in the world of abstract philosophy, abandoning the essentials of "base living" in order to do so (like sleep, food, and sex). This is clearly doomed to failure (just as were the desperate attempts to preserve the British Victorian Empire in the face of rising poverty and political unrest in the countries all around them prior to World War I).

So, threaded throughout the world that we create in this staging of *Love's Labours Lost*, my ambition would be to find those hints of the darker realities of the world outside this "little academe" that the Duke dreams of creating. Some of those hints might lie in the edginess of Costard's behavior with his "betters"; the suppressed desperation of the Princess's mission (i.e., finding allies, political and financial, for her father's government before it falls); the scars of prior regional conflicts on some of the play's characters (an eye patch for Don Armado? Or a limp and a cane? Old war wounds that perhaps explain his lapses into fantastical behavior at times? And Moth as a war orphan?); and a schoolmaster left with very few children to instruct. I imagine a newspaper headline read by Berowne in the first scene, briefly noted by the audience ("WAR IN THE BALKANS: Political unrest spreads"); servants who shift the scenery dressed in natty looking attire, signs of an over-extended and insolvent aristocracy; and Hessian soldiers that accompany Marcade (obviously now in their custody) when she announces the news of the King's death in France at the close of the play.

Thus, in spite of the romantic comedy and occasionally silly escapades that occur in this brief, idyllic interlude of romance in an isolated country garden in Navarre, a tidal wave of societal change is waiting without the garden's rusted, antique gates. The ladies feel this instinctively even as they arrive in Navarre, although they find some pleasure in putting it aside and being "young" again, if only for awhile. The men, by the end of the play, are realizing it. It is the end of childhood for them all, and their onrushing adulthood promises unexpected hardships, physical and emotional. Change is coming, and for the aristocratic *status quo* it brings with it a dying fall.

AS THE PLAY BEGINS:

The Duke of Navarre, a man in his twenties, is a provincial governor in search of a purpose in life. He is intellectually curious, a rabid reader of philosophy, history, the sciences, and literature; but knowing him, one wonders how much of his almost nerd-y pursuit of this book knowledge stems from his fundamental social ineptness, particularly in matters involving the opposite sex. He is virtually clueless about affairs of the heart, having had little prior experience except vicariously, through his avid studies of poetry, literature and biology. He surrounds himself with three fellows, "courtiers" of a sort, who resemble the famous Duke of Clarence/James Whistler/Oscar Wilde social circle of the Victorian Age, only without the more worldly and risqué behavior that those men became known for. However, two of these fellows (Berowne and Longaville) have some romantic experiences under their belts (so to speak!); and Dumaine, the youngest, although lacking their level of sophistication with the ladies, is very eager to catch up.

Unfortunately, it seems to be not in the cards, for as the play begins the Duke reveals his latest plan for the immediate future: he and his comrades (lacking a war to seek glory in, or a sport to find fame with, or anything of any consequence happening in their immediate future—these men are definitely of the "idle class," bordering on the "twits" that Monty Python skewered so effectively) will find their fame and immortality by becoming the most serious and preeminent bookworms of their time. They will study EVERYTHING. If *Jeopardy* had been invented, their goal would be to become its all-time champions—at least, that is the Duke's brilliant intention. And, in order to do that most effectively, the Duke believes that they must swear off every fleshly distraction that could hamper their success: wine, women, song, sleep, etc. Longaville, cynical, bored and game for anything (and secretly certain that he can get around any restrictions, if necessary), agrees. Dumain, eager to please his slightly older comrades, also quickly signs on to the idea. Berowne, the most practical (and jovially quarrelsome and challenging) of the group, attempts to point out the silliness and impracticality of the idea, but is quickly ridiculed into going along with it by his pals.

Almost immediately, the Duke is reminded of what is on his political agenda for the coming week, and of course it presents an immediate obstacle to his grand plan: the young Princess of France is due to arrive, an emissary from the King, her father, an old political ally of the Duke's own late sire. The Duke is unaware, however, of the urgency behind the Princess's visit, and it is only suggested by the circumstances revealed in the play's early scenes. It is a time of great social unrest throughout Europe, a time when the lower economic classes are beginning to feel their muscle and find a determination to shrug off the oppression of their "masters." And the King of France, long one of the more ostentatious of the old guard social order, is feeling the heat, and in dire need of coins in the treasury in order to deal with the bubbling caldron that his country is becoming.

What to do? Knowing that the young Duke of Navarre's father has passed on, the King of France devises a fiction wherein there remains an outstanding debt to be paid to France by Navarre, now assumed to be his son's responsibility. Knowing that passing this fiction off as fact is a bold gamble, the King decides to try to disguise it by distracting the Duke from paying too much attention to historical facts; he will do this by sending his daughter as messenger, a young lady largely unaware of her attractiveness, herself accompanied by three carefully chosen young women from her retinue. The King of France has done his planning well: he believes that the bookish, inexperienced young Duke will be ripe for his daughter's charms, and he is aware that each lady he has chosen as one of his daughter's travelling companions has an individual romantic history of sorts with each of the Duke's companions. With just a bit of good fortune (France hopes), the hapless young men will be so focused upon their beauteous guests that they will repay him the fictional debt without undue protest.

Knowing that much is at stake politically for her father and her homeland, the Princess carries a burdensome responsibility. Although gifted with intelligence and wit that easily outmatches the Duke's, she has never been completely confident in her ability to charm the male of the species; nor is she confident that she will be clever enough to carry out her country's mission. Although he believes that his daughter has more than enough skill, beauty and ability to achieve her mission, he nonetheless dispatches his trusted counselor, Boyet, and the Princess's childhood governess, Marcade, to help keep the plan on track. And if the Duke of Navarre falls strongly enough for his daughter to propose a marriage? Well, all the better; an alliance with Navarre could be extremely beneficial in view of France's currently fragile political state.

As the Duke of Navarre ponders the problems posed by the briefly forgotten arrival of the French entourage, a few other related problems arise: Dull, the local Constable, arrives at the estate with Costard, a well-known local rascal (and one of the Duke's groundskeepers) in tow. Beneath the jokes and yokel-like role-playing that Costard's behavior exhibits, the man is clever, conniving, and more than a little contemptuous of the pretensions of the upper classes, an opportunist revolutionary of sorts. It seems that he has knowingly disregarded the Duke's silly edict about all of the estate's personnel adhering to the monastic-type life he has recently decreed, and has been caught dallying with a local dairymaid, Jaquenetta. Frustrated and distracted by the problem of how to handle the Princess of France, the Duke quickly directs that Costard be given unto his eccentric foreign estate neighbor, Don Armado, to serve an informal penitential servitude.

Little is known about Armado's background; but he seems quite the character, and the Duke and his pals enjoy the amusing distraction that Armado often provides them. However, behind his eccentricity lies more than a hint of a melancholy past. Armado shows physical signs of having fought in various unspecified engagements in past years; and he is accompanied by a young girl, Moth (whom we will gender-switch for our production), who is at the doorstep of womanhood, and whom Armado "adopted" years ago when she was a starving child in some war-ravaged country. Perhaps his tendency toward addled silliness in matters of love and philosophy also represents the consequences of past traumas in his life, connected with his soldiering days of years ago.

Also on the fringes of this strange society, living in rural isolation on the Duke's decaying, aristocratic, Chekhovian estate, we find Holoferness, the country schoolteacher with urbane scholarly pretensions, and Lady Natalie (another gender-switched role, changed from "Nathaniel"), his wealthy old-maid admirer who longs for the male attention that has always eluded her. They too will play a part in the antics of the play, as the young ladies and men come together in youthful attraction, shattering their oaths and pretensions. Yet amid all the comedy of young love, a darker world lies beyond the ivy-covered towers of the Duke's estate; a world that is moving from the spring and summer of bloom and promise steadily toward the devastating autumn and winter of another war that will eventually reach, engulf and change forever the idyllic and naïve worlds of Navarre and France.

THE CHARACTERS:

THE DUKE OF NAVARRE: He has spent much of his life as something of a literary, philosophical policy wonk. He loves reading, debating, exploring theories, and playing out various scenarios in his imagination. His nature secretly leans toward the romantic, but he is very uncertain of his "gifts" in that realm. Thus, his library has always been a wonderful refuge. His appearance is somewhat unkempt, given his stature; someone needs to make his fashion choices for him, as it's not in his realm of interest. He has a keen wit and sense of humor, but not so much when the joke is on him.

BEROWNE: A great lover of life and pleasure, in all their aspects. He is as much at home with a book of poetry as he is on a playing field. Not a hedonist, he is nonetheless confused why anyone would be willing to sacrifice an opportunity to thoroughly enjoy himself, and never considers that his taking of personal pleasure might ever cause pain or unhappiness for others; thus, we begin to have an understanding of what might have occurred in his prior relationships with women, particularly Rosaline. A likeable and energetic young man, quick with a joke (even when it's at his own expense).

DUMAIN: The youngest of the four comrades, extremely eager to please. He is thrilled to be chosen as worthy for the Duke's attention and companionship—a courtier in training—and determined to demonstrate his "can do" attitude. However, saying "yes" to everything means that he is expected to follow through successfully, and this occasionally eludes him. He seems quite naïve, energetic, and a little lost at times—like a cuddly puppy dog.

LONGAVILLE: Studiedly bored, laconic, with an "I've seen it all, so don't try to impress me" attitude. Coolly sophisticated, he has a sarcastic wit that he treasures as one of his greatest assets. He believes himself to be a new, undiscovered Oscar

Wilde, and thinks that he is devastatingly attractive to the ladies, as well as admired by his envious male compatriots. This is partly accurate, as Dumain certainly admires him; but Berowne and the Duke, while liking him, see the real person behind the crafted facade.

THE PRINCESS OF FRANCE: A remarkably intelligent young lady, introspective and contemplative by nature. She is very well-read, has grown up without a mother (raised by Marcade, the governess/tutor), and has no experience of romance beyond what she has learned from her library. Her father is an ailing monarch of a nation in a precarious political situation, fighting off rebels both external and internal. She has been sent on this mission to Navarre, in rather desperate times, with her father's hope that her youth and beauty will bring success to procuring the funding and support that his government direly needs. However, she is far from confident or secure that she is a) beautiful, and b) up to the crucial task. Because of her family's circumstances and her upbringing, she has missed much of a "normal" girlhood, and feels the loss.

ROSALINE: The Princess's foremost lady-in-waiting. Clearly more experienced in affairs of the heart than her mistress, Rosaline has a past that involves an affair (Brief? Substantial?) with Berowne that ended badly. She knows the sting of a man's betrayal in love, and does not forgive nor forget easily. As a result, she lives behind a wall of cynical and hard-edged wit, particularly sharpened by her disappointment in how she has been treated by past lovers. She has a dark, mysterious melancholy air at times; at other times, she quickly finds her laughter, and provokes the same from her fellow ladies. She has a mercurial temperament, and can move between moods suddenly. Her volatility indicates a passionate personality.

KATHERINE: A bubbly young lady by nature, she seems a perfect match for the boyish and inexperienced Dumain. She seems determinedly optimistic and happy, and is therefore a valued comrade for the Princess, who has dealt with more than her share of troubles in recent years. We discover some reason for her determination not to burden herself with focusing on the darker side of things in one of the play's latter scenes: she lost a beloved older sister some years ago, who apparently pined and died after an unsuccessful love affair. This exchange with Rosaline is one of the only times in the play that her sunshine demeanor drops and we glimpse the vulnerable (but tough) young lady underneath. Most of the time she's giggly, and enjoys being just that.

MARIA: Perhaps the most enigmatic of the four ladies that attend the Princess, she reveals little about herself in the play's various encounters. She keeps her own counsel, but there appears in her a depth that is both attractive and seemingly unsounded. She can easily join in the merriment of the other young ladies when it erupts, but is a more private personality than the others. Her careful guardedness, her sense of reserve, and her economy of wit are the qualities that the verbose and self-satisfied Longaville finds the most intriguing.

MARCADE: Although she has limited stage time and words to say, Marcade is a sobering and grave presence, a reminder at key moments that a darker world exists at the edges of the exuberant young romantic escapades at the center of the play. As the Princess's governess/tutor, Marcade was the closest person to a mother that she had when she was young, and thus her announcement of the King of France's death at the climax of the play carries a familial gravity as well as a political one. She presents a stern demeanor, but cares deeply for her charge, as she knows that the Princess is growing up in a challenging political time.

BOYET: The Princess of France's counselor and advisor, assigned by the court and her father to keep her and her diplomatic/political mission to Navarre on track. Very sophisticated and with a wry and sharp sense of humor, his is more than a match for any of the would-be wits of the Duke of Navarre's court. Although worldly and knowledgeable in a variety of areas, and quite keen to help fulfill the Princess's mission, Boyet has his amorous and earthy side too. He greatly enjoys watching the youngsters around him play the game of love, and is not above a few suggestively flirtatious soirees with the young ladies in his charge—all in fun, of course. In this, he very much reflects the French view of sex and romance.

DULL: He is one of those delightful, bureaucratic authority figures that Shakespeare paints so well, very much akin to Dogberry and Elbow in *Much Ado About Nothing* and *Measure for Measure*. He is a blunt, straightforward, "what's all this, then?" police officer (obviously based on the London model that hasn't really changed in centuries, as Monty Pyton's depictions clearly show us) and feels uncomfortably out of his depth dealing with aristocracy, royalty, foreign eccentrics, and pseudo-intellectuals. He laughs little if at all and tries to do everything "by the book"; he is a mutton-and-potatoes man, baffled by the caviar crowd.

COSTARD: One of the more intriguing characters of the play, and one that could be approached as a charming dunce—OR (as I would like to explore) a clever country lad who gets what he wants by making everyone else think he is a simple guy, easy to fool; while, in fact, he is having a marvelous time manipulating them into corners and mazes of his own devising. I see him as a Moliere-type servant in the manner of La Fleche in *The Miser*, realizing that there is much to be gained by not letting others who believe they are smarter than you discover that *you* are actually much smarter than *them*. (For example: he impregnates Jaquenetta, but cleverly devises a situation that makes Don Armado and others believe that Armado is responsible for the child.)

JAQUENETTA: A young, sultry and voluptuous country wench who has known from puberty exactly how to wrap silly men around her little finger, and thus get exactly what she wants from them. She has found a perfect mate/partner/lover in Costard. Although she has nowhere near his level of wit, she has great instincts for "the grift", and knows how to use her charms effectively. She and Costard are the perfect con artist team, and they can play dumb with a wink and a nod to one another.

DON ARMADO: A stranger in a strange land, I see Armado not as a bumbling idiot (as he is often played), but someone with a somewhat checkered and murky past, someone who is a dreamer—yet something of a naïve fool, from some perspectives—in the Don Quixote mode. Sometime in the past, he was a soldier, who dreamed of ideals and honors, and yet never quite had the intelligence to see his dreams fulfilled. As a result, he became an easy foil for those around him, as his idealism can easily be seen as pompous, self-aggrandizing, and pretentiously silly. Perhaps he sustained a head wound in some past battle in this tumultuous, part-mythic Europe in which our version of the play is set; and perhaps this adds to the general sense of foggy unawareness of reality that often surrounds him?

MOTH: An obvious nickname, given to this young girl because of her small stature. In our version, she seems to be a child growing into a young woman, who is frustrated because (in spite of her intelligence and her approaching adulthood) she is still seen by others as a little girl. I suspect that Don Armado found her many years ago (during one of his battlefield exploits or expeditions?), and has never stopped thinking of her as his little "orphan." However, Moth (now his housekeeper and serving girl) is starting to see herself as the protector of Armado, who (she feels) seems to be growing less able to deal with the real world as the years pass. She loves Armado almost as she would a dodgy uncle, and is often frustrated that he will not realize that she is now a young woman, not a child.

HOLOFERNESS: Another of Shakespeare's favorite types to have some fun with, the pretentiously intellectual country schoolmaster who believes that he is miles above all of those around him and should have been at the helm of some major university. He is pedantic, obsessed with demonstrating his bookish education at every opportunity, believes that the world around him ought to be as fascinated with trivialities as he is, rather contemptuous of them if they're not . . . and almost completely out of touch with human nature. He is a brilliant demonstration of what the Duke and his boys might be heading for if they actually made good on their vow at the beginning of the play.

LADY NATALIE: A delightful mixture of propriety and hidden longings, a middle-aged country lady who is a perfect eccentric match for Holoferness ("If only he would see it!" she thinks). She truly admires Holoferness's educational superiority to the rough country peasant types that inhabit the fringes of our version of Navarre, and secretly (and often NOT so secretly) harbors a strong crush on this man of her dreams. She only knows of actual romance from the 3-volume novels that she reads (a stack of them on her bedside table), but would truly like some first-hand experience. Nonetheless, she's too shy to be as bold with Holoferness as she would like to be. A wonderfully quirky lady. (Think Elsa Lanchester at about age 40, wearing a country squire outfit of tweeds and a deerstalker hat, perhaps?)

PRODUCTION APPROACHES AND AMBIENCE (A TALE OF TWO WORLDS):

The music that I've tentatively settled on as appropriate for the world that I'd like to create are the piano sketches of Erik Satie. They seem to strike the right balance of playfulness with a wistful sadness.

As I've alluded to earlier, I'm not interested in slavishly following a particular historical time period: prop newspaper headlines should refer to such general situations as "Unrest in the Balkans", "Bank Collapses Feared", or "Riots in Paris." The precarious situation of Europe prior to World War I should be our general model, but what I envision is something of a "parallel universe" with reference points to western history models, without worrying unduly about anachronisms. The Parisian women should look alluring to the men, even if that means that the strait-laced look of the 1910's need to be relaxed a bit. Each subset of lovers—the women of Paris and the men of Navarre—should probably have two sets of basic attire, one for formal occasions (the welcoming of the women in Act II, Scene i), and another for all of the informal running around. The soldiers who escort Marcade in at the play's close should look Prussian, Hessian or Eastern European (whichever appears the most hard and threatening). Holoferness and Lady Natalie should look akin to English country garden types, with Holoferness's clothes looking the worse for wear, and Lady Natalie's looking eccentrically mannish. (Jodhpurs and a peaked cap, with tweedy riding jacket? I even see her carrying a shotgun in very Elsa Lanchester-ish style.) Dull's attire should resemble a standard British copper of the early 20th century, and Costard and Jacquenetta appear to be the recognizable stable lad and country wench (a la Willam and Audrey in *As You Like It*). Don Armado's costume should look something like a foreign legion officer's (perhaps more exotic), although threadbare and fallen into a state of disrepair. As noted before, Moth is a war orphan that he adopted during an earlier campaign that is growing into a young woman as his ward. None of these latter folks have much wealth, for most of that is held by the Parisian envoy and the Navarre aristocrats.

The general scenery of the play is that of a once manicured and carefully maintained country estate garden that is now falling into slow decay from a lack of interest, money and supervision. Stone walls (if visible) appear to be starting to crumble, flowerbeds have overflowed their confinements, and ivy and foliage is beginning to reclaim the space. In other words, order is slowly giving way (inevitably) to the wildness of nature. Pieces of lawn furniture adorn the enclosure where the boys enjoy their backyard sunshine, and when Don Armado and Moth first appear, Moth is laying down an afternoon picnic for her guardian. Once the Princess and her ladies arrive on the estate grounds, the scene simply continues to revolve around various areas outdoors on Navarre's grounds, with specific variances of locale suggested by strategic shifts in periaktoi-type walls, arches and/or columns; however, it is vital that the stage always maintain a sense of overall openness, never so burdened with structures that it appears claustrophobic. Perhaps some sort of platform—or gazebo—in the upstage area would facilitate the presentation of the "Nine Worthies" presentation at the play's conclusion, complete with makeshift curtain set up by its Company? And of course, there needs to be at least three distinct hiding places to serve the lads when they're eavesdropping on one another's sonneteering.

In overall mood and lighting ambience, the "tale of two worlds" *mise en scene* should also be emphasized. Perhaps the course of the play moves slowly through the acts from bright morning to deepening twilight. Or maybe the gardens show brilliant colors of autumn, juxtaposed against the false promise of a late Indian summer. Once glorious/now decayed; autumn leaves/Indian summer sunshine; wealth falling into disrepair—all are antithetical symbols that are underscored by the play itself. The young women's grasp of real-world practicality vs. the men's capricious fantasies; the academic vs. the actual; idealized love vs. the challenges of the real thing; vows and honor vs. manipulation and equivocation; love and renewal vs. death and decay. As in all of his plays, it is the balance, it is the measuring of one against the other that most fascinates Shakespeare. Truth lies in the argument itself, not in its conclusion. Even the concluding song, followed by the final line, stresses the contrasting antithetical elements: "The words of Mercury are harsh after the songs of Apollo. You that way; we this way."

Author Photo by: Logan Falk-Woodruff

DAVID MONTEE was formerly the Director of Theatre at the Interlochen Center for the Arts for 21 years, and has directed and acted in over 150 stage productions over the course of his professional and educational career. During the past three decades, he has directed or performed in over half of the Shakespeare canon. Before embarking upon a teaching career some thirty years ago, he acted professionally in New York City, Boston, and regionally, and continues an active performance career alongside his work in the classroom.

Dr. Montee has received educational awards from every institution at which he has taught in his thirty years of teaching. He has been cited numerous times by *Who's Who Among America's Teachers* and named as a Distinguished Teacher by the U.S. Department of Education's Presidential Scholars program twice, in 2001, and again in 2009. In 2004, he was awarded the Coca-Cola Distinguished Teacher in the Arts from the National Foundation for Advancement in the Arts. Many of his former students have performed over their subsequent professional careers in featured roles on television, in films, on Broadway, and with prestigious stage companies throughout the United States and internationally, including the Public Theatre's Shakespeare in Central Park series at the Delacorte Theatre, the Acting Company, the Williamstown Theatre Festival, the Old Globe Theatre in San Diego, the Seattle Repertory Theatre, the Guthrie Theatre, the Oregon Shakespeare Festival, the American Players' Theatre, the Utah Shakespeare Theatre, and the Royal Shakespeare Company venues in both London and Stratford.